UNDERSTANDING
ENGLISH
GRAMMAR

FOURTH EDITION

Martha Kolln

The Pennsylvania State University

MACMILLAN PUBLISHING COMPANY
New York

MAXWELL MACMILLAN CANADA
Toronto

MAXWELL MACMILLAN INTERNATIONAL
New York   Oxford   Singapore   Sydney

Editor: Eben Ludlow
Production Supervisor: Bert Yaeger
Production Manager: Francesca Drago
Text Designer: Angela Foote
Cover Designer: Robert Freese

This book was set in Caledonia by Publication Services, Inc. and was printed and bound by Quebecor Printing Book Press. The cover was printed by Lehigh Press.

Macmillan Publishing Company
866 Third Avenue, New York, New York 10022

Macmillan Publishing Company is part of the Maxwell Communication Group of Companies.

Maxwell Macmillan Canada, Inc.
1200 Eglinton Avenue East
Suite 200
Don Mills, Ontario M3C 3N1

Library of Congress Cataloging in Publication Data

Kolln, Martha
      Understanding English grammar / Martha Kolln. — 4th ed.
          p.   cm.
      Includes index.
      ISBN 0-02-366072-4
      1. English language—Grammar.   I. Title.
PE 1112.K64   1994
428.2—dc20   93-3099
                                                                  CIP

Printing: 1   2   3   4   5   6   7   Year: 4   5   6   7   8   9   0

PREFACE

The purpose of *Understanding English Grammar* is to help students understand the system of rules underlying the grammar of English, to help them understand in a conscious way the system that, if they are native speakers, they already know subconsciously. Throughout the book the students are encouraged to see themselves as language experts and to develop a positive attitude about grammar.

Understanding English Grammar does not describe or advocate one particular grammar theory. Rather, it draws upon all of the theories, the old and the new, as each contributes to the understanding of a concept. For example, it uses that visual aid of the traditional grammarian, the sentence diagram, along with the sentence pattern formulas of the structuralists and the generative rules and branching diagrams of the transformationalists. This eclectic method makes use of whatever will help illuminate the systematic nature of our language and help students experience the consciousness raising that the study of grammar can and should be.

Part I, which is new to this edition, introduces such issues as language development, correctness, usage, and language change. These discussions will be of special interest to the future teachers in your classes.

Part II, on syntax, begins with a description of the ten sentence patterns. I begin in this way, with the largest unit of grammar rather than with individual words or sounds, so that the students will come to understand the sentence as a series of slots, or functions, filled by structures that take on a variety of forms, from single words to phrases and clauses. Later, when the students read about word classes, which have fairly detailed descriptions, the sentences they have been analyzing and diagramming constitute an organizing framework for those details.

Part II also includes chapters on the expanded verb phrase, on nominals, and on ways of reordering or transforming basic sentences. Part III describes our system of expanding the basic patterns with adverbials, adjectivals, sentence modifiers, and coordination. Part IV takes up morphology and parts of speech, with separate chapters for form classes, structure classes, and pronouns. I should emphasize that instructors who prefer the more traditional approach of studying words before sentence patterns will find it easy to begin the course with Part IV. The occasional references to the sentence patterns in those chapters should not be a problem for the students. Part V discusses rhetorical grammar, the application of grammar knowledge to composition.

There are exercises throughout the chapters to reinforce the principles of grammar as they are introduced. Answers to the exercises, which are provided in a section at the end, give the book a strong self-instructional quality. New to this edition are exercises entitled "Investigating Language," which will stimulate class discussion, calling on students to tap their innate language ability.

Each chapter ends with a list of key terms, which is a new feature of this edition, a section of practice sentences (for which answers are not provided), and a series of questions for discussion that go beyond the concepts covered in the text. In addition to the main text, there are appendixes covering phonology and an introduction to transformational grammar. The students will also find the glossary of terms extremely helpful.

Many of the changes in this fourth edition of *Understanding English Grammar* are the result of my correspondence and conversations with teachers who have used the book, along with several enjoyable visits to classes in other colleges.

Several of the changes will be readily apparent to those of you who have used an earlier edition of the book. The most obvious is the new Chapter 1, "The Gift of Language," an addition that many teachers suggested. Another change you'll notice is that the nominal chapter now follows immediately after the early chapters on sentence patterns and verbs. This change, putting the nominal discussion before those of adverbials and adjectivals, greatly simplifies the important concept of noun phrase substitutes. Other new features, already mentioned, are the inductive "Investigating Language" exercises and the chapter-ending "Key Terms." Another change is the expanded discussion of transformational grammar, which has been shifted to the Appendix section. And throughout the chapters there are expanded explanations, discussions, and exercises.

Supplementing the fourth edition of the text is an *Instructor's Manual*, which includes analyses of the practice sentences, suggested answers for the discussion questions, and some suggestions for using the book. The *Instructor's Manual* is available from your Macmillan representative.

With this new edition of *Understanding English Grammar* there is now available a workbook, *Exercises for Understanding English Grammar*, which I have written in response to the many teachers and students who have asked for more practice. The workbook contains exercises to accompany the first nine chapters of the text, many of which call for students to compose sentences, and a tenth chapter of sentence-combining exercises. To keep the self-instructional quality that teachers appreciate, I have included answers to half of the items in each exercise, where answers are appropriate. In addition, there are chapter-ending "test exercises" without answers, which can be used for testing and review.

The study of grammar is not just for English majors or for future teachers: It is for people in business and industry, in science and engineering, in law and politics. Every user of the language, in fact, will benefit from the consciousness raising that results from the study of grammar. The more that speakers, writers, and readers know consciously about their language, the more power they have over it and the better they can make it serve their needs. It is very gratifying to me that many thousands of students in schools throughout the country have experienced their consciousness raising with *Understanding English Grammar.*

ACKNOWLEDGMENTS

A great many of the changes in this new edition are the result of questions and suggestions from both teachers and students. I am grateful to all those who have called and written to discuss the book and to tell me about their grammar classes.

I wish to acknowledge the following individuals who gave me so much help:

Lettie J. Austin, Howard University
Gwen Brewer, California State University, Northridge
Ron Buckalew, The Pennsylvania State University

Lee Campbell, Marquette University
John F. Carson, Kent State University, Stark Campus
Sandra Clark, Anderson University
Sandra L. M. Coyle, Jacksonville University
Carol I. Croxton, University of Southern Colorado
Virginia F. Dailey, St. Edwards University
Elsie M. Deal, Edinboro University of Pennsylvania
Dorothy Disterheft, University of South Carolina
Elizabeth-Anne F. Duke, Virginia Commonwealth University
Connie Eble, University of North Carolina at Chapel Hill
Robert W. Funk, Eastern Illinois University
Elizabeth Stevens Girsch, The University of Michigan
John Hagge, Iowa State University
Deane McLure Hargrave, Northern Arizona University
Charles L. Houck, Ball State University
David Jolliffe, University of Illinois at Chicago
James Kenkel, Eastern Kentucky University
Anne LeCroy, East Tennessee State University
Lee Little, Western Kentucky University
Stanley Matyshak, St. Norbert College
Paul R. Meyer, New Mexico State University
James K. P. Mortensen, University of Texas at El Paso
Barbara Patrick, Rowan College of New Jersey
John G. Rechtien, St. Mary's University
Herbert J. Roth, Southwestern Adventist College
Deborah Schaffer, Eastern Montana College
Ann W. Sharp, Furman University
Ronald Shook, Utah State University
R. Baird Shuman, University of Illinois at Urbana–Champaign
Maggi Sokolik, Texas A&M University
Hector A. Torres, University of New Mexico
Cindy L. Vitto, Rowan College of New Jersey
Nancy Yee, Fitchburg State College

I reserve special thanks for four reviewers who evaluated the final manuscript in detail and offered many useful suggestions, every one of which I considered carefully and a great many of which I followed:

Robert W. Funk, Eastern Illinois University
John Hagge, Iowa State University

Lee Little, Western Kentucky University

R. Baird Shuman, University of Illinois at Urbana–Champaign

Again, it has been a pleasure to work with the folks at Macmillan: Bert Yaeger, who guided the book through production; and Eben Ludlow, friend and editor.

And, finally, I acknowledge once more the love and support of my ever-expanding family, which, with this edition, now includes Denny and Shelley and Devon and Riley.

Martha Kolln

CONTENTS

PART VI
GLOSSARY OF GRAMMATICAL TERMS   391

I

INTRODUCTION

Biofeedback: A technique for teaching people to become aware of their involuntary bodily processes, such as temperature, heart rate, and blood pressure, in order to control them by a conscious mental effort.

No, you didn't pick up the wrong book. This isn't a biology text in disguise. But that definition of *biofeedback,* a concept you may have heard about in connection with alternative medicine, can be applied to the study of language to explain what *Understanding English Grammar* is all about.

Linguafeedback: A technique for teaching people to become aware of their involuntary language processes—sounds and words and sentences—in order to develop a conscious understanding of their innate, subconscious language competence.

The goal of biofeedback is physical and mental health; the goal of "linguafeedback" is similar: to help you recognize your competence and to give you confidence in your own language ability.

Basic to the lessons of linguafeedback is this idea of competence. Even before you started kindergarten, you were competent—in fact, an expert—in your native language. So when you study the grammar of your language, you are bringing to a conscious level of understanding a system of rules that you somehow already "know."

1

In Chapter 1 we will take up that subject of expertise; we'll look also at language variation and change, at the difference between usage rules and grammar rules, and at the issue of correctness. In all of these discussions—in all of the chapters—remember that, as with biofeedback, the key word to success in this technique of linguafeedback is *awareness*. The purpose of *Understanding English Grammar* is to help you become consciously aware of your innate language competence.

1

The Gift of Language

Do you remember the scene from Walt Disney's *Pinocchio* when the Blue Fairy appears at Gepetto's cottage and touches his newly carved wooden puppet with her magic wand? Pinocchio blinks his eyes and looks around. "I can move," he says. Then, realizing what he has just done, he adds, "I can talk."

"Yes, Pinocchio," the Blue Fairy explains. "I've given you life."

"Life?" he asks. "Am I a real boy?"

It turns out, of course, that Pinocchio is not yet a "real boy." He must first prove himself brave, truthful, and unselfish. "To make Gepetto's wish come true will be up to you," the Blue Fairy tells him.

"Up to me?"

"You must choose between right and wrong."

"How will I know?" Pinocchio wonders.

"Your conscience will tell you."

"What are conscience?" he asks.

As you recall, Pinocchio and Jiminy Cricket, his official conscience, have their ups and downs before the Blue Fairy returns to pronounce Pinocchio a "real boy." But from a linguist's point of view, she has already done so—the moment she endowed Pinocchio with the gift of language.

LANGUAGE DEVELOPMENT

Although we didn't acquire our speech at the touch of a wand, there is still something almost magical in our human gift of language. Unlike Pinocchio, we grew up in a language environment; we heard our language spoken before we could begin to speak it ourselves. We listened for quite a long time—for most of us, close to a year or more—before we joined in the conversation. And we certainly didn't begin the way Pinocchio did, with his well-formed sentences. We began with single words, naming the people and the objects in our environment. It took several months before we had devised a system for putting words together, following our own set of rules for forming sentences: "Cookie allgone." "Mommy go bye-bye." Gradually our language came to resemble that of the adults in our speech community.

By the time we started school, we were experts.

Well, almost experts. There were still a few gaps in our system. For example, we didn't start using verb phrases as direct objects (I like *reading books*) until perhaps second grade; and not until third or fourth grade did we use *although* or *even if* to introduce clauses (I'm going home *even if you're not*). But for the most part, our grammar system was in place.

The operative word in this drama of language development is *system.* Somehow children in every speech community in every part of the world develop a system of rules—an internal computer program of sorts— that enables them to process and to generate language. All of us are endowed with this internalized system, a linguistic marvel that can go into action without a moment's hesitation, inventing sentences, putting together combinations that fit the occasion. In day-to-day situations our inventions tend to be fairly predictable: "Hi, how's it going?" "Sorry I'm late." But other situations call for unique combinations, and we come up with those sentences automatically, too. We invent them all the time, original sentences that have never been said before. In fact, our computer-like system is so spectacular that we are able to generate an infinite number of grammatical sentences.

THE RULES OF GRAMMAR

Underlying this almost magical language ability is the system of rules we call grammar. When you study grammar you are bringing to a conscious level of awareness the rules of the language that you already "know" subconsciously.

This language ability is yours, of course, no matter what your native language happens to be. If your native language is not English, your knowledge of English grammar will be different from that of native speakers. Unless you began speaking English at a very young age, you will probably never have the extent of subconscious knowledge that a native speaker does. On the other hand, you can certainly develop just as much—if not more—conscious knowledge. It's possible, in fact, that the level of your conscious knowledge may already exceed that of some native speakers in your class, especially if you were introduced to English through textbooks. In your English classes, when you learned the rules for constructing sentences, you also learned labels for their parts; you learned a language for talking about the language, something your classmates may not have learned—or may have forgotten.

Pinocchio's conversation with the Blue Fairy illustrates the kinds of rules that native speakers of English have internalized and that nonnative speakers have to pay attention to and practice. For example, like all children, Pinocchio asked questions:

> Am I a real boy?
> How will I know [the difference between right and wrong]?

The first is what we call a **"yes/no" question,**[1] one in which the expected answer is either *yes* or *no*. In order to ask it, Pinocchio reversed the subject and verb. The underlying statement looks like this:

> I am a real boy.

The other question required another maneuver: Besides the subject-verb switch—actually the **auxiliary,** in this case—he added the **interrogative** word *how* in order to elicit particular information. Here the underlying statement is

> I will know [somehow].

The unknown element, the "somehow," is the information being asked for.

In English we elicit unknown information by using such interrogatives as *how, who, what, when, where,* and *why*. These words always

---

[1] The words and phrases in boldface are defined in the Glossary of Grammatical Terms, beginning on page 391.

appear at the opening of the question—even if the information being elicited appears elsewhere in the underlying statement:

> *What* should we have for dinner?
> We should have [something] for dinner.

At this point you may be wondering if in fact the questions in our language actually begin as statements and then get changed by some internal rule. We surely don't go through a two-step process like that when we ask questions—or do we? To speculate in this way is to think about language the way that linguists do:

> How do children develop this computer-like ability, this system of grammar rules that produces language?
> What, specifically, are the rules?

Linguists, scientists whose field of study is language, are looking for answers to basic questions like these about this human gift.

It's clear that in addition to asking questions Pinocchio has also internalized the system for using **pronouns.** As we would expect, the Blue Fairy addresses Pinocchio as *you:* "I have given you life." In responding, he refers to himself, correctly, as *I:* "Am I a real boy?" When she discusses his future, using the phrase "up to you," he again responds with the appropriate pronoun: "Up to me?" Here the pronoun is the object of the preposition *to,* not the subject. These responses illustrate the rules determining the **case** of pronouns, the distinction between the subjective *I* and the objective *me.* Native speakers have internalized this particular rule. You've probably never heard anyone say "Is me a real boy?" or "It's up to I."

Another part of Pinocchio's grammar system is illustrated by his response when the Blue Fairy refers to his conscience: "What are conscience?" This time his question doesn't sound like one that a native speaker would ask. It sounds as if Pinocchio has made his first mistake. (And that, by the way, is the linguists' definition of **ungrammatical:** something that a native speaker wouldn't say.)

But listen carefully to the word *conscience.* Compare it with similar words that have a final *s* sound, such as *talents.* Not knowing the meaning of *conscience,* Pinocchio did what the rest of us do in acquiring our language: He analogized. Words such as *talents* are plural, he might have thought, so *conscience* must be plural too.

===== *Investigating Language 1.1* =====

If you've been around small children, you may have heard sentences similar to these:

1. She goed to the store.
2. I eated the cookies.
3. I see two mouses.

Even though these sentences are ungrammatical (from the standpoint of adult language), they illustrate certain rules that the speakers have internalized. What are those rules? Why don't they produce grammatical sentences?

To answer these questions, write your adult version of the three sentences:

1. _____.
2. _____.
3. _____.

Now rewrite your sentences, substituting the correct form of the word in parentheses for the problem word.

1. (walk) _____.
2. (bake) _____.
3. (house) _____.

Your adult sentences should illustrate why analogizing—learning by analogy—did not work for the children.

As you have just seen, verbs like *eat* and *go* and nouns like *mouse* are different from other members of their word classes in the way that the past tense of the verbs and the plural of the nouns are formed. You'll discover, as we study the grammar of English, that even though the rules are highly systematic there are exceptions to almost all of them. If you are a native speaker of English, you have somehow internalized the exceptions along with the rules—and you pay no attention to them. *Goed* and *eated* and *mouses* dropped out of your system a long time ago. If, on the other hand, you are not a native speaker, if you have only recently begun your study of English, then you have to learn consciously such exceptions as the irregular noun plurals and verb tenses. In our study of the system, we'll look at both the rules and the exceptions.

LANGUAGE VARIATION

Not every child who learns English ends up with exactly the same adult language. Different parts of the country, different levels of education, different ethnic backgrounds—all of these situations produce differences in language communities. One of the positive contributions that television has made to our education is the demonstration of such differences. In less mobile, preelectronic times, Americans, especially those in isolated small towns, could go through life rarely hearing dialects other than their own. (We define *dialect* as the variety of a language spoken in a particular region or community.) Now we regularly hear speakers from all parts of the country and all parts of the world. At times the English we hear is so different, in fact, that it can sound like another language. Some of the dialogue in British movies and TV programs, for example, can be downright indecipherable.

Sometimes the differences we hear sound like grammatical errors. What else are we to think when we hear people say "He just upped and left" or "I might could go" or "Y'all come back soon" or "He be working"? We don't see such sentences in formal writing, nor do we hear them in television news reports or in presidential addresses to Congress. Are such sentences **grammatical?** Perhaps a personal anecdote will help you discover the answer.

Shortly after I moved to central Pennsylvania from the West Coast I heard people saying sentences I had never heard before: "My car needs fixed" and "My hair needs washed" and "Let the door open." My grammar rules had never produced these sentences. I say instead, "My car needs to be fixed" or "My car needs fixing" and "Leave the door open." However, in the central and western parts of Pennsylvania and in nearby areas of bordering states, children develop rules that do produce such sentences. So are they grammatical? They are part of the language system of a million or more people. Of course they're grammatical. Who among us has the authority to declare the language of a million people ungrammatical?

Many of the sentences that get labeled "ungrammatical" are simply usages that vary from one dialect to another, what we sometimes call regionalisms. The Southern *y'all* or *you all* and the Philadelphia *youse* and the Appalachian *you-uns* (or *y'uns*) are all ways of pluralizing the pronoun *you*. It's probably accurate to say that the majority of speech communities in this country don't have a plural form of *you*—but some do, and these plurals are part of their grammar.

We don't hear regionalisms like "I might could go" and "y'all" and "the car needs fixed" on the nightly news because they are not a part of what is called "standard English." However, the word *standard* can be misunderstood. Modern linguists maintain that every dialect of English is standard within its speech community and that to label only one dialect as standard is to imply that others are somehow inferior, or substandard. Here, however, we are using the word *standard* as the label for the status dialect, the one that is used in newscasts, in formal business transactions, in courtrooms, in all sorts of public discourse.

In addition to regionalisms, ethnic influences, and differing levels of education—all of which contribute to variations among communities and individuals—the speech situation makes a difference. Even children understand that the language they use with their playmates is different from the language they use with adults. The negative "huh-uh" on the playground is likely to become "no thank you" when the school principal is asking the question. And certainly the language that broadcasters use on the air or that lawyers use in the courtroom is not the same as the language they use at the breakfast table with their family or at the bowling alley with their friends. The situation makes a difference.

In written language, too, what is appropriate or effective in one situation may be inappropriate or ineffective in another. The language you use in letters to your family and friends is noticeably different from the language you use when applying for a job. Even the writing you do in school varies, depending on the situation. The language of the personal essay you write in your composition class has an informality that would be inappropriate for a business report or a history research paper. As with speech, the purpose and the audience make all the difference.

USAGE RULES AND GRAMMAR RULES

It's important to recognize that these variations in language—dialect differences among speech communities or variations resulting from the speech or writing situation—are not distinctions between "grammatical" and "ungrammatical" language. The grammar rules of central and western Pennsylvania produce "The car needs washed"; the grammar rules of many Southern speech communities produce "Y'all come back soon." Even though neither conforms to what we are calling the status dialect, both are grammatical.

So it's important to understand the difference between rules of grammar and rules of usage—sometimes called "linguistic etiquette." Rules of usage are imposed by society. Often a sentence that gets labeled "ungrammatical" is simply one that in a given situation may be inappropriate—or, in someone's opinion, is unacceptable. You may recall how Professor Higgins, in *My Fair Lady*, changed Eliza Doolittle's social class by changing her speech. "The rain in Spain stays mainly in the plain" was a pronunciation lesson.

The well-known issue of *ain't* provides a good illustration of the difference between our internal rules of grammar and our external—social—rules of usage. You may have assumed that pronouncements about *ain't* have something to do with "incorrect" grammar—but they don't. The word itself, the contraction of *am not*, is produced by an internal rule, the same rule that gives us *aren't* and *isn't*. Any negative bias you may have against *ain't* is strictly a matter of linguistic etiquette. (And, as you can hear for yourself, many speakers of English harbor no such bias.) Written texts from the seventeenth and eighteenth centuries show that *ain't* was once a part of standard conversational English in both England and America. It was sometime during the nineteenth century that the word became stigmatized for public discourse and marked a speaker as uneducated or ignorant. It's still possible to hear *ain't* in public discourse, but only as an attention-getter:

> If it ain't broke, don't fix it.
> You ain't seen nothin' yet.

And of course it's used in written dialogue and in both written and spoken humor. But despite the fact that the grammar rules of millions of people produce *ain't* as part of their native language, for many others it carries a stigma.

===== *Investigating Language 1.2* =====

The stigma attached to *ain't* has left a void in our language: We now have no first-person equivalent of the negative questions *Isn't it?* and *Aren't they?* You will discover how we have filled the void when you add the appropriate tag questions to these sentences. The tag question is a common way of turning a statement into a question. Two examples will illustrate the structure:

> The Blue Fairy is magic, isn't she?
> Jiminy Cricket is a fine fellow, isn't he?

1. The weather is nice today, _____ ?

2. You are my friend, _____ ?

3. I am your friend, _____ ?

You'll notice that you can turn those tag questions into statements by reversing them. Here are the examples: *She isn't. He isn't.*
Now reverse the three that you did:

1. _____ .

2. _____ .

3. _____ .

You have probably discovered the problem that the banishment of *ain't* has produced. It has left us with something that sounds like an ungrammatical structure. Given the linguists' definition of *ungrammatical*—something that a native speaker wouldn't say—would you call "Aren't I?" ungrammatical or grammatical? Explain.

In summary, then, our attitude about *ain't* is an issue about status, not grammar. If the network newscasters and the president of the United States and your teachers began to use *ain't* on a regular basis, its status would eventually change. Teachers and presidents and newscasters don't avoid *ain't* because it's nonstandard: *It's nonstandard because such people avoid it.*

THE ISSUE OF CORRECTNESS

Can we really be saying that *ain't* is "grammatical" English, that it's "correct"? How about "She don't like me" and "I don't have no money" and "He be working"? Are they correct?

Where shall we turn for answers to questions about correctness? To grammar books? To dictionaries? There was a time when people did just that, when such reference books were written mainly for the purpose of instruction, to change the way people used language, to teach them to speak and write "proper" English so that they could move up the ladder of success. Today, however, the purpose of most grammar books and dictionaries is descriptive rather than prescriptive—to describe how people actually use language, not how someone says it should be used.

The question of correctness implies a set of standards, and a set of standards implies an authority who sets them and regulates them and polices them. Who should we choose as our authorities? Or do the authorities get to choose themselves?

=== *Investigating Language 1.3* ===

Writers of letters to "Dear Abby" regularly complain about the unacceptable language they hear. In a column devoted to her readers' pet peeves on the subject of the "misuse of words and other irritants," Abby included the following:

1. People use the word "snuck" instead of "sneaked." Although "snuck" somehow sneaked into the dictionary, it's not used by people who use proper English.
2. Now lend me your ear: Don't use "loan" as a verb, as in, "Loan me a twenty." It should be, "Lend me a twenty." "Loan" is a noun; "lend" is a verb.
3. The month of February has two "Rs" in it—but we keep hearing "Feb-yoo-ary."

Abby obviously thinks that these are mistakes in grammar and pronunciation. What does the dictionary have to say about them? The following entries are from *Webster's Ninth New Collegiate Dictionary* (Merriam-Webster, 1991).[2]

---

[2]By permission. From *Webster's Ninth New Collegiate Dictionary* © 1991 by Merriam-Webster Inc., publisher of the Merriam-Webster ® dictionaries.

¹**sneak** \ 'snēk\ *vb* **sneaked** \ 'snēkt\ *or* **snuck** \ 'snək\ ; **sneak·ing** [akin to OE *snīcan* to sneak along, OHG *snahhan* to creep—more at SNAIL] *vi* (1596) **1:** to go stealthily or furtively: SLINK **2.** to act in or as if in a furtive manner **3:** to carry the football on a quarterback sneak ~ *vt:* to put, bring, or take in a furtive or artful manner < ~ a smoke> *syn* see LURK—**sneak up on:** to approach or act on stealthily

¹**loan** \ 'lōn\ *n* [ME *lon,* fr. ON *lān;* akin to OE *lǣn* loan, *lēon* to lend, L *linquere* to leave, Gk *leipein*] (bef. 12c) **1 a:** money lent at interest **b:** something lent usu. for the borrower's temporary use **2 a:** the grant of temporary use **b:** the temporary duty of a person transferred to another job for a limited time **3:** LOANWORD
²**loan** *vt* (13c): LEND—**loan·able** \ 'lō-nə-bəl\ *adj*
usage Most recent commentators accept the use of *loan* as a verb as standard. It has been in use at least since the time of Henry VIII but became widely used first in the U.S. About 100 years ago a prominent American critic denounced the use, apparently basing his objections on a misunderstanding of Old English. Even though they are based on a mistake, these same objections may still be heard today

Feb·ru·ary \ ÷ 'feb-(y)ə-, wer- ē, 'feb-rə-\ *n* [ME *Februarie,* frm. OE *Februarius,* fr. L, fr. *Februa,* pl., feast of purification; perh. akin to L *fumus* smoke] (bef. 12c): the 2d month of the Gregorian calendar
usage Dissimilation may occur when a word contains two identical or closely related sounds, resulting in the change or loss of one of them. This happens regularly in *February,* which is more often pronounced \ 'feb-(y)ə-,wer-ē\ than \ 'feb-rə-,wer-ē\ , though all of these variants are in frequent and acceptable use. The \ y\ heard from many speakers is not an intrusion but rather an alternative pronunciation of the unstressed vowel *u* after a consonant, as in *January* and *annual.*

What does the information about pronunciation and meaning in the dictionary actually represent? Do you agree with Abby and the readers who complained about these "irritants"?

Our language has a great many words like *snuck* and *ain't* that are judged ungrammatical even though the words are produced by our internalized grammar rules—and even though they are spoken by many people. So if we accept the linguists' definition of *grammatical*— "language produced by the rules of a native speaker"—then we obviously cannot label these words as "ungrammatical."

"Is it correct?" is generally the wrong question—or, at least an incomplete one. A more accurate question would be "Is it correct in this situation?" or "Is it appropriate?" Remember, there are many variations in this language of ours. **Standard Written English,** the version that has come to be the standard for written public discourse—for newspapers and books and for most of the writing you do in school and on the job—is the version of our language that this book describes, the written version of the prestige dialect.

Where did this description of Standard Written English come from? Is it the work of "prominent American critics," like the one referred to in the dictionary's discussion of *loan?* In fact, that's exactly what it is. It is the work of many such critics and grammarians and authors of dictionaries through the years who have taken it upon themselves to describe—and sometimes to prescribe—the prestige dialect, the version of English used by the respected writers and speakers of their day. Those writers and speakers don't say "I don't have no money" and "She don't like me" and "He be working" and "They snuck in"—at least not in their public discourse. They say "I don't have any money" and "She doesn't like me" and "He is working" and "They sneaked in," and these forms are the ones that get included in the grammar books as the "standard."

So the issue of correctness and the issue of standards are determined by the situation. On the nightly news and in the Senate chamber, *ain't* and *he don't* and the double negative would be inappropriate; they would violate the standards of those institutions. In the opinion of many language observers, of course, those usages are grammatical errors no matter where they are spoken. Dear Abby isn't the only self-proclaimed authority on "proper English." But remember that every dialect in every speech community includes ways of speaking that some critic somewhere would call improper.

And how about the classroom? Should teachers call attention to the nonstandard words and phrases in their students' language? Should teachers "correct" them? These are questions that the National Council of Teachers of English (NCTE) has addressed in a document called "Students' Right to Their Own Language." The resolution reads, in part,

> We affirm the students' right to their own patterns and varieties of language—the dialects of their nurture or whatever dialects in which they find their own identity and style. Language scholars long ago denied that the myth of a standard American dialect has any validity.... A nation proud of its diverse heritage and its cultural and racial variety will preserve its heritage of dialects.

But teachers also have an obligation to teach students to read and write Standard English, the language of public discourse and of the workplace that those students are preparing to join. There are ways of doing that without making students feel that the language spoken in their home, the language produced by their own internal grammar rules, is somehow inferior. Certainly one way is to study language differences in an objective, nonjudgmental way and to discuss individual and regional and ethnic differences, the differences in levels of formality, and the differences between speech and writing.

LANGUAGE CHANGE

Another important aspect of our language that is closely related to the issue of correctness is language change. A great many of the usages that bother language critics, including Abby and her irritated readers, are simply new ways of using words, the introduction of new meanings, or new forms that are starting to take over. The verb *sneak,* for example, seems to be going the way of *dig* and *stick:* The irregular *dug* and *stuck* have completely replaced *digged* and *sticked.* Another verb to keep our eye on is *drag.* The irregular *drug* ("Look at what the cat *drug* in") is sneaking in, too—but not quite as fast as *snuck.*

Among the changes that language critics deplore is the *-ize* ending that gets added to adjectives and nouns to produce verbs like *finalize* and *prioritize.* According to *Webster's Dictionary of English Usage* (Merriam-Webster, 1989), such newly coined words have been raising hackles since 1591, when *-ize* as a word-forming suffix was first mentioned. Apparently, every *-ize* word has had to go through its probationary period:

> Critics were upset by Noah Webster's inclusion of *demoralize, Americanize,* and *deputize* in his 1828 dictionary.... [T]he issue roared into the 20th century, where *finalize* replaced *jeopardize* as the object of the most heat and least rationality. (568)

In summary, the *Dictionary* asks, "Who today blinks at *popularize, formalize, economize, legalize, politicize, terrorize,* or *capitalize?*"

Change is inevitable in a living organism like language. The change is obvious, of course, when we compare the English of Shakespeare or of the King James Bible to our modern version. But we certainly don't have to go back that far to see differences. We can see and hear change happening all around us, especially if we consider the new words required for such fields as medicine, space science, and computer technology. *Webster's Ninth New Collegiate Dictionary* reports that *biofeedback* arrived as recently as 1971. As for *linguafeedback*—you witnessed its arrival back on page 1.

Another place we can find evidence of change is *Pinocchio*—not in Walt Disney's version this time, but in translations of the original, an Italian children's book, written in the 1880s by Carlo Collodi. The following passages are from two different translations of Collodi's *Pinocchio*, written almost sixty years apart. You'll have no trouble distinguishing the language of 1925 from the language of 1983:

 1a. Fancy the happiness of Pinocchio on finding himself free!
  b. Imagine Pinocchio's joy when he felt himself free.

 2a. Gallop on, gallop on, my pretty steed.
  b. Gallop, gallop, little horse.

 3a. But whom shall I ask?
  b. But who can I possibly ask?

 4a. Woe betide the lazy fellow.
  b. Woe to those who yield to idleness.

 5a. Hasten, Pinocchio.
  b. Hurry, Pinocchio.

 6a. Without adding another word, the marionette bade the good Fairy good-by.
  b. Without adding another word, the puppet said good-bye to his good fairy.

In both cases the translators are writing the English version of 1880 Italian, so the language is not necessarily idiomatic 1925 or 1983 English. In spite of that constraint, we can recognize—as you've probably figured out—the first item in each pair as the 1925 translation. Those sentences include words that we simply don't use anymore, that would sound out of place in a conversation—or even a fairy tale—of the 1990s: *betide, hasten, bade.* The language of 1925 is simply not our language. In truth, the language of 1983 is not our language either, but it's a great deal closer.

===== *Investigating Language 1.4* =====

The difference between the two translations in the first pair of *Pinocchio* sentences is connected to the word *fancy*, a word that is still common today. Why did the 1983 translator use *imagine* instead? What has happened to *fancy* in the intervening decades?

The third pair involves a difference in grammar rather than vocabulary, the change from *whom* to *who*. What do you suppose today's language critics would have to say about the 1983 translation? How is that change related to what you read earlier about language variety?

The last pair includes a spelling change. Check the dictionary to see which is "correct"—or is *correct* the right word? The dictionary includes many words that have more than one spelling. How do you know which one to use?

Finally, provide evidence to demonstrate the accuracy of the assertion that the language of 1983 is not our language.

KEY TERMS IN CHAPTER 1

Correctness	Language variation
Dialect	Pronoun
Grammar rules	Regionalisms
Grammatical	Standard Written English
Internalized rules	Ungrammatical
Interrogative	Usage rules
Language change	Yes/no question

II

THE GRAMMAR OF BASIC SENTENCES

You might have been surprised to learn, when you read Chapter 1, that you're already an expert in grammar—and have been since before you started school. Indeed, you're such an expert that you can generate completely original sentences with those internal grammar rules of yours—sentences that have never before been spoken or written. Here's one to get you started:

> *At this very moment, I [Insert your name] am reading page 19 of the fourth edition of* Understanding English Grammar.

The occasion for that sentence has never happened before, so you can be fairly sure that it's original. Perhaps even more surprising is the fact that the number of such sentences you can produce is infinite.

When you study the grammar of your native language, then, you are studying a subject you already "know"; you are bringing to a conscious level of understanding the subconscious, intuitive gift of language that you began to develop in infancy. So in a sense you will not be learning grammar in this course; you will be learning "about grammar." If you're not a native speaker, you will probably be learning both grammar and about grammar; the mix will depend on your background and experience.

That intuitive expertise of yours makes the study of grammar different from the study of every other subject in the curriculum. You probably know a lot about certain other subjects: You may have memorized the multiplication tables in fifth grade—and you've never forgotten them;

you may understand the laws of physics; you may know a great deal about Shakespeare's sonnets; you may be a computer hack or a film buff or an expert bird watcher. But that kind of acquired knowledge pales in comparison to your subconscious language expertise. It's important that you understand what you are bringing to this course—even though you may have forgotten all those "parts of speech" labels you once consciously learned. The unconscious, or subconscious, knowledge that you have can help you if you will let it. The discussions and the exercises are designed to help you put your intuition to work, to help you bring your grammar expertise to a conscious level and to use it more confidently.

We will begin the study of sentence grammar, the subject known as **syntax,** by examining basic sentence patterns, the underlying framework of sentences, looking for both their common and their distinguishing features. A conscious knowledge of the basic patterns will provide a foundation for understanding the sentence expansions and variations that come later. In Chapter 3 we will examine the expanded verb, the system of auxiliaries that makes our verbs so versatile. In Chapter 4 we will look at alternatives for the noun phrase slot. And in Chapter 5 we will look at the ways we have of transforming our basic sentences for a variety of purposes.

2

Sentence Patterns

To understand English grammar is to understand the structure of sentences—and vice versa: To understand sentences is to understand grammar. That job of understanding may seem impossible when you realize that the potential number of sentences a speaker can produce is infinite. But of course it's not impossible. What makes it possible is the systematic nature of sentence structure and the limited number of elements that make up the sentences. So despite the infinite possibilities, the number of basic sentence forms, or patterns, is decidedly finite—in fact, the total is very small. Ten **sentence patterns** account for the underlying skeletal structure of almost all the possible grammatical sentences in English.

The patterns are much simpler than most of the sentences that we actually use in speech and writing, but to understand the expanded sentences, we must first understand the simple skeletons that underlie them. Probably the easiest way to think about those sentence skeletons is to recognize them as a series of slots, or functions, each one of which is filled by a particular structure, or form. Let's take a simple example:

The students studied their assignment.

It's fairly obvious, even if you haven't studied grammar before, that the sentence can be divided into three separate slots:

The students   studied   their assignment.

And if you were asked to come up with similar sentences, substituting other words in the slots, you could come up with a long list:

My sister	collects	baseball cards.
Our team	won	the trophy.
That car	needs	four new tires.

This is one way, then, to think about sentences: as a series of slots, or functions. And when we examine the sentence patterns further, we will do just that, recognizing that some of them have two slots, some three, and some four.

Before looking at those multiple slots, we will simplify the design somewhat and look at all of the ten sentence patterns as binary, or two-part, structures. The two branches represent the two components that make up the sentence: the subject and the predicate. An example of each pattern follows:

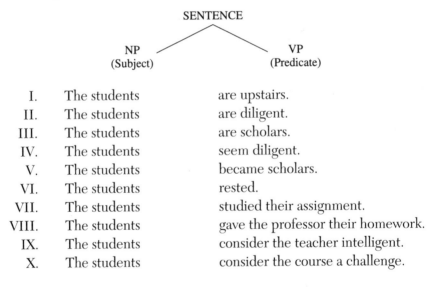

SENTENCE

NP   VP
(Subject)   (Predicate)

I.	The students	are upstairs.
II.	The students	are diligent.
III.	The students	are scholars.
IV.	The students	seem diligent.
V.	The students	became scholars.
VI.	The students	rested.
VII.	The students	studied their assignment.
VIII.	The students	gave the professor their homework.
IX.	The students	consider the teacher intelligent.
X.	The students	consider the course a challenge.

This list illustrates the two basic constituents of every sentence: (1) the NP, or **noun phrase,** which functions as the **subject;** and (2) the VP, or **verb phrase,** made up of the **predicating verb** together with its complements and modifiers, which functions as the **predicate.**

The terms *noun phrase* and *verb phrase* may be new to you, although you've undoubtedly encountered *noun* and *verb* and *phrase* before. A **phrase** is any group of two or more words that function as a unit within a sentence. A phrase always includes a head, or **headword,** along with its modifiers and/or complements. The head of a noun phrase is a noun; the head of a verb phrase, a verb. We'll soon encounter prepositional, adjectival, and adverbial phrases as well. It's important to recognize that in each of the sample sentences the subject is the complete noun phrase, *the student*—not just the noun headword, *student.*

Another term you're probably familiar with is **clause.** It, too, is a group of words, but unlike the phrase, the clause has a subject and a predicate. The sentences illustrating the ten sentence patterns are clauses. (We could, in fact, call them—and this chapter—"clause patterns" to be more accurate.) But there is a difference in meaning between *sentence* and *clause.* Not all clauses are sentences, and often a single sentence will include more than one clause. We'll look more carefully at this distinction in Chapter 4, where we first examine clauses that are not independent sentences.

The subject of the sentence, as its name suggests, is what the sentence is about—its topic. The predicate is what is said about the subject. The two parts can be thought of as the topic and the comment. This relationship underlies every sentence, including those in which the subject is unstated but clearly understood:

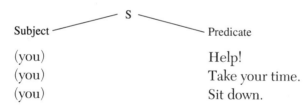

Subject	Predicate
(you)	Help!
(you)	Take your time.
(you)	Sit down.

No matter what your experience with grammar has been, your intuition will often be sufficient for figuring out the two basic parts of the sentence. For example, if you were asked to divide the following sentences into subject and predicate, you could probably do so with no problem:

The county commissioners have passed a new ordinance.
The mayor's husband spoke against it.
The mayor was upset with him.
Several residents of the community spoke in favor of it.
The merchants in town are unhappy.
This new law will prohibit billboard advertising on major highways.

Chances are that you made your divisions correctly—after these subjects:

> The county commissioners
> The mayor's husband
> The mayor
> Several residents of the community
> The merchants in town
> This new law

You were probably able to make those divisions on the basis of your intuition. But if you want to check your intuition, one trick that can help you figure out where the subject ends and the predicate begins is to substitute a **pronoun** for the subject. The pronoun, you will discover, stands in for the entire noun phrase. You will also discover that you use such pronouns automatically:

> They   have passed a new ordinance.
> He   spoke against it.
> She   was upset with him.
> They   spoke in favor of it.
> They   are unhappy.
> It   will prohibit billboard advertising on major highways.

===== *Investigating Language 2.1* =====

Another way of calling on your intuition in order to discover where the subject of a sentence ends and the predicate begins is to turn the statement into a yes/no question. You saw some examples with Pinocchio's questions in Chapter 1. Here are some further examples:

> The commissioners have passed a new ordinance.
> <u>Have</u>   the commissioners _____   passed a new ordinance?

> This new law will prohibit billboard advertising.
> <u>Will</u>   this new law_____   prohibit billboard advertising?

As you see, the first word in the predicate—in both of these cases, the auxiliary verb—shifts to the opening position of the sentence. You'll notice that its path has underlined the subject for you. Some of the following examples are more complicated, but you'll discover that in every case, when you turn them into yes/no questions, you automatically shift the auxiliary, thus identifying the subject:

1. _____ The business owners in town are complaining.

2. _____ The committee studying the billboard issue has recommended a different ordinance.

3. _____ All the townspeople and students should vote.

Now confirm your decision by substituting a pronoun for the subject you have identified.

Recognition of this subject–predicate relationship, the common element in all of the patterns, is the first step in the study of sentences. Equally important for the classification of sentences into patterns is the concept of the verb as the central, pivotal slot in the sentence. Notice that in the ten sample sentences on page 22 the subjects are identical: *The students*. The sentence pattern categories are determined by variations in the predicates—variations in the verb and in the slots following the verb. So although the categories are called *sentence patterns,* a more accurate label might be *predicate patterns*.

FORM AND FUNCTION

Because the variations among the sentence patterns are in the predicates, we group the ten patterns according to their verbs: the **be patterns**, the **linking verb** patterns, the **intransitive verb** pattern, and the **transitive verb** patterns.

The patterns are shown as formulas, with each slot labeled according to *form*. The abbreviations used in the formulas stand for *noun phrase [NP], adverbial of time or place [ADV/TP],* and *adjectival [ADJ]*. The subscript numbers you will see in some of the patterns show the relationship between noun phrases: Identical numbers (such as those in Patterns III and V, where both subscript numbers are 1) mean that the two noun phrases have the same referent; different numbers (such as those in Pattern VII, where the subscript numbers are 1 and 2) denote different referents. The **referent** is the thing (or person, event, concept, etc.) that the noun or noun phrase stands for. You'll come to understand noun phrase referents in the discussions of the separate patterns.

The labels **noun phrase, verb, adjective**, and **adverb** refer to form. Equally important for understanding the patterns are the labels that name the slots according to **function**, the terms given in parentheses in the patterns. Take a brief look first at the labels for the first two slots: In all the patterns the first slot is the **subject**, the second is the **predicating verb**. It's in the slots following the verb that the differences among the patterns appear. You'll notice that all the patterns except Pattern VI, the intransitive pattern, have at least one slot following the verb; the last three patterns have two. In Pattern I, the verb is followed by an adverbial of time or place. The slots in the other patterns are called **complements**, structures that *complete* the verb: **subjective complement, direct object, indirect object**, and **objective complement**. Three of the complement slots in the ten patterns are adjectives (or, to be more accurate, adjectivals); the rest are noun phrases.

This list of patterns, with their slots labeled according to form and function, may look formidable at the moment. But don't worry—and don't try to memorize all this detail. It will fall into place as you come to understand the separate patterns.

The be Patterns

I	**NP** (subject)	*be* (predicating verb)	**ADV/TP** (adverbial)
	The students	*are*	*upstairs*
II	**NP** (subj)	*be* (pred vb)	**ADJ** (subj complement)
	The students	*are*	*diligent*
III	**NP$_1$** (subj)	*be* (pred vb)	**NP$_1$** (subj comp)
	The students	*are*	*scholars*

The Linking Verb Patterns

IV	**NP** (subj)	**linking verb** (pred vb)	**ADJ** (subj comp)
	The students	*seem*	*diligent*
V	**NP$_1$** (subj)	**lnk verb** (pred vb)	**NP$_1$** (subj comp)
	The students	*became*	*scholars*

The Intransitive Verb Pattern

VI	**NP** (subj)	**intransitive verb** (pred vb)
	The students	*rested*

The Transitive Verb Patterns

VII	**NP$_1$** (subj)	**transitive verb** (pred vb)	**NP$_2$** (direct object)	
	The students	*studied*	*their assignment*	
VIII	**NP$_1$** (subj)	**trans verb** (pred vb)	**NP$_2$** (indirect object)	**NP$_3$** (dir obj)
	The students	*gave*	*the teacher*	*their assignment*
IX	**NP$_1$** (subj)	**trans verb** (pred vb)	**NP$_2$** (dir obj)	**ADJ** (obj comp)
	The students	*consider*	*the teacher*	*intelligent*
X	**NP$_1$** (subj)	**trans verb** (pred vb)	**NP$_2$** (dir obj)	**NP$_2$** (obj comp)
	The students	*consider*	*the course*	*a challenge*

===== *Investigating Language 2.2* =====

Because noun phrases play such prominent (and multiple) roles in our sentences, it might be helpful at this point to look briefly at nouns, one of our four **form classes**. This exercise will help you discover the features of our grammar that determine the classification of a word as a noun.

One way to put your intuition to work is to look at some sentences that a native speaker would never say:

> *I borrowed book from friend.[1]
> *I often borrow book from friend.
> *Unfortunately, I lost my friend book.

On the blanks below, write your grammatical version of those three sentences:

_____

_____

_____

There's more than one possibility, of course. But if you compare your answers with those of your classmates, you will probably discover that most of you have added a **determiner**, a noun signaler, to *book* and *friend* in sentence 1; turned *book* and *friend* into *books* and *friends* in sentence 2; and turned *friend* into *friend's* in sentence 3.

By doing what you did—making those kinds of changes—you have classified *book* and *friend* as nouns. You have, in effect, demonstrated two defining characteristics of nouns:

1. A noun is a word that can be made plural and/or possessive.
2. A noun is a word that is signaled, or marked, by a determiner.

(The most common determiners are the articles, *a* and *the*. You've seen a number of others in our sample sentences in this chapter: *my, their, this*. For more about determiners, see Chapter 12.)

You can now use your definition as a "rule of thumb" for figuring out if a word is indeed a noun: "Can I make it plural and/or possessive?" and "Can I use *the* with it?" In the case of most nouns, the answer to one or both questions will be "yes."

---

[1]The asterisk before a sentence signals that it is ungrammatical or in some way unacceptable to a native speaker.

For further discussion: You may recall the traditional definition of *noun* as "the name of a person, place, or thing." In what respects does our new definition differ from that one?

THE *BE* PATTERNS

The first three formulas state that when a form of *be* serves as the main, or predicating, verb, an adverbial of time or place, or an adjectival, or a noun phrase will follow it. The one exception to this rule—and, by the way, we can think of the sentence patterns as descriptions of the rules that our internal computer is programmed to follow—is a statement simply affirming existence, such as "I am." Aside from this exception, Patterns I through III describe all the sentences in which a form of *be* is the predicating verb. (Other one-word forms of *be* are *am, is, are, was, were, being,* and *been*; the expanded forms include *have been, was being, might be,* and *will be.*)

PATTERN I: NP *be* ADV/TP

The students are upstairs.
The teacher is here.
The next performance will be soon.

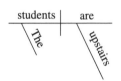

The ADV in the formula stands for *adverbial,* a modifier of the verb. The ADV that follows *be* is, with certain exceptions, limited to *when* and *where* information, so in the formula for Pattern I we identify the slot as ADV/TP, meaning "adverbial of time or place."[2] In the sample sentences *upstairs* and *here* designate place; *soon* designates time.

We are labeling this slot filler as an **adverbial** rather than simply an adverb because the adverbial information is often expressed by a structure other than a simple adverb. One of the most common adverbial structures is the **prepositional phrase,** a two-part structure consisting of a preposition—a word such as *in, out, up, down, over,*

---

[2]See Question 4 at the end of this chapter for examples of these exceptions.

under, between, for, from—and its object, most commonly a noun or noun phrase.

> The students are in the library.
> The next performance will be on Monday.

The diagram of Pattern I shows the adverb below the verb, which is where all adverbials are diagrammed. The diagram for the adverbial prepositional phrase is a two-part framework with a slanted line for the preposition and a horizontal line for the object.

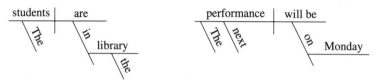

(Because the prepositional phrase is such a common structure in the sentences you'll be seeing as examples, you might find it useful at this point to read about prepositions in Chapter 12.)

PATTERN II: NP *be* ADJ

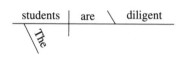

The students are diligent.
The price of steak is ridiculous.
The play was dull.

In this pattern the **complement** that follows *be* is an adjectival. In the language of traditional grammar, this slot is the **subjective complement**: The adjectival both completes the verb and modifies or describes the subject.[3]

At this point you may be wondering how you can recognize a Pattern II sentence when you're not sure what an adjective is. To answer this question, look for a word that will fill both slots in the following frame:

> The _____ NOUN is very _____.

---

[3]More specifically, the traditional label for the subjective complement in Pattern II (and IV) is *predicate adjective;* the traditional label for the NP in Pattern III (and V) is *predicate nominative.* We will use the more general term *subjective complement* for both adjectives and noun phrases.

Only an adjective will fit. For example, when we insert the sample subjective complements into both slots of the frame, we recognize the resulting sentences as grammatical; they are acceptable to a native speaker:

> The diligent student is very diligent.
> The ridiculous price is very ridiculous.
> The dull play is very dull.

There are a few adjectives that don't fit both slots—only one or the other—but most adjectives do; and any word that does fit both is unquestionably an adjective.

Besides adjectives, we sometimes find prepositional phrases filling the subjective complement slot in Pattern II sentences. Such phrases name an attribute of the subject, just as adjectives do:

> He is out of his mind.
> She is in a bad mood.

The diagram for the prepositional phrase in a complement position has that same two-part framework. We attach that frame to the main line by means of a pedestal; in this way the structure is immediately identifiable in terms of both form (prepositional phrase) and function (subjective complement).

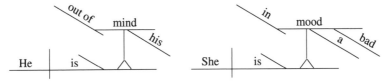

To figure out that such sentences do not belong to Pattern I, you can usually think of an adjective, a single descriptive word, that could substitute for the phrase:

> He is crazy.
> She is cranky.

Moreover, you can easily rule out Pattern I because such phrases do not supply information of time or place.

PATTERN III: NP₁ *be* NP₁

The students are scholars.
Professor Mendez is my math teacher.
The tournament was an exciting event.

students | are \ scholars

The NP, of course, fills the subject slot in all of the patterns; in Pattern III a noun phrase following *be* fills the subjective complement slot as well. The numbers that mark the NPs indicate that the two noun phrases have the same referent. For example, when we say "Professor Mendez is my math teacher," the two NPs, "Professor Mendez" and "my math teacher," refer to the same person. The subjective complement renames the subject; *be*, the main verb, asserts identification or characterization. We could restate the sample sentences:

> The students may be characterized as scholars.
> Professor Mendez is being identified as my math teacher.
> The tournament is being characterized (or identified) as an exciting event.

===== *Exercise 1* =====

Draw vertical lines to isolate the slots in the following sentences; identify each slot according to its form and function, as the example shows. Then identify its sentence pattern.

Example: This vacation | has been | wonderful. (Pattern ___II___)
           NP | be | Adj.
         Subject | Pred vb | Subj Comp

1. Brian's problem is serious. (Pattern _____)

2. The horses are at the gate. (Pattern _____)

3. The excitement of the fans is really contagious. (Pattern _____)

4. Brevity is the soul of wit. [Shakespeare] (Pattern _____)

5. The final exam will be at four o'clock. (Pattern _____)

6. The kids are being unusually silly. (Pattern _____)

7. The Wongs have been terrific neighbors. (Pattern _____)

8. Those joggers are out of shape. (Pattern _____)

9. The basketball team is on a roll. (Pattern_____)

10. A foolish consistency is the hobgoblin of little minds. [Ralph Waldo Emerson] (Pattern _____)

Now do a traditional diagram of each sentence, like those you have seen next to the patterns. (See pages 50–53 for notes on the diagrams.)

THE LINKING VERB PATTERNS

The term *linking verb* applies to all verbs other than *be* completed by a subjective complement—an adjectival or a noun phrase that describes, characterizes, or identifies the subject. (We should note that in many grammar books describing verb classes *be* is not separated from linking verbs. Here we are doing so in order to emphasize the special qualities of *be*, which has variations of both form and function that other verbs do not. However, it is certainly accurate to think of Patterns II and III as the "linking *be*.")

PATTERN IV: NP V-lnk ADJ

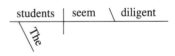

The students seem diligent.
I grew sleepy.
The soup tastes salty.

In these sentences an adjectival fills the subjective complement slot; it describes or names an attribute of the subject, just as in Pattern II. In many cases, a form of *be* can be substituted for the Pattern IV linking verb with a minimal change in meaning: *I grew sleepy* and *I was sleepy* are certainly close in meaning. On the other hand, sentences with *be* and *seem* could have significant differences in meaning.

Pattern IV is a common category for verbs of the senses; besides *taste*, the verbs *smell, feel, sound,* and *look* often link an adjective to the subject.

The soup smells good.
The dog looks sick.

And again, as with Pattern II, an adjectival prepositional phrase some-times fills the subjective complement slot:

> The piano sounds <u>out of tune</u>.
> The fighter seems <u>out of shape</u>.

A complete list of all the verbs that pattern with subjective comple-ments would be fairly short. Besides the verb *seem* and the verbs of the senses, others on the list are *appear, become, get, prove, remain,* and *turn*. But just because the list is short, don't try to memorize it. All of these verbs, with the possible exception of *seem,* hold membership in other verb classes too—transitive or intransitive or both. The way to recognize linking verbs is to understand the role of the subjective complement, to recognize the form of the structure following the verb and its relationship to the subject.

PATTERN V: NP$_1$ V-lnk NP$_1$
The students became scholars.
My uncle remained a bachelor.

In this pattern a noun phrase fills the subjective complement slot following the linking verb. As the formula shows, the two noun phrases have the same referent, just as they do in Pattern III. We should note, too, that very few of the linking verbs mentioned in connection with Pattern IV will fit in Pattern V; most of them take only adjectivals, not noun phrases, as subjective complements. The two most common linking verbs that do take noun phrases are *become* and *remain*.

Again we should remember that the most common link between two noun phrases with the same referent is *be* (Pattern III). And often the substitution of *be* for the linking verb in Pattern V makes little difference in meaning.

===== *Exercise 2* =====

Draw vertical lines to identify the sentence slots, as in Exercise 1. Then label them according to their form and function. Identify the sentence pattern. Diagram each sentence.

1. The baby looks healthy. (Pattern _____)

2. The old neighborhood gang has remained good friends. (Pattern _____)

3. Exotic birds are becoming popular family pets. (Pattern _____)

4. The piano sounds out of tune. (Pattern _____)

5. Ryan looks like his older brother. (Pattern _____)

6. You look a mess! (Pattern _____)

7. That spaghetti smells wonderful. (Pattern _____)

8. Your idea seems very sensible. (Pattern _____)

THE OPTIONAL SLOTS

Before looking at the last five patterns, we will examine an optional **slot**, the adverbial slot, which can appear in every sentence pattern. It is useful to think of the two or three or four slots in the basic patterns as sentence "requirements," the elements needed for sentence completeness. But it's obvious that many, if not most, of our sentences include information beyond the basic requirements—words or phrases that answer such questions as *where, when, why, how, how often,* and the like. Because the sentences are grammatical without them, we consider the elements filling these adverbial slots as "optional." You'll recall that in the case of Pattern I, however, the ADV/TP slot, the adverbial of time or place, is required. But a Pattern I sentence can include the optional adverbials, too, along with its required time and/or place adverbial:

> The fans were in line (*where?*) for tickets to the play-offs (*why?*).
> The plane was on the runway (*where?*) for an hour (*how long?*).

All ten sentence patterns can include optional adverbials, which can come at the beginning or end of the sentence or even in the middle. And no sentence is limited to just one adverbial structure; a sentence can have any number of adverbials, providing information about time, place, manner, reason, and the like.

I stopped <u>at the deli</u> (*where?*) <u>for some bagels</u> (*why?*). (Pattern VI)

<u>On Saturday night</u> (*when?*) the library was almost deserted. (Pattern II)

Mario <u>suddenly</u> (*how?*) hit the brakes. (Pattern VII)

No matter where they occur in the sentence, all adverbials are diagrammed as modifiers of the verb; the adverbs go on diagonal lines and prepositional phrases on a two-part line below the verb:

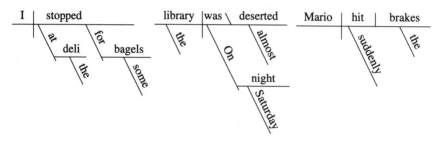

These and other forms of adverbials are discussed in detail in Chapter 6.

THE INTRANSITIVE VERB PATTERN

PATTERN VI: NP V-int

The students rested.

John slept.

The visitors from El Paso arrived.

This formula describes the pattern of intransitive verb sentences. An **intransitive verb** has no complement—no noun phrase or adjectival—following. It's true, however, that such skeletal sentences are rare in both speech and writing; most Pattern VI sentences have information other than the simple subject and verb. You're likely to find adverbial information added:

The students rested <u>after their long trip</u>.

John slept <u>soundly</u>.

The visitors from El Paso arrived <u>on schedule</u>.

You may have noticed that the diagram of this pattern looks a great deal like that of Pattern I, with no complement following the verb on the main line. But there is a difference: The adverbial in Pattern I is not optional; it is required. Another important difference between Patterns I and VI is in the kind of adverbials the sentences include. Pattern I nearly always has a structure that tells where or when. The optional adverbial of Pattern VI, however, is not restricted to time and place information; it can answer other questions, such as *why* or *how* or *how long*. We can say, "John *slept* soundly" or "John *slept* for an hour" (Pattern VI), but we cannot say, "John *was* soundly" or "John *was* for an hour."

Exceptions to the Intransitive Pattern. Unlike the linking verb patterns, with their handful of verbs, the intransitive category has thousands of members. And among them are a few verbs that require an adverbial to make them complete (much like the required adverbial in Pattern I). For example, the following sentences would be ungrammatical without the adverbial:

> My best friend resides in Northridge.
> The boys sneaked past the watchman.
> She glanced at her watch.

Reside and *sneak* and *glance* are intransitive verbs, but if you read these sentences without the adverbial, it will be obvious that they're incomplete. We could provide a new sentence pattern for this category of intransitive verbs, but since the number is so small, we will simply consider them exceptions to the usual Pattern VI formula.

Intransitive Phrasal Verbs. **Phrasal verbs** are common structures in English. They consist of a verb combined with a preposition-like word, known as a **particle**; together they form an **idiom**. The term *idiom* refers to a combination of words whose meaning cannot be predicted from the meaning of its parts; it is a set expression, or formula, that acts as a unit. In the following sentence, the meaning of the underlined phrasal verb is not the meaning of *up* added to the meaning of *made*:

> We made up.

Rather, *made up* means "reconciled our differences."

In the following sentence, however, *up* is not part of the verb:

We jumped up.

Here *up* is simply an adverb modifying *jumped*. The meaning of *jumped up* is the meaning of the adverb *up* added to *jumped*. The two diagrams demonstrate the difference:

Another way to demonstrate the properties of verbs such as *made up* and *jumped up* is to test variations of the sentences for parallel results. For example, adverbs can often be shifted to opening position:

Up we jumped.

But notice the ungrammatical result in the case of *made up*:

*Up we made.

Here are some other Pattern VI sentences with phrasal verbs. Note that the first two include optional adverbials.

We turned in at midnight.
The union finally gave in to the company's demands.
Tony will pull through.
My favorite slippers wore out.
The party broke up.

In each case the phrasal verb has a special meaning that is different from the meaning of its parts: Here *gave in* means "capitulated"; *pull through* means "recover"; *broke up* means "ended."

====== *Exercise 3* ======

Before you diagram these sentences, you'll have to decide if the word following the verb is an *adverb* or a *particle* or a *preposition*. Try both the movability test and the meaning test to help you decide on the slot boundaries. Then diagram the sentences.

1. The car turned in a complete circle.
2. The boys turned in at midnight.
3. The baby turned over by himself.
4. The students turned around in their seats.
5. A big crowd turned out for the parade.
6. The fighter passed out in the first round.
7. He came to after thirty seconds.
8. Susan came to the party late.
9. Two witnesses came forward with new evidence.
10. Bill came for his coat.

THE TRANSITIVE VERB PATTERNS

Unlike intransitive verbs, all **transitive verbs** take one or more complements. The last four formulas classify transitive verbs according to the kinds and number of complements they take. All transitive verbs have one complement in common: the **direct object**. Pattern VII, which has only that one complement, can be thought of as the basic transitive verb pattern.

PATTERN VII: NP$_1$ V-tr NP$_2$
The students studied their assignment.
The lead-off batter hit a home run.
That car needs four new tires.

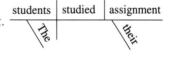

In these sentences the noun phrase following the verb, the **direct object**, has a referent different from that of the subject, as indicated by the different numbers in the formula. Traditionally, we think of the transitive verb as an action word: Its subject is considered the doer and its object the receiver of the action. In many Pattern VII sentences this meaning-based definition applies fairly accurately. In our Pattern VII sample sentences, for instance, we can think of *their assignment* as the receiver of the action *studied* and *a home run* as a receiver of the action *hit*. But sometimes the idea of *receiver of the action* doesn't apply at all:

> Our team won the game.
> We enjoyed the game.

In both of these sentences, we would certainly be more accurate to say that *game* names the action rather than receives it. And in the sentence about the car needing new tires and in this one—

> Red spots covered her neck and face—

we are describing a situation rather than an action. So although it is true that many transitive verbs are action words and many direct objects are receivers, this meaning-based way of analyzing the sentence doesn't always work.

We can also think of the direct object as the answer to a *what* or *whom* question:

> The students studied (*what?*) geometry.
> Devon helped (*whom?*) her little brother.

However, the question will not differentiate transitive verbs from linking verbs; the subjective complements in Patterns III and V also tell *what*:

> Pat is a doctor. (Pat *is what?*)
> Pat became a doctor. (Pat *became what?*)

The one method of distinguishing transitive verbs that works almost every time is the recognition that the two noun phrases have different referents. We don't have to know that *study* and *hit* and *need* are transitive verbs in order to classify the sentences as Pattern VII; we simply recognize that the two noun phrases, the one before the verb and the one following, do not refer to the same thing. Then we know that the second noun phrase is the direct object.

An exception occurs when the direct object is either a **reflexive pronoun** (John cut *himself*) or a **reciprocal pronoun** (John and Mary love *each other*). A **pronoun** (*himself, each other, I, me, he, she, it, they,* etc.) is a word that takes the place of a noun phrase. In these sentences with reflexive and reciprocal pronouns, the two NPs, the subject and the direct object, have the same referent, so the numbers 1 and 2 in the formula are inaccurate. In terms of the referents of the NPs, these sentences actually resemble Pattern V, the linking verb pattern. But clearly the purpose and sense of the verbs—*cut* and *love* in the case of these examples—are not like those of the linking verbs. Rather than institute a separate sentence pattern for these exceptions, where the difference is not in the verbs, we include these sentences in Pattern VII, simply recognizing that when the direct object is a reciprocal or reflexive pronoun the formula numbers are inaccurate.

Transitive Phrasal Verbs. Many of the idiomatic phrasal verbs belong to the transitive verb category, and like other transitive verbs they take direct objects. Compare the meaning of *came by* in the following sentences:

> He came by his fortune in an unusual way.
> He came by the office in a big hurry.

In the first sentence, *came by* means "acquired"; in the second, *by the office* is a prepositional phrase that modifies the intransitive verb *came*, telling where:

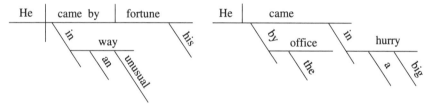

You can also demonstrate the difference between these two sentences by transforming them:

> By which office did he come?
> *By which fortune did he come?

It is clear that *by* functions differently in the two sentences.

The transitive phrasal verbs include both two- and three-word strings:

> I don't go in for horse racing.   _____
> I won't put up with your nonsense.   _____

The dog suddenly <u>turned</u> on its trainer.   _____

The principal <u>passed out</u> the new regulations.   _____

I finally <u>found out</u> the truth.   _____

You can test these as you did the intransitive phrasal verbs, by finding a single word that has the same general meaning. On the blank lines write the one-word substitutes.

===== *Exercise 4* =====

Identify the form and function of the sentence slots; then identify the sentence pattern. (Remember to be on the lookout for phrasal verbs.) Diagram each sentence.

1. The boys prepared a terrific spaghetti dinner. (Pattern _____)

2. An old jalopy turned into our driveway. (Pattern _____)

3. The ugly duckling turned into a beautiful swan. (Pattern _____)

4. The fog comes on little cat feet. [Carl Sandburg] (Pattern _____)

5. On Sundays the neighbor walks his dog at 6:00 A.M. (Pattern _____)

6. I can't make out the address on this envelope. (Pattern _____)

7. After two months, the teachers called off their strike. (Pattern _____)

8. Everyone was reminiscing at our class reunion about the good old days. (Pattern _____)

9. My best friend from high school majors in English at Portland State. (Pattern _____)

10. The mass of men lead lives of quiet desperation. [H. D. Thoreau] (Pattern _____)

PATTERN VIII: NP₁ V-tr NP₂ NP₃

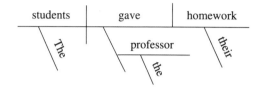

The students gave the professor their homework.
The judges awarded Mary the prize.
The clerk handed me the wrong package.

In this pattern, *two* noun phrase complements follow the verb. Again, the three different subscript numbers on the three NPs indicate that the three noun phrases all have different referents. (When the referents are the same, the numbers are the same, as in Patterns III and V.) The first slot following the verb is the indirect object; the second is the direct object. Even though both Patterns VII and VIII use transitive verbs, they are easily distinguished, since Pattern VII has only one NP following the verb and Pattern VIII has two.

We traditionally define **indirect object** as the *recipient of the direct object* or as the person *to whom* or *for whom* the action is performed. In most cases this definition applies accurately. A Pattern VIII verb—and this is a limited group—usually has a meaning like "give," and the indirect object usually names a person who is the receiver of whatever the subject, NP₁, gives. As with Pattern VII, however, the most accurate way to distinguish this pattern is simply to recognize that all three noun phrases have different referents: In the first sample sentence, *the students, the professor,* and *their homework* all refer to different people or things. Incidentally, in the third Pattern VIII sample sentence, a pronoun rather than a noun phrase fills the indirect object slot.

An important characteristic of the Pattern VIII sentence is the option we have of shifting the indirect object to a position following the direct object, where it will be the object of a preposition:

The students gave their homework to the professor.
The judges awarded the prize to Mary.
The clerk handed the wrong package to me.

With some Pattern VIII verbs the preposition will be *for* rather than *to*:

> Jim's father bought him a new car.
> Jim's father bought a new car <u>for him</u>.

When the direct object is a pronoun rather than a noun phrase, the shift is required; without the prepositional phrase, the sentence would be ungrammatical:

> The students gave it to the professor.
> *The students gave the professor it.
> Jim's father bought it for him.
> *Jim's father bought him it.

You'll notice that the shift will not alter the diagram. The indirect object is diagrammed as if it were the object in an adverbial prepositional phrase—even when there is no preposition:

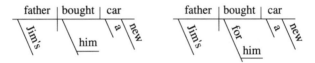

It's also important to understand that the shift of the indirect object from the slot following the verb to that of object of the preposition does not mean that the sentence pattern changes. Remember that the sentence patterns represent verb categories. Pattern VIII covers the "give" group of verbs, those that include both a direct object and a "recipient" of that object. In other words, there are two possible slots for that recipient, the indirect object, in the Pattern VIII sentence.

In the discussion of Pattern VII we noted that when the direct object is a reflexive or reciprocal pronoun (*myself, themselves, each other,* etc.) its referent is identical to that of the subject. The same system of identity applies in Pattern VIII when reflexive or reciprocal pronouns fill the indirect object slot, as they often do:

> Jill gave *herself* a haircut.
> We gave *each other* identical Christmas presents.

For these examples, the referent numbers 1, 2, and 3 do not apply to the three NP slots. *Jill* and *herself* refer to the same person; so do *we* and *each other.* In most Pattern VIII sentences, all three NPs have different referents, represented by the numbers 1, 2, and 3.

PATTERN IX: NP₁ V-tr NP₂ ADJ

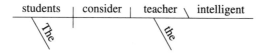

The students consider the teacher intelligent.
The teacher made the test easy.
The boys painted their hockey sticks blue.

In this pattern the direct object, NP₂, is followed by a second complement, an adjective that modifies or describes the direct object; this is the **objective complement**. The relationship between the direct object and the objective complement is the same as the relationship between the subject and the subjective complement in Patterns II and IV. In Patterns II and IV the subjective complement describes the subject; in Pattern IX the objective complement describes the direct object. We could say, in fact,

The teacher is intelligent.
The test is easy.
The hockey sticks are blue.

The function of the objective complement is twofold: (1) It completes the meaning of the verb; and (2) it describes the direct object.

When we remove the objective complement from a Pattern IX sentence, we are sometimes left with a grammatical and meaningful sentence: "The boys painted their hockey sticks." (This is now Pattern VII.) However, most Pattern IX sentences require the objective complement; the meaning of the first two examples under the Pattern IX formula would change without it:

The students consider the teacher.
The teacher made the test.

Pattern IX is a small class, with relatively few verbs, most of which appear equally often in Pattern VII, where they take the direct object only. Other verbs commonly found in this pattern are *prefer, like,* and *find.* Some Pattern IX verbs, such as *consider* and *make,* also commonly appear in Pattern X.

PATTERN X: NP$_1$ V-tr NP$_2$ NP$_2$

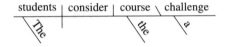

The students consider the course a challenge.
The students elected Barbara chairperson.
They named their dog Sandy.

Just as both adjectives and noun phrases can be subjective complements, both adjectives and noun phrases also serve as objective complements. In Pattern X the objective complement is a noun phrase, one with the same referent as the direct object, as indicated by the numbers in the formula. Its twofold purpose is much the same as that of the adjectival objective complement in Pattern IX: (1) It completes the meaning of the verb; and (2) it renames the direct object. And, again, we can compare the relationship of the two noun phrases to that of the subject and subjective complement in Pattern III:

The course is a challenge.
Barbara is the chairperson.

In fact, the possibility of actually inserting the words *to be* between the direct object and the following slot can serve as a test for Patterns IX and X. That is, if *to be* is possible, then what follows is an objective complement. Which of the following sentences will pass the "to be" test?

Taro finds his job easy.
Taro found his job easily.
Pam found her job the hard way.
Taro takes his job seriously.
Pam finds her job a challenge.

If you have decided that the first and last sentences in the list could include *to be,* you have identified objective complements. The other three, you'll discover, end with adverbials that tell "how" about the verb.

Sometimes the objective complement is signaled by *as*, which we call an **expletive**, or operator:

> We elected Tom *as* our secretary.
> We refer to him *as* "Mr. Secretary."
> I know him *as* a good friend.

In some cases, the *as* is optional; in other cases, it is required. With the verbs *refer to* and *know*, for example, we cannot add the objective complement without *as*:

> *We refer to him "Mr. Secretary."
> *I know her a good friend.

The expletive is diagrammed just before the objective complement but above the line:

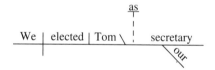

This use of *as* is discussed further on pages 325–326.

═══ *Exercise 5* ═══════════════════════════════

First identify the sentence slots according to their form and function to help you identify sentence patterns. Then diagram the sentences. (*Note:* The list includes sentences representing all four verb classes: *be,* linking, intransitive, and transitive.)

1. The neighborhood kids drive my mother crazy. (Pattern _____)

2. She describes them as a menace to the neighborhood. (Pattern _____)

3. On Friday the weather suddenly turned colder. (Pattern _____)

4. Yesterday Luis bought himself an expensive leather coat at Nordstrom's. (Pattern _____)

5. England's soccer fans have a reputation for wild behavior. (Pattern _____)

6. My boss at the pizza parlor promised me a raise. (Pattern _____)

7. Hector's party broke up at midnight. (Pattern _____)

8. The voters elected Bill Clinton president in 1992. (Pattern _____)

9. Joe cut himself a huge piece of cake. (Pattern _____)

10. Alaska became the fiftieth state in 1959. (Pattern _____)

11. According to the 1980 census, Wyoming is our least populous state. (Pattern _____)

12. Some people consider Minnesota's winters excessively long. (Pattern _____)

13. Our team plays Indiana in the Holiday Invitational Tournament on Saturday night. (Pattern _____)

14. I ordered you a cheeseburger with onions. (Pattern _____)

15. Professor Moore assigned the class six chapters for Monday. (Pattern _____)

DIAGRAMMING THE SENTENCE PATTERNS

The traditional sentence diagram is a visual aid to help you remember the patterns, to understand their common features, and to distinguish their differences. On page 49, where all ten diagrams are shown together, you can see the relationships among them. For example, the two linking verb patterns closely resemble the two *be* patterns, II and III, above them. Likewise, the intransitive verb pattern, VI, placed at the left of the page, looks exactly like the main line of Pattern I. Finally, the slanted line that separates the subjective complement from the verb in the *be* and linking verb patterns, II through V, depicts a relationship similar to that of the objective complement and object in Patterns IX and X, which are also separated by a slanted line. You might find it useful to label the slots on the diagrams according to their functions (subject, subjective complement, direct object, indirect object, objective complement).

The be *Patterns*

I. NP *be* ADV/TP

II. NP *be* ADJ

III. NP₁ *be* NP₁

The Linking Verb Patterns

IV. NP V-lnk ADJ

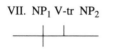

V. NP₁ V-lnk NP₁

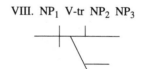

The Intransitive Verb Pattern

VI. NP V-int

The Transitive Verb Patterns

VII. NP₁ V-tr NP₂

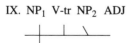

VIII. NP₁ V-tr NP₂ NP₃

IX. NP₁ V-tr NP₂ ADJ

X. NP₁ V-tr NP₂ NP₂

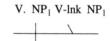

PUNCTUATION AND THE SENTENCE PATTERNS

There is an easy punctuation lesson to be learned from the sentence patterns with their two or three or four slots:

DO NOT PUT SINGLE COMMAS BETWEEN THE REQUIRED SLOTS.

That is, never separate—

- the subject from the verb.
- the verb from the direct object.
- the direct object from the objective complement.
- the indirect object from the direct object.
- the verb from the subjective complement.

For example, in these two sentences there is no place for commas:

The sportswriters considered the game between the Lions and the Panthers one of the truly great games of the football season.
All of the discussion groups I took part in during Orientation Week were extremely helpful for the incoming freshmen.

So even though the noun phrases that fill the slots may be long, the slots are never separated by commas. A pause for breath does not signal a comma. Often we do have sentences in which punctuation is called for *within* a noun phrase slot, but even then the rule applies: no single commas between the required slots.

The one exception to this rule occurs when the direct object is a direct quotation following a verb like *say*. Here the punctuation convention calls for a comma before the quoted words:

He said, "I love you."

NOTES ON THE DIAGRAMS

Except for a few modifications, this method of diagramming follows the Reed and Kellogg system, which dates back to the late nineteenth century and traditional school grammar. The diagram provides you with a visual framework for organizing details of the sentence patterns, recognizing their similarities and differences, and understanding the relationship of their parts. Doing the diagram forces you to account for every structure in the sentence.

The diagram is not perfect by any means. One major drawback is that it does not maintain word order. And there are a number of sentence structures that it does not represent accurately. But for the most part, for most of our sentences, the diagram provides a valuable visual aid.

The Main Line. The positions on the main horizontal line of the diagram represent the slots in the sentence pattern formulas. Only two required slots are not included on the main line: the adverbial (see Pattern I) and the indirect object (see Pattern VIII). The vertical line that bisects the main line separates the subject and the predicate, showing the binary nature of the sentence. The other vertical and diagonal lines stop at the horizontal line:

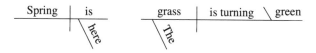

The Noun Phrase. The noun phrases we have used so far are fairly simple; in Chapter 7 we will identify a wide variety of structures that can modify and expand the noun. But now we will simply recognize the feature that all noun phrases have in common—the noun head, or headword. This is the single word that fills the various NP slots of the diagrams; it always occupies a horizontal line. The modifiers slant down from the noun headword:

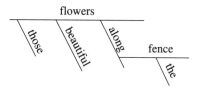

Qualifiers of adjectives are placed on diagonal lines attached to and parallel with the adjective:

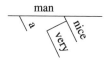

The Verb Phrase.   The complements are set off from the verb:

1. The subjective complement follows a diagonal line. The line slants toward the subject to show their relationship:

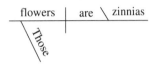

2. The direct object always follows a vertical line:

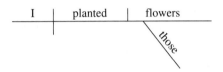

   Note that only Patterns VIII through X have this vertical line following the verb: the only patterns with a direct object.

3. The objective complement is set off from the direct object by a line that slants toward the object:

   I | consider | zinnias \ beautiful

4. The indirect object is placed below the verb. We can understand the logic of this treatment of the indirect object when we realize that it can be expressed by a prepositional phrase without changing the meaning or the pattern of the sentence. Both of these sentences are Pattern VIII :

      The students gave the teacher an apple.

      The students gave an apple to the teacher.

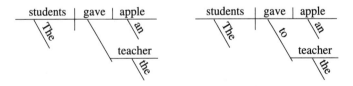

5. Adverbs are placed on slanted lines below the verb; they are modifiers of the verb:

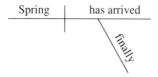

6. Like the qualifiers of adjectives, qualifiers of adverbs are placed on diagonal lines attached to the adverb:

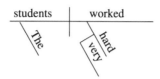

The Prepositional Phrase. The preposition is placed on a diagonal line, its object on a horizontal line attached to it. The prepositional phrase slants down from the noun or verb it modifies. When the prepositional phrase fills the subjective complement slot, it is attached to the main line by means of a pedestal:

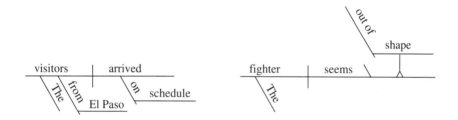

Punctuation. There are no punctuation marks of any kind in the diagram, other than apostrophes.

KEY TERMS IN CHAPTER 2

In this chapter you've been introduced to the basic vocabulary of sentence grammar. Even though this list of key terms may look formidable, some of the terms are already familiar, and those that are new will become more familiar as you continue the study of sentences. You'll discover, too, that the patterns and their diagrams, as shown on page 49, provide a framework for helping you organize many of these concepts.

Adjectival	Particle
Adjective	Phrasal verb
Adverb	Phrase
Adverbial	Predicate
Be patterns	Predicating verb
Clause	Preposition
Complement	Prepositional phrase
Determiner	Pronoun
Direct object	Reciprocal pronoun
Form	Referent
Function	Reflexive pronoun
Headword	Sentence pattern
Indirect object	Subject
Intransitive verb	Subjective complement
Linking verb	Transitive verb
Noun phrase	Verb
Objective complement	Verb phrase
Optional slot	

SENTENCES FOR PRACTICE

Identify the form and function of the sentence slots; identify the sentence pattern; diagram.

1. In the evening Chicago's skyline is a beautiful sight.
2. After the picnic the teacher rounded up the kindergartners for the long return trip.
3. My uncle is moving to Arizona for his health.
4. The asparagus in our garden grows really fast during June.
5. Our grocer calls asparagus the Rolls Royce of vegetables.
6. In 1992 scientists announced an important breakthrough in their research on the AIDS virus.
7. Tall oaks from little acorns grow. [David Everett].
8. Our math teacher assigned everyone in the class six pages of homework.
9. According to the afternoon papers, the police are looking into the sources of the reporter's information.

10. Our art history class was at the museum for three hours on Tuesday afternoon.
11. Some people find modern art very depressing.
12. Jeff pleaded innocent.
13. For most of the morning the kids have been in a very grumpy mood.
14. Some soccer teams in Europe have canceled their games with English teams because of the fans' wild behavior.
15. Cosmetic surgery has become a growth industry in this country.
16. Our oil supply from the Middle East may be in jeopardy.
17. Something is rotten in the State of Denmark. [Shakespeare]
18. The rules of Japanese baseball seem very strange to Americans.
19. In Japanese baseball the ideal score is a tie.
20. Athletes from 171 countries competed in the 1992 Summer Olympics in Barcelona.

QUESTIONS FOR DISCUSSION

1. Here are some pairs of sentences that look alike. Think about their sentence patterns; diagram them to demonstrate their differences.

The teacher made the test hard.
The batter hit the ball hard.

My husband made me a chocolate cake.
My husband made me a happy woman.

We set off through the woods at dawn.
We set off the firecrackers at dawn.

2. The following sentences are either Pattern I or Pattern II; in other words, the prepositional phrases following *be* are either adverbial or adjectival. What test can you use to distinguish between them?

The mechanic is under the car.
The mechanic is under the weather.

The teacher is in a bad mood.
The teacher is in the cafeteria.

The students were in a frenzy.
The students were in a parade.

3. Very few verbs are restricted to a single category. Verbs like *taste* and *feel* commonly act as linking verbs, but they can fit into other classes as well. Identify the patterns of the following sentences:

The cook tasted the soup.
The soup tasted good.

I felt the kitten's fur.
The fur feels soft.

The farmers in Iowa grow a lot of wheat.
The wheat grows fast in July.
We grew weary in the hot sun.

She appeared tired.
Black clouds appeared suddenly on the horizon.

4. Some sentences in English are not represented by one of the ten patterns described in this chapter. Among those that don't fit very well are certain sentences with *be* as the main verb:

The book is about black holes.
The potato salad is for the picnic.
I am from San Francisco.
I am in favor of the amendment.
The misunderstanding was over a scheduling conflict.
Pat and Jen are among the most popular students in our class.

The prepositional phrases in these sentences are different from those we saw in Patterns I and II. How would you characterize the difference? A paraphrase of the sentence might help you to determine a possible pattern. And in the following *be* sentences, the noun phrase in subjective complement position is different from those we saw in Pattern III. Do these sentences belong in Pattern III? If not, where do they belong?

My shoes are the wrong color.
This new wallpaper is an odd pattern.

And in what way does the following sentence change our understanding of the *be* patterns?

The time is now.

5. Consider the following sentences:

The roast weighs five pounds.
The roast cost twenty dollars.

Because the slot following the verb is filled by an adverbial, we classify these sentences as Pattern VI, as intransitive verbs. But some linguists include such verbs in the "midverb" category. Explain their rationale for doing so. Could you also make a case for including them in Pattern VII with the transitive verbs instead of in Pattern VI?

6. People commonly say "I feel badly" when discussing their physical or mental condition. Using your understanding of sentence patterns, explain why this is sometimes considered an ungrammatical sentence. Assuming that "I feel badly" is indeed questionable, how do you explain the acceptance of "I feel strongly about that"?

7. What is unusual about the following sentence? Think about the sentence pattern:

The waitress served me my coffee black.

8. We have seen sentences in which prepositional phrases function as subjective complements. Can they be objective complements as well?

9. You have learned that one way to distinguish particles from prepositions in some sentences that look alike is to test the words for movability:

Joe turned *on* the light.
Joe turned the light *on*.

Joe turned *on* the bridge.
*Joe turned the bridge *on*.

I will look *up* the words.
I will look the words *up*.

I will look *up* the hall.
*I will look the hall *up*.

It is also interesting to discover that our use of pronouns is determined to a certain extent by the position of the particle:

> Joe turned *the light* on.
> Joe turned *it* on.
> Joe turned on *the light*.
> *Joe turned on *it*.

Try the same kind of substitutions in the following sentences:

> Joe brought up the laundry from the basement.
> He brought up an unexpected topic.
> The suspect made up a phony alibi.
> The police eventually found out the truth.

Now formulate rules regarding movability and the use of pronouns that can help us recognize phrasal verbs.

10. A sentence is **ambiguous** when it has more than one possible meaning. You can illustrate the two meanings of the following sentences by diagramming each in two different ways. Think about sentence patterns and the referents of the noun phrases.

> Herbert found his new bride a good cook.
> Rosa called her mother.

11. Identify the slot boundaries of the following sentences; label their form and function:

> He took the loss of his job hard.
> She takes her job seriously.

How do these sentences differ from the patterns you have learned?

Here are three more sentences. In what way do they differ from our patterns? (*Reminder*: Think about the optional adverbial slot.)

> Christopher put his toys away.
> Shirley set the books on the table.
> Sue placed the manuscript on Stanley's desk.

If we were to include new patterns to account for these groups of sentences, where in our scheme of ten patterns would we include them?

3

Expanding the Main Verb

In Chapter 2 we described the predicating verb as the central, or pivotal, slot in the sentence. The sentence patterns are, in fact, verb phrase patterns, with the verb determining the functions that follow. Most of the predicating verbs used in the sample sentences so far have been single words: *are, is, studied, gave, consider, became.* We call such verb forms the simple present or simple past tense. But the verbs we use in our everyday speech and writing are often expanded forms that include additional verb forms called **auxiliaries**:

Predicating Verb

	Auxiliary	Main verb	
The students	have	been	unhappy.
John	may	become	a scholar.
The teacher	has	given	us too much work.
The baby	is	sleeping	upstairs.
The students	should	elect	Barbara chairperson.
The students	will	study	tonight.

(*Note:* We are using the term **predicating verb** as a label for the entire verb string—including auxiliaries and the main verb—that fills the verb slot in the sentence patterns.[1])

---

[1]Another term sometimes used to describe the main verb is **finite verb**. The contrasting term **nonfinite** refers to verbs when they function as adverbials, adjectivals, and nominals.

These six auxiliary–verb combinations represent only a small sample of the possibilities for expanding our verbs. With little or no effort our linguistic computer can come up with many other two-word variations—and with three- and four-word strings as well:

> The students will be studying all afternoon.
>
> The baby has been sleeping all morning.
>
> They should have been studying harder.

We have still only scratched the surface.

In this examination of the verb, we want to understand the system underlying our ability to expand it as we do; we want to discover all the verb's possible expansions and to recognize the variations in meaning they can convey. Using *to eat* as our example, we will first look at some of the ways in which we use this verb in everyday situations. (In labeling a verb, we traditionally use the **infinitive** form, which consists of the present tense, in this case *eat*, preceded by *to*, known as the "sign of the infinitive.")

> I eat an apple every day.
>
> I ate one this morning.
>
> I have eaten an apple every day this week.
>
> I should eat oranges as well.
>
> My sister eats the seeds and all.
>
> I am eating a peach at the moment.
>
> I had eaten all the grapes by the time you arrived.
>
> I have been eating junk food all evening.
>
> I was eating both candy and pretzels last night.
>
> I will eat only two candy bars today.
>
> I might have eaten only one yesterday; I forget.
>
> I may be eating a gourmet dinner at Carol and Jim's tonight.

This partial list of the possibilities includes all the forms of the word *eat* itself: *eat, ate, eats, eaten, eating.* (The only verb in English with more than five forms is *be*, with eight: *be, am, are, is, was, were, been,* and *being*.) Anyone familiar with a foreign language will appreciate the simplicity of this small set of only five. A speaker of French or Spanish, instead of adding auxiliaries to express differences as we do, can simply add a different ending, or inflection, to the verb. French verbs, for instance, have more than seventy different inflections to express differences in person, number, tense, and mood.

A speaker of English uses only two different forms (*eat*, *eats*) to express the present tense in first, second, and third person, both singular and plural:

	SINGULAR	PLURAL
1st person	I eat	we eat
2nd person	you eat	you eat
3rd person	he eats she eats it eats	they eat

The speaker of French uses five forms in the present tense; in only the first- and third-person singular are the forms alike:

	SINGULAR	PLURAL
1st person	*je mange*	*nous mangeons*
2nd person	*tu manges*	*vous mangez*
3rd person	*il mange*	*ils mangent*

The speaker of English uses only one form to express the simple past tense:

	SINGULAR	PLURAL
1st person	I ate	we ate
2nd person	you ate	you ate
3rd person	he ate	they ate

Again, the speaker of French uses five, all different from the first set. In fact, for the various tenses and moods the speaker of French uses fourteen such sets, or conjugations, all with different verb endings.

THE FIVE VERB FORMS

Before looking at the system for adding auxiliaries, we will name the five verb forms so that we can conveniently discuss them, using labels that reflect our emphasis on form rather than meaning. (The traditional names are shown in parentheses.)

1. eat	the base form	(present tense)
2. eats	the *-s* form	(3rd-person singular)
3. ate	the *-ed* form	(past tense)
4. eating	the *-ing* form	(present participle)
5. eaten	the *-en* form	(past participle)

A comparison of *eat*, which is an irregular verb, with the regular verb *walk* will provide the rationale for the labels *-ed* and *-en*:

1. base form	eat	walk
2. *-s* form	eats	walks
3. *-ed* form	ate	walked
4. *-ing* form	eating	walking
5. *-en* form	eaten	walked

In the language of traditional grammar, a verb is **regular** when both its simple past tense and its past participle (forms 3 and 5) are formed by adding the inflectional ending *-ed* (or, in some cases, *-d* or *-t*); this means that the past tense and the past participle of regular verbs are always identical in form. This description applies to most verbs. Only a small number, one hundred or so, are **irregular**, although, like *eat*, they are among the verbs we use most frequently. (Incidentally, regular verbs are sometimes referred to as *weak verbs*, irregular verbs as *strong verbs*.) But because we need to distinguish the past tense and the past participle, we give them different labels. The regular past tense inflection (*-ed*) provides the label for the past tense; the *-en* form of irregular verbs such as *eat* (and *drive*, *give*, *break*, *speak*, *choose*, etc.) provides the past participle label.

═════ *Exercise 6* ═════

Fill in the blanks with the four additional forms of the verbs listed on the left. If you have a problem figuring out the *-ed* form, simply use it in a sentence with *yesterday*: "Yesterday I _____ ." If you have trouble figuring out the *-en* form, use it in a sentence with *have*: "I have _____ ."

BASE	-S FORM	-ed FORM	-ing FORM	-en FORM
1. go	_____	_____	_____	_____
2. break	_____	_____	_____	_____
3. come	_____	_____	_____	_____
4. move	_____	_____	_____	_____
5. expect	_____	_____	_____	_____
6. put	_____	_____	_____	_____
7. drink	_____	_____	_____	_____
8. think	_____	_____	_____	_____
9. like	_____	_____	_____	_____
10. feel	_____	_____	_____	_____
11. lose	_____	_____	_____	_____
12. pass	_____	_____	_____	_____
13. meet	_____	_____	_____	_____
14. beat	_____	_____	_____	_____
15. lead	_____	_____	_____	_____
16. read	_____	_____	_____	_____
17. say	_____	_____	_____	_____
18. drive	_____	_____	_____	_____

===== *Investigating Language 3.1* =====

One way to think about the tricky verbs *lie* and *lay* is in terms of their sentence patterns: One is intransitive (Pattern VI) and one is transitive (Pattern VII). Read the following information adapted from *Webster's Ninth New Collegiate Dictionary*; then fill in the blanks, as you did for the irregular verbs in Exercise 6.

lie/ (intran) **lay**/; **lain**/; **lying** 1 a. to be or to stay at rest in a horizontal position; be prostrate: REST, RECLINE (~motionless) (~asleep) b. to assume a horizontal position—often used with *down*.

lay/ (tran) **laid**/; **laying**/ (bef 12c) 1: to beat or strike down with force 2 a: to put or set down b: to place for rest or sleep; esp: BURY 3: to bring forth and deposit (an egg).

BASE	-s FORM	*-ed* FORM	*-ing* FORM	*-en* FORM
1. lie	_____	_____	_____	_____
2. lay	_____	_____	_____	_____

Now identify the verbs in the following sentences as transitive or intransitive and indicate the base form of the verb: Is it *lie* or *lay*?

1. I should lay the papers in neat piles on the table. _____

2. The cat has never lain so still before. _____

3. Yesterday he lay very still. _____

4. I laid the baby on the bed for her nap. _____

5. I lay on the beach for two hours yesterday. _____

If you are accustomed to hearing people say "I'm going to lay down for a nap" or commanding their dogs to "lay down," you may think that the last sentence in the list sounds wrong. It's not unusual to hear people say "I laid on the beach." In fact, it is so common that at the end of the definition for *lay*, just quoted, the dictionary includes *lie* as an intransitive synonym—and labels it "nonstandard." In other words, when you say "lay down," you are using *lay* as a synonym for the intransitive *lie*. (If your dog responds only to standard usage, you'll have to say "lie down.") The reason for the common nonstandard usage becomes clear when you examine the five forms of the two verbs: Both sets include *lay*.

EXPANDING THE VERB

The subtle differences in verb meanings we are able to express result not from variations in the verb itself, with its limit of five forms, but rather from the auxiliaries we add. Here again are the versions of *eat* from the list of sentences on page 60:

1. eat	5. eats	9. was eating
2. ate	6. am eating	10. will eat
3. have eaten	7. had eaten	11. might have eaten
4. should eat	8. have been eating	12. may be eating

What is the system underlying these one- and two- and three-word verb strings? How many more variations are there? What rules and restrictions of our system would have to be included in a computer program designed to generate all the possible variations?

To discover the system, we will make some observations about these twelve variations of *eat*, observations that apply to all verbs in English, both regular and irregular:

1. The base form is used both alone [1] and with *should* [4] and *will* [10].
2. The *-ed* and *-s* forms are used alone [2 and 5].
3. The *-en* form is used after a form of *have: had* [7] and *have* [3, 8, and 11].
4. The *-ing* form is used after a form of *be: am* [6], *been* [8], *was* [9], and *be* [12].

We can state these last two observations in terms of a formula:

(have + -en) + (be + -ing)

This formula means that we can use *have* as an auxiliary, but when we do, we follow it with the *-en* form of the verb; it also states that we can use the *-ing* form of the verb, but when we do, we precede it with a form of *be*. The parentheses mean "optional." This simply means that *have* + *-en* and *be* + *-ing* are optional auxiliaries; that is, a grammatical verb string does not require either or both of them.

What further observations can we make about our list of verbs?

5. If both *have* and *be* are used [8], they appear in that order.
6. Besides *have* and *be*, we have another kind of auxiliary: *should, will, may,* and *might*. We call these **modal auxiliaries (M)**.
7. When a modal appears [4, 10, 11, 12], it is the first word in the string.

Now we can add another element to the formula:

(M) + (have + -en) + (be + -ing)

8. A form of *eat*, the **main verb (MV)**, is always the last word in the string.

(M) + (have + -en) + (be + -ing) + MV

The MV does not appear in parentheses in the formula because it is not optional; it is a part of all the verb strings. Now the formula reads as follows: In generating a verb string, we can use a modal auxiliary if we choose; when we do, it comes first. We can also choose *have*; when we do, the *-en* form follows it. We can also choose *be*; when we do, the *-ing* form follows. When we use more than one auxiliary, they appear in the order given: modal, *have, be*.

M {will} + eat = will eat

have + -en + eat = have eaten

be + -ing + eat = am {is, are} eating

will + have + -en + eat = will have eaten

will + be + -ing + eat = will be eating

The arrows in the foregoing strings show the *-en* and *-ing* attached to the following word. What happens to the *-en* when we choose both *have* and *be*?

have + -en + be + -ing + eat = have been eating

Because the *-en* (and the *-ing*) get attached to whatever follows, here the *-en* produces *been*, the *-en* form of *be*.

So far we have a simple but powerful formula, capable of generating a great many variations of the verb. But something is missing. How can it generate *had eaten* [7] and *was eating* [9]? What exactly is different about them? *Had* and *was* are past tense (*-ed*) forms of *have* and *be*. This means we have to add one more component to the formula: **tense**, which refers to *time*. Among the five forms of the verb, you will recall, the present and past forms are the only tenses, so **T** will represent either present or past tense. Here, then, is the complete formula for the **verb-expansion rule**:

$$\textbf{T} + \textbf{(M)} + \textbf{(have + -en)} + \textbf{(be + -ing)} + \textbf{MV}$$

You might find the branching diagram helpful for visualizing the rule:

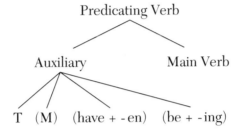

Predicating Verb

Auxiliary   Main Verb

T   (M)   (have + -en)   (be + -ing)

=== *Investigating Language 3.2* ===

The branching diagram illustrates the predicating verb as a two-part structure: an auxiliary and a main verb. Those two parts are obvious in a sentence such as

> We *had eaten* by the time you arrived.
>
> *or*
>
> I *was eating* when you arrived.

Sometimes the two parts of the predicating verbs are not as obvious:

> He *eats* too fast.
> Beth already *ate*.

Look again at the formula, and remember that parentheses mean "optional." The components of the verb that are shown without parentheses are required—and there are two of them.

In sentences with *eats* and *ate*, then, what does the auxiliary consist of?

We can think of T as a tense marker that attaches itself to whatever follows it—that is, to the first word in the string, either M, *have*, *be*, or the main verb. So to generate *had eaten* and *was eating*, we choose *past* as the tense marker:

$$past + have + \text{-}en + eat = had\ eaten$$

$$past + be + \text{-}ing + eat = was\ \{were\}\ eating$$

When there is no auxiliary word intervening, the tense gets attached to the main verb, thus producing either the simple past tense or the simple present.

$$past + eat = ate$$

$$pres + eat = eat\ \{eats\}$$

(It's clear then that the auxiliary in sentences with *ate* or *eats* is simply T.)

If we choose M, the modal auxiliary will carry the tense marker:

past + will + eat = would eat

pres + shall + eat = shall eat

past + can + have + -en + eat = could have eaten

past + can + have + -en + be + -ing + eat = could have been eating

pres + will + be + -ing + eat = will be eating

So now the formula is complete. Here is what it says: In generating a verb string, there are only two requirements—tense, either present or past, and the main verb; the other components of the auxiliary are optional. The tense marker will apply to the first word in the string. We have the option of using three different kinds of auxiliaries: modal, *have*, and *be*. When we use more than one, we use them in that order. The formula also specifies that with *have* we use the *-en* form of the following auxiliary or verb; with *be*, the *-ing* form of the following verb. The last word in the string is the main verb.

=== *Exercise 7* ===

What is the expanded verb that each of the following strings will produce? (Assume in each case that the subject is *Fred*.)

1. pres + have + -en + work
2. past + be + -ing + work
3. pres + have + -en + be + -ing + play
4. past + be + -ing + be
5. pres + be + -ing + have
6. pres + have + -en + have
7. past + have + -en + have
8. past + have + -en + be + -ing + be

THE MODAL AUXILIARIES

The **modal auxiliaries** are so named because they affect what is called the **mood** of the verb. Mood refers to the manner in which a verb is expressed, such as a fact, a desire, a possibility, or a command. The modals convey conditions of probability, possibility, obligation, or necessity: I *may* eat; I *could* eat; I *should* eat; I *must* eat. These are known as the **conditional mood**. (We should also note that the modals *will* and *shall* produce what in traditional terminology is called the future tense: *will eat* and *shall eat*.)

The modals differ from the auxiliaries *have* and *be*, both of which can fill the role of main verb in addition to their auxiliary role. The modals never fill the main verb slot, nor do they have all five forms that verbs have.[2] They have a maximum of two forms, the base form and the *-ed*: *can/could, will/would, shall/should, may/might*. Although we call these forms *present* and *past*, they do not necessarily indicate present and past time; these are simply labels indicating the form of the modal. For example, in the sentence "I may eat" (present), the act of eating is not going on; in "I might eat" (past) the act of eating is not over; in fact, in

---

[2]Sometimes modals appear without verbs in **elliptical sentences**, where the main verb is understood but not expressed:

Who'll cook the spaghetti? I *will*.
May I join you? Yes, you *may*.

both cases it may never happen. Rather, the present and past forms of *may* indicate degrees of probability regarding present and future events. We should note, too, a difference in the base form of verbs and of modals: The base form of the verb combines with *to* to form the infinitive, which can play a number of roles in the sentence; the base form of the modal does not. We say "to eat," but we do not say "to shall."

In addition to these four modals, which include past forms, there are two that have only one form: *must* and *ought to*. One other modal-like auxiliary with two forms is *have to/had to*. It differs from the regular auxiliary *have* in that it fills the modal slot in the verb expansion rule. We refer to it as "modal-like" because it does not pattern with *have* + *-en* and *be* + *-ing* as freely as the other modals do. Incidentally, its past form, *had to*, also supplies the past meaning of *must*: "I *must* go today. I *had to* go yesterday."

The modal auxiliaries enable us to express subtle variations in the meaning of our sentences:

> <u>Would</u> you lend me ten dollars?
>
> <u>Will</u> you lend me ten dollars?
>
> <u>Could</u> you lend me ten dollars?
>
> <u>Can</u> you lend me ten dollars?

These questions express subtle differences—in the degree of politeness, in the extent of the speaker's expectation of getting the money or hesitation in asking, in the perception of the ability of the person addressed to lend the money. In spite of such subtleties, a native speaker has little trouble in choosing the precise modal to fit the social situation. (But we must admit that programming the computer to consider the social nuances would be a challenge.)[3]

---

[3] A group of British linguists has called the modal verbs "one of the most problematic areas of English grammar." The complications include not only differences in meaning from one context to another, but also significant differences in the various parts of the English-speaking world and changes that are taking place. They point out that increasingly "the forms associated with American English are becoming the norm" (Randolph Quirk, Sidney Greenbaum, Geoffrey Leech, and Jan Svartvik, *A Comprehensive Grammar of the English Language*, Longman, 1985, p. 220).

===== *Exercise 8* =====

What is the expanded verb that each of the following strings will produce?

1. pres + shall + be + -ing + go
2. past + shall + have + -en + go
3. past + will + come
4. pres + may + have + -en + be + -ing + play
5. past + may + play
6. past + can + have + -en + drink

Write a complete sentence for each of the verbs. Do your sentences include adverbials of time? Should they?

THE SUBJUNCTIVE MOOD

Before leaving the subject of the verb moods, we should mention another one you may be familiar with: the **subjunctive**. The subjunctive mood is not a matter of adding modal auxiliaries, as the conditional is. Rather, it is simply a variation of the verb that we use in special circumstances. For example, after verbs that convey a strong suggestion or recommendation, we often use a *that* clause:

> We suggested that Mary go with us.
>
> Kathy insisted that Bill consult the doctor.
>
> The doctor recommended that Bill stay in the hospital.
>
> I move that the meeting be adjourned.

The use of the base form of the verb in these *that* clauses is an example of the subjunctive mood. Notice that even for a third-person singular subject, which would normally take the -s form, we have used the base form: Mary *go*; Bill *consult*; Bill *stay*; the meeting *be*. Other verbs that commonly take clauses in the subjunctive mood are *command*, *demand*, *ask*, *require*, *order*, and *propose*.

The subjunctive *that* clause also modifies certain nouns and adjectives related to commands, suggestions, and the like:

The suggestion <u>that Bill see the doctor</u> was a good one.

The doctor's insistence <u>that Bill stay in the hospital</u> took us by surprise.

It is advisable <u>that he get a thorough checkup.</u>

It is imperative <u>that Bill follow the doctor's orders.</u>

The subjunctive mood also occurs when *be* is the main verb in *if* clauses that express a wish or a condition contrary to fact:

<u>If I were you,</u> I'd be careful.

<u>If Joe weren't so lazy,</u> he'd probably be a millionaire.

<u>If my parents were rich,</u> I wouldn't need a bank loan.

In clauses such as these, *were* is the standard form of *be*, no matter what the subject. However, the use of *was* is also fairly common in sentences like the second example:

<u>If Joe was here,</u> he'd agree with me.

In writing, however, the subjunctive *were* is the standard form.

ASPECT OF THE VERB

The auxiliaries *have* (with *-en*) and *be* (with *-ing*) indicate what we call the **aspect** of the verb, referring to whether the action of the verb is completed or in progress. With our variations in the aspect, we can express both limited and extended actions in the present and the past:

I <u>had</u> eaten dinner....

I <u>have</u> eaten dinner....

I <u>had been</u> eating dinner....

I <u>was</u> eating dinner....

I <u>am</u> eating dinner....

Although we have no future tense among our five forms of the verb, we can express the future with the modals *shall* and *will*, with *be* + *-ing* + *go*

("I'm going to eat soon"), or with *be + about* + V ("I am about to leave"), or by using an adverbial in connection with the present tense ("The bus leaves at noon").

The traditional grammarian labels verbs with *have + -en* as perfect tenses and those with *be + -ing* as progressive. So a verb form labeled "past perfect tense, indicative mood," simply means "past + *have + -en* + V." **Indicative** (in contrast to conditional) names the mood that refers to a sentence dealing with fact, not probability, or a question about a fact.

USING THE VERB FORMS

Following are examples of our most common verb forms; their traditional labels are shown in parentheses.

Base form and -s form (SIMPLE PRESENT)

I live in Omaha.

The news comes on at six.

The leaves on our maple tree turn
  absolutely golden in October.

Milton's poetry speaks to
  everyone.

Habitual or timeless present

I understand your position.

Present point in time

Pres + be + -ing + MV (PRESENT PROGRESSIVE)

I am working at Wal-Mart.

John is taking philosophy this
  term.

Present action of limited duration

Note that both of these present forms can indicate future time with the addition of an appropriate adverbial:

The bus leaves at *seven*.

We're having pizza *tonight*.

Past + *MV* (SIMPLE PAST)

I <u>moved</u> to Omaha last March.

Diane <u>passed</u> her law board

exam.   *Specific point in time*

The computer <u>swallowed</u> all of

my data.

Note that with an appropriate adverbial, this form can indicate a period of time in the past:

I <u>studied</u> Spanish *for three years in high school.*

Past + *be* + *-ing* + *MV* (PAST PROGRESSIVE)

A baby <u>was crying</u> during the   *Past action of limited*
entire ceremony this morning.   *duration (often to show*

I <u>was trying</u> to sleep last night   *one particular action*
during the party, but it was   *during a larger span of*
no use.   *time).*

Pres + *have* + *-en* + *MV* (PRESENT PERFECT)

The leaves <u>have turned</u> yellow   *A completed action*
already.   *extending from a point*

I <u>have finished</u> my work.   *in the past to either*
                                           the present or the near
I <u>have memorized</u> several of   *present or occurring*
Frost's poems.   *at an unspecified past*
                                           time.

Past + *have* + *-en* + *MV* (PAST PERFECT)

The hikers <u>had used</u> up all
their water, when finally
they found a hidden spring.   *Past action completed*
The students <u>had finished</u> only   *before another action in*
the first page of the test by   *the past.*
the time the bell rang.

Pres* + *have* + *-en* + *be* + *-ing* + *MV (PRESENT PERFECT PROGRESSIVE)

The authorities <u>have been looking</u>
for the arson suspect since
last Sunday.

*Past action continuing
into the present.*

Past* + *have* + *-en* + *be* + *-ing* + *MV (PAST PERFECT PROGRESSIVE)

The authorities <u>had been looking</u>
for the suspect even before
the fire broke out.

*Continuing past
action completed
before another
action in the past.*

EXCEPTIONS TO THE RULE

The verb-expansion rule is simple, but it is powerful. With it we can expand the verb slot in all the sentence patterns to express a great many variations in meaning. Given the variety of modals we have, which we can use with or without *have* + *-en* and *be* + *-ing*, the number of possible variations adds up to fifty or more for most verbs. However, we rarely use all the possibilities for any given verb. Our system restricts the use of some, and others we simply have no occasion for. Although we may say,

He has been eating.

we would probably never say,

*They have been remaining friends.
or
*Tiffany is resembling her mother.

We would probably say, instead,

They have remained friends.
and
Tiffany resembles her mother.

And when we hear someone say,

*He is seeming happy.
or

*The price of steak is being ridiculous.

or

*I am preferring my coffee black.

or

*Paul is owning a BMW.

we are probably correct in concluding that we are hearing a nonnative speaker of English.

Like the preceding examples, most of the exceptions involve the restriction of *be* + *-ing* with linking verbs, with *be* as main verb, and with a small number of transitive verbs that refer to mental processes, such as *prefer*, *know*, and *like*, or states, such as *own*, *resemble*, and *weigh*. We normally use the progressive aspect (*be* + *−ing*) when the action or condition has a natural endpoint, a logical time of conclusion. Compare the ungrammatical examples here with the progressive examples given in the preceding section.

Under some circumstances *be* + *-ing* may be perfectly acceptable in these patterns:

> He is being silly.
> He is becoming a scholar.
> She is becoming scholarly.
> She is preferring a lot of strange things today.

In Pattern I (NP *be* ADV/TP), on the other hand, the restriction is unequivocal: *be* + *-ing* never appears as an auxiliary:

> The students have been upstairs.
> *The students are being upstairs.
> *The bus is being here soon.

Certainly there are other auxiliary strings we rarely have occasion to use; nevertheless, there remain dozens of ways we can expand all of our verbs. The verb-expansion rule describes the system for doing so.

THE AUXILIARY *DO*

So far we have not discussed sentences in which a form of *do* acts as an auxiliary: *do* is not listed among the modal auxiliaries, nor is it a part of the verb-expansion rule, as *have* and *be* are. Then where in the system does it fit? Here are three sentences that include the auxiliary *did*, the past form of *do*:

> I <u>did</u>n't buy the cat food.
>
> <u>Did</u> you remember to buy some?
>
> Yes, I <u>did</u> remember.

All three of these—the negative statement, the question, and the emphatic sentence—are what we call transformations of basic sentences. Our built-in system of grammar requires that before a sentence can be transformed in one of these ways it must have either an auxiliary or a form of *be*. When there is no auxiliary or *be* as part of the main verb in the basic sentence, we add the **"stand-in" auxiliary** *do*.

The use of *do* in these transformations is discussed in more detail in Chapter 5.

THE PASSIVE VOICE

In all the sentences we have examined so far, the subject serves as **agent** or actor, the performer of the action that the verb describes. We call this an active relationship: the **active voice**. In the transitive verb patterns (VII–X), the opposite relationship, the **passive voice**, is also possible. A passive sentence results when the direct object—the original "receiver of the action"—or, in the case of Pattern VIII, the indirect object becomes the subject.

The traditional diagram of Pattern VII shows the changing roles of the two NPs:

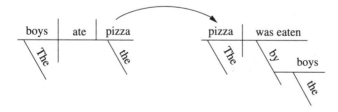

The passive transformation involves three steps:

1. The original direct object, NP_2, becomes the subject.
2. *be* + *-en* is added to the active verb.

3. The original subject, NP_1, becomes the object of the preposition *by*. This third step is optional; the passive sentence is grammatical without the prepositional phrase.

The first of these steps is obvious; the second might not be, especially in sentences like the following:

The committee discussed the report. (*Active*)
The report was discussed by the committee. (*Passive*)

The addition of *be* (in this case, *was*) is obvious, but the addition of *-en* is not. The change shows up clearly, however, when we analyze the components of the active verb:

past + discuss = discussed

When we add *be* + *-en*, we always insert it just before the main verb:

past + **be** + **-en** + discuss = was discussed

In other words, in the active version of the sentence, *discussed* is the *-ed* form (the past); in the passive version, *discussed* is the *-en* form.

===== *Investigating Language 3.3* ==========================

You can use your understanding of the auxiliary rule to help you identify the voice of verbs. Here, for example, are two sentences, each of which has a two-word verb string:

Scientific advances in medicine have changed our lives.
Insulin was discovered in 1921.

Both *change* and *discover* are regular verbs, so their *-ed* and *-en* forms are identical. Let's decide first which form we have here. Is it possible that in these two sentences the verbs are the *-ed* forms, the past tense? Or, to put the question another way, Is it possible that the words *change* and *discover* are carrying the T, the tense marker, in these sentences? Look again at the verb-expansion rule (the auxiliary rule):

T + (M) + (have + -en) + (be + -ing) + MV

Remember that the T (either present or past) attaches itself to the first word it comes to. Clearly, then, the answer to the questions is "no": The two sentences have auxiliary words—*have* (present) and *was* (past)—that are carrying the T: so *changed* and *discovered* are not the *-ed* form. In fact, we can state as a rule without exception that a main verb can be the *-ed* form (the simple past tense) *only* when it stands alone—that is, only when it has no auxiliary word.

So we've established that the verbs *changed* and *discovered* are the *-en* forms. Where did those *-en* forms come from? Look again at the rule (and we can think of the rule shown here as the "active rule"). The only *-en* it includes is the one that goes with the auxiliary *have*. That means that our sentence with "have discovered" must be active.

The active rule also says that when *be* is an auxiliary an *-ing* verb will follow. When a sentence shows up with the auxiliary *be* (i.e., a form of *be*) that is *not* followed by an *-ing* verb, we know that the auxiliary cannot have been generated from the active rule: So the sentence with *was discovered* must be passive. (*Note*: Recall step 2 of the passive transformation: "Add *be* + *-en* to the active verb.")

Here, then, are four rules about verbs we can extract from our auxiliary and passive rules. Think of these as helpful "rules of thumb" that will heighten your awareness of verbs:

> **Rule 1:** A verb without an auxiliary is always active.
> **Rule 2:** When the main verb ends in *-ing*, it is active.
> **Rule 3:** If an *-en* main verb is preceded by a form of *have*, it is active.
> **Rule 4:** If an *-en* main verb is preceded by a form of *be*, it is passive.

Now apply these rules of thumb as you identify the voice of the following sentences as either active (A) or passive (P). In the parentheses, write the number of the rule that helped you decide.

> I have eaten too much again. A or P (   )
> Amy's car was stolen during the night. A or P (   )
> I finally finished my homework. A or P (   )
> We were studying for the exam. A or P (   )

Here's another sentence with an expanded verb—this time with two auxiliary words:

> The candidates <u>have been criticized</u> for their stand on health care.

You can extract an even easier rule of thumb for such sentences. Review the verb-expansion rule; then finish the rule by filling in the blank:

> **Rule 5:** If the auxiliary *be* is *not* followed by _____, the sentence is passive.

Here's another sentence:

> The candidates <u>were being criticized</u> by the media.

And another rule to extract:

> **Rule 6:** If the verb string has two forms of _____ as auxiliaries, the sentence is passive.

These are not rules to memorize. They are simply ways of helping you use your awareness of auxiliaries as you analyze sentences. Remember that the difference between the active and passive verbs is the *be*+*-en* component that we add to the active to form the passive:

> *Passive:* **T + (M) + (have + -en) + (be + -ing) + be + -en + MV**

(*Note:* This discussion should make clear that the words *past* and *passive* are not related: *past* refers to tense; *passive* to voice. A verb in the passive voice can be either present or past tense.)

====== *Exercise 9* ======

Transform the following active sentences into the passive voice, retaining the same verb tense and aspect.

1. My roommate wrote the lead article in today's *Collegian*.
2. Bach composed some of our most intricate fugues.
3. My brother-in-law builds the most expensive houses in town.
4. He is building that expensive apartment complex on Allen Street.
5. The county commissioners will discuss a new tax collection system at their next meeting.

Now change these passive sentences to the active voice.

1. The football team was led onto the field by the cheerleading squad.
2. The cheerleaders are chosen by a committee in the spring.
3. Several apartments in our building have been burglarized recently.
4. A shipment of fresh lobsters should be delivered soon.
5. A special election was held on Tuesday.

(Note that in sentences 3, 4, and 5 the agent is missing. In order to change them to the active voice, you will have to supply a subject.)

Diagramming the Passive. You have probably noticed that the diagram of the passive Pattern VII sentence looks exactly like the diagram of a Pattern VI:

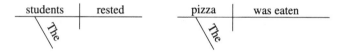

But don't make the mistake of thinking that the sentence pattern has changed; it has not. "The pizza was eaten" is a Pattern VII sentence, a *passive* Pattern VII. With the passive transformation rule, we have added a new dimension to the job of identifying sentence patterns. We now have to ask, "Is it active or passive?" Your rules of thumb will help you answer that question.

The other three transitive verb patterns can also undergo the passive transformation. In most Pattern VIII sentences, the indirect object serves as the subject of the passive:

PATTERN VIII:

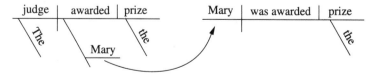

In this pattern, where we have two objects following the verb—both an indirect and a direct—we retain the direct object in the passive transformation. Traditional grammarians refer to this as the **retained**

object. Another possibility in Pattern VIII is to use the direct object as the subject of the passive, as we do in Pattern VII, and then retain the indirect object:

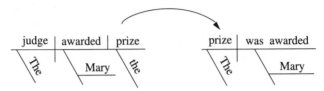

The resulting sentence has a somewhat formal or old-fashioned sound: "The prize was awarded Mary." A more common version includes the preposition *to*: "The prize was awarded to Mary."

In the active voice of Patterns IX and X again two complements, the direct object and the objective complement, follow the verb; but in these two patterns only the direct object can serve as the subject of the passive transformation:

PATTERN IX:

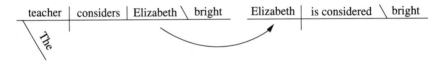

PATTERN X:

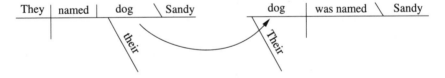

The diagrams of these passive sentences look like those of the linking verb and *be* patterns, where a subjective complement describes or renames the subject. The relationship of the direct object and the objective complement remains exactly what it was in the active voice; so when the object becomes the subject, it follows that the objective complement becomes the subjective complement. How, then, do we distinguish these passives from Patterns IV and V?

Elizabeth is considered bright.
Their dog was named Sandy.

Remember your rules of thumb: When a form of *be* appears as an auxiliary without *-ing* following, the verb is passive. And because only transitive verbs can undergo the passive transformation, *is considered* and *was named* cannot be linking verbs.

You might find it useful to add these passive diagram frames to page 49:

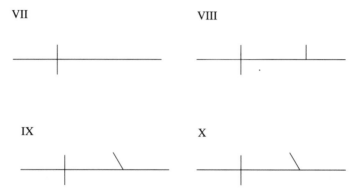

The ties between the transitive verb and the passive voice are so strong—there are so few exceptions—that we can almost define "transitive verb" in terms of this relationship. In other words, a transitive verb is a verb that can undergo the passive transformation. There are a few exceptions, including *have*, one of our most common verbs. In only a few colloquial expressions does *have* appear in the passive voice: "A good time was had by all," "I've been had." Another use of *have* in the passive voice occurs as a modifier: "There were no tickets to be had." But in most cases *have* sentences cannot be transformed:

> I had a cold.
> *A cold was had by me.
>
> Juan has a new car.
> *A new car is had by Juan.

Other verbs that fit Pattern VII but are rarely transformed into passive are *lack* ("He lacks skill in debate") and *resemble* ("Mary resembles her mother"). Linguists sometimes classify these as "midverbs" and assign them to a separate sentence pattern. But on the basis of form (NP₁ V NP₂), we will classify these sentences as Pattern VII and simply look on them as exceptions to the passive rule.

====== *Exercise 10* ======

Change the voice of the following sentences, turning the active ones into passive, the passive into active.

1. We will probably elect a Republican as mayor next year.
2. Gold had been found in Alaska long before the Gold Rush in California.
3. Some older students are being given academic credit for "life experience."
4. The road crew finally repaired the potholes in our street.
5. The city is raising the subway fare to sixty cents next week.
6. Remedial math courses are sometimes referred to in a pejorative way as "bonehead math."
7. Dozens of UFOs have been sighted in our area during the past few years.
8. Six chapters should be studied before the next exam.
9. Lake Michigan is sometimes called America's inland ocean.
10. In the 1970s New Jersey legalized casino gambling.
11. The company has finally given Maria the recognition she deserves.
12. In 1993, Janet Reno was confirmed as our first female attorney general.

USING THE PASSIVE VOICE

The terms *active* and *passive* describe the relationship between the subject and the verb; they mean precisely what they say. In most active sentences, the subject—the actor or agent—is active; the subject is doing something:

The boys ate the pizza.
The judge awarded Mary the prize.

In the passive transformation the relationship between subject and verb is different: It is passive; the subject is doing nothing. In the passive sentence the relationship between the subject and the verb remains what it was between the direct object and verb of the same active sentence: The subject is the receiver of the action or, perhaps to be more accurate, the objective or goal. The former subject of the active verb, if it is still in the sentence, remains the agent or actor:

> The pizza was eaten by the boys.
> Mary was awarded the prize.

If you're like many students, your first introduction to the passive voice may have appeared in the margin of a freshman theme where your teacher left the cryptic message "pass." This meant either "Why are you using the passive voice?" or, more likely, "Don't use the passive." But is the passive voice always wrong or second best?

Consider the foregoing passive sentences. If pizza is the topic at hand, shouldn't *pizza* serve as the subject of the sentence? In the other example, it's not the judge we're talking about; it's Mary who got the prize, so why not use *Mary* as the subject? In this case it's also possible to make *Mary* the subject without using the passive:

> Mary earned the prize.
> Mary won the prize.

The passive—"Mary was awarded the prize"—removes the emphasis from Mary as active winner to Mary as passive recipient. And how about the pizza?

> The pizza disappeared.

In these examples, instead of insisting on the underlying active sentences, with *the judge* and *the boys* as subjects, we found an active verb that would substitute for the passive one. But certainly the passive voice is sometimes the best choice. For instance, the agent may be obscured in history or simply have no bearing on the discussion:

> In 1905 the streets of Patterson, California, were laid out in the shape of a wheel.

> Oregon's economy is closely tied to the lumber industry.

> The Vikings have had a bad press. Their activities are equated with rape and pillage and their reputation for brutality is second

only to that of the Huns and the Goths. Curiously, they also have been invested with a strange glamour which contradicts in many ways their fearsome image.

—JAMES GRAHAM-CAMPBELL AND DAFYDD KIDD, *The Vikings*

The authors' purpose in the third passage is not to explain who equates the Vikings with rape and pillage or who invests them with glamour. The use of the passive puts these statements in the category of accepted beliefs. Sometimes the agent is unknown, as in the first passive verb of the following passage:

So far as we know, from Einstein's Special Theory of Relativity, the universe is constructed in such a way (at least around here) that no material object and no information can be transmitted faster than the velocity of light.

—CARL SAGAN, *Broca's Brain*

And in the following sentence, the prepositional phrase provided by the passive transformation emphasizes the Churchillian style:

Never in the field of human conflict was so much owed by so many to so few.

—WINSTON CHURCHILL, August 20, 1940

The passive voice is especially common—and deliberate—in technical and scientific writing, in legal documents, and in lab reports, where the researcher is the agent, but to say so would be inappropriate:

I increased the temperature to 450° for one hour. (*Active*)
The temperature was increased to 450° for one hour. (*Passive*)

In some instances the passive voice is simply more straightforward:

Joe was wounded in Vietnam.

And sometimes, in order to add modifiers to the agent, we put it where we can do so more conveniently, at the end of the sentence:

Early this morning my little poodle was hit by a delivery truck traveling at high speed through the intersection of Beaver and Allen Streets.

The passive voice is discussed further in Chapter 14.

KEY TERMS IN CHAPTER 3

Active voice	Modal auxiliary
Agent	Passive voice
Aspect	Regular verb
Auxiliary	Stand-in auxiliary
Conditional mood	Subjunctive mood
Indicative mood	Tense
Irregular verb	Verb-expansion rule
Main verb	

SENTENCES FOR PRACTICE

Identify the components of the main verb in each of the following sentences. Your answers will be in the form of verb strings, such as those given in Exercise 8.

1. The press has recently labeled our new senator a radical on domestic issues.
2. During the campaign everyone was calling him reactionary.
3. The teacher should have given the class more information about the exam.
4. According to the students, their teacher was being downright secretive.
5. In Florida the Coast Guard is now confiscating the boats of drug runners.
6. Some sports reporters have called the new Orioles stadium at Camden Yards the architecture of nostalgia.
7. The president may soon name three women to top posts in the Department of State.
8. Our company will try a new vacation schedule in the summer.

9. All the workers are taking their two-week vacations at the same time.

10. Pat has been jogging regularly for six years.

11. Until last week, Mario had never told me his middle name.

12. Many large firms are now hiring liberal arts majors for management positions.

13. Employers value them for their analytical ability.

14. The suspect's alibi may have been a lie.

15. I should have been studying on a regular basis throughout the semester.

16. People are constantly teasing me about my southern accent.

17. Apparently they have never heard a southern accent around here before.

18. Writers have produced almost 2,500 works about the *Bounty* mutiny during the past 200 years.

Decide which of these sentences can be transformed into the passive voice, and then do so. Identifying their sentence patterns will help you in making that decision. Remember that to form a passive verb you must add *be* + *-en* to the active verb string. Remember also that the active and passive versions of the sentence have different subjects.

QUESTIONS FOR DISCUSSION

1. "I've already ate" is a fairly common nonstandard usage in our country. Explain how it deviates from the standard usage described by the verb-expansion rule. Compare it with "I've already tried"; can you discover a logical reason for the nonstandard usage? Does that particular nonstandard form ever occur with regular verbs?

2. The verb *get* shows up quite regularly with other verbs. Identify the patterns of these sentences, all of which include a form of *get*:

They got married in July.
The window got broken.
The dog got lost.
I get tired at basketball games.
The cookies always get eaten before they get cold.
I got there too late.

Should we alter the passive rule to account for any of these sentences? How does "The window was broken" differ from "The window got broken"?

3. A few years ago the tourist bureau of Pennsylvania came up with a slogan to encourage visitors: "You've got a friend in Pennsylvania." When the slogan was put on the Pennsylvania license plate, letters to the editor and complaints to the governor began. "Ungrammatical," "uncouth," "ungraceful," and "disgraceful" were some of the epithets used. Are those criticisms justified? Why or why not?

4. The difference between two such sentences as

He is tall.   *and*   He is silly.

is obviously in the adjective that fills the subjective complement slot. We cannot say

*He is being tall.

but we can say

He is being silly.

so there must be a fundamental difference between the two adjectives.

The contrast is between **stative** and **dynamic** qualities—the one describing a state, usually permanent, and the other a changing quality. What is there about *be* + *-ing* that makes this restriction seem logical? Can you think of other stative adjectives (other than *tall*) that are restricted from the subjective complement slot with *be* + *-ing*?

Perhaps a better way of describing the contrast between *silly* and *tall*—between silliness and height—concerns the presence or absence of volition, the power of choice. Which of the following adjectives describe characteristics that are willed: *young, tough, nice, red, absorbent, reckless, round*? Can these adjectives serve as subjective complements with *be* + *-ing*?

5. Consider further restrictions on *be* + *-ing*:

*Mary is resembling her mother.
*The blue dress is fitting you.

Can we speak of dynamic and stative or willed and nonwilled qualities of verbs as well as of adjectives? Consider the following verbs: *assume, suit, equal, enjoy, desire, agree with, mean, know, contain, lack, like.* Do any of these have restrictions? Why?

6. Do nouns carry such distinctions, too? Try the following nouns in the subjective complement slot of Pattern III: *a doctor, a nuisance, a hero, a nice person, a gentleman, a hard worker, a construction worker.* Here is the slot: "He is being —." Can all of them be used with *be +* *-ing*? What conclusions can you draw about NPs? Does volition, or the power of choice, make a difference?

7. In the following sentences, what does *'s* stand for?

> He's had enough.
> Mary's not here.
> She's already gone.
> She's already left.
> He's finished.

Now consider the following sentences:

> Are you done?
> Mike is already gone.

In what way do they appear to violate our verb-expansion rule?

8. How does the auxiliary in "He's finished" and "Mike's already gone" help explain the auxiliaries in the following sentences from Shakespeare and the King James Bible:

> Laertes is come.
> His lordship is walked forth.
> When they were come to Bethlehem.
> My father is gone wild into his grave.

In what way is the Modern English verb system different from that of the early seventeenth century?

9. All the following sentences include the auxiliary *must*, which commonly has a meaning of necessity or obligation. Demonstrate its meaning in these sentences by paraphrasing each of them—that is, by coming up with a sentence that means the same thing.

You must have seen Lisa; she walked right by you.
You must be exhausted.
It's such a lovely day for a picnic; you must have had a wonderful time.
You mustn't bother with the dishes; I'll do them later.
You must have been a beautiful baby.
We must try the new Chinese restaurant on College Avenue.

10. You probably would have no occasion to use some of the following sentences. Which ones?

Pam drinks coffee.
Tracy drinks a cup of coffee.
Tom cannot eat most shellfish.
Jeff is eating most shellfish.

What would you be more likely to say in their place? Why?

11. In addition to the modals *will* and *shall*, we can express the future with the simple present tense or present progressive aspect when we include an appropriate adverbial:

The bus leaves at seven.
Mark graduates tomorrow.
John is coming on Saturday.
The plane is taking off at noon.

But not every future event can be expressed with those verb forms:

Carlos will probably win the race tomorrow.
*Carlos is probably winning the race tomorrow.

The sun will shine tomorrow.
*The sun shines tomorrow.

Think of other future events—considering whether they are facts or probabilities, scheduled or nonscheduled events, with or without a specific endpoint. Formulate a rule for expressing the future.

4

The Noun Phrase Functions: Nominals

In this chapter we continue the discussion of form and function that began in Chapter 2 by looking at the NP slots in the sentence patterns, focusing on forms other than noun phrases—namely, clauses and verb phrases—that fill those NP slots.

Among the new terms you learned in Chapter 2 were *adverbial* and *adjectival*, terms that denote functions. *Adverbial* refers to any structure, or form, that does what an adverb usually does—that is, modify a verb. *Adjectival* refers to any structure that does what an adjective usually does—modify a noun. We used those terms for functions right from the start in our study of the sentence patterns because right from the start we were using prepositional phrases as adjectivals and adverbials in the sample sentences. But you'll notice that we have not used the parallel *-al* term for noun, *nominal*, until now. In the discussion of sentence patterns we stuck to the label of form; we labeled the subject and direct object and the other functions simply as NP, mainly for the sake of simplicity.

Now it's time for the term **nominal**, the official label for the NP function. All of those NP slots you learned about—subject, direct object, indirect object, subjective complement, objective complement, and object of the preposition—are actually nominal slots. Before we get to those other nominal forms, however, we will look at one other nominal function, one that does not show up in the sentence patterns—an optional nominal slot called the **appositive**.

APPOSITIVES

You can think of the appositive as a nominal companion, a structure that renames the nominal; it is also referred to as a noun in apposition:

My best friend, Meda, lives in California.

I really like Ron, the butcher at Giant Foods.

You can easily understand the optional nature of the appositive; those sentences would be grammatical without that added information. On the diagram the appositive occupies a place right next to the noun, or other nominal structure, that it renames:

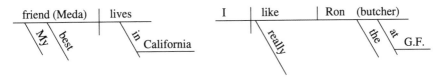

Because these appositives add information to noun phrases, it would probably be equally accurate to classify them as adjectivals. But they are different from other adjectivals in that they can substitute for the nouns they rename:

Meda lives in California.

I really like the butcher at Giant Foods.

The appositive can introduce the sentence when it modifies the subject:

An ex-Marine who once played professional football, the security guard in our building makes us feel secure, indeed.

The world's largest winery, Gallo bottles 250,000 cases of wine daily.

No matter where in the sentence the appositive is placed, in the diagram it will be shown in the same slot as the nominal it renames:

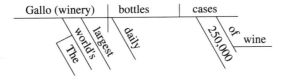

We will look further at appositives in Chapter 7 in connection with the punctuation of restrictive and nonrestrictive modifiers and in Chapter 14 in connection with colons and dashes.

NOMINAL CLAUSES

What is a clause? When is a clause nominal?

The label **clause** denotes a form: a group of words with a subject and a predicate. The ten sentence patterns described in Chapter 2 have this form. The branching diagram, you'll recall, illustrates the two parts:

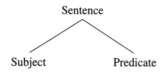

In other words, the ten sentence patterns are essentially clause patterns.

From the standpoint of mechanical conventions, we can define **sentence** as a word or group of words that begins with a capital letter and ends with a period or other terminal punctuation. (In terms of spoken sentences, we would refer to terminal "juncture" rather than punctuation.) A more complete definition, one that includes the criterion of meaning as well as form, would read as follows:

> A **sentence** is a word or group of words based on one or more subject–predicate, or clause, patterns; the written sentence begins with a capital letter and ends with terminal punctuation.

This definition eliminates "Wow!" and "The very idea!" and "Rats!" as sentences, but it includes imperatives, such as "Help!" with its underlying clause "You help me."

All sentences, then, are clauses, but not all clauses are sentences. In the following sentences, for example, the direct object slot contains a clause rather than a noun phrase. These are examples of **nominal clauses** (sometimes called "noun clauses"):

> I know that the students studied their assignment.
> I wonder what is making Tracy so unhappy.

These nominal clauses are examples of **dependent clauses**—in contrast to **independent clauses**, those clauses that function as complete sentences. (In later chapters we will see other dependent clauses, some that function as adverbials and others as adjectivals.) In traditional terms, any sentence that includes a dependent clause of any kind is known as a **complex sentence**.

In the discussion of noun phrases in Chapter 2, you learned the trick of substituting a pronoun (*it* or *he* or *she* or *they* or *something*) to determine the boundaries of the NP slot. That trick is especially useful when the nominal slot is filled by a clause, as in the two previous examples:

I know it.
I wonder something.

The pronoun substitutes for the entire nominal slot.

To diagram a sentence with a nominal clause, simply attach the clause

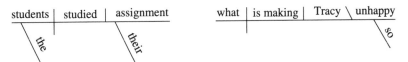

to the main line by means of a pedestal (just as we did in Chapter 2 when a prepositional phrase filled the subjective complement slot):

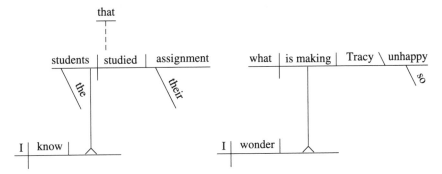

These two sentences also illustrate the two kinds of introductory words that signal nominal clauses: **interrogatives**, such as *what*, and the **expletive** *that*. As the diagrams illustrate, the two are different: The interrogative fills a grammatical role in the clause that it introduces—in this case, that of subject; the expletive does not.

(*Diagramming note:* The pedestal can be attached to the clause wherever it is convenient to do so. The expletive is placed above the clause it introduces and attached with a broken line, again wherever convenient.)

The Expletive That.

The term **expletive** refers to a sentence element that plays no grammatical role itself; the expletive is an operator of sorts, an added element that enables us to manipulate a structure for reasons of emphasis and the like. The expletive *that* enables us to embed one sentence as a nominal in another sentence. In the previous example, the Pattern VII sentence "The students studied their assignment" becomes a direct object. We should note that this clause introducer sometimes goes by other names: It is often called a "nominalizer," which is certainly an accurate label, and sometimes a "subordinator." The term that we are using here, "expletive," emphasizes its role outside of the clause itself. The diagram illustrates that added-on quality.

The expletive *that* can turn any declarative sentence into a nominal clause:

The guests from El Paso will arrive soon.	→	I hope that the guests from El Paso will arrive soon.
The common cold is caused by a virus.	→	That the common cold is caused by a virus has been clearly established by science.

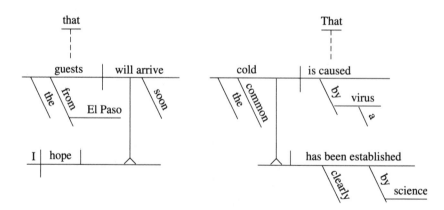

When the *that* clause fills the direct object slot, as in the first example, the sentence may be grammatical without the expletive:

I hope the guests from El Paso will arrive soon.

When the clause is in subject position, however, the expletive is required:

*The common cold is caused by a virus has been clearly established by science.

Two other nominal functions for *that* clauses are as appositives and as subjective complements:

The idea that our powerful defense couldn't stop the Wolverines was unthinkable to the fans.

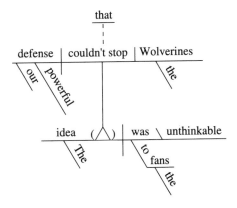

Like most appositives, the *that* clause could actually replace the head-word *idea*:

That our powerful defense couldn't stop the Wolverines was un-thinkable to the fans.

Another fairly common appositive occurs in sentences with *it* as the subject, where a *that* clause at the end of the sentence actually explains what *it* stands for:

It is unbelievable that we actually lost that game.

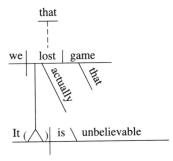

The sentence would be equally grammatical without *it*, with the clause in the subject position:

That we actually lost that game is unbelievable.

The *it* construction allows the writer to change the rhythm of the sentence, to put more emphasis on the clause by delaying it.

In the following example the *that* clause functions as the subjective complement in a Pattern III sentence:

The reason for our defeat was that their backfield outsmarted us on
every play.

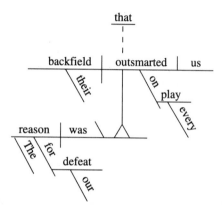

Interrogatives.   One of the sample sentences we saw earlier included a nominal clause introduced by the interrogative *what*:

I wonder *what* is making Tracy so unhappy.

Other interrogatives, or question words, that introduce nominal clauses are *who, whose, whom, which, where, when, why,* and *how*. Unlike the expletive, the interrogative always plays a grammatical role in its own clause. In the sentence about Tracy, *what* functions as the subject. In the following sentence, *what* is the direct object in its clause:

I wonder *what* our history midterm will cover.

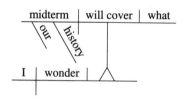

In both of these examples, the *what* clause functions as the direct object. Another common function is that of subject:

Where you are going is no business of mine.

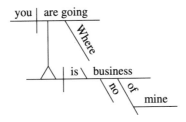

Where is an interrogative adverb, so it acts as an adverb in its clause. The interrogative pronoun *who* will be the subject in its own clause:

Who will be at the party remains a mystery.

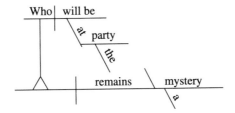

Who can also be the subjective complement in its clause:

I don't know *who* that stranger is.

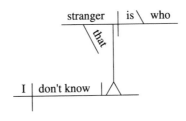

In the following sentences *what* and *which* function as determiners:

I wonder *which* brand of yogurt has the least fat.

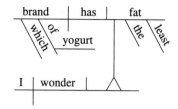

I wonder *what* brand I should buy.

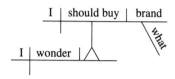

The interrogative pronoun *whose*, the possessive case of *who*, also acts as a determiner in its clause. Recall that the determiner slot is the usual place for possessive nouns and possessive personal pronouns too.

I wonder *whose* car this is.

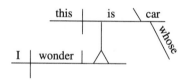

The interrogative *whom* will act as an object in its clause. When it is the object of a preposition, it may not be the first word in the clause, as in the famous line by John Donne:

Never send to know for *whom* the bell tolls.

In everyday speech we rarely introduce a clause with *for whom* or *to whom* or *by whom*; we are more likely to use *who* instead of *whom* and to end the clause with the preposition:

Bill told me who he bought the flowers for.
I wonder who Mary is going to dance with.

At the beginning of the clause, *who* seems a more logical form, perhaps, because *who* is the subjective case form and the subject generally fills the opening position. But the diagrams clearly show *he* and *Mary* as the subjects and *whom* as object of the prepositions:

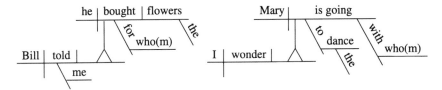

Even though *whom* may sound awkward or too formal for everyday speech, the conventions of edited English call for *whom* in formal writing. If you want to avoid the formality of

Bill told me whom he bought the flowers for,

there are always alternatives:

Bill told me who is getting the flowers.
Bill told me the name of the person he bought the flowers for.
Bill said he bought the flowers for Kathy.

Yes/No Interrogatives.   Besides the questions introduced by interrogatives that ask for specific information, we also ask questions that call for a *yes* or *no* response. The interrogative clauses based on yes/no questions are introduced by two expletive-like elements, *if* and *whether* (*or not*):

I can't remember if I turned off the television.

Whether or not I turned it off doesn't matter.

We consider these introductory words as expletives because, like the expletive *that*, they play no part in the clause. They simply act as operators that allow us to use yes/no questions as nominal clauses:

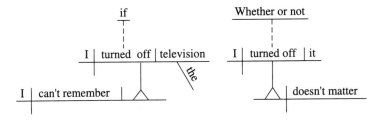

Punctuation of Nominal Clauses.   As many of the examples illustrate, sentences with nominal clauses can get fairly long. But with one exception, the punctuation of these sentences remains exactly the same as the punctuation of the basic sentence: no single commas between the sentence pattern slots. The exception occurs when the direct object is a direct quotation. The standard convention calls for a comma between a verb like *say* or *reply* and the quote:

He said, "I will meet you at the gym at five o'clock."

═══ *Exercise 11* ═══

Underline the nominal clause in each of the following sentences. In the parentheses, identify its function in the sentence: What NP slot does it fill?

1. I wonder where I put my math book. (   )
2. Why you stayed out so late is no business of mine. (   )
3. The counselor couldn't remember who had volunteered for cleanup duty. (   )
4. Percy wondered if we could come for the weekend. (   )
5. My problem in English class is that I don't really understand poetry. (   )
6. I can't decide which gym class I should take. (   )
7. It doesn't seem fair that an exam is scheduled on the day before Thanksgiving break. (   )
8. I wish he would explain his explanation. [Lord Byron] (   )
9. How the Panama Canal was built is a story of high drama. (   )
10. Our basketball fans think it's great that we're getting a new athletic center. (   )

NOMINAL VERB PHRASES

Nominal clauses have all the features of full sentences, including a **finite verb**—that is, a predicating verb generated by the verb-expansion rule, which we examined in Chapter 3. Finite verbs—as opposed to **nonfinite verbs**—are also called *tensed verbs*. And if you remember the components of the auxiliary, you'll understand that term: A tensed verb includes T, the present or past tense marker. Bear in mind that when you studied the nominal clause, you were again studying the basic sentence patterns you learned in Chapter 2.

Now we turn to nominals of another—but related—form: the verb phrases. These phrases are essentially reduced clauses—again, our familiar sentence (clause) patterns—but this time *without* subjects and *without* tensed verbs. You may recall in the list of the ten sentence patterns in Chapter 2 that the same subject was used in all ten sample sentences. The purpose was to emphasize that the distinctions among the patterns are in the predicates. Although they are called *sentence* patterns, a more accurate label might be *predicate*, or *verb phrase*, patterns. Understanding this concept will help you to understand the idea that verb phrases have sentence patterns, just as clauses do—even when those verb phrases fill NP, or nominal, slots.

Nominal verb phrases come in two basic forms: (1) the *-ing* verb, known as a **gerund** when it functions as a nominal; and (2) the **infinitive**, the base form of the verb usually signaled by *to*, which is called "the sign of the infinitive." Here are examples of these two verb phrases as nominals, in this case as direct objects:

Teenagers enjoy <u>playing computer games.</u>

Teenagers like <u>to play computer games.</u>

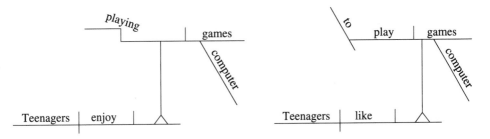

The diagrams show the nominal verb phrases filling the direct object slot, connected to the main line by pedestals (just as the nominal clauses are connected). You can also see that in these examples the nominal verb phrases themselves include direct objects. Clearly, they are Pattern VII verb phrases: Underlying them both is the Pattern VII sentence,

Teenagers play computer games.

The gerund is diagrammed on a two-step line, the infinitive on a two-part line exactly like that of the prepositional phrase.

In our earlier discussions of the direct object function, we identified the parameters of the slot—its beginning and ending—by substituting a pronoun. The substitution works here too:

> Teenagers enjoy <u>something</u>.
>
> Teenagers like <u>it</u>.

Gerunds.   Because they are nounlike, we can think of gerunds as names. But rather than naming persons, places, things, events, and the like, as nouns generally do, gerunds, because they are verbs in form, name actions or behaviors or states of mind or states of being. In our example, *playing computer games* names an activity.

All the sentence patterns can serve as the source of gerunds. And because they are verbs, the gerunds will include all the complements and modifiers that tensed verbs include. In the following example, an adverbial prepositional phrase modifies the intransitive verb *going*, a Pattern VI gerund:

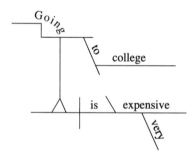

Except for its two-step line, the diagram of the gerund looks exactly like the predicate half of its underlying sentence:

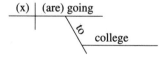

A Pattern I gerund, like the Pattern I sentence, will have an adverbial of time or place:

> The teacher is here ⟶ the teacher's being here

Note that we convert *is* into the *-ing* form and its subject into the possessive case:

The teacher's being here surprised us.

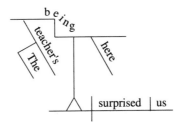

This gerund names an activity or state of being; that state is the "something" that surprised us. In this diagram the subject of the gerund is shown as a modifier; it has become a determiner of sorts, playing the same role that possessive nouns and pronouns ordinarily play: *John's* hat, *his* hat, *the teacher's* hat, *the teacher's* being here.

A gerund derived from a Pattern II sentence will include a subjective complement:

John's being angry surprised Mary.
or
His being angry surprised Mary.

Note that *angry* fills the subjective complement slot in the gerund phrase just as it did in the underlying sentence:

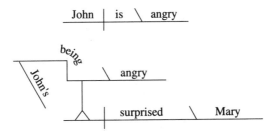

All of the NP slots can be occupied by gerunds:

Direct Object: My brother enjoys collecting stamps.
Subjective Complement: My brother's hobby is collecting stamps.

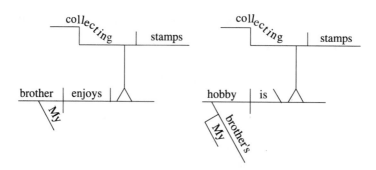

In these gerund phrases the underlying sentence is Pattern VII: *My brother collects stamps.*

> **Object of Preposition:** We gave the children a bigger allowance for keeping their rooms spotless.

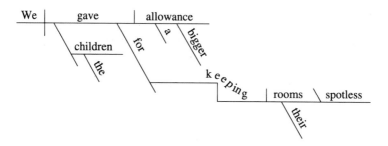

Here the sentence underlying the gerund phrase is Pattern IX: *The children keep their rooms spotless.*

> **Appositive:** My hobby, building computers, is expensive.

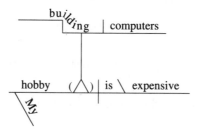

That was a great idea, cooking hamburgers on the grill.

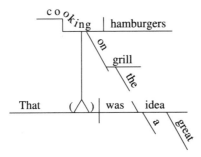

In these sentences the gerund renames, in the first, a noun phrase (*my hobby*) and, in the second, a pronoun (*that*). In both cases a Pattern VII sentence underlies the gerund phrase: *I build computers; Someone is cooking hamburgers on the grill.*

═══════ *Exercise 12* ═══════

Identify the sentence pattern of each gerund phrase and the part that the gerund phrase plays in the sentence. Diagram the sentences.

1. Your complaining to the boss will only make matters worse.
2. Mark was arrested for going through a red light.
3. I really dislike weeding the garden.
4. My mother's hobby is growing roses.
5. Finding Japanese beetles in her prize roses simply ruins her day.
6. My roommate obviously enjoys giving me a bad time.
7. It is nice being here with you.
8. The tranquil bays of Lake Michigan make swimming there a pleasure.
9. Instead of feeling angry with me, you should thank me for being so honest.
10. Our latest fix-up project, painting the house green, was a disaster.

The Subject of the Gerund.   In Exercise 12, only the first sentence has a gerund in which its subject—i.e., the gerund's subject—is a part of the gerund phrase itself. In items 2 and 3, the subject of the sentence is the subject of the gerund as well, a common occurrence. The subject of the gerund will generally be left unstated when it names a general, rather than a particular, action or behavior:

Raising orchids requires patience.

One of the most popular forms of exercise in our neighborhood is jogging.

Becoming a lawyer is not easy.

As we saw in earlier examples, when the subject of the gerund is part of the gerund phrase, it will often be in the possessive case:

The teacher's being here surprised us.

John's being angry surprised Mary.

Your complaining to the boss will only make matters worse.

Although the possessive case may sometimes sound excessively formal or even incorrect, it is the form considered correct in formal writing.

When the subject of the gerund includes postheadword modifiers, we generally omit the possessive inflection. We would say

I appreciated his giving me a lift,

or

I appreciated Bill's giving me a lift,

but we would probably not say

I appreciated the man next door's giving me a lift.

Instead we would say simply

I appreciated the man next door giving me a lift.

It's not unusual to hear people say,

I appreciated *him* giving me a lift,

but, technically, this version makes the man himself, rather than his action, the object of the appreciation.

Dangling Gerunds.   You've probably heard about dangling participles (you'll read about them in Chapter 7). Dangling gerunds are not quite as well known. Like the dangling participle, the dangling gerund occurs when its subject is neither stated nor clearly implied. This situation arises at times when the gerund serves as the object in an opening or closing prepositional phrase:

> After cooking the snails in white wine, none of the guests would eat them.
>
> In filling out the form, an original and two copies are required.
>
> The rust spots must be carefully sanded and primed before giving the car its final coat of paint.

We certainly have no problem understanding such sentences; the message comes through. In fact, "dangling" may be too strong a word; these sentences don't have the obvious weakness that you'll see in those with dangling participles. Of the three sentences preceding, the first is probably the least acceptable; here the activity named by the gerund is a specific, one-time event, and we expect the subject of the gerund to be the first available noun. So it appears that *none of the guests* did the cooking. One alternative is to expand the opening phrase into a clause, turning *cook* into the main verb of the clause:

> After I cooked the snails in white wine, none of the guests would eat them.

Another version would leave *cooking* as a gerund, but its subject is now clearly stated:

> After I went to all the trouble of cooking the snails in white wine, none of the guests would eat them.

But even when the verbs refer to general, rather than specific, activities, there tends to be a vagueness in these dangling gerund phrases, simply because we are programmed to expect the subject of the sentence to serve as the subject of the gerund as well, as in the following revisions:

> After cooking the snails in white wine, *I* couldn't get any of the guests to eat them.

In filling out the forms, *you* will need an original and two copies.

Before giving the car its final coat of paint, sand the rust spots carefully and paint them with primer.

In the last example the subject of both the gerund and the main clause is the understood *you*.

═══ *Exercise 13* ═══════════════════════════

Improve the following sentences by providing a clear subject for the gerund.

1. Before starting to bake a cake, the ingredients should be assembled.
2. Heavy meals should be avoided before swimming.
3. In making a career decision, my counselor was a big help.
4. After storing the outdoor furniture in the garage, there was no room left for the car.
5. Our backpacks got really heavy after hiking up that steep mountain trail.

Infinitives.   In their nominal roles, infinitives, like gerunds, name actions or behaviors or states of being. And like the gerunds, infinitives can be derived from all the sentence patterns. In the following sentence, a Pattern VII infinitive fills the subject slot in a Pattern III sentence:

Subject: To fly a helicopter is one of my goals.

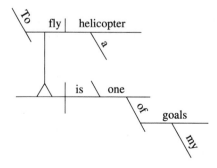

At first glance you may confuse the infinitive with a prepositional phrase, such as *to school* or *to the store; to* appears in both constructions, and the traditional diagrams are similar. But there is an important difference in form: In the prepositional phrase, a nominal—usually a noun or noun phrase—follows *to*; in the infinitive a verb phrase follows *to*.

Direct Object: Since ancient times, people have attempted to fly.

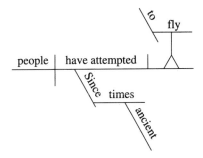

Note that the infinitive *to fly* is intransitive in this sentence: a Pattern VI infinitive. In the previous example the same infinitive has a direct object: Pattern VII.

Subjective Complement: My current plan is to change my major to marketing.

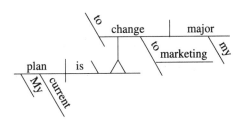

Appositive: My parents aren't very enthusiastic about my plans for spring break, to hitchhike to Florida.

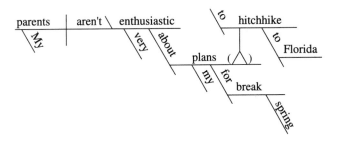

Here the idea stated in the infinitive renames the object in the preposi-tional phrase, *plans*. You saw a similar delayed appositive in the discussion of nominal clauses.

It would be exciting to be a helicopter pilot.

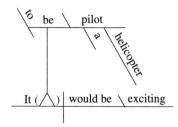

In the preceding sentence the infinitive is the actual subject; the pronoun *it* allows us to delay the subject for greater emphasis. The diagram distorts the word order of the sentence, but it clearly shows the underlying meaning: *To be a helicopter pilot would be exciting.* This use of *it* is sometimes called the anticipatory *it*.

Hamlet's famous infinitive phrase is in apposition to *that*:

To be or not to be, that is the question.

===== *Exercise 14* =====

Underline the nominal infinitives in the following sentences. Identify the sentence pattern of the main clause; identify the sentence pattern of the infinitive phrase; identify the function of the infinitive.

1. To put off unpleasant tasks may produce unpleasant consequences.
2. It was embarrassing to see myself on television in speech class today.
3. I have not yet begun to fight. [John Paul Jones]
4. To survive midterms is my only goal at the moment.
5. The goal in a Japanese baseball game is to tie.
6. No Japanese team wants to show up another team.
7. To tie is to save face.
8. The worst solitude is to be destitute of sincere friendship. [Francis Bacon]
9. Pat has decided to become a vegetarian.
10. It was a big mistake to paint the kitchen cupboards purple.

═════ *Investigating Language 4.1* ═══════════════

One of the common roles for gerunds and infinitives is that of direct object. And if you pay attention to the sentences we've used to illustrate that function, you may notice something their verbs have in common. Here are some of the examples:

> Teenagers *enjoy* playing computer games.
> Teenagers *like* to play computer games.
> I really *dislike* weeding the garden.
> No Japanese team *wants* to show up another team.
> Pat has *decided* to become a vegetarian.

Remember that gerunds and infinitives name something, as most nominals do, but what they name are activities rather than objects or people. If you try using gerunds or infinitives as objects of such transitive verbs as *hit* or *eat*, you'll discover they won't work. Activities cannot be hit or eaten.

We actually have a name for this subgroup of verbs that take other verbs as direct objects, verbs such as *enjoy* and *like* and *decide*. They are called **catenatives**, from the word *catenate*, which means "to form into a chain or linked series." We can, in effect, form a chain of words:

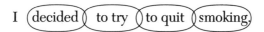

I (decided)(to try)(to quit)(smoking)

In general, the catenatives are mental processes or resolutions.

But there's a certain arbitrariness in the way catenatives work. For example, what would be your first thought if you heard someone say, "Teenagers enjoy to play computer games"? Chances are, you'd identify the speaker as foreign. For some reason, with the word *enjoy* a native speaker uses gerunds but not infinitives.

You can classify catenatives into three groups: (1) those that can take gerunds, (2) those that take infinitives, and (3) those that take both. Think about your own use of the language; then assign these verbs to one of the three groups.

> agree, attempt, avoid, continue, decide, dislike, expect, forget,
> hate, hope, like, love, prefer, remember, start, try, want

Can you think of other verbs that should be on the list? Do you and your classmates agree in all cases, or are there some that are open to question?

The Subject of the Infinitive.   In most of the infinitive sentences we have seen so far, the subject of the tensed verb is also the subject of the infinitive. However, when an infinitive has a general meaning, the sentence may not include that infinitive's actual subject. The situation is especially common when the infinitive occupies the subject slot:

> To raise orchids requires patience.
>
> To go to college is not cheap.

We saw the same situation with the gerund. Where the topic under discussion is a general activity rather than a specific one, the subject of the gerund is omitted:

> Raising orchids requires patience.
>
> Going to college is not cheap.

In neither the infinitive nor the gerund examples are the sentences about specific orchid raisers or college goers.

In some cases with infinitives, however, the subject of the infinitive will be expressed in a prepositional phrase:

> For Beth to go to college will not be cheap.
>
> For reporters to check their facts thoroughly is the first rule of news writing.

Prepositional phrases with embedded infinitives also occur in the direct object position after certain catenative verbs:

> Beth's family hopes for her to go to college.
>
> I would like for you to change your mind.
>
> I prefer for you to handle the arrangements.

The diagram of these sentences illustrates the structure as essentially a reduced clause. The vertical line between the object of the preposition and the infinitive indicates the subject/predicate boundary:

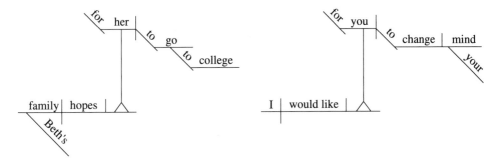

Most of the verbs that can appear in such sentences are also grammatical without the preposition:

> Beth's family wants her to go to college.
> I would like you to change your mind.
> I prefer you to handle the arrangements.

With or without the preposition, the diagram will show that subject/predicate relationship:

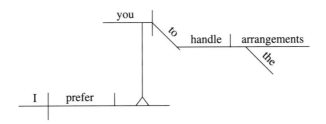

In these examples, a single slot follows the tensed verb. But that is not always the case:

> We *asked* the boys to clean the garage.
>
> We *persuaded* the boys to clean the garage.

In the case of these two verbs, we have both a "somebody" and a "something" following the verb; so rather than analyze these sentences as Pattern VII, we would analyze them as Pattern VIII, with the "someone" as an indirect object:

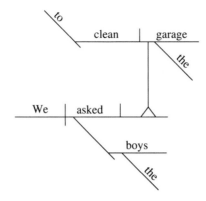

You could make the argument that *ask* and *persuade* are not "give" verbs; nor do they have a "recipient." (You'll recall from Chapter 2 that the indirect object is the recipient of the direct object in the Pattern VIII sentences with "give" verbs.) However, the two slots clearly have different referents, so the Pattern VIII formula, with its NP_2 and NP_3, seems to fit.

We can also test the sentences by transforming them into the passive voice:

> The boys were asked to clean the garage.
> The boys were persuaded to clean the garage.

The fact that we have split up "the boys to clean the garage" is evidence that the structure has two parts, that it fills two slots. In the earlier examples (*Beth's family wants her to go to college; I would like you to change your mind*), we cannot separate the infinitive from its subject.

Complementary Infinitives. We should mention one other use of the infinitive, even though it is not a nominal: the so-called **complementary infinitive**, a completer of the verb. We take it up here simply because it looks so much like the nominal infinitive following a catenative verb:

> I am going to eat less sugar.

This sentence not only resembles but also means much the same as

> I plan to eat less sugar.

or

I am planning to eat less sugar.

However, in the sentence with *going to*, *eat* is the main verbal idea; *am going* actually serves as a modal-like sign of the future. In the second, *plan* is the main verb, and the infinitive is the direct object: *To eat less sugar* is the "something" that I plan. The diagrams demonstrate the difference.

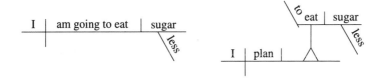

The verbs *be* and *have* sometimes take complementary infinitives too:

The parade is to start at noon.

The marchers have to arrive by eleven.

Here the main verbal ideas are *start* and *arrive*, not *is* and *have*.

There is a modal-like quality in the complementary infinitives; *will* could easily substitute for *is to* or *am going to* and *must* for *have to* with little change in meaning. In fact, in Chapter 12, you'll see that the list of "marginal modals" includes *have to*.

KEY TERMS IN CHAPTER 4

Appositive	Independent clause
Catenative verb	Infinitive
Clause	Interrogative
Complementary infinitive	Nominal
Complex sentence	Nominal clause
Dangling gerund	Nominal verb phrase
Dependent clause	Nonfinite verb
Direct quotation	Predicating verb
Expletive *that*	Sentence
Finite verb	Tensed verb
Gerund	Yes/no interrogative

SENTENCES FOR PRACTICE

Draw vertical lines to show the sentence slots. Label the form of the structure that occupies each slot. Identify the sentence pattern of each verb phrase and clause. Diagram the sentences.

1. I wonder what Jeff's problem is.
2. I think that I know what the solution to Jeff's problem is.
3. My friend Chondra said that she would call me today.
4. The president announced that he has decided to propose a tax cut during this session of Congress.
5. Where you will be in ten years is an intriguing question.
6. My little horse must think it queer,
   To stop without a farmhouse near.
   [Robert Frost, "Stopping by Woods on a Snowy Evening"]
7. Ling-ling, the giant panda at the Washington zoo, died in December 1992 at the age of twenty-three.
8. For some students the cost of going to college is moving out of reach.
9. To fly through the air—to soar like a bird—has always been my dream.
10. I know how men in exile feed on dreams. [Aeschylus]
11. Being a good homemaker has been the goal of most women in our culture for many generations.
12. My roommate is wondering why finding a job in his field, petroleum engineering, is so difficult.
13. I haven't figured out which Shakespeare play is my favorite.
14. The U.S. Customs Service reports that smuggling birds from the Caribbean has become a big business.
15. Our biological rhythms play a crucial role in determining how alert we feel.
16. It takes 248 years for Pluto to orbit the sun.

QUESTIONS FOR DISCUSSION

1. Show by a diagram how the sentences in the following sets are different. Identify their sentence patterns.

My brother is getting into trouble again.
My problem is getting into law school.

I went to work.
I want to work.

2. What is the source of the ambiguity in the following sentence?

I disapprove of her smoking.

If the smoker were male instead of female, how would the sentence be stated? Would it still be ambiguous?

3. What are the two possible meanings of the following ambiguous sentence?

The shooting of the hunters was a wanton act.

In what way is the traditional diagram inadequate to account for that ambiguity?

4. One of the most common roles for nominals is as object of the preposition. In the following sentences, identify the form of that object in the underlined prepositional phrases:

This afternoon I took a nap after exercising.

Before starting my exercise program, I had a thorough physical examination.

Until recently, I did very little exercise.

After my physical, I began doing calisthenics gradually.

From then on, I began to be careful about my diet, too.

For the truly obese, strenuous exercise can be dangerous.

5. In Chapter 3 we examined the passive voice of finite verbs. Can gerunds and infinitives be passive?

6. In speech a fairly common way of expressing purpose is the use of the infinitive *to try* with *and*:

I'm going to try and finish my homework before lunch.

Given what you know about catenative verbs, how would you judge the correctness (perhaps *precision* is a better word than *correctness*) of "try and finish"? How does the structure differ from *go and see* in the following sentence?

> We should go and see what they're doing.

7. In the discussion of the catenative verbs in this chapter, we note that not all transitive verbs will take other verbs as objects. We wouldn't find *eat* and *hit* and *read*, for example, with other verbs as their direct objects. If this is true, then how do we account for such sentences as the following:

> We ate his cooking.
> Tom hit his pitching.
> I read her writing.

In considering this question, you might find it useful to think about the sentence pattern of *cook, pitch,* and *write*.

5

Transforming the Basic Patterns

The ten sentence-pattern formulas described in Chapter 2 represent the underlying framework of almost all the sentences we speak and write. For example, underlying the sentence you just read, the first one in this paragraph, is a basic Pattern VII sentence:

The formulas	represent	the framework.
NP_1	V-tr	NP_2

The two NP slots have been expanded with a variety of phrases and clauses, but the underlying subject and verb and direct object are there, in order, just as the formula describes them; you can pick out the basic skeleton with little trouble.

But it's not always so easy. We don't always use straightforward statements (**declarative sentences**) like that one; sometimes we alter the word order to ask questions (**interrogative sentences**); sometimes we suppress the subject and give commands (**imperative sentences**); sometimes we shift the object or complement before the subject for special emphasis (**exclamatory sentences**):

Interrogative:	Have you ever found those books you lost?
	Where do you think you lost them?
Imperative:	Find those books.
Exclamatory:	What a helpful librarian we have!

The ten sentence-pattern formulas describe basic declarative sentences; all ten patterns can undergo the transformations that turn them into these other three sentence types. In this chapter we will look briefly at the three alternatives; we will also take up two other transformations that, like the passive voice, alter the word order and emphasis of certain basic sentences: the *there* transformation and the cleft sentence.

INTERROGATIVE SENTENCES

One of the first lessons in the study of a foreign language is how to turn statements into questions. In our native language, of course, we begin asking questions automatically, without lessons, at an early age. A child's questions develop along with statements in stages, beginning with one- and two-word strings—"Why? Where go?"—progressing in a short time to more complicated constructions—"Can I go with Daddy? Where is Daddy going?"

The two questions about Daddy, although they look similar, represent two basic kinds of questions we have in English: the "**yes/no question**" and the "**wh-question**," or interrogative-word question. Both kinds of questions are transformations of basic sentences in which one or more elements are shifted from their usual sentence positions.

In the yes/no question, we shift the auxiliary—or the first auxiliary, if there is more than one—to the beginning of the sentence:

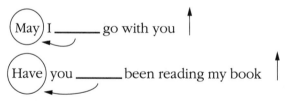

For most speakers of English, the yes/no question is also signaled by rising intonation at the end, as indicated by the arrow (and indicated in writing by the question mark).[1] The yes/no question, as its label suggests,

---

[1]One of the dialect distinctions in parts of central Pennsylvania (and perhaps in other parts of the country as well) is the absence of this rising intonation. For many speakers who are natives of the area, yes/no questions have the same intonation pattern as statements and *wh*-questions:

May I go with
you.

permits "yes" and "no" as appropriate answers, although other answers are also possible:

> *Q:* May I go with you?   *A:* We'll see.
> *Q:* Have you been reading my book?   *A:* Do you mind?

We diagram the question as we would the statement underlying it. And because the diagram includes no marks of punctuation, our only clue to its original question form is the capitalized auxiliary:

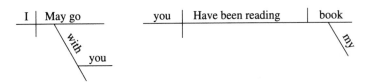

The *wh*-question is somewhat more complicated than the yes/no question in that it involves two movement operations. It begins with a question word, or interrogative, that elicits specific information, such as *why, where, when, who, what,* and *how.* These are the same interrogatives we saw in Chapter 4 introducing nominal clauses. In the question about Daddy, the information asked for, represented by the interrogative word, fills the optional adverbial slot in a Pattern VI sentence:

Where is Daddy going?

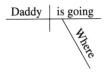

The interrogative can also fill an NP slot:

What have you been reading?

you | have been reading | What

Some interrogatives act as determiners:

Whose car are you taking?

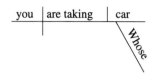

Which brand is cheapest?

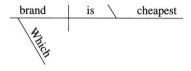

As the preceding examples show, the slots of the basic sentence pattern of a question will be out of order because the interrogative word always comes first, no matter what grammatical function it has. However, when the information being elicited is a *who* or *what* that fills the subject slot, then normal word order is maintained:

Who	broke	the window?
What	is making	that noise?
NP_1	V-tr	NP_2

The other difference between the *wh*-question and the statement is the shifted first auxiliary:

Where (is) Daddy ____ going? (Daddy is going where?)

What (have) you ____ been reading? (You have been reading what?)

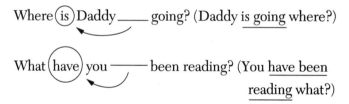

Again, this shift will not occur when the interrogative fills the subject slot:

What is happening in there?

Who has been eating my porridge?

Investigating Language 5.1

Like the interrogative sentences you have seen in this chapter, the nominal clauses introduced by interrogatives are also questions, either asked or answered, stated or implied. You can demonstrate that concept by completing the following sentences. Finish filling in the blank NP slots, using questions similar to those in the foregoing discussion (the introductory interrogative word has been supplied):

I wonder *what* _____ .

Whose _____ is a mystery to me.

Joe wants to know *why* _____ .

How _____ is really none of my business.

If you take those interrogative clauses out of their sentences and turn them into questions, you'll discover one change you'll have to make. What is that one difference between interrogative nominal clauses and complete sentences?

THE "STAND-IN" AUXILIARY

So far the system of transforming statements into questions seems fairly simple; certainly we should be able to program a computer to replace a sentence slot with the appropriate interrogative word and to shift the first auxiliary. But a complication arises in certain sentences that have no auxiliary. Consider the possible questions contained in the following statement:

Denny polishes his car every week.

There are no complications with a *who* question, where the word order remains the same:

Who polishes his car every week?

But a yes/no question or one that asks *what* or *how often* or *why* introduces another step into the process:

What does Denny polish every week?
How often does Denny polish his car?

>Does Denny polish his car every week?
>Why does Denny polish his car every week?

Turning these questions back into statements, we end up with a new element:

>Denny <u>does</u> polish his car every week.

Does polish is not one of the verb strings we can generate from the verb-expansion rule. The choice of auxiliaries under that rule is limited to the modals and to forms of *have* and *be*; *do* is not among them. But in the original sentence—"Denny polishes his car every week"—there is no auxiliary. And because we need an auxiliary for the auxiliary shift in the question transformation, we add a form of the **"stand-in" auxiliary**, *do*. In this case we have used *does*; if the underlying sentence had been in the past tense instead of the present, we would have used *did*:

>Denny <u>polished</u> his car last night.
>
><u>Did</u> Denny polish his car last night?

Like the other auxiliaries, *do* carries the tense, so the past tense has shifted from the verb *polish* to the auxiliary *do*. The addition of *do* as a stand-in auxiliary is known as the **do transformation**.

Incidentally, the *do* transformation does not apply to sentence Patterns I, II, and III, even when there is no auxiliary. When a form of *be* is the main verb, the *be* itself does the shifting:

>The teacher is at her desk → Is the teacher at her desk?
>
>The pizza was expensive → Was the pizza expensive?
>
>I am a real boy → Am I a real boy?

The *do* transformation also applies in two circumstances other than questions: in both negative sentences and emphatic sentences.

Negative Sentences.   Negative sentences are similar to questions in their need for an auxiliary or for *be* as the main verb to carry the negative marker and the tense. Some sentences are easy to transform into negatives:

The mayor should apologize to the city council members.
The council members have been concerned about her outburst.
The council is planning a special session to discuss the problem.

When a sentence has an auxiliary, as these three do, we simply add *not* after the first auxiliary:

The mayor should not apologize.
The council members have not been concerned.
The council is not planning.

The same rule applies when *be* is the predicating verb, with or without an auxiliary:

The mayor was not angry.

But when there is no auxiliary or *be* in the sentence, it doesn't work to simply add *not*:

The mayor resigned → *The mayor resigned not.
                    *The mayor not resigned.

The only way we can add *not* is to provide an auxiliary: Once again the stand-in *do* comes into play:

The mayor resigned → The mayor did not resign.
The council believes she will resign → The council does not believe . . .

In the sentence with *resigned*, we have used *did*; in the one with *believes*, we have used *does*. You'll recall from the verb-expansion rule that tense is applied to the first auxiliary in the verb string; that system also applies when the auxiliary is *do*. We have automatically shifted the past tense from *resigned* and the present tense from *believes*.

If these sentences with *not* sound somewhat formal, it's probably because you're used to seeing and hearing negatives with contractions—*n't* rather than *not*: *shouldn't* apologize, *haven't* been concerned, *isn't* planning, *wasn't* angry, *didn't* resign, *doesn't* believe. The difference between the two is a matter of emphasis. The uncontracted *not* gets a great deal more stress than the contracted form.

An alternative to *not* is a negative with built-in adverbial emphasis—*never*, a combination of *not* and *ever*; it will automatically get the loudest stress:

> She will probably <u>never</u> resign.

To diagram a negative sentence, place the *not* or *never* on a slanted line under the verb, as you do other adverbs; the contracted *n't* can remain attached to the auxiliary on the main line:

Emphatic Sentences.   In statements spoken with normal intonation, the loudest stress generally occurs after the verb, on the complement or modifier:

> Denny is polishing his CAR.
> I'm going HOME tomorrow.
> He's reading your BOOK.

One way to make the statement more emphatic is to shift stress to the auxiliary:

> He IS polishing his car.
> I AM going home tomorrow.
> He IS reading your book.

But in the absence of an auxiliary, a form of *do* can be added to carry the stress:

> He polishes his car every week → He DOES polish his car every
>   week.
> He polished his car yesterday → He DID polish his car yesterday.

When the *do* transformation is applied to a verb in the past tense, such as *polished*, the *do* will carry the past marker, as it does in negative statements and questions. Note that the resulting emphatic verb is *did polish*; the main verb is the base form, *polish*.

In its role as a stand-in auxiliary, *do* has no effect on meaning. It merely acts as kind of operator that enables us to add emphasis to sentences not containing auxiliaries or *be* and to transform them into negatives and questions. The emphatic *do* is much more common in speech than in expository prose.

IMPERATIVE SENTENCES

Imperative sentences, or **commands,** take the base form of the verb without auxiliaries:

> Be careful.
> Help yourself.
> Kiss me again.
> Tell me a story.

Note that the example with *be* demonstrates that the verbs of imperative sentences differ from those of other sentences in having no tense.

In most imperative sentences the subject is the understood *you*, the personal pronoun that refers to the person or persons being addressed. Although commands can be made from all the sentence patterns, there are some verbs that rarely produce imperative sentences: *resemble, lack, seem*. These are among the stative verbs generally—verbs that refer to a state rather than an action; and many are the same verbs that are not expanded with *be* + *-ing*, which we saw in Chapter 3 as exceptions to the verb-expansion rule. (See also Discussion Questions 4 and 5 at the end of Chapter 3.)

===== *Investigating Language 5.2* =====

Notice that the simple commands in the foregoing list are positive; another command that most of us use fairly often is the negative kind: "Don't do this" and "Don't do that." Here are some more examples:

Don't be silly.
Don't do anything I wouldn't do.
Don't forget to take out the garbage.

You'll notice that they all have the auxiliary *do*. Why is that?
And here's another with *do*:

Do be careful.

That one isn't negative: Why does it need *do*?
In answering these *why* questions, consider what you know about the form of the verb in commands and what you know about our use of the stand-in auxiliary.

In the imperative sentences we have seen so far, the subject is the understood *you* and the verb is the base form. As you probably discovered in thinking about negative commands, it's because we use the base alone, with neither tense nor an auxiliary word, that we need to add *do* when we make the command negative or emphatic. Those are two circumstances that require auxiliary words.

There are exceptions to the general rule about the understood *you*: Sometimes the *you* is not understood, it is stated:

You behave yourself.
Now don't you forget to write.
You do the best you can.

And sometimes the subject is not the second person *you*. In the following sentences, the first two are third person; the last is first person:

Somebody help Julie with the dishes.
Don't anybody move.
Let's go to the movies.

You've probably learned about the concept of **person** in your composition and literature classes in connection with point of view. In this book you'll study it in connection with personal pronouns in Chapter 13.

You might want to look over that discussion just to understand better the principle underlying imperative sentences and to recognize the subtleties of these exceptions to the standard "you" command.

EXCLAMATORY SENTENCES

We usually think of the **exclamatory sentence**, or exclamation, as any sentence spoken with heightened emotion, written with an exclamation point:

> I hate purple!
> Take that cat out of here this minute!
> Don't anybody move!

But in terms of form, the first sentence immediately preceding is *declarative*, a straightforward statement, and the other two are *imperative*. In contrast, what we call the exclamatory transformation includes a shift in word order that focuses special attention on a complement:

> What a helpful librarian we have!
> How very peaceful the countryside is!
> What a hard-working president we elected!

The *what* or *how* that introduces the emphasized element is added to the underlying sentence pattern:

> We have a helpful librarian. (Pattern VII)
> The countryside is very peaceful. (Pattern II)
> We elected a hard-working president. (Pattern VII)

The exclamation mark signals the reader that the sentence (or sentence fragment, in some cases) is expressing excitement or emotion that goes beyond standard intonation. In reading such sentences aloud, we use both higher pitch and louder stress. Whether or not a sentence includes the actual transformation—with the shift of the complement and the addition of *what* or *how*—we recognize the exclamation by its intonation pattern and its signal of the exclamation mark. To understand the significance of that mark to the written language, read the following pairs aloud and listen to your voice:

Have you ever seen such a mess?
Have you ever seen such a mess!

Is this rain ever going to stop?
Is this rain ever going to stop!

Is our football team good this year?
Is our football team good this year!

In the last sentence, as in the second example, the addition of *ever* would make the exclamatory nature of the sentence even more pronounced.

The written language, of course, cannot convey the subtleties of the meaning that the spoken language can, although punctuation certainly helps. In the following section we'll see some other tools that writers have to control the reader's intonation.

═══ *Exercise 15* ═══

Diagram the following sentences, each of which has undergone one or more of the transformations that you have learned about: passive, interrogative, negative, imperative, and exclamatory. You'll find it useful to identify the sentence patterns. (*Note*: Be alert for clauses and verb phrases in NP slots, which you learned about in Chapter 4.)

1. Where have all the flowers gone?
2. Cut everyone a piece of that delicious birthday cake.
3. Call me Ishmael. [Herman Melville]
4. Should the students be allowed into the gym before eight on the night of the dance?
5. How far that little candle throws his beams. [Shakespeare]
6. Has the social committee decided what the theme of the dance will be?
7. Don't be deceived by the flattery of strangers.
8. What a jerk I am sometimes!
9. Does going to a movie tonight appeal to you?
10. Give my regards to Broadway. [George M. Cohan]

OTHER SENTENCE TRANSFORMATIONS

The sentence types we have just seen—interrogative, imperative, and exclamatory—are variations of the basic declarative sentence that apply with few exceptions to all ten sentence patterns. In Chapter 3 we studied the passive voice, the result of a transformation that applies to the transitive verb patterns. We will now look briefly at two other fairly common transformations that alter word order for purposes of emphasis in certain kinds of sentences.

The **There Transformation.**   Like the exclamatory sentence, the ***there* transformation** includes an introductory word that plays no grammatical role in the basic sentence pattern. It also includes a shift in word order: The unstressed *there*, known as an **expletive**, introduces the sentence; the subject of the sentence follows *be:*

> There's a fly in my soup.
> There's an error message on the computer screen.

To diagram a *there* transformation, we must identify the underlying pattern. As the diagram shows, *there* has no grammatical function in the basic sentence:

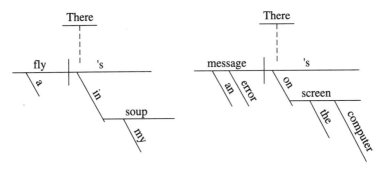

When we use the *there* transformation, we are taking advantage of the natural rhythm of language. In general, our language is a series of valleys and peaks, a fairly regular pattern of unstressed and stressed syllables:

Sentences usually begin with an unstressed valley. And more often than not, that first, unstressed slot is the subject. But the *there* transformation changes that usual word order: When the unstressed *there* fills the opening slot, it delays the subject until that first peak position of stress.

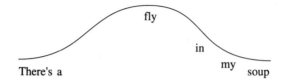

The *there* transformation applies in fairly limited circumstances. It applies when the subject of the sentence is indefinite: "*a* fly" or "*an* error message" rather than "*the* fly" or "*the* error message." The indefinite article is a signal that the subject of the *there* transformation is new information; we use the definite article, *the*, for old, or known, information. We might have occasion to say,

> Thére's that fly that knows good soup.

if a particular fly under discussion lands in the soup. But clearly this is a known fly, so this is not the unstressed *there*. The stress it carries marks it as an adverb providing information of place (it's called the "locative" adverb, from the word *location*). The same is true of

> Thére's that error message I told you about.

In these sentences with definite subjects, we have simply shifted the order of the basic sentence pattern, as we sometimes do to emphasize adverbials:

> Here's your book.
> Right off the end of the pier plunged the getaway car.

The expletive *there* is always unstressed; the adverb *there*, when it opens a sentence, is nearly always stressed—providing an exception to the normal rhythm pattern of that opening unstressed valley we just saw. The adverb *there*, besides providing information of place, often acts as a kind of pointer. For example, read the following pair of sentences aloud and notice the difference in meaning and stress of the two *theres*:

> There's a piece of the jigsaw puzzle missing.
> There it is, on the floor.

You can almost see the finger pointing in the case of the second *there*.

In addition to the indefinite subject, the *there* transformation usually has a form of *be* either as the main verb or, in the case of the transitive and intransitive patterns, as an auxiliary. Pattern I (NP *be* ADV/TP) is the most common pattern we transform with *there*; Patterns II and III, in which *be* acts as a linking verb, will not accept the *there* transformation.

The form of *be* will, of course, depend on the tense and on the number of the subject, whether singular or plural:

> There *were* some problems with the heat in our new apartment.
> There *has* been a problem with the plumbing, too.

But an exception to the general rule of **subject–verb agreement** occurs with the *there* transformation. A compound subject, which we usually treat as plural, may take the *-s* form of *be* under some circumstances:

> There was some great blocking and some fine running and passing in Saturday's game.

In this sentence "there were" would be awkward, even though the subject is compound.

The *there* transformation without a form of *be* is also possible, but such sentences are not very common:

> There came from the alley a low moaning sound.
> There followed a series of unexplained phenomena.
> There remains an unanswered question.

Listen to the difference between these sentences and those with *be*. These have a tight, controlled quality about them. Notice also that when a verb other than *be* follows *there* it shares the stress with the subject.

You will read more about the rhythm of sentences and about the *there* transformation as a tool for the writer in Chapter 14.

===== *Exercise 16* =====

Identify the function of *there* in the following sentences. Is it the expletive or is it the locative adverb? Also identify the sentence patterns.

1. There's often a flock of blackbirds lining the telephone wire in our neighborhood.
2. There they are now.
3. There's nothing to do tonight.
4. There's always TV to watch.
5. There's Henry across the street.
6. There he goes.
7. Isn't there a spelling checker on your word processor?
8. There but for the grace of God go I.

The Cleft Sentence.   Another sentence variation that provides a way to shift the focus of attention is the cleft transformation, so called because it divides a clause into two parts: It cleaves it. The **cleft sentence** allows a writer to accomplish by means of word order what a speaker can do by varying the point of main stress or loudness. For example, in the following sentence a speaker can change the focus or meaning simply by putting stress on different words:

MARY wrecked her motorcycle in Phoenix during the Christmas break. (It wasn't Diane who did it.)

Mary wrecked her MOTORCYCLE in Phoenix during the Christmas break. (Not her car.)

Mary wrecked her motorcycle in PHOENIX during the Christmas break. (Not in Albuquerque.)

Mary wrecked her motorcycle in Phoenix during the CHRISTMAS break. (Not Thanksgiving.)

Because the conventions of writing do not include capital letters for words that should get main stress, as shown in the preceding sentences, the writer's intended emphasis may not always be clear. The cleft transformation solves the problem. In one kind of cleft sentence the main subject is *it* with a form of *be* as the main verb. In reading the following sentences aloud, you'll notice that you automatically stress the word or phrase following *was:*

> It was <u>Mary</u> who wrecked her motorcycle in Phoenix during the Christmas break.
> It was <u>her motorcycle</u> that Mary wrecked in Phoenix during the Christmas break.
> It was <u>in Phoenix</u> that Mary wrecked her motorcycle during the Christmas break.
> It was <u>during the Christmas break</u> that Mary wrecked her motorcycle.

Another kind of cleft sentence uses a *what* clause in subject position. Note that the added *was* separates the original sentence into two parts:

> Mary wrecked her motorcycle.
> What Mary wrecked <u>was</u> her motorcycle.

Sometimes *what* shifts the original verb phrase into subject position. Again, a form of *be* is added as the main verb:

> A branch in the road <u>caused the accident</u>.
> <u>What caused the accident</u> was a branch in the road.

> Thick fog <u>reduced the visibility to zero</u>.
> <u>What reduced the visibility to zero</u> was the thick fog.

You'll notice in both the *it* and *what* clefts that the sentence pattern of the main clause has changed, a change that does not occur with the other transformations.

The cleft transformations produce sentences that are quite complicated structurally, with clauses filling certain slots in the patterns, so we will not be concerned here with their diagrams. The *what* cleft produces nominal clauses in subject position, like the sentences you saw in Chapter 4. In Chapter 14 the cleft transformations are discussed in terms of their rhetorical effects.

KEY TERMS IN CHAPTER 5

Cleft sentence	Locative adverb
Command	Negative sentence
Declarative sentence	Person
Do transformation	Stand-in auxiliary
Emphatic sentence	Subject–verb agreement
Exclamatory sentence	*There* transformation
Expletive *there*	*Wh*-question
Imperative sentence	*What*-cleft
Interrogative sentence	Yes/no question
It-cleft	

SENTENCES FOR PRACTICE

Using the transformations you have studied in this chapter (interrogative, imperative, exclamatory, "there," and cleft), write as many variations of the following sentences as you can.

1. Hundreds of angry women were protesting the candidate's position on abortion at yesterday's political rally in the student union.

2. Myrtle's special marinated mushrooms added a festive touch to the salad.

3. A big family is moving into the apartment upstairs next week.

4. A strange man was lurking suspiciously on the neighbor's front porch last night.

5. The encroachment of civilization on wilderness areas bothers a great many environmentalists.

6. Women athletes from all over the world made an impressive showing at the 1992 Olympic Games in Barcelona.

7. A month of unseasonably warm weather almost ruined the ski season last winter.

8. An old stone bridge near our home is a popular subject for local photographers.

9. Several gangs of kids in the neighborhood are cleaning up the empty lot on the corner.

10. Computer viruses are becoming a serious problem.

QUESTIONS FOR DISCUSSION

1. Do we ever need the stand-in auxiliary *do* for a passive sentence? Why or why not?

2. How many transformations has the following sentence undergone? *Don't be fooled!* What is unusual about the sentence? (Hint: Remember Question 1.)

3. Why do the following sentences from Shakespeare and the King James Bible sound strange to our twentieth-century ears? What particular change that has taken place in the language do these sentences illustrate?

> Let not your heart be troubled.
> Know you where you are?
> Wherefore weep you?
> Revolt our subjects?
> I came not to send peace, but a sword.

4. In this chapter we looked briefly at our system for turning sentences into questions, a process that sometimes requires *do*. The tag question is another method for turning statements into questions:

> John is washing his car, <u>isn't he?</u>
> Perry should wash his too, <u>shouldn't he?</u>

Add the tags that turn the following statements into questions:

Harold has finally stopped smoking, _____?

The students are not studying Latin, _____?

Bev finished her book on schedule, _____?

Tim and Joe are good carpenters, _____?

Kris is a good carpenter, too, _____?

She builds beautiful cabinets, _____?

Now look at the system you followed for adding these questions. How many steps are involved? Imagine writing a computer program so that it, too, could generate tag questions. What are the steps you would have to include?

Here are three more tags to supply:

Harold should stop smoking,   _____?

Harold ought to stop smoking,   _____?

Harold may stop smoking soon,   _____?

Take a poll among your friends to get their responses to these three. Do all the respondents agree? Do they follow the procedure you described in the first set? What do these tags tell you about the changing nature of the language?

5. Add tag questions to the following sentences:

There's a good movie on TV tonight,   _____?

There were a lot of students absent today, _____?

Now explain why some linguists prefer to call *there* the subject of the sentence rather than an expletive. Give other evidence to support or refute that argument.

6. We usually think of contractions (*doesn't, shouldn't, I'll, he'd*, etc.) as optional, informal variations of verbs. And we generally think of them as forms that are best avoided in formal writing. Consider the following sentences in this light. Are the foregoing assumptions true?

Can't you come with me?
Doesn't the sunset look beautiful this evening?
Hasn't everyone tried to conserve energy?
Are you sure he'll try hard enough to win?
I'm very hungry.

7. In Chapter 2 we looked briefly at sentence variations that help us distinguish verb–particle combinations (phrasal verbs) from verb–adverb combinations:

We jumped up → Up we jumped.
We made up → *Up we made.

The cleft transformation, introduced in this chapter, can also be useful in identifying properties of verbs:

> He came by the office in a big hurry.
> He came by his fortune in an unusual manner.

> Where he came was by his office.
> *Where he came was by his fortune.

> Joe turned on the bridge and looked around.
> Joe turned on the light and looked around.

> It was on the bridge that Joe turned and looked around.
> *It was on the light that Joe turned and looked around.

Here are some other pairs that look alike. Use transformations to demonstrate their differences:

> The student looked up the word.
> The teacher looked up the hall.

> Sharon called up the stairs.
> Karen called up the club members.

> An old jalopy turned into the driveway.
> Cinderella's coach turned into a pumpkin.

8. You can demonstrate the ambiguity of the following negative sentences by adding two possible follow-up sentences to each:

> I'm not taking Math 10 because it's so easy.
> He did not kill his wife because he loved her.

9. The following aphorism is ambiguous, too:

> No news is good news.

Restate the sentence in two ways to demonstrate its two meanings.

III

MODIFICATION AND COORDINATION

As you study the four chapters on sentence expansions in Part III, you will be building on your knowledge of the basic sentence patterns you learned in Chapter 2. You will expand those patterns with modifiers of the verb (Chapter 6), modifiers of the noun (Chapter 7), and modifiers of the sentence as a whole (Chapter 8); finally, you will put together sentences and their parts into coordinate structures (Chapter 9).

FORM AND FUNCTION

One way to organize all of these new details of sentence structure is to think in terms of the two-sided analysis that was introduced in Chapter 2: form and function. The labels designating *form* that you have learned include the names of word classes such as noun, verb, adjective, adverb, and preposition; the various phrases you have come to recognize—noun phrase, verb phrase, prepositional phrase—are also form designations. We recognize, and can label, the form of a structure like "the student" as a noun phrase, "to the store" as a prepositional phrase, and "eating pizza" as a verb phrase—all on the basis of their forms. That is, we needn't see those structures in sentences in order to recognize their forms.

Until we give those structures a context, however, we have no way of discussing their *functions*. In Chapter 4, you'll recall, we looked at verb phrases that fill NP, or nominal slots:

143

I enjoy *eating pizza*.

Now that it's in a sentence, we can talk about *eating pizza* in terms of both form and function: In form it's a verb phrase (in this case, a gerund); in function it's a direct object. In Chapter 7, you'll see verb phrases just like this one functioning as adjectivals, the modifiers of nouns:

The kids *eating pizza* are having a good time.

And in Chapter 6, you'll see infinitive verb phrases functioning as adverbials, telling why:

We're going downtown *to eat pizza*.

The following outline will be helpful to you in understanding the two-sided analysis of form and function and in organizing the details of sentence expansions.

FORM	FUNCTION
Word	**Nominal**
noun	subject ˙
verb	subjective complement
adjective	direct object
adverb	indirect object
	objective complement
Phrase	object of preposition
noun phrase	appositive
verb phrase	
gerund	**Adverbial**
infinitive	modifier of (<u>verb</u>)
participle	
prepositional phrase	**Adjectival**
	subjective complement
Clause	objective complement
independent sentence	modifier of (<u>noun</u>)
nominal clause	
adverbial (subordinate) clause	**Sentence Modifier**
adjectival (relative) clause	

You'll discover that all of the general functions listed on the right—nominal, adverbial, adjectival, and sentence modifier—can be carried out by all of the general forms listed on the left—words, phrases, and clauses. As an illustration of this principle, turn to the table of contents and read the headings for Chapter 6. You will see that the chapter title names and defines a function: "Modifiers of the Verb: Adverbials." The major subheadings name the five forms that carry out that function: Adverbs, Prepositional Phrases, Noun Phrases, Verb Phrases, and Clauses.

In this section of the book we will again use the sentence diagram to illustrate the various ways of expanding sentences, first with adverbials, then with adjectivals, sentence modifiers, and coordinated structures. The sentences are beginning to get long and complex, it's true; however, if you remember to consider the two-sided analysis of form and function, the diagrams will enhance your understanding. Each of the various forms we have discussed—noun phrase, prepositional phrase, verb phrase, clause—has a particular diagram, no matter what its function in the sentence. For example, a prepositional phrase is always diagrammed as a two-part structure, with the preposition on the diagonal line and the object of the preposition on the attached horizontal line; a noun phrase is always diagrammed with the headword on the horizontal line and its modifiers attached below it.

Always begin your analysis of a sentence by identifying the underlying pattern, one of the ten basic sentences you diagrammed in Chapter 2. Then analyze each of the slots to see how it has been expanded; adverbials will slant down from the verb; adjectivals will slant down from the noun headword, and so on. If you take these expansions one step at a time, asking yourself questions about form and function, you'll come to understand the system that produces the sentences of your language.

6

Modifiers of the Verb: Adverbials

Although only one of the sentence patterns has an adverbial in a required slot—Pattern I: NP *be* ADV/TP—the symbol for an optional adverbial, (ADV), could be added to all ten formulas. Adverbial information—structures telling where, when, why, how, and so on—is common in every sentence pattern. And no sentence is limited to a single adverbial. In the following sentence, each of the underlined structures—an adverb, a prepositional phrase, and a clause—adds adverbial information to the verb *gasped*:

> The audience gasped <u>nervously</u> <u>throughout the theater</u> <u>when the magician thrust his sword into the box.</u>

> The audience gasped (*How?*) nervously.
> The audience gasped (*Where?*) throughout the theater.
> The audience gasped (*When?*) when the magician thrust his sword into the box.

Even though all the adverbials in the preceding sentence follow the verb, there is really no fixed slot for most adverbials; in fact, movability is one of their most telling characteristics, and, for the writer, one of the most useful. In the preceding sentence, for example, there are several possibilities for ordering the three adverbials:

146

When the magician thrust his sword into the box, the audience
nervously gasped throughout the theater.

Throughout the theater the audience gasped nervously when the
magician thrust his sword into the box.

The position may depend on the writer's emphasis, on the rhythm of the
sentence, or simply on the desire for sentence variety.

In Pattern I sentences the adverbial of time or place nearly always
follows the verb, although even with this pattern there are certain
exceptions:

The committee members are here.

Here they are.

We should note that other adverbials can be added to Pattern I sentences
with the same versatility with which they are added to the other patterns:

The committee members are finally here.

At noon the teacher was in the library to do some research.

But no matter what positions the adverbials occupy—whether at the
beginning, middle, or end of the sentence—the traditional diagram will
show them as modifiers of the verb:

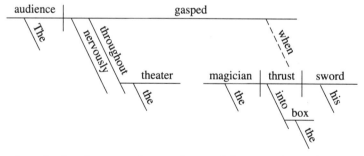

Even though the diagram shows the modifiers in the order that they
appear in the sentence, an exact reading of the diagram may still not be
possible. For instance, this one does not show whether *nervously* comes
before or after *gasped*. But because the purpose of diagramming is to
illustrate visually the relationship of the various parts of the sentence, an
exact left-to-right reading of the diagram is not necessarily important.

The preceding sample sentence includes structures of three different forms functioning adverbially: an adverb, a prepositional phrase, and a clause. Other structures that provide adverbial information are noun phrases and verb phrases. In this chapter we will take up each of these forms in its role as adverbial.

ADVERBS

The words we recognize as adverbs most readily are the adverbs of **manner**—the *-ly* words, such as *nervously*, *quietly*, and *suddenly*. These adverbs, derived from adjectives, usually tell "how" or "in what manner" about verbs:

They gasped nervously	=	in a nervous manner
They talked quietly	=	in a quiet manner
It stopped suddenly	=	in a sudden manner

The manner adverbs are probably the most movable of all the adverbials; they can appear before or after the verb, as well as at the beginning or end of the sentence:

Suddenly the wind shifted.

The wind suddenly shifted.

The wind shifted suddenly.

Notice that all three versions of the sentence are diagrammed the same; the only clue to word order is capitalization:

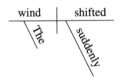

A single-word adverb can even come within the verb string, between the auxiliary word and the main verb:

The roof was suddenly blown off by a strong gust of wind.

Or between auxiliaries:

I have <u>actually</u> been working on my term project.

In all positions the manner adverbs can be marked by qualifiers, words such as *very, quite, so,* and *rather*:

<u>Quite suddenly</u> the crowd grew restless.

The old woman crooned <u>very softly</u>.

The airline employees handled our luggage <u>rather carelessly</u>.

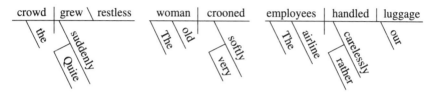

And like the adjectives they are derived from, these adverbs can be compared by combining with *more*:

<u>More suddenly</u> than the police expected, the crowd grew restless.

The sails flapped <u>more and more furiously</u> as the wind grew stronger.

Although the superlative degree, *most*, is much more common with adjectives than with adverbs, it has a strong effect when we do use it with adverbs. It nearly always shifts the main stress to the adverb or the following word:

We <u>most certainly</u> will be at the hearing.

Reginald testified <u>most reluctantly</u> about the party.

Besides the *-ly* adverbs, many other single-word adverbs provide information of time, place, frequency, and the like: *now, then, nowadays, today, often, always, sometimes, seldom, never, here, there, everywhere,* and many others.

I <u>still</u> jog <u>here</u> <u>sometimes</u>.

<u>Nowadays</u> I <u>seldom</u> swim.

Some of these, like the manner adverbs, can be qualified and compared:

> I should jog more often.
> Nowadays Judd and Betty jog quite often.

Although movability is a characteristic of all single-word adverbs, the various subclasses are bound by certain restrictions as to order. For example, in the following sentence, the adverbials of place and time cannot be reversed:

> I am going there now.
> *I am going now there.
> Now I am going there.
> *There I am going now.

And although we would say

> Often I jog here.
> I often jog here.

a native speaker of English would rarely say

> Here I jog often.

and would never say

> *I here jog often.

The rules governing the order and movement of adverbs are quite complex, but as native speakers we are unaware of that complexity; our linguistic computers are programmed to follow the rules automatically.

=== *Investigating Language 6.1* ===

The adverbs of frequency (or *non*frequency), such as those in the following sentences, are among our most movable.

1. My friends and I have pizza <u>frequently</u>.
2. I <u>generally</u> order mushrooms on my pizza.
3. <u>Occasionally</u> I order peppers.
4. <u>Sometimes</u> I order extra cheese.
5. <u>Seldom</u> do I order hot sausage.
6. <u>Never</u> will I order anchovies.
7. I <u>rarely</u> finish the whole thing.

The movability of adverbs enables the writer to change the emphasis in the sentence in subtle ways. Interestingly, however, the seven adverbs in this list don't always behave alike. Notice what has happened in sentences 5 and 6: What's different about those two? Are there any others in the same category? Formulate a rule to account for the placement of frequency adverbs.

PREPOSITIONAL PHRASES

The **prepositional phrase** is our most common structure of modification, appearing regularly as a modifier of both nouns and verbs.

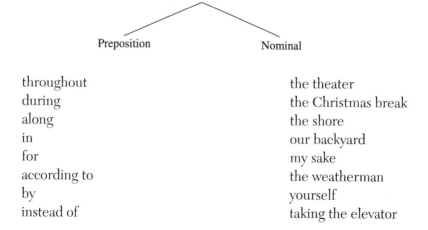

Preposition	Nominal
throughout	the theater
during	the Christmas break
along	the shore
in	our backyard
for	my sake
according to	the weatherman
by	yourself
instead of	taking the elevator

As the branching diagram illustrates, the prepositional phrase is a binary structure, consisting of a preposition and a noun phrase or other nominal structure, known as the object of the preposition. You'll find a long list of simple (one-word) and phrasal (two- or three-word) prepositions in Chapter 12.

The term **prepositional phrase** is a label referring to *form*. Even out of context we can identify a structure such as *during the Christmas break* as a prepositional phrase in form; but only when it appears in a sentence can we label its *function*—either as adjectival, a modifier of a noun ("The weather *during the Christmas break* was unseasonably mild"), or as adverbial, a modifier of a verb ("I worked for the Post Office *during the Christmas break*").[1]

Adverbial prepositional phrases provide the same kind of information as adverbs do:

Direction

We hiked
$\begin{cases} \text{toward the pond.} \\ \text{beyond the ridge.} \\ \text{across the field.} \end{cases}$

Place

We fished
$\begin{cases} \text{on the bank.} \\ \text{along the shore.} \\ \text{near the island.} \\ \text{in the pond.} \\ \text{under the pier.} \end{cases}$

Specific Time

We arrived
$\begin{cases} \text{at noon.} \\ \text{on Wednesday.} \end{cases}$

Duration

We hiked
$\begin{cases} \text{until three o'clock.} \\ \text{for several days.} \\ \text{during the term break.} \\ \text{throughout the winter.} \end{cases}$

---

[1] On rare occasions the prepositional phrase appears in an NP slot, usually as the name of a time or place:

> After lunch will be too late.
>
> Beyond the baseline is foul territory.

Manner

She walked <u>with dignity</u>.

I sunbathe <u>in the nude</u>.

I went <u>by myself</u>.

Measure

She won <u>by a mile</u>.

He came <u>within an inch</u>.

Means

She does her best work <u>with a palette knife</u>.

They cleared the land <u>through sheer determination</u>.

Cause or Reason

We went out <u>for a pizza</u>.

We were late <u>because of the storm</u>.

In the diagram the adverbial prepositional phrase is always attached to the verb:

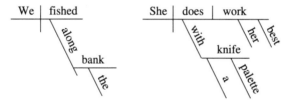

Some prepositional phrases have modifiers that qualify or intensify them, just as adjectives and adverbs do:

He arrived <u>shortly</u> before noon.

The house was built <u>directly</u> over the water.

In the diagram the modifier will be attached to the preposition:

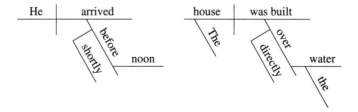

Sentences often have more than one adverbial prepositional phrase:

We hiked in the woods for several hours on Saturday.

And like adverbs, adverbial prepositional phrases can occupy several positions, with those referring to time often more movable than those referring to place, especially when both appear in the same sentence:

For several hours on Saturday we hiked in the woods.

On Saturday we hiked in the woods for several hours.

We are less likely to say:

In the woods we hiked on Saturday for several hours.

In general, an adverbial with main focus will occupy a slot at or near the end of the sentence. But no matter where in the sentence they appear—whether at the beginning, the middle, or end—in the diagram the adverbial prepositional phrases will be attached to the verb:

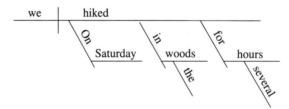

=== *Exercise 17* ===

Diagram the following sentences, paying particular attention to the adverbs and prepositional phrases that function adverbially. Bear in mind that the nominals you studied in Chapter 4 (gerunds, infinitives, and nominal clauses) can also have adverbials as modifiers.

1. In winter we burn wood for our heat.
2. We can heat our house very efficiently in cold weather because of its good insulation.
3. In an interview with *Time* reporters, the president promised that he has some new approaches for the economy up his sleeve.

4. The economy invariably becomes an issue in every election.
5. For middle-aged people, doctors often recommend climbing stairs regularly instead of taking elevators.
6. It is important for all of us to exercise regularly.
7. My grandmother always insists on having her lunch precisely at noon.
8. Keeping the spotted owl habitat undisturbed is still an important goal for environmentalists.
9. During an election year, the environment inevitably becomes big news.
10. Man is by nature a political animal. [Aristotle]

Because prepositional phrases can modify both verbs and nouns, ambiguity is fairly common. The prepositional phrase in the following sentence, for example, could be interpreted as meaning either "with whom" or "which problems":

They discussed their problems <u>with the teacher.</u>

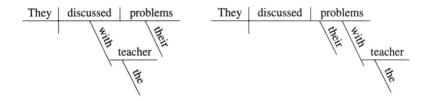

Sometimes the difference between the two possible interpretations is simply a matter of emphasis:

I'll see you at the party <u>on Saturday.</u>

Here the question is whether *on Saturday* modifies the noun *party* or the verb *see*. If we can move the prepositional phrase without distorting the meaning, then it must be adverbial—it must modify *see*—because only adverbial prepositional phrases are movable. So if it's possible to reverse the order of the two prepositional phrases and say

I'll see you <u>on Saturday</u> at the party,

or to make *on Saturday* the sentence opener,

> On Saturday I'll see you at the party.

then *on Saturday* is clearly adverbial. If, however, the phrase specifies Saturday's party as opposed to Friday's party, then the function is to modify the noun *party*, and shifting its position would distort the meaning. In a conversation the speaker's intonation would make the meaning clear. But even in context the intention of the writer may not be clear. There is often no way of knowing which interpretation is more accurate:

> I'll see you at [the party on Saturday].
> *or*
> I'll see you [at the party] [on Saturday].

In a sentence such as this, where the two interpretations mean essentially the same thing, the ambiguity is not really a problem for the reader or listener. But in the earlier example—"They discussed their problems with the teacher"—a genuine question of meaning does exist. In speech, meaning is rarely a problem, and when it is, the listener can ask for clarification. But the solitary reader has no one to ask, "What do you mean?" or "How's that again?" So the writer has an obligation to make such questions unnecessary. Understanding when modifiers are ambiguous is important for writers; avoiding ambiguity is a requirement of clear writing.

===== *Exercise 18* =====

Rewrite each of the following sentences in two ways to show its two possible meanings.

1. I'm going to wax the car in the garage.
2. We watched the game on the porch.
3. I hid from the neighbors upstairs.
4. Fred tripped his teammate with the bat.
5. Susan washed the stones she found in the river.

NOUN PHRASES

Noun phrases that function adverbially form a fairly short list of words and phrases designating time, place, manner, and quantity. Here are some of them:

We walked home. ———————————

I'm leaving Monday morning. ———————————

I'm going your way. ———————————

Every day he studied two hours. ———————————

I travel a great deal. ———————————

We are flying tourist class. ———————————

I sent the package airmail. ———————————

The Boy Scouts hiked single file down the trail. ———————————

He arrived this evening. ———————————

These noun phrases may look suspiciously like direct objects or subjects, but if you remember to think about the kind of information that adverbials contribute to the sentence, you should have no trouble in distinguishing them from nominals. In the blank following each sentence, write the adverbial question that the noun phrase answers.

These noun phrases work like prepositional phrases—like prepositional phrases with missing prepositions. The traditional grammarian labels them **adverbial objectives** and diagrams them as though they were the objects in prepositional phrases:

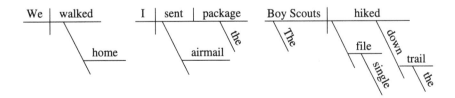

In some of these sentences the preposition is optional: (*on*) Monday morning, (*for*) two hours, (*by*) airmail, (*in*) single file. This method of diagramming the adverbial noun phrase acknowledges both its *form*—a noun headword on a horizontal line with or without modifiers—and its *function*—a modifier of the verb.

═════ *Investigating Language 6.2* ═══════════

In Chapter 2, when you first studied the sentence patterns, you were advised to think in terms of the referents of the NPs in determining the sentence patterns. For example, you can distinguish Pattern V,

Carmen became a doctor [NP_1 V NP_1]

from Pattern VII,

Carmen called a doctor [NP_1 V NP_2]

by recognizing the relationship that the two NPs have to each other. That is, when you see an NP with a referent different from that of the subject, you can assume that it's a direct object and that the verb is transitive:

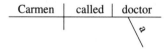

In Chapter 3, you learned about another test for determining if a verb is transitive: Can you make the sentence passive? Can you say "A doctor was called (by Carmen)"? In this case, the answer is yes. This means that the verb is transitive and the sentence is Pattern VII.

Now we come to a complication of sorts—sentences that look like Pattern VII:

We arrived home.
I work Sundays.

In both cases the verb is followed by an NP with a referent different from that of the subject. What test can you apply to show that *arrived* and *work* are not transitive verbs?

Here's a pair that might fool you. How can you show that they belong to different patterns? What tests can you apply?

Terry is flying the plane.

Terry is flying first class.

You'll want to bear in mind the kind of information that adverbials and direct objects contribute, the kinds of questions that they answer.

══════ *Exercise 19* ═══════════════════════

Underline the adverbials in the following sentences and identify their forms. Then identify the sentence patterns. In making your judgments, you'll want to think about the kind of information that each slot contributes to the sentence.

1. Pete is working nights this week.
2. I was awake the whole night.
3. I'll see you soon.
4. This morning Pam threw away the leftover spaghetti.
5. George will do dishes next time.
6. I love weekends.
7. Bill works weekends.
8. At the first sign of winter the birds flew south.

VERB PHRASES

The most common form of the verb in an adverbial role is the infinitive, the base form of the verb with *to*. In Chapter 4 we saw infinitives functioning as nominals; here the same form modifies verbs:

Mom cashed a check <u>to give Jody her allowance</u>.

I went home early <u>to get ready for the party</u>.

Jennifer took on two paper routes <u>to earn money for camp</u>.

Remember that the infinitives—*to give, to get,* and *to earn*—are not simply verbs with *to*; they are entire verb phrases, complete with complements and modifiers.

Underlying the first infinitive is a Pattern VIII sentence:

Mom gave Jody her allowance.

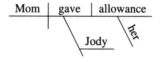

When we turn that predicate into an infinitive, the relationship of the complements and the verb stays the same, as the diagram of the infinitive shows. We have a Pattern VIII infinitive, an adverbial that tells why, in a Pattern VII sentence:

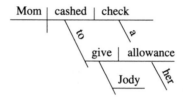

Underlying the *get* infinitive phrase is a Pattern IV sentence:

I got ready for the party.

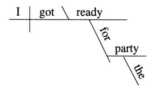

And underlying the *earn* phrase is a Pattern VII sentence:

Jennifer earned money for camp.

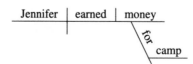

The Pattern IV sentence is now a Pattern IV infinitive phrase; the Pattern VII sentence is now a Pattern VII infinitive phrase. The *get* phrase has

been added to a Pattern VI sentence (*I went home*), the *earn* phrase to
a Pattern VII (*Jennifer took on two paper routes*):

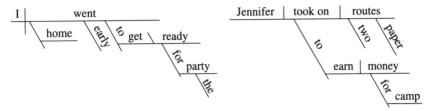

Note, too, that the subjects of the sentences are also the subjects of the
infinitives.

In the first and third sentences, where the infinitive phrases follow
nouns, *check* and *routes*, they may appear to modify those nouns. The
clue that says otherwise is the meaning "in order to" that underlies
almost all adverbial infinitives; they answer the question *why*:

> Mom cashed a check in order to give Jody her allowance.
>
> I went home early in order to get ready for the party.
>
> Jennifer took on two paper routes in order to earn money for camp.

In fact, we often include *in order*, especially in introductory position:

> In order to earn money for camp, Jennifer took on two paper
> routes.

In diagramming the expanded version, you can treat it like a phrasal
preposition, with "in order to" on the diagonal line.

There are exceptions. Occasionally an infinitive functions adverbially
without the meaning of "in order to," but such sentences are uncommon
in speech:

> The detective glanced out the window only to see the suspect slip
> around the corner.
>
> I arrived at the auditorium only to find every seat taken.

These infinitives have an almost main-verb rather than adverbial quality.
We could, and probably would, more often say:

The detective glanced out the window <u>and saw</u> the suspect slip
around the corner.

I arrived at the auditorium <u>and found</u> every seat taken.

Other exceptions, which are fairly common idioms, occur with the verbs
come and *live*:

I've <u>come to believe</u> in UFOs.

I've <u>come to understand</u> your point of view.

You'll <u>live to regret</u> that remark.

The *-ing* verbs occasionally act adverbially, too, as in the following
sentences:

He drank his beer <u>standing at the bar</u>. (*How?*)

The kids came <u>running out of the house</u>. (*How? Where?*)

Betsy went <u>swimming</u>. (*Where?*)

Dangling Infinitives.   We noted that the subject of the sentence is also the subject of the adverbial infinitive. When this is not
the case, the infinitive is said to "dangle." You'll recall that the same
"dangling" problem can occur with gerunds in prepositional phrases. In
the following sentences, the infinitive phrases have no stated subject:

<u>To keep farm machinery in good repair</u>,   a   regular   maintenance
schedule is necessary.

For decades the Superstition Mountains in Arizona have been
explored in order <u>to find the fabled Lost Dutchman Mine</u>.

Certainly the problem with these sentences is not a problem of
communication; the reader is not likely to misinterpret their meaning.
But in both cases a kind of fuzziness exists that can be cleared up with
the addition of a subject for the infinitive:

<u>A farmer</u> needs a regular maintenance schedule <u>to keep the farm
machinery in good repair</u>.

For decades <u>people</u> [or <u>adventurers</u> or <u>prospectors</u>] have explored the Superstition Mountains in Arizona <u>to find the fabled Lost Dutchman Mine.</u>

===== *Exercise 20* =====

Underline all the adverbial modifiers in the following sentences. Identify the sentence pattern of the main clause; then identify the sentence pattern of the adverbial and nominal verb phrases. Diagram the sentences.

1. Our cat often jumps up on the roof to reach the attic window.
2. Sometimes she even climbs the ladder to get there.
3. Last night the television set buzzed strangely during an electrical storm.
4. I had just gone into the kitchen to fix some popcorn.
5. We went downtown last Saturday to check out the sidewalk sales.
6. First I bought the children winter boots at the new shoe store.
7. Afterward we stayed home to watch the playoff game with Uncle Dick.
8. To keep my weight under control this winter, I have decided to give up popcorn.

CLAUSES

In Chapter 4 you studied the dependent clauses that fill nominal roles in sentences. The term *dependent*, in contrast to *independent*, refers to any clause that is not itself a complete sentence. In that discussion you learned that all sentences are clauses but not all clauses are sentences.

Another set of contrasting labels traditionally given to clauses (in addition to *independent* and *dependent*) is *main* and *subordinate*. It's accurate to say that the terms *main clause* and *independent clause* are synonymous—and, in fact, are used interchangeably. With their counterparts, however, there is a difference: *Dependent* and *subordinate* are not generally used interchangeably.

The term *subordinate clause* is often restricted to those dependent clauses that are introduced by subordinating conjunctions—words like *since* and *if* and *because* and *when*. That definition rules out the nominal clauses: As you recall, nominal clauses are introduced by expletives and interrogatives. (It also rules out the adjectival clauses, which we will take up in Chapter 7: They are introduced by relative pronouns and relative adverbs.)

In form a subordinate clause consists of a sentence—any declarative sentence—to which a subordinating conjunction has been added as an introducer. For example, we used a *when* clause at the opening of this chapter in a sentence illustrating the various forms that adverbials take:

> The audience gasped nervously throughout the theater <u>when the</u> <u>magician thrust his sword into the box.</u>

That clause is a complete sentence made incomplete—made dependent—by the subordinator *when*. Unlike the interrogatives that introduce nominal clauses, the subordinators do not have a role in their own clause. Rather, their role is to establish the relationship of that clause to the main clause.

Traditionally, these subordinate clauses have been considered adverbial. Certainly, the *when* clause in the sentence about the magician is a straightforward clause of time. But there are other subordinate clauses that are less clearly adverbial, especially those introduced by such subordinating conjunctions as *although, if,* and *whereas*; these clauses are related more to the sentence as a whole. For that reason, you will see subordinate clauses in two places: here in this chapter as adverbials and in Chapter 8 as sentence modifiers. (You'll find a long list of subordinators under the heading "Conjunctions" in Chapter 12.)

Included here in the adverbial chapter, then, are some examples of clauses that answer such adverbial questions as *where, when,* and *why,* as you'll see in the following sentences:

> <u>After the Blue Jays won the World Series in 1992,</u> the citizens of Toronto went crazy.
>
> Harold held his partner on the dance floor <u>as if she were made</u> <u>of glass.</u>

You should eat some breakfast <u>before you take that exam</u>.

I never take the subway home at night <u>because my family worries about me</u>.

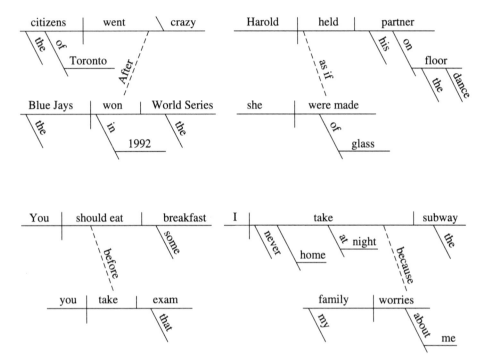

Adverbial clauses also function as modifiers in verb phrases that are themselves modifiers—such as the adverbial infinitive phrases we saw earlier:

I went home early *to get ready for the party <u>before the guests arrived</u>*.

The underlined clause added to the infinitive phrase is clearly adverbial, telling "when" about *get ready*; it does not tell "when" about the verb *went*, the main verb, nor is it likely to be construed as a modifier of the whole sentence.

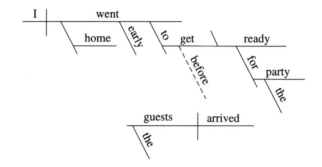

═══════ *Exercise 21* ═══════

Both *when* and *where* hold membership in two word classes. As **subordinators**, they introduce adverbial clauses; as **interrogatives** they introduce nominal clauses. In the parentheses, identify the function of the *where* and *when* clauses in the following sentences. Are they adverbial or nominal? If the clause is nominal, identify the NP slot that it fills. (*Helpful hint*: Remember the trick of substituting a pronoun, such as *something*, to identify a nominal.) Also identify the sentence patterns of both the independent and dependent clauses.

1. Julie couldn't remember where she had left her keys.

   (_____)

2. Rob lost his keys when his backpack was stolen.

   (_____)

3. When I get in late, my roommate gets upset.

   (_____)

4. I think that when I get in is my own business.

   (_____)

5. The starship *Enterprise* regularly ventures where explorers have never gone before.   (_____)

6. When you have decided where we should have dinner, give me a call.

   (_____)

7. I learn by going where I have to go. [Theodore Roethke]

   (_____)

8. Where you spend your time says something about you.

   (_____)

Before you can do a diagram of a sentence, you have to ask—and answer—questions about function and patterns. You've already come up with most of that information, so diagramming these eight sentences should give you no trouble.

PUNCTUATION OF ADVERBIALS

You may have noticed in the examples that some opening adverbials are set off by commas and some are not. Their punctuation is sometimes a matter of choice, especially in the case of phrases. Generally a short prepositional phrase or noun phrase or an adverb will not be set off:

Saturday morning we all pitched in and cleaned the garage.
By noon we were exhausted.
Hastily they gathered their books and left the room.

With longer prepositional phrases there is a choice:

At the top of the hill the hikers sat down to rest.
At the end of a long and exhausting morning, we all collapsed.

When the end of the adverbial slot is not readily apparent, the comma will be needed to prevent misreading:

During the winter, vacation days are especially welcome.
In the middle of the night, winds from the north brought subzero
    temperatures and the end of Indian summer.

The two opening adverbial structures that are *always* set off by commas are verb phrases and clauses—no matter what their length:

> To earn money for camp, Jennifer took on two paper routes.
> To succeed, you'll need self-discipline.
> When the speech finally ended, the audience broke into applause.

When an adverbial interrupts the verb phrase for a special effect, it will be set off by commas:

> I finally bought, on my birthday, a brand new car.
> The stranger asked me, quite openly, for my credit card number.

When the opening phrase is parenthetical—more clearly a comment on the whole sentence than a straightforward adverbial—then a comma is called for:

> According to all the polls, the incumbent was expected to win.
> On the other hand, not everyone was surprised at the outcome of the election.
> Luckily, no one was hurt.

The punctuation of sentence modifiers is discussed in Chapter 8.

===== *Investigating Language 6.3* =============================

It's not at all unusual for inexperienced writers to punctuate subordinate clauses as complete sentences. It's probably the most common sentence fragment that teachers encounter.

> The children have been quite bored this summer. Because the swimming pool has been closed since July.
> Although we had a lot of rain last spring. Apparently the drought is not over yet.

Given what you know about sentence slots, can you explain why writers would make that mistake? In the second example, what's the difference between *although* and *apparently*?

If you listen carefully to the intonation of subordinate clauses and complete sentences, you will hear the difference. Read the clauses aloud:

> because you were here
> since Joe went away
> if he knows the truth

Now read them without the subordinator:

> You were here.
> Joe went away.
> He knows the truth.

You can probably hear the pitch of your voice dropping at the end of the last three. In the set with subordinators, your pitch would normally stay more level on the last word. (Even if you didn't read them with that contrast, you probably could do so to illustrate the difference.)

There's another way of reading that first group: as if they were answers to questions. In fact, such sentence fragments are common in conversation:

> Q. Why did you come back?   A. Because you were here.
> Q. How long have you lived alone?   A. Since Joe went away.
> Q. Will Mike ever forgive you?   A. If he knows the truth.

Does this reading help explain why writers make punctuation errors? What can a writing teacher do to help students understand and correct their punctuation?

KEY TERMS IN CHAPTER 6

Adverb	Adverb of time
Adverb of frequency	Adverbial
Adverb of manner	Adverbial clause
Adverb of place	Adverbial infinitive

Adverbial noun phrase	Main clause
Adverbial prepositional phrase	Movability
Ambiguity	Sentence fragment
Dangling infinitive	Subordinate clause
Dependent clause	Subordinating conjunction
Independent clause	

SENTENCES FOR PRACTICE

Underline the adverbials in the following sentences and identify their forms. For additional practice, identify the sentence patterns and diagram the sentences. Remember also to identify the sentence patterns of all nominal and adverbial verb phrases and clauses.

1. By the end of the fifth inning, the playoff game had already become boring.

2. When the fall foliage shows its colors in New England, thousands of tourists go there to enjoy nature's astonishing display.

3. On Halloween night the members of our sorority decided to go out into the neighborhood to trick-or-treat.

4. We expectantly rang every doorbell on the block to fill our bags with goodies.

5. Some of the neighbors firmly declared that they were saving their treats for the little kids.

6. The recent rally on Wall Street probably occurred because of the optimistic news about interest rates.

7. According to the *Wall Street Journal*, the deficit is considered our most serious domestic problem.

8. Because of a lyme disease outbreak in several counties, fewer hunters applied for licenses in 1993.

9. Cowards die many times before their death. [Shakespeare]

10. Be silent always when you doubt your sense. [Alexander Pope]

11. Diane has to take nineteen credits to graduate this semester.

12. Susan plans to stay home on Friday to fix a special gourmet dinner for her roommates.

13. During the month of December there will be dozens of holiday specials on television.

14. Where were you when I needed a shove to get my car to the garage for repairs?

15. Never in the field of human conflict was so much owed by so many to so few. [Winston Churchill]

16. It is undesirable to believe a proposition when there is no ground whatever for supposing it true. [Bertrand Russell]

QUESTIONS FOR DISCUSSION

1. Consider the differences in meaning in these two pairs of sentences. How do you account for the differences? Do the differences involve different sentence patterns?

> Mel stopped to talk to Walt.
> Mel stopped talking to Walt.
>
> Mel started talking to Walt.
> Mel started to talk to Walt.

2. How would you analyze the following sentences, which were spoken in a television interview by an attorney whose client had been accused of murder:

> You're not talking a traffic ticket here. You're talking somebody's life.

In considering the sentence patterns and the referents of the noun phrases, you might think that *talking* is a transitive verb. Is it?

3. How do you account for the difference in meaning of the following sentences? Why is "in the mountains" so important?

> After his retirement, Professor Jones lived for six months in the mountains.
> After his retirement, Professor Jones lived for six months.

4. A school official who had signed an admission certificate for a foreign student was taken to court by the U.S. Immigration Service. The government maintained that the official had broken the law by signing

the certificate in Europe. The official disagreed; he maintained that the regulation was ambiguous. Here's the regulation. Who was right?

> This certificate may be signed and issued only by an authorized official in the United States after he has determined that the student is eligible.

(P.S. The case was settled out of court.)

5. As you know, single-word adverbs are often movable, producing a number of variations in a sentence. How many acceptable variations can you produce by adding the adverb *frequently* to the following sentence?

> I have had colds this year.

Are there any slots in the sentence where *frequently* is clearly unacceptable?

6. One of our most movable words in English is *only*. How many variations of the following sentence can you produce by inserting it?

> Joe eats raw vegetables for dinner on Sunday evenings.

Explain the difference in meaning that *only* produces by adding a negative clause to each version of your sentence, as shown in the following example:

> Only Joe eats raw vegetables for dinner on Sunday evenings; Mary doesn't.

7. Recently a banner was hung across a city's main street to recognize the local bus company's ten years of service to the community. On it was printed the company's name, followed by the verb phrase "serving our community" and, in bold print, these three words:

SAFELY   ECONOMICALLY   FRIENDLY

What suggestion could you have made to the banner committee if they had asked for your advice?

CHAPTER
7
Modifiers of the Noun: Adjectivals

As you know, a nominal occupies at least one slot in every sentence pattern—that of subject. In six of the ten patterns, nominals occupy one or more slots in the predicate as well: direct object, indirect object, subjective complement, and objective complement; and in every prepositional phrase a nominal serves as the object of the preposition—and the most common form for nominals is the noun phrase. Most of the NPs used in the sample sentences have been simple two-word phrases: *the students, a scholar, an apple, their assignment.* But in the sentences we actually speak and write, the noun phrases are frequently expanded with modifiers—not only with adjectives, the basic noun modifier, but with other nouns and noun phrases, with prepositional phrases, verb phrases, and clauses. We refer to the function of all such modifiers in the noun phrase as **adjectival**.

We can think of the noun phrase as a series of slots (in much the same way as we looked at the expanded verb), with the determiner and noun headword as the required slots and the modifiers before and after the headword as optional:

$$\text{NP} = \underline{\text{Det}} \quad \underline{(\ \ )} \quad \underline{(\ \ )} \quad \underline{\begin{array}{c}\text{NOUN}\\ \text{HEAD-}\\ \text{WORD}\end{array}} \quad \underline{(\ \ )} \quad \underline{(\ \ )} \quad \underline{(\ \ )}$$

Because of their frequency in the sentence and the variety of structures we use to expand them, noun phrases provide a remarkable range of possibilities for putting ideas into words. In this chapter we will look at

173

these possibilities, and we will come to appreciate the systematic nature of modification in the noun phrase.

THE HEADWORD

Filling the **headword** slot in the noun phrase is, of course, the noun, the word signaled by the determiner. We usually define a noun as the name of a person, place, thing, event, concept, or the like—a meaning-based definition. But a better way to identify nouns, as you learned in Chapter 2, is to use your intuition: Is the word signaled by a determiner—or could it be? Can you make it plural? Also, an understanding of the system of pre- and postnoun modifiers in the noun phrase will make the identification of the noun headword an easy matter.

Recognition of the headword of the noun phrase, incidentally, can be a help in preventing problems of subject–verb agreement. Such problems can arise when a postheadword modifier includes a noun itself:

> *The stack of instruction forms were misplaced.

> *The complicated instructions on the new income tax
>   form really confuses me.

With just a few exceptions, it is the number, either singular or plural, of the headword in the subject noun phrase that dictates the form of the verb in the present tense. In the preceding sentences, the writer has used the wrong noun in making the verb selection. *Stack* and *instructions* are the headwords; *forms* and *form* are simply parts of postnoun modifiers.

> The stack was misplaced.

> The *stack* of instruction forms was misplaced.

> The instructions confuse me.

> The complicated *instructions* on the new income tax
> form really confuse me.

The exceptions to this system involve noun phrases with certain "collective" nouns and pronouns in which the modifier rather than the headword determines the verb:

> A bunch of my friends are coming over for dinner.
>
> Some of the cookies are missing.
>
> Some of the cake is missing.

This topic, along with other details of determiners, is discussed further in the "Determiner" section of Chapter 12.

THE PRENOUN MODIFIERS

The Determiner.   The **determiner**, one of the structure classes, is the word class that signals nouns. This class includes *articles, possessive nouns, possessive pronouns,* and *demonstrative pronouns,* as well as a variety of other common words. When you see one of these words, you can be fairly sure you're at the beginning of a noun phrase.

The native speaker rarely thinks about determiners; they are automatic in speech. But for the writer, the determiner's role is something to think about. For example, as the first word of the noun phrase, and thus frequently the first word of the sentence and even of the paragraph, the determiner can provide a bridge, or transition, between ideas. The selection of that bridge can make subtle but important differences in emphasis:

> This attempt at reconciliation proved futile.
>
> The attempt at reconciliation . . .
>
> Their attempt . . .
>
> Every such attempt . . .
>
> All their attempts . . .
>
> Those attempts . . .

In selecting determiners, writers have the opportunity not only to make such distinctions but also to help their readers move easily from one idea to the next in a meaningful way.

Some nouns, of course, are used without determiners: proper nouns (*John, Berkeley*), noncountable nouns (*salt, water*), abstract nouns (*justice, grief*), and sometimes plural count nouns (*apples, students*). You will read more about these categories in Chapter 11.

Adjectives and Nouns.   These two word classes generally fill the slots between the determiner and the headword. When the noun phrase includes both an adjective and a noun as modifiers, they appear in that order; they cannot be reversed:

DETERMINER	ADJECTIVE	NOUN	HEADWORD
the	little		boy
the		neighbor	boy
the	little	neighbor	boy
an	ancient	marble	bathtub
that	nervous	test	pilot
my	new	kitchen	table

We do not say, "My kitchen new table" or "The neighbor little boy."

The adjective slot frequently includes more than one adjective; all of them modify the headword:

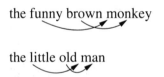

You'll notice that there are no commas in the preceding noun phrases, even though there are several modifiers before the noun. But sometimes commas are called for. A good rule of thumb is to use a comma if it is possible to insert *and* between the modifiers. We would not talk about "a little and old man" or "a funny and brown monkey." However, we would say "a strange and wonderful experience," so in using these two adjectives without *and*, we would use a comma:

a strange, wonderful experience

That comma represents juncture in speech—a pause and slight shift in pitch. Read the following pair of sentences aloud and listen to the difference in your voice:

On the table stood a little black suitcase.
On the table stood an ugly, misshapen suitcase.

In general, the system calls for a comma between two adjectives when they are of the same class, for instance, when they are both subjective qualities such as "strange" and "wonderful" or "ugly" and "misshapen." However, in the earlier example—*funny brown monkey*—the adjectives *funny* and *brown* are not alike: "funny" is a subjective, changing quality; "brown" is an objective, permanent quality.

The adjective can also be qualified or intensified:

the extremely bright young lady

a really important career decision

In this situation we often have occasion to use a hyphen to make the relationship clear:

a half-baked idea
the moss-covered stones
a Spanish-speaking community
a bases-loaded home run

Hyphens are especially common when the modifier in the adjective slot is a participle (the -*ing* or -*en* verb), as in the previous examples: *baked, covered, speaking,* and *loaded* are participles. And because participles are verbs, they are also commonly modified by adverbs:

a well-developed paragraph
the fast-moving train
the low-hanging clouds
this highly publicized event
a carefully conceived plan

The hyphen rule here is fairly straightforward: The -*ly* adverbs (such as *highly, carefully, really,* and *extremely*) do not take hyphens; other adverbs (such as *well* and *fast* and *low*) do take hyphens.

Other classes of words also need hyphens when the first modifier applies not to the headword but to the second modifier:

> high-technology industries
> two-word verbs
> all-around athletes
> free-form sculpture

In these modifiers, if the hyphen were eliminated, the reader would not necessarily know that *two* does not apply to *verbs*, nor *all* to *athletes*, nor *free* to *sculpture*.

Another occasion for hyphens in the preheadword position occurs when we use a complete phrase in the adjective slot:

> an off-the-wall idea
> the end-of-the-term party
> a middle-of-the-road policy
> my back-to-back exams

When a phrasal modifier fills the subjective complement slot in the sentence pattern, however, the hyphens are generally omitted:

> Our party will be at <u>the end of the term</u>.
> My exams during finals week are <u>back to back</u>.

In certain idioms they would probably be retained:

> Her idea seemed off-the-wall to me.
> The policy he subscribes to is strictly middle-of-the-road.

The position in the sentence can also affect the earlier hyphenated examples:

> The paragraph was well developed.
> The industry did research in high technology.

You might have been surprised to see nouns as modifiers of other nouns. It's possible, too, that in earlier grammar classes you called such nouns "adjectives." If you did, it's probably because you didn't have the term *adjectival*, the label that refers to the function of all modifiers in the noun phrase.

There are very few, if any, nouns that cannot function as modifiers of other nouns. Here's a vocabulary exercise to test that statement. Begin with a common noun, such as *light* or *tree* or *house*. Use it as a modifier; then use the noun you modified as a modifier—and see how far you can keep the chain going: *tree farm—farm building—building code—code word—word game—game player—player piano—piano bench—bench warmer—warmer oven—oven light. . . .* If you get stuck, you can go back and change a word to start a new path.

Another feature of prose that might make you aware of the effect of noun modifiers is the problem of "modifier noun proliferation"—a problem that you as a writer should be aware of. This proliferation of noun modifiers occurs when a modified noun becomes the modifier of still another noun. For example, when the committee in charge of the cafeteria becomes the "school cafeteria policy committee" and their meetings then become the "school cafeteria policy committee meetings," you can imagine what the reports of those meetings then become!

In the diagram of the noun phrase, no matter where in the sentence it appears and no matter how many modifiers it includes, the headword is on a horizontal line with the determiner, adjective(s), and modifying noun(s) slanting down from it:

When the modifiers themselves have modifiers, either qualifiers or other nouns, the diagram will make that clear:

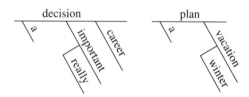

When the determiner is a possessive noun, it may have a determiner of its own: my daughter's car, the car's electrical system:

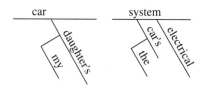

As the diagram illustrates, it is the whole phrase, "my daughter" and "the car," that has been made possessive. You can show that *my daughter's* and *the car's* constitute a single modifier of the headword by substituting a possessive pronoun: <u>her</u> car; <u>its</u> electrical system.

=== *Exercise 22* ===

Underline the determiner and the headword of each noun phrase in the following sentences. Identify the form of any modifiers that fill slots between them. Punctuate the noun phrases with commas and hyphens, if necessary.

1. The department's personnel committee met in the main office Monday night.
2. I am impressed with the new Sunday brunch menu at the cafeteria.
3. I found an expensive looking copper colored bracelet in the subway station.
4. The committee has worked hard to make this year's homecoming celebration a really festive occasion.
5. The bicycle safety commission will discuss the new regulations at their regular meeting this noon.
6. Her lovely gracious manner was apparent from the start.
7. My poor old cat probably won't last through another extreme winter.
8. There was a splendid old table at the auction.

9. For dessert, Connie served a creamy delicious chocolate mousse.
10. A commonly held notion among my cynical friends is that big business lobbyists run this country.

THE POSTNOUN MODIFIERS

The postheadword position in the noun phrase may contain modifiers of many forms; when there is more than one, they appear in this order:

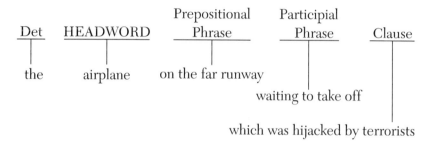

In this section we will look at all of these structures that follow the headword, beginning with the most common postnoun modifier, the prepositional phrase.

Prepositional Phrases. The **adjectival prepositional phrase**, which modifies a noun, is in form identical to the adverbial prepositional phrase described in Chapter 6. In its adjectival role the prepositional phrase identifies the noun headword in relation to time, place, direction, purpose, origin, and the like:

The *people* across the street rarely speak to the neighbors.

The security *guard* in our building knows every tenant personally.

I have always admired the lovely *houses* along Sparks Street.

The *meeting* during our lunch hour was a waste of time.

Jack is a *man* of many talents.

Because the prepositional phrase itself includes a noun phrase, the adjectival prepositional phrase demonstrates the recursiveness of the language—the embedding of one structure in another of the same kind:

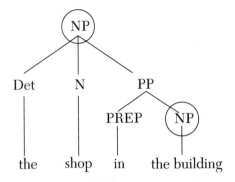

Such recursiveness occurs in many parts of the sentence: a sentence within a sentence, a noun phrase within a noun phrase, a verb phrase within a verb phrase. In the case of the adjectival prepositional phrase, we nearly always have a noun phrase within a noun phrase. And we needn't stop with one embedding; we could continue branching that NP at the bottom of the diagram with another Det + N + PP, which would produce yet another NP:

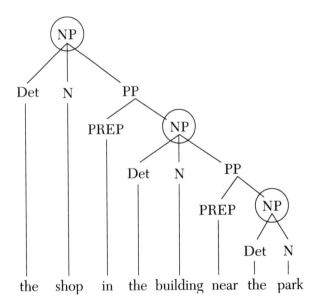

Such strings, though fairly common, especially at the end of the sentence, are sometimes open to ambiguity:

> My sister manages the flower shop in the new brick building near the park on Center Street.

Our linguistic computer most readily associates a modifier with the nearest possible referent:

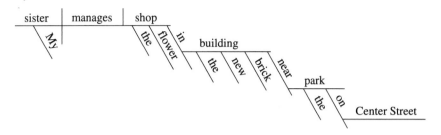

If a different meaning is intended—if, for example, it is the building rather than the park that is on Center Street—the writer must make that clear: "the flower shop in the brick building on Center Street that is near the park."

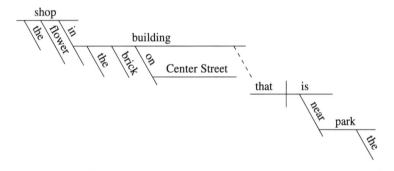

In the discussion of adverbial prepositional phrases in Chapter 6, we described another source of ambiguity—the modifier that could be either adjectival or adverbial:

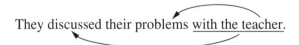

They discussed their problems <u>with the teacher</u>.

The ambiguity arises because the adverbial phrase often comes at the end of the sentence, which is also a common position for the noun phrase modifier. Here's another ambiguous example:

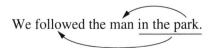

We followed the man <u>in the park</u>.

There are always alternatives to ambiguity, ways of recasting a sentence to make it clear:

> We followed the man who was in the park.
>
> *or*
>
> We followed the man through the park.
>
> *or*
>
> We followed the man as he strolled in the park.

Unlike the adverbial prepositional phrase, which is often movable, the adjectival prepositional phrase always stays with the noun it modifies; and with few exceptions it follows the noun. Occasionally a prepositional phrase appears in prenoun position, as we saw earlier; in such cases it is usually written with hyphens; and because it is so rare, it always calls attention to itself:

> the across-the-street neighbors
> the club's after-hours activities
> an out-of-the-way place
> an off-the-wall idea

===== *Exercise 23* =====

Underline the adjectival prepositional phrases in the following sentences. If any of them are ambiguous, rewrite them to clear up the ambiguity.

1. A young man with a cast on his left foot hobbled down the street.
2. I will meet you in the lobby of the museum near the visitors' information booth.
3. The party after the game at Bob's must have been a riot.
4. The threat of computer viruses is causing concern among scientists.
5. The computer world is being threatened by an enemy from within.
6. The textbook for my science course was written by a Nobel laureate from Stanford.

Participial Phrases. The **participle**—the *-ing* or *-en* form of the verb—is another of the nonfinite verbs, those verbs that function in ways other than as predicating verbs. Like gerund and infinitive phrases,

participial phrases have all the characteristics of verb phrase patterns, including complements and adverbial modifiers:

> The students taking the SAT look nervous.
>
> The helicopter hovering over the roof scared the dogs.
>
> Do you recognize those boys acting so foolish?

You'll easily recognize the sentence patterns underlying the participles:

> The students are taking the SAT. (Pattern VII)
> The helicopter is hovering over the roof. (Pattern VI)
> Those boys are acting so foolish. (Pattern IV)

In the diagram the participle is attached to its subject on a diagonal line that bends to become a horizontal line, which accommodates any complements and/or modifiers it may have:

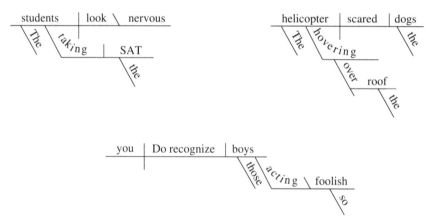

You'll notice that the participle is diagrammed exactly like the predicate of the sentence that underlies it:

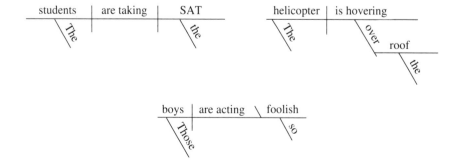

The only difference in the participle is the absence of the auxiliary *be* with tense.

As the examples illustrate, participles that are formed from transitive verbs will have direct objects (taking the *SAT*), and those from linking verbs will have subjective complements (acting *so foolish*). And all participles, just like verbs in all the sentence patterns, may be modified by adverbials of various forms. Note the adverbial prepositional phrase that modifies *hovering*.

In the following sentence we have added an adverbial noun phrase, *this morning*.

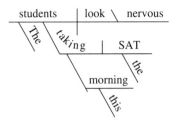

Here are three key points that will help you understand participles:

1. Verbs from all four classes—*be*, linking, intransitive, and transitive—can function as participles.
2. All the NP slots can include participles (or participial phrases) as modifiers: direct objects, subjective complements, objective complements, indirect objects, objects of prepositions, as well as subjects.
3. The noun that the participle modifies is its subject. That is, the relationship between the headword of the noun phrase in which the participle is embedded and the participle itself is a subject–verb relationship. In a diagram, the participle is connected to its own subject.

═══════ *Exercise 24* ═══════

Turn each of the following sentences into a noun phrase with a postnoun participial phrase. Use that noun phrase in a sentence.

Example: Two dogs are fighting over the bone.
Sentence: I recognize *those two dogs fighting over the bone.*

1. An expensive sports car is standing in the driveway.
2. The students are cramming for their history test.

3. The baby is sleeping upstairs in the crib.
4. The fans are lining up at the ticket office.
5. A huge crowd is watching the parade.
6. The students are feeling upset about their tuition increase.

Prenoun Participles. When a participle is a verb alone, a single word, with no complements or phrasal modifiers, it will usually occupy the adjective slot in preheadword position:

Our snoring visitor kept the household awake.

The barking dog next door drives us crazy.

The old hound growled at every passing stranger.

In this position, an adverb sometimes modifies the participle:

Our loudly snoring visitor kept the household awake.

The peacefully sleeping baby was a joy to watch.

We've also seen hyphenated adverb–participle modifiers in preheadword position:

John Henry was a hard-driving man.

Passive Participles. The participles we have seen so far are the *-ing* form of the verb (traditionally called the *present participle*); and the sentences underlying them are in the active voice. Another common form of the participle is the *-en* form, the past participle:

The houses designed by Frank Lloyd Wright are national treasures.

The car driven by the front runner has developed engine trouble.

We can figure out the sentences underlying these *-en* participles by again adding a form of *be*:

The houses were designed by Frank Lloyd Wright.

The car was driven by the front runner.

Both of these underlying sentences are passive transformations: The modifiers they produce are **passive participles**. (You will recall from Chapter 3 that in active voice verbs the auxiliary *be* is followed by the *-ing* form of the verb, not the *-en*.)

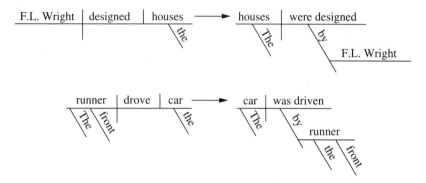

Remember, we produce a passive sentence by adding *be* + *-en* to the verb, so the passive verb is always the *-en* form. When we turn such sentences into participles, we will automatically have the *-en* form:

> We stored the record collection in the attic. (*Active*)
>
> The record collection was stored in the attic. (*Passive*)

With the deletion of *was*, this passive verb phrase will become a passive participle: *stored in the attic*.

> The record collection stored in the attic collected dust all summer long.
>
> I completely forgot the record collection stored in the attic.

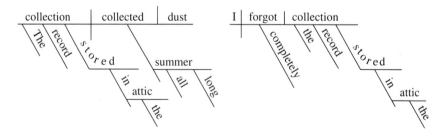

A participle derived from a passive Pattern IX or X sentence will include a subjective complement:

My brother is considered the area's best foreign car mechanic.

When we delete *is*, the result is a noun phrase with a postheadword passive participial phrase, which we can then use in another sentence:

> My brother, considered the area's best foreign car mechanic, drives
> an old Chevy pickup.

Because these last two examples of passive participles are derived from regular verbs, the *-en* form ends in *ed* rather than *en*. The participles are obviously passive rather than active, however, because with few exceptions the active voice participle will be the *-ing* form.

━━━━━ *Investigating Language 7.2* ━━━━━━━━━━━━━━━━

In your study of verbs in Chapter 3, you learned that all verbs have *-ing* and *-en* forms (although the *-en* ending—the past participle—is more often spelled *-ed*). You've also seen the way verbs function. They're not always in the predicate slot: Sometimes they're gerunds, occupying nominal slots. Like other nominals, *gerunds are names—the names of activities.* Sometimes the *-ing* and *-en* verbs are adjectivals, modifiers of nouns, known as participles. And *participles, you'll recall, modify their own subjects.*

But our language also has some *-ing* and *-en* words that are adjectives (although perhaps made from verbs). Do you remember the test for adjectives? You can usually (but not always) *qualify adjectives with* very.

With that short summary in mind, consider the modifiers in the following noun phrases. Where did they come from?

a walking stick	_____	a rocking chair	_____
a drinking fountain	_____	a fishing pole	_____
a charming person	_____	a broken window	_____

a willing worker	_____	the warning bell	_____
my unwashed hands	_____	an unbroken line	_____
the singing waiters	_____	a standing ovation	_____
a meeting place	_____	a dancing partner	_____
an interesting topic	_____	his pitching arm	_____

Label them as adjective (A), participle (P), or gerund (G). Are any of them ambiguous, requiring more than one label? (*Note:* Sometimes a paraphrase will help: *a stick for walking.*)

Movable Participles.   We can think of the postheadword slot in the noun phrase as the "home base" of the participle, as it is of the adjectival prepositional phrase. But unlike the adjectival prepositional phrase, the participial phrase can shift to the beginning or end of the sentence when it modifies the subject:

> <u>Built by Frank Lloyd Wright in 1936</u>, the Kauffman house at Fallingwater is one of Western Pennsylvania's most valued architectural treasures.
> <u>Hoping for good weather</u>, we planned our class picnic for Saturday.
> We planned our class picnic for Saturday, <u>hoping for good weather</u>.

In introductory position, the participial phrase often includes the auxiliary *have:*

> <u>*Having found* the camp deserted</u>, we assumed that the hunters had returned to civilization.
> <u>*Having felt* sick all night</u>, I decided to skip my morning classes.

You'll notice in these examples that it's the auxiliary that ends in *-ing*, not the verb. The verbs in the participial phrases—*found* and *felt*—are *-en* forms. But that makes sense if you think about the verb-expansion rule from Chapter 3. One component of that rule is *have* + *-en*: In other words, we never use the auxiliary *have* without an *-en* form following it. That rule applies to participles as well as to predicating verbs.

Passive participles can also have auxiliaries—either *being* or *having been*. You'll notice in the following two examples that even though these are passive participles they include *-ing*; but they also include *be* + *-en*, the passive auxiliary:

> The award *being presented* this morning is for the sorority's out-
> standing volunteer.
>
> *Having been fired* from my job in the bookstore, I didn't feel like
> talking to anyone.

The passive participle is sometimes a single word, in which case it will appear in prenoun position:

> The broken window should be replaced.

The passive participle in prenoun position can also be modified by an adverb:

> We followed a well-worn path.

═══ *Exercise 25* ═══════════════════════════════

Underline the participles in the following sentences; identify their sentence patterns. Diagram.

1. The award given every year to the outstanding volunteer has been announced.
2. Carrying their supplies on their backs, the Boy Scout troop trudged up the mountain to find a campsite.
3. We gave the singing waiters at Ziggy's an extra big tip.
4. A noisy crowd of students gathered yesterday to demonstrate against the tuition hike recently approved by the college trustees.
5. Finding the price reasonable, we rented the apartment on the spot.
6. We planned our class picnic for Saturday, hoping that the good weather would hold.

7. Having felt sick all night, I decided to skip my morning classes.
8. The teachers' union has finally approved the last two disputed sections of the contract offered by the school district.

Dangling Participles.   The introductory participial phrase provides a good way to add variety to sentences, to get away from the standard subject opener. But it carries an important restriction: The participle can begin the sentence *only* if it modifies the subject—that is, when the subject of the participle is also the subject of the sentence and is in regular subject position. Otherwise, the participle dangles. Simply stated, a dangling participle is a verb in search of a subject:

> *Having swung his five iron too far to the left, Joe's ball landed precisely in the middle of a sand trap.

(The ball did not swing the five iron; Joe did.)

> *Still smiling blandly at the newsmen, a cream pie from somewhere in the crowd struck the senator squarely in the face.

(The cream pie was not smiling; the senator was.)

A common source of the dangling participle, as well as other kinds of danglers, is the sentence with a "delayed subject." Two common delayers are the *there* transformation and the generalized *it*.

> *Having moved all the outdoor furniture into the garage, there was no room left for the car.

In this *there* transformation, the subject of *having moved* does not appear at all. But even when the subject is part of the sentence, the participle will dangle if the subject is not in normal subject position:

> *Knowing how much work I had to do yesterday, it was good of you to come and help.

In this sentence the subject of the participle, *you*, is there, but it appears in the predicate rather than in the usual subject position. As readers and listeners, we process sentences with certain built-in expectations. Our linguistic computers are programmed to attach an introductory participle to the first logical subject offered. The dangling participle causes a malfunction in the program.

Incidentally, moving the participle to the end of the sentence does not solve the problem of the dangler. Even there we expect the participle to modify the subject:

> *Joe's ball landed precisely in the middle of a sand trap, <u>having swung his five iron too far to the left.</u>

Probably the most efficient way to revise such a sentence is to expand the participial phrase into a complete clause. That expansion will add the missing subject:

> <u>After *we* moved all the outdoor furniture into the garage,</u> there was no room left for the car.
>
> It was good of you to come and help yesterday <u>when *you* learned how much work I had to do.</u>

Another common source of the dangling participle is the passive sentence:

> *<u>Having worked hard since 6 A.M.,</u> the project was completed before noon.

Here the problem arises because the passive transformation has deleted the agent, which is also the subject of the participle. Transforming the sentence into the active voice will solve the problem.

> <u>Having worked hard since 6 A.M.,</u> *we* completed the project before noon.

===== *Exercise 26* =====

Rewrite the following sentences to eliminate the dangling participles.

1. Having endured rain all week, the miserable weather on Saturday didn't surprise us.
2. Having hiked five miles uphill, my backpack must have weighed a ton.
3. Hoping for the sixth win in a row, there was great excitement in the grandstand as the band played "The Star Spangled Banner."
4. Guarding his bone as though it were his last meal, it was fascinating to watch the dog react to strangers.
5. Working ten hours a day, six days a week, Jan's first novel was completely finished in six months.
6. Exhausted by the hot weather, there was nothing to do but lie in the shade.
7. Wearing their new uniforms proudly, we watched the band march across the field and form a huge "O."
8. Having spent nearly all day in the kitchen, that superb gourmet dinner was worth the effort.

The Participle as Objective Complement. You'll recall from Chapter 2 that two of the required slots in the sentence patterns, two functions, are filled by adjectivals: the subjective complement in Patterns II and IV and the objective complement in Pattern IX. In most cases, those slots are filled by adjectives. We did see some examples, however, of prepositional phrases as subjective complements:

The teacher was in a bad mood this morning.

The piano sounds out of tune.

And we could easily come up with prepositional phrases as objective complements as well:

We found the teacher in a bad mood this morning.

I consider your behavior out of line.

The objective complement slot can also be filled by a participle:

I could feel my heart beating faster.

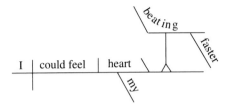

Again, we make use of the pedestal in the diagram to attach the participle's characteristic bent line to the objective complement slot on the main line.

What this diagram says is that "my heart beating faster" is not a single noun phrase; it is two separate structures. You can test that conclusion by substituting a pronoun for the direct object:

I could feel <u>it</u> beating faster.

Clearly, there are two slots following the verb, both of which are required for the sense of the sentence.

Here are two further examples of participles as objective complements:

The police found the government's star witness <u>murdered</u>.
Indiana Jones found the cave <u>filled with pitfalls</u>.

To understand the difference between a participle as objective complement and the participle as part of the direct object, compare the previous example to another version:

Indiana Jones found a cave filled with snakes.

With a pronoun substituting for the direct object, the sentence would read simply:

Indiana Jones found <u>it</u>.
or
Indiana Jones found <u>something</u>.

The Pattern IX sentence with the pronoun, however, would have two slots. A fairly reliable way to determine if the sentence has an objective complement is to insert *to be*:

Indiana Jones found it *to be* filled with pitfalls.

Relative Clauses.   Like the adverbial clause that modifies verbs, the **relative,** or **adjectival, clause** is a dependent clause; as a clause in form, it is a sentence pattern, complete with subject and predicate. The only difference between the relative clause and a complete sentence is the introductory word, the relative: It may be a relative pronoun (*who, whose, whom, which, that, whoever, whatever,* etc.) or a relative adverb (*where, when, why*).

The **relative pronoun** (1) renames the headword, which is the antecedent of the pronoun, and (2) plays the part of a nominal in the clause:

The people *who* live across the street always share their surplus
vegetables.

The traditional diagram clearly shows the relationship of the clause to the noun it modifies:

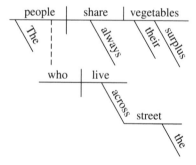

You'll notice that some of these *wh*-relatives (*who, whose, whom, which, where, when, why*) look exactly like the interrogatives, the introducers of questions and nominal clauses. But there's an important difference: There is no question involved in the relative clause, no question being asked or answered or alluded to.

It is important to recognize that the underlying meaning of the relative clause is *The people live across the street.* The relative pronoun substitutes for *the people.* The broken line connects the pronoun to its antecedent, the headword of the noun phrase; the relative pronoun *who* fills the subject slot in its clause.

In the next sentence, the relative pronoun *that* is the direct object in the relative clause; its antecedent, *the solution*, is the subject of the main clause. The relative clause is embedded as a modifier in that subject noun phrase:

> The solution that Chris worked out in just minutes had eluded me for hours.

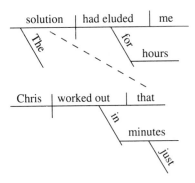

Remember that any noun in the sentence can have a clause as a postnoun modifier; that is, the noun phrase *the solution that Chris worked out* could fill a different NP slot:

> I still don't understand the solution that Chris worked out.

In the next sentence the possessive relative pronoun, *whose*, acts as a determiner in the clause, the part that possessive pronouns usually play:

> Do you know the people whose car we bought?

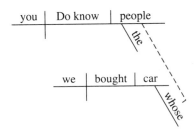

The broken line connects *whose* to its antecedent, *the people*—in other words, *the people's car*. And here the noun phrase with the embedded clause functions as the direct object.

In the following sentence, the relative pronoun *that* acts as the subject of its clause:

The museum in Johnstown that commemorates the city's frequent floods has some astonishing pictures.

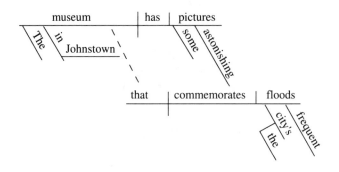

=== *Investigating Language 7.3* ===

It might be useful to interrupt this discussion of relative clauses for a moment and consider the word *that*—a word with many disguises. This is not the first time we have seen *that*. We have seen it as a determiner:

That salad looks delicious.

Here the name it goes by is **demonstrative pronoun** (the three other demonstratives are *this, these,* and *those*). One way to recognize the demonstrative disguise is to substitute one of its fellow demonstratives: If *this* or *these* or *those* can be substituted, *that* is clearly a demonstrative. And in this case, all three alternatives would work—"this salad" or "these salads" or "those salads."

But we have also seen *that* as an introducer of nominal clauses, where it goes by the name of **expletive:**

I think that she likes me.

An important feature of the expletive is that it plays no part in the clause it introduces: "She likes me" is a complete sentence: All of its slots are filled. The expletive *that* simply enables us to use that complete sentence to fill a nominal slot in another sentence.

Now we come to the **relative pronoun** *that*:

> The solution that Chris worked out had eluded me.

This *that* differs from the expletive in important ways:

1. It's a pronoun, so it has an antecedent—a nominal that it refers to or renames. In this example, the antecedent of *that* is "the solution": *Chris worked out the solution.* The antecedent of the relative pronoun is *always* the headword of the noun phrase that contains the relative clause. And remember that's where relative clauses are found: in noun phrases as postnoun modifiers.
2. The relative pronoun *that* plays a part in its own clause—that is, in the clause it introduces. The roles that relative pronouns play in relative clauses are the same roles that pronouns always play. For example, in the clause "that Chris worked out," *that* is the direct object.

Here are some other sentences with the word *that*. Label the *that* in each. Is it a demonstrative pronoun (DP) (remember the substitution trick)? Is it an expletive (EX)? Is it a relative pronoun (RP)?

> You choose a color that you like. _____
>
> I know who made that mess. _____
>
> I think that she did it on purpose. _____
>
> The books that I need for chemistry class are expensive. _____
>
> I suspect that the books that I need for art history will be expensive
>
> too. _____, _____

You can check your answers by doing a diagram to make sure that you've identified the *that* correctly.

Here's the first sentence in the list you just saw. The relative pronoun *that* is the direct object in its clause:

You choose a color <u>that you like.</u>

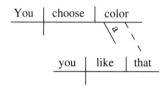

And here's an important feature when *that* is the direct object: The sentence would be equally grammatical without *that*:

You choose a color you like.

The relative *that* is often deleted, but the deletion is possible only when the pronoun functions as an object in its clause, not when it acts as the subject.

The objective case relative, *whom*, like the relative *that*, can often be deleted too. The following *whom* clause illustrates another principle: The *case* of the relative is determined by the part it plays in its own clause:

A woman [whom] my mother knew in high school has invited me to dinner.

Even though the *whom* is deleted, it will have a place on the diagram; it is "understood." The deleted word can be shown in brackets, or it can be replaced by an x:

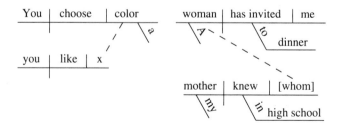

Sometimes we substitute *that* in order to avoid the awkwardness or formality of *whom*. Some writers, however, consider *that* unacceptable in reference to people:

A man that I knew in the army called me last week.

In this example, we would be more likely to simply delete the relative. For a nonrestrictive clause, however, the relative pronoun is required:

Sergeant Major Miller, whom I knew in the army, called me last week.

In speaking this sentence we are more likely to say *who* instead of *whom*; most listeners wouldn't notice the difference.

===== *Exercise 27* =======================================

Underline the adjectival clauses in the following sentences. Identify (1) the role of the relative in its clause and (2) the sentence pattern of the clause.

1. I don't like the new kitchen chairs that we bought.
2. The man I love loves me.
3. This morning my wife's best friend, Allison, returned the book by Toni Morrison that she had borrowed last month.
4. Vitamin C, which some people consider a defense against the common cold, is relatively inexpensive.
5. King Edward VIII gave up the throne of England for the woman he loved.
6. It is not only fine feathers that make fine birds. [Aesop]
7. Professor Carter, who taught history at Emory University, is our former president.
8. We're going to the concert that the jazz band is giving this afternoon on the lawn.
9. A weed is a plant whose virtues have not been discovered. [Ralph Waldo Emerson]
10. I understand that the killer bees, which are gradually moving north, have now reached Texas.

The clauses that are introduced by the **indefinite,** or expanded, **relative pronouns** are traditionally classified as adjectival clauses:

I will give the prize to <u>whoever scores the most points.</u>

On the surface this relative clause looks like a nominal, rather than an adjectival, clause; it looks like the object of the preposition. We could certainly make a case for that analysis. But we can also make a case for the traditional analysis of this clause because of its underlying meaning, which is illustrated in the diagram that follows: "I will give the prize to [the person who] scores the most points." The expanded relatives are called *indefinite* because there is no specific noun they refer to, but there is an understood, or general, reference underlying these relatives.

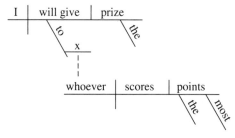

This sentence again illustrates the concept of case: The case of the relative pronoun is determined by its role in the relative clause, not by the role of the clause. In this sentence the clause follows the preposition; however, the relative pronoun is the subject of *scores* within its clause, so its case is subjective (*whoever*), not objective (*whomever*).

─────── *Exercise 28* ───────

Select the case of the relative pronoun in the following sentences.

1. Tell me the name of the man (who, whom) you are planning to marry.
2. The boss offered double overtime to (whoever, whomever) would work on Super Bowl Sunday.
3. Teresa is the candidate (who, whom) we are campaigning for.
4. I will ask (whomever, whoever) I want to the party.
5. (Whoever, Whomever) leaves the room last must turn out the lights.
6. Our senator, (who, whom) we have always considered an honorable man, seems reluctant to talk about his campaign funds.

All the relative pronouns fill slots in the clauses that nouns normally fill. However, some adjectival clauses are introduced not by relative pronouns but by the relative adverbs *where, when,* and *why.* In these clauses the relative replaces an adverbial structure in its clause. The relative adverb *where* introduces clauses that modify nouns of place:

> Newsworthy events rarely happen in the small *town* <u>where I was born.</u>

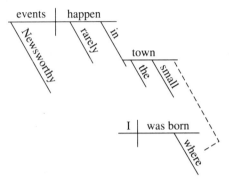

Note in the diagram that the relative adverb *where* modifies the verb *was born* in its own clause; however, the clause itself is adjectival, modifying *town.*

When clauses modify nouns of time:

> We are all looking forward to *Tuesday,* <u>when results of the audition will be posted.</u>

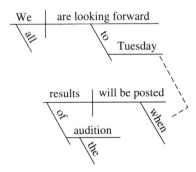

Why clauses modify the noun *reason:*

> I understand the *reason* <u>why Margo got the leading role.</u>

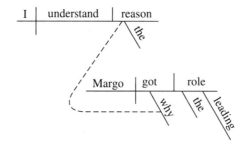

Where, when, and *why* clauses are often equally acceptable, and some-times smoother, without the relative:

> I understand the reason Margo got the leading role.
> We are looking forward to the day the results will be posted.

Sometimes *that* takes the place of the relative adverb:

> I understand the reason that Margo got the leading role.
> We are looking forward to the day that the results will be posted.

In diagramming these sentences, we would have to recognize the underlying meaning of *that* as an adverbial. Here it is not the relative pronoun *that*, which would fill an NP slot in the sentence. In the last example, "the day that" is another way of saying "the day on which"; the clause itself, however, is adjectival, the modifier of a noun.

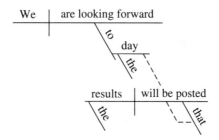

PUNCTUATION OF CLAUSES AND PARTICIPLES

The question regarding punctuation of clauses and participles is the question of restrictive versus nonrestrictive modifiers. Put simply, the question is "Should I set off the phrase or clause with commas?"

In answering this question, the writer must think about the referent of the noun being modified. Is it clear to the reader? In the case of a singular noun, is there only one possible person (or place or thing, etc.) to which the noun can refer? In the case of plurals, are the limits understood? If there is only one, the modifier cannot restrict the noun's meaning any further: The modifier is therefore **nonrestrictive** and will be set off by commas. It might be useful to think of these commas as parentheses and the modifier as optional; if it's optional, we can assume it's not needed to make the referent of the noun clear.

If the referent of the noun is not clear to the reader—if there is more than one possible referent or if the limits are not known—the purpose of the modifier is quite different: to restrict the meaning of the noun. Thus the modifier in this case is **restrictive** and is not set off by commas. You may find the terms *defining* and *commenting* easier to understand than *restrictive* and *nonrestrictive*.[1] Does the modifier define (restrict) the noun or does it merely comment on (not restrict) it?

Notice the difference in the punctuation of the following pair of sentences:

> The football players wearing shiny orange helmets stood out in the crowd.
> The football players, wearing shiny orange helmets, stood out in the crowd.

In the first sentence the purpose of the participial phrase is to define *which* football players stood out in the crowd. We could illustrate the situation by depicting a crowd of football players on the field, some of whom are wearing *shiny orange helmets;* they are noticeable—they *stand out in the crowd* of football players—because the others are wearing drab, dark helmets or perhaps no helmets at all. In the second sentence the modifier merely comments on the players—it does not define them. An illustration of this situation might show a group of orange-helmeted football players signing autographs in a crowd of children; those players would stand out in that crowd with or without orange helmets. The modifier does *not* tell *which* football players stood out in the crowd; they *all* did. (And, incidentally, they were all wearing orange helmets.)

---

[1] These terms are used by Francis Christensen in *Notes Toward a New Rhetoric* (New York: Harper & Row, 1967), pp. 95 ff.

Context, of course, will make a difference. What does the reader already know? For example, out of context the clause in the following sentence appears to be restrictive:

> The president <u>who was elected in 1932</u> faced problems that would have overwhelmed the average man.

Ordinarily we would say that the noun phrase *the president* has many possible referents; the *who* clause is needed to make the referent clear; it defines and restricts *the president* to a particular man, the one elected in 1932. But what if the reader already knows the referent?

> Franklin Delano Roosevelt took office at a time when the outlook for the nation was bleak indeed. The president, <u>who was elected in 1932</u>, faced decisions that would have overwhelmed the average man.

In this context the clause is simply commenting; the referent of the noun phrase *the president* is already defined by the time the reader gets to it. Many times, however, context alone is an insufficient determinant; only the writer knows if the clause defines or comments. The reader can only take the writer's word—or punctuation—at face value:

> The rain began with the first drumbeat. Only the band members <u>who were wearing rain gear</u> stayed reasonably dry. Everyone else at the parade, spectators and marchers alike, got wet.

Without commas the clause restricts the meaning of the noun phrase *the band members*; it defines those band members who stayed dry. With commas we would assume that all the band members were wearing rain gear.

Francis Christensen emphasizes that the writer must also be aware of what the reader might infer from the restrictive clause or phrase. "When the modifier is restrictive, the sentence makes one statement and implies its opposite; and what it implies is just as important as what it states."[2] In other words, in the preceding sentence the clause *who were*

---

[2]Christensen, p. 98.

wearing rain gear implies that some band members were *not* wearing rain gear and did *not* stay reasonably dry. In the case of the football players, the modifier in the first sentence, the one with the restrictive participial phrase, suggests the presence of football players who were *not* wearing shiny orange helmets and did *not* stand out in the crowd. That implication is built into the restrictive modifier. If such an opposite statement is not true, the writer must be careful to avoid giving the reader the wrong impression. In writing the sentence with commas, the writer would no longer be identifying or defining a *subgroup* of dry band members or football players; with commas, the clauses become comments about the *entire group*.

So in reaching a decision about commas, the writer must take into account (1) what the reader knows (Is the referent clear without this information?) and (2) what the reader will infer if the modifier is restrictive.

Avoiding Comma Errors. The writer who uses commas at every pause in the sentence probably uses too many commas. In speech we often pause between the subject and the verb or between the verb and the direct object—that is, between the slots in the sentence pattern; but in writing we never separate these slots with commas. A simple pause, then, does not signal a comma. The pause that signals a comma usually includes a change in pitch.

Reading a sentence aloud as you would normally speak can be useful in identifying such changes. If you wanted to distinguish the dry band members from the wet ones, for example, you would probably speak the sentence with the loudest stress on *rain,* with secondary stress on *dry:*

The band members wearing rain gear stayed dry.

The line indicates the normal pitch or **intonation** contour, showing rising pitch over the loudest syllable and falling pitch at the end. The intonation contour of the sentence with a nonrestrictive modifier is quite different:

The band members, wearing rain gear, stayed dry.

The nonrestrictive modifier has an intonation contour separate from that of the main sentence, so that this sentence has three main stress points.

In reading the sentence aloud, you'll especially notice a difference in the stress you give to *band;* it is longer and louder than it is in the other version, with its single intonation contour. And if you listen carefully to the words *members* and *gear,* you'll detect a slight rise in pitch at the very end of the words. That is the pitch rise that is often signaled by a comma.

Actually this sentence probably sounds strange when you hear yourself say it; it has an unnatural, stilted quality. That quality occurs because we rarely speak in sentences with nonrestrictive modifiers in postnoun position. This is an important difference between speaking and writing. In making punctuation decisions about such modifiers, the writer can take advantage of this difference by reading the sentence aloud.

In the case of participial phrases that modify the subject, the writer has another useful test: Can the modifier be shifted to the beginning or end of the sentence? If that shift does not change the meaning, the modifier is nonrestrictive. The restrictive participial phrase will remain within the noun phrase, whereas the nonrestrictive phrase can introduce the sentence and sometimes follow it:

Wearing rain gear, the band members stayed reasonably dry.

In the case of the relative clause, the relative pronoun provides some clues for punctuation:

1. The adjectival *that* clause is always restrictive; it is never set off by commas.
2. The *which* clause is generally nonrestrictive; it is set off by commas. You can test a *which* clause by substituting *that*; if it works, the clause is restrictive, and if not, it is nonrestrictive. NOTE: There is an exception to this general rule about *that* in restrictive and *which* in nonrestrictive clauses: Only *which* functions as the object of a preposition; *that* does not. So the relative in that position will be *which* whether the clause is restrictive or nonrestrictive:

I probably won't get either of the jobs for which I applied.
Pat got a terrific new job, for which I also applied.

3. If the relative can be deleted, the clause is restrictive:

The bus (that) I ride to work is always late.
The woman (whom) I work with is always early.

The next two rules of thumb apply to both clauses and phrases:

4. After any proper noun the modifier will be nonrestrictive.

Herbert Hoover, elected president in 1928, was the first president born west of the Mississippi River.

5. After any common noun that has only one possible referent the modifier will be nonrestrictive:

My youngest sister, who lives in Oregon, is much more domestic than I.
The highest mountain in the world, which resisted the efforts of climbers until 1953, looks truly forbidding from the air.

===== *Exercise 29* =====

Identify the postnoun modifiers in the following sentences as restrictive or nonrestrictive by adding commas if needed.

1. My parents who retired to Arizona in 1992 love the dry climate there.
2. The town where I was born which has a population of 3,000 offers very little in the way of entertainment for teenagers.
3. My favorite television show which I watch every chance I get is "Cheers."
4. The reruns of "Cheers" that I like the best are the early ones with the Shelley Long character.
5. Neither the senator nor his wife sitting next to him on the speakers' platform looked very enthusiastic about being there.
6. Westerners generally understand very little about the Middle East where much of the world's oil is located.
7. On weekends I sometimes work for my oldest sister who runs a day-care center.

8. The driver of the bus that I take to work knows her regular passengers by name.
9. The International Date Line which is an imaginary line at 180° longitude was fixed at the location on the earth exactly opposite Greenwich, England.
10. The list of animal species that had become extinct as of 1980 includes fifty-eight species of birds.

MULTIPLE MODIFIERS

So far we have used examples of noun phrases with a single post-headword modifier, either a clause or a phrase. But we often have more than one such modifier, and when we do, the order in which they appear is well defined: prepositional phrase, participial phrase, relative clause:

> the security guard [in our building] [who checks out the visitors]
> the woman [from London] [staying with the Renfords]
> the DC-10 [on the far runway] [being prepared for takeoff]
>   [which was hijacked by a group of terrorists]

In a traditional diagram, all the noun modifiers in both pre- and postposition are attached to the headword:

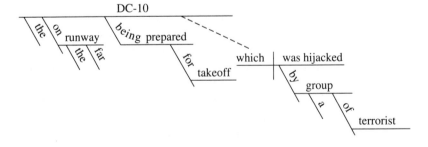

A change in the order of modifiers would change the meaning:

> the DC-10 being prepared for takeoff, which was hijacked by a group of terrorists on the far runway

Here the prepositional phrase no longer specifies *which* DC-10; it has become an adverbial modifier in the relative clause, modifying *was hijacked*. In this version DC-10 has only two postheadword modifiers, not three:

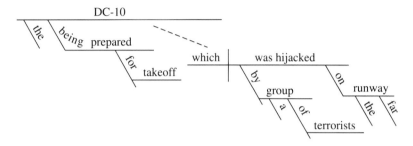

Just as ambiguity may result from a string of prepositional phrases, these multiple modifiers, too, are sometimes open to more than one interpretation:

> the driver of the bus standing on the corner
> a friend of my sister who lives in Tampa

In context these noun phrases may or may not be clear to the reader. In any case, the ambiguity is easily avoided:

> the driver of the bus who was standing on the corner
> the driver of the bus parked at the corner

> my sister's friend who lives in Tampa
> my sister in Tampa's friend (or, my sister in Tampa has a friend who . . .)

OTHER POSTNOUN MODIFIERS

Infinitives. The infinitive—the base form of the verb preceded by *to*—can serve as a modifier in the postnoun position. As a verb, it will have all the attributes of verbs, including complements and modifiers, depending on its underlying sentence pattern:

> the way to be helpful
> the time to start

the party after the play to honor the director

the best place in San Francisco to eat seafood

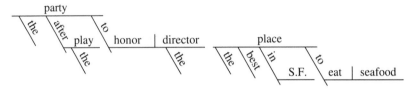

As the last two examples illustrate, the infinitive can be separated from the headword by another modifier. These examples also illustrate another common feature of the adjectival infinitive: Its subject may not be the noun it modifies; its subject is frequently just understood—the object in an understood prepositional phrase:

> That was a nice thing [for you] to do.
> Fisherman's Wharf is not necessarily the best place in San Francisco [for one] to eat seafood.

Noun Phrases.   Nouns or noun phrases of time and place can follow the headword:

> the party last night
> the ride home

These adjectival noun phrases are diagrammed just as the adverbial noun phrases are—on horizontal lines:

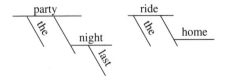

Adjectives.   Qualified adjectives and compound adjectives, which usually occupy the preheadword position, can follow the headword if they are set off by commas:

the neighbors, <u>usually quiet</u>

the neighborhood, <u>quiet and peaceful</u>

Like the nonrestrictive participles, these nonrestrictive adjectives can also introduce the sentence when they modify the subject:

<u>Usually quiet</u>, the neighbors upstairs are having a regular brawl tonight.

<u>Quiet and peaceful</u>, the neighborhood slept while the cat burglars made their rounds.

Adverbs. Even adverbs can occupy the postheadword position in the noun phrase:

That was my idea <u>exactly</u>.

The people <u>here</u> have no idea of conditions <u>there</u>.

KEY TERMS IN CHAPTER 7

Adjectival	Intonation
Adjectival clause	Nonrestrictive modifier
Adjectival infinitive	Participial phrase
Adjectival prepositional phrase	Participle
Adjective	Passive participle
Case	Postnoun modifier
Dangling participle	Prenoun modifier
Demonstrative pronoun	Relative adverb
Determiner	Relative clause
Headword	Relative pronoun
Indefinite relative pronoun	Restrictive modifier

SENTENCES FOR PRACTICE

Draw vertical lines between the slots of the sentence patterns. Mark the headword of each NP with an X, the determiner with a D; underline the pre- and postheadword modifiers; then label each according to its form. Circle any pronouns that fill NP slots.

For further practice, identify the sentence patterns and diagram the sentences. Remember that all verb phrases and clauses functioning as nominals and adverbials and adjectivals also have identifiable sentence patterns.

1. The student in my history class whose written notes I borrowed has been absent since the midterm exam.

2. The initials engraved inside my ring are BFJ.

3. My neighbor's husband, who has always been a strong union man, refused to cross the picket line that the clerical workers organized at the mill where he is a foreman.

4. The company's reorganization plan, voted down last week, called for the removal of all incumbent officers.

5. At midnight Cinderella's beautiful coach, in which she had been driven to the ball, suddenly became a pumpkin again.

6. The fish rising to the surface of the stream are the ones that usually begin to feed at this time of evening.

7. I discovered that the old gentleman in Union Square, whom I met last week, will talk to whoever will listen to him.

8. The play's the thing wherein I'll catch the conscience of the king. [Shakespeare]

9. Uneasy lies the head that wears the crown. [Shakespeare]

10. It is a truth universally acknowledged, that a single man in possession of a good fortune must be in want of a wife. [Jane Austen]

11. Calling Pearl Harbor Day a day that would live in infamy, President Roosevelt asked Congress for a declaration of war.

12. Having been a police officer in downtown Atlanta for thirty years, my neighbor grew restless after he retired from the force.

13. The town where I lived until I reached my fifteenth birthday is in the foothills of the beautiful Ozarks.

14. Beauty in things exists in the mind which contemplates them. [David Hume]

15. In the nineteenth century the French, in their failed attempt to build a canal across Panama, lost 20,000 lives.

16. The clown, acting out pantomimic movements to entertain the children, was not very funny.

QUESTIONS FOR DISCUSSION

1. Generate a noun phrase according to each of the following formulas:

  A. det + adj + HEADWORD + participial phrase
  B. det + adj + noun + HEADWORD + clause
  C. det + adj + HEADWORD + prep phrase + part phrase
  D. det + noun + HEADWORD + part phrase + clause

Use your NPs in sentences as follows:

  Use A as the direct object of a Pattern VII sentence.
  Use B as the object of a preposition.
  Use C as an indirect object.
  Use D as the direct object in a relative clause.

2. In our description of the noun phrase we saw that the headword slot is filled by a word that is a noun in form. Would you consider these underlined noun phrases as exceptions to the rule?

  The rich are different from other people.

  I was late for our meeting.

  You clean the upstairs, and I'll do the downstairs.

3. One of the sample sentences we used in this chapter has an ambiguous modifier. Explain the source of the ambiguity.

  My brother is considered the area's best foreign car mechanic.

4. In this chapter we discussed the recursive quality of the noun phrase—that is, the embedding of one noun phrase in another. Give a sentence in which a relative clause is embedded in another relative clause; give another in which a participle is embedded in another participial phrase; another with a participle in a relative clause; another with a relative clause in a participial phrase.

5. Without this embedding quality of English we could not delight in "The House That Jack Built." Using either a branching diagram (see

Appendix B) or a traditional diagram, illustrate the embeddings in this sentence:

> This is the cow with the crumpled horn that tossed the dog that worried the cat that killed the rat that ate the malt that lay in the house that Jack built.

Can you leave out any of the *thats*?

6. We quoted Francis Christensen as saying that restrictive modifiers make one statement and imply the opposite. What opposite statements can you infer from the following?

> All the students with an average of 90 or higher will be excused from the final.
> The flight controllers who saw the strange lights in the sky became firm believers in UFOs.
> The football players wearing white uniforms stood out in the crowd.

How would the meaning of these sentences change if the postnoun modifiers were set off by commas?

7. What is the source of the ambiguity in the following sentences?

> Tony buried the knife he found in the cellar.
> Fred tripped his teammate with the baseball bat.

Diagram each in two ways to show its two possible meanings.

8. Speech can convey meaning that writing cannot. Read the following sentence in two ways to show two different meanings:

> The affluent Japanese travel all over in America.

Now write the sentence in two ways to show the difference.

9. The traditional grammarian would label the *who* clause in this famous line by Shakespeare an adjectival clause. Why? Why is it not nominal? How would you as a twentieth-century speaker word this statement?

> Who steals my purse steals trash.

10. Both of the following sentences include an adjectival infinitive as a modifier of *decision;* and in both, the expletive *as* introduces an objective complement. But there's an important difference between them. Diagram both sentences to illustrate the difference.

> The Jaycees are hailing the decision to admit women as a landmark.
> The Jaycees are hailing the decision to admit women as members.

11. In *The Book of Lists* (Morrow, 1977), David Wallechinsky, Irving Wallace, and Amy Wallace describe a comma "that cost the government two million dollars before Congress could rectify the error." Here's the expensive sentence:

> All foreign fruit, plants are free from duty.

The clerk who wrote the rule was supposed to use a hyphen instead of a comma. Explain the difference.

12. In the summer of 1984 the writers of the Republican party's platform made headlines with their dispute about a comma. The first draft declared that Republicans "oppose any attempts to increase taxes which would harm the recovery and reverse the trend to restoring control of the economy to individual Americans."

The conservative wing of the party insisted on inserting a comma. Their version said that the Republicans would "oppose any attempts to increase taxes, which would harm the recovery and reverse the trend to restoring control of the economy to individual Americans."

Remember that a restrictive modifier says one thing and implies its opposite. What is the implication in the first version? Explain the difference between the two versions.

(P.S. The version with the comma was approved.)

13. Sometimes a verb phrase at the end of a sentence adds information that is more clearly adverbial than it is adjectival:

> Pat spent the whole evening <u>cleaning house</u>.

Here the purpose of the verb phrase, rather than being simply to comment about Pat, is to tell "how" about the verb. In reading the sentence aloud, you will not hear the pause that signifies a comma.

Consider the following sentences. How should you punctuate them? The decision about whether to set off the final verb phrase is not always clear-cut. In making your decision, read the sentence aloud; then ask yourself how the verb phrase functions: Is it adverbial or is it adjectival? (You might try positioning the modifier elsewhere in the sentence. Does the meaning change?)

My uncle made his fortune selling real estate.

My uncle worked hard all his life selling real estate and insurance.

Pete spent the night sleeping in the car.

Amy crossed the finish line smiling at the judges and spectators.

Marcia came to visit me last night crying her eyes out.

The neighbors fled from their burning apartment making good use of their new fire escape.

The neighbors fled from their burning apartment carrying as many of their valuables as their arms would hold.

We ended the homecoming celebration singing around the bonfire.

8

Sentence Modifiers

Like the modifiers of nouns and verbs, modifiers of the sentence as a whole also come in the form of single words, phrases, and clauses. In general, these modifiers resemble adverbials: The information they contribute is, for the most part, adverbial information—time, place, manner, and the like; and most single-word sentence modifiers are adverbs in form. The choice of whether to call a certain phrase or clause a sentence modifier or a verb modifier is, in fact, sometimes hard to make; there are few definitive rules. Within a sentence the sentence modifier will usually be set off by commas, but at the beginning or end of the sentence it may not be. As a result, often the only structures classified as sentence modifiers are those that are clearly parenthetical or independent in meaning or those in which an obvious contrast exists, as in the following pair:

> Clearly, he did not explain the situation.
> He did not explain the situation clearly.

This contrast in meaning shows the difference between the two functions of *clearly*: It is a **sentence modifier** in the first sentence but an adverbial in the second.

The single-word sentence modifier is often set off by a comma. We can usually identify its relationship to the sentence as a whole even without the obvious contrast in meaning that a word such as *clearly* illustrates: It generally makes a comment or value judgment about the sentence.

Invariably, the dress or pair of shoes I like best is the one with the
highest price tag.

Luckily, the van didn't get a scratch when it hit the ditch.

Undoubtedly, we will see interest rates gradually rise.

The book you want is out of print, unfortunately.

But not all sentence modifiers are separated by commas:

Perhaps the entire starting lineup ought to be replaced.

Here it is fairly clear that *perhaps* raises a question about the idea of the
sentence as a whole. If it were moved to a position within the sentence,
it would probably be set off by commas:

The entire starting lineup, perhaps, ought to be replaced.

So the absence of a comma after an introductory modifier does not
rule it out as a sentence modifier; but neither does the presence of a
comma rule it in. As we saw in the earlier chapters on noun and verb
modifiers, both adjectivals and adverbials can sometimes be shifted to
the opening position. That shift does not in itself make them sentence
modifiers. For example, in the following sentences the introductory
phrases are adjectival, modifiers of the subject:

Hot and tired, we loaded the camping gear into the station wagon
for the long trip home.

Limping noticeably, the runner rounded third base and managed
to beat the throw at home plate.

Verb modifiers in introductory position are somewhat more open
to interpretation as sentence modifiers, because adverbials do tend
to add information that relates to the whole idea. In Chapter 6 we
classified phrases like the following as modifiers of the verb, although
admittedly the designation is somewhat arbitrary; a case could be made
for such modifiers to be classified as sentence modifiers rather than
adverbials:

To polish his skills for his trip to Las Vegas, Tim plays poker every night.

Almost every Monday morning, I make a vow to start counting calories.

On a day like today, I prefer to stay in bed.

The less clearly a modifier is related to a particular part of the sentence, the more clearly we can classify it as a modifier of the sentence as a whole. English has many idiomatic expressions—unvarying formulas that have an independent or parenthetical quality—that are clearly sentence modifiers. Unlike the three adverbial examples given earlier, the introductory modifiers in the following sentences are not added for information such as *when* or *where* or *why*:

Frankly, I didn't expect sailing to be so much work.

To our amazement, the driver of the Corvette walked away from the accident.

To my regret, I've never seen the Grand Canyon.

Speaking of the weather, let's decide on the place for our picnic.

To tell the truth, I have never read *Silas Marner*.

Besides the adverb, these examples include two prepositional phrases, a participial phrase, and an infinitive phrase.

You might think that the last two sentence modifiers in the list, which are verb phrases in form, look suspiciously like the danglers that we have seen in earlier discussions of gerunds and infinitives and participles. But it's probably accurate to say that, in contrast to those earlier examples, *speaking of the weather* and *to tell the truth* have achieved the status of independent idiomatic expressions, or set phrases.

You'll notice that there are no diagrams in this chapter to help you visualize the sentence modifiers. All of the other modifiers—the adverbials and adjectivals—get attached to the noun or verb they modify. But the traditional diagram really has no good way of showing a structure that is related to the sentence as a whole. However, since you already know how to diagram verb phrases and noun phrases and clauses, you should have no trouble visualizing the internal structure of these sentence modifiers, even though you aren't actually diagramming them.

NOUNS OF DIRECT ADDRESS: THE VOCATIVES

Another structure set off by a comma is the noun or noun phrase of direct address, known as a **vocative**.

> Ladies and gentlemen, please be seated.
> Jennifer, your date is here.

Although the vocative is not a modifier in the same sense that other structures are, in that it does not modify the meaning of the sentence, it does have a relationship to the sentence as a whole. And like other modifiers, it can come at the beginning, middle, or end of the sentence:

> We certainly hope, my dear friends, that you will visit again soon.
> I promise you won't see me here in court again, your honor.
> Tell us, Mr. President, how your new tax plan will benefit the economy.

The purpose of the vocative, as the term "direct address" implies, is to direct the writer's or speaker's message to a particular person or group. (In most cases it's the speaker's message: This structure is much more common in speech than in writing.) And, as the foregoing examples illustrate, the vocative can express the attitude of the writer or speaker and reflect the tone, whether formal or informal, serious or light, familiar or distant. In that sense, certainly, the vocative is a "sentence modifier." It can affect the meaning of the words.

INTERJECTIONS

The **interjection**—usually a single word or short phrase—can also be considered as a modifier of the sentence as a whole:

> Oh, don't frighten me like that!
> Wow! That's not what I expected.

The traditional view of grammar treats the interjection as one of the parts of speech, probably because there is no other way to categorize such "nonwords" as *oh* and *ah* and *wow* and *ouch*. However, many words that we recognize as nouns and verbs are also used as exclamatory sentence modifiers of this kind:

> <u>Heavens</u>, I don't know what to say.
>
> <u>Good grief</u>! Don't confuse me with the facts!
>
> <u>My word</u>! This will never do.

Like the vocatives, interjections are much more likely to occur in speech than in writing (other than written dialogue).

It would seem logical to consider these as interjections of the same kind as *oh* and *wow*; however, we do not put all such "interjections" into a single parts-of-speech class, as the traditional grammarians do; such a classification distorts the principle on which we make judgments about word categories. Except for *oh* and *ah* and *whew* and a few others, we recognize interjections strictly by their exclamatory, or emotional, function in the sentence. It's true, of course, that the familiar definitions given to the traditional eight parts of speech are not necessarily consistent in their criteria; for example, nouns and verbs are defined according to their meaning (as names and as actions) and adjectives and adverbs by their function (as modifiers). Nevertheless, out of all eight traditional "parts of speech," only the interjection category is denoted strictly by sentence function, rather than as a word type; that is, the other seven traditional parts of speech (noun, verb, adjective, adverb, pronoun, preposition, and conjunction) are names of word classes. It is for this reason that the interjection is not included in our inventory of structure words, described in Chapter 12, but, rather, is included here as one kind of sentence modifier.

===== *Exercise 30* =====

Underline any sentence modifiers in the following sentences.

1. Amazingly, the money held out until the end of the month.
2. The twins look amazingly alike.

3. Well, I plan to stay, myself.
4. Myself, I plan to stay well.
5. Strangely, he seemed to look right through me.
6. I thought he looked at me strangely.
7. Without a doubt our team will win the league championship.
8. We will no doubt win the league championship.
9. I told my friend I was not interested in her scheme.
10. I told you, my friend, that I am not interested.

SUBORDINATE CLAUSES

In Chapter 6 we looked at the adverbial clauses, recognizing that they, too, often seem to relate to the sentence as a whole rather than to the verb specifically. Those introduced by *where*, *when*, *before*, and *after* seem to be the most "adverbial" of all in that they convey information of time and place about the verb; but certainly we could make an equal case for classifying even these as sentence modifiers. **Subordinate clauses** introduced by such subordinators as *if*, *because*, *since*, *as*, and *although* seem even more clearly to modify the idea of the whole sentence, because the subordinator explains the relationship of one idea to another:

> *If* you promise to be there, I'll go to Sue's party.
> I'll go to the party *because* you want me to.
> I'll go with you, *although* I would rather stay home.
> We'll have scrod for dinner *if* the fish market has it at a reasonable price.
> *Because* you prefer it, we'll have scrod instead of sole.

The phrasal subordinators, too, may relate one complete clause to another:

> *Provided that* the moving van arrives on schedule, we'll be ready to leave by three o'clock.
> All the members of the city council, *as far as* I know, voted in favor of the new dog ordinance.

(See page 321 for a list of the simple and phrasal subordinators.)

Some of the interrogatives and expanded relatives introduce conditional clauses that are clearly sentence modifiers:

Whatever decision you eventually make, I'll support you.

Whichever route we take, there's no way we'll get there on time in this traffic.

Now matter *how much* overtime I work, my paycheck never seems to stretch far enough.

The subjunctive *if* clauses that we saw in Chapter 3 can also join this list of clauses that say something about the sentence as a whole:

If I were you, I'd skip the party.

Punctuation of Subordinate Clauses.   In opening position the subordinate clause is always set off by a comma; in closing position, punctuation is related to meaning. As a general rule, when the idea in the main clause is conditional upon or dependent upon the idea in the subordinate clause, there is no comma. For example, the idea of the main clause—the opening clause—in the following sentence will be realized only if the idea in the subordinate clause is carried out; thus here the main clause depends on the *if* clause:

I'll go to Sue's party if you promise to be there.

But in the next sentence the subordinate clause does not affect the fulfillment of the main clause:

I'm going to the party that Sue's giving on Saturday night, even though I know I'll be bored.

The distinction between these two functions is comparable to the restrictive/nonrestrictive distinction we examined in connection with adjectivals in Chapter 7. If the subordinate clause "defines" the situation, it will not be set off from the main clause; if it simply "comments," it will take the comma.

In general *even though* and *although* are preceded by commas; *if* and *because* are not. The point to be made here is that the subordinator relates the idea in its clause to the idea in the main clause, so the subordinate clause clearly functions as a modifier of the sentence as a whole—even though it is not preceded by a comma. But in opening position, the clause is always followed by a comma. The use of the comma with final subordinate clauses is probably one of the least standardized of our punctuation rules. The final criteria must be readability and clarity for the reader.

═══ *Exercise 31* ═══════════════════════

Add commas to the following sentences, if necessary.

1. We left the party as soon as we politely could.
2. Jim agreed to leave the party early and go bowling with us although he was having a good time.
3. When the storm is over we can head for home.
4. We might as well put on the coffee since we're going to be here for another hour.
5. I know that Jerry and I will never be able to afford that much money for rent even if it does include utilities.
6. I won't be able to stay in this apartment if the rent goes any higher.
7. I won't be able to stay in this apartment even if the rent stays the same.
8. If you can't stand the heat get out of the kitchen. [Harry Truman]

═══ *Investigating Language 8.1* ═══════════

Examine the following pairs of sentences. You will probably agree that one of the two in each pair is ungrammatical, something a native speaker would be unlikely to say:

Although she was tired, Michelle worked out in the gym for over an hour.
She was tired, but Michelle worked out in the gym for over an hour.

Because they worked overtime, Meg and Mickey were expecting a big paycheck.
They worked overtime, but Meg and Mickey didn't get a very big paycheck.

In examining sentences, you probably noticed the conjunctions involved: *Although* and *because* are among the subordinators that you've seen in this chapter; *but* is a coordinating conjunction. If you agree that one of the two is ungrammatical, how would you explain to a nonnative speaker of English the rule that native speakers follow? In considering what makes the sentences ungrammatical, you'll want to think about pronouns and their antecedents, as well as the movability of clauses.

Elliptical Clauses.   Many subordinate clauses are **elliptical**— that is, certain understood words are left out:

> While [we were] waiting for the guests to arrive, we ate all the good
>
>   hors d'oeuvres ourselves.
>
> When [I am] in doubt about the weather, I always carry an um-
>
>   brella.

As a reader, you have no problem understanding either of those elliptical clauses: In both cases the missing words, the subject of the elliptical clause, show up as the subject of the main clause.

What would happen if that understood subject did not show up? The result would be a fuzzy sentence, similar to those we have seen with dangling participles and gerunds and infinitives. Like the opening verb phrase, the elliptical element sets up certain expectations in the reader; it's the writer's job to fulfill those expectations. Consider what you expect in the main clause following these elliptical openers:

> *When late for work, the subway is better than the bus.
>
> *If kept too long in hot weather, mold will grow on the bread.
>
> *While driving to the game on Saturday, an accident tied up traffic
>
>   for over an hour.

As with many of the dangling structures we have seen, the message of the sentence may be clear; but there's simply no reason for a writer to set up a situation in which the reader must make the connections—and must do so in a conscious way. Those connections are the writer's job. In some cases only the elliptical version is grammatical:

> I'm a week older than Bob.
> My sister isn't as tall as I.
> *or*
> I'm a week older than Bob is.
> My sister isn't as tall as I am.

We would never include the entire clause:

> *I'm a week older than Bob is old.
> *My sister isn't as tall as I am tall.

In both of these examples, we are comparing an attribute of the subjects of the two clauses. But the ellipses in such comparisons can produce ambiguity when the main clause has more than one possible noun phrase for the subordinate clause to be compared with:

> The Rangers beat the Dolphins worse than the Broncos.
> Joe likes Mary better than Pat.

In these sentences we don't know whether the comparison is between subjects or objects because we don't know what has been left out. We don't know whether

> The Rangers beat the Dolphins worse than ⎱   the Rangers beat the Broncos.
> *or*
> the Broncos beat the Dolphins.

> Joe likes Mary better than ⎱   Joe likes Pat.
> *or*
> Pat likes Mary.

The comparison in the clauses with *as_____ as* can become a problem when an alternative comparison is added. Here is how such comparisons should read:

> Our team is as good as, or better than, the Wildcats.

But sometimes the writer (or speaker) omits the second *as*:

> *Our team is as good, or better than, the Wildcats.
> *My sister is just as strong, or stronger than, you.

These omissions do not result in ambiguity, but the sentences clearly have a grammatical problem—an incomplete comparison.

Incidentally, these clauses of comparison are actually modifying adjectives—*older, tall, worse, better, good,* and *strong*—the qualities that are being compared, rather than modifying the sentence as a whole. We are discussing them here with the sentence modifiers because of the shared elliptical feature.

====== *Exercise 32* ======

Rewrite the three sentences on page 227, including a subject in the elliptical clause. You may have to make changes in the main clause as well.

> When late for work, the subway is better than the bus.
> If kept too long in hot weather, mold will grow on the bread.
> While driving to the game on Saturday, an accident tied up traffic for over an hour.

Now rewrite the following sentences, supplying the words missing in the elliptical clauses. Are the sentences clear?

1. I picked up a Midwestern accent while living in Omaha.
2. My accent is not as noticeable as Carlo's.
3. Holmes hit Ali harder than Norton.
4. If necessary, strain the juice before adding the sugar.
5. While waiting at the train station in Lewistown, there was no place to sit.
6. If handed in late, your grade will be lowered 10 percent.
7. Love goes toward love, as schoolboys from their books.
   But love from love, toward school with heavy looks. [Shakespeare]
8. The weather in Little Rock is not as humid as New Orleans.

ABSOLUTE PHRASES

The **absolute phrase** (also known as the *nominative absolute*) is a structure independent from the main sentence; in form the absolute phrase is a noun phrase that includes a postnoun modifier. The modifier is commonly an *-en* or *-ing* participle or participial phrase, but it can also be a prepositional phrase, an adjective phrase, or a noun phrase. The absolute phrase introduces an idea related to the sentence as a whole, not to any one of its parts:

> Our car having developed engine trouble, we stopped for the night at a roadside rest area.
>
> The weather being warm and clear, we decided to have a picnic.
>
> Victory assured, the fans stood and cheered during the last five minutes of the game.

Absolute phrases are of two kinds—with different purposes and different effects. (Moreover, both are structures generally used in writing, rather than in speech.) The preceding sentences illustrate the first kind: the absolute that explains a cause or condition. In the first sentence, the absolute phrase could be rewritten as a *because, when,* or *since* clause:

> When our car developed engine trouble,
>
> *or*
>
> Since our car developed engine trouble,   we stopped for
>
> *or*   the night. . . .
>
> Because our car developed engine trouble,

The absolute construction allows the writer to include the information without the explicitness that the complete clause requires. In other words, the absolute phrase can be thought of as containing all the meanings in the three versions shown here rather than any one of them.

In the following sentence the idea in the *because* clause could be interpreted as the only reason for the picnic:

> Because the weather was warm and clear, we decided to have a picnic.

The absolute construction, on the other hand, leaves open the possibility of other reasons for the picnic:

The weather being warm and clear, we decided to have a picnic.

It also suggests simply an attendant condition rather than a cause.

In the second kind of absolute phrase, illustrated by the sentences following, a prepositional phrase (*above his head*), adjective phrase (*alert to every passing footstep*), or noun phrase (*a dripping mess*), as well as a participle (*trembling*), may serve as the postnoun modifier. This second kind of absolute adds a detail or point of focus to the idea stated in the main clause:

Julie tried to fit the key into the rusty lock, her hands trembling.

The old hound stood guard faithfully, his ears alert to every passing footstep.

Hands above his head, the suspect advanced cautiously toward the uniformed officers.

Her hair a dripping mess, she dashed in out of the rain.

One interesting difference between the two kinds of absolute constructions is the kind of paraphrase each can undergo. As we saw earlier, the first kind—the absolute of cause or condition—can be expanded into a subordinate clause introduced by such words as *because* or *since* or *when*. But if the absolute phrase of detail or focus—the second kind—is expanded into a clause, it will become the main clause of the sentence, not the subordinate one:

Julie's hands trembled as she tried to fit the key into the rusty lock.

The old hound's ears were alert to every passing footstep as he faithfully stood guard.

The suspect held his hands above his head as he advanced cautiously toward the uniformed officers.

This underlying meaning suggests that the idea in the absolute construction may be the main focus of the sentence, even though grammatically and structurally it occupies a subordinate role.

Another way of paraphrasing the absolute construction is to make it the object of the preposition *with*:

> Julie tried to fit the key into the rusty lock with her hands trembling
> (or with trembling hands).
> The old hound stood guard with his ears alert to every sound.

This paraphrase gives the former absolute phrase the role of manner adverbial, a role that may not render the meaning accurately. Again, the absolute construction enables the writer to avoid that specific adverbial suggestion and to sharpen the impact of the sentence by focusing on a detail of the whole.

This technique of focusing on a detail allows the writer to move the reader in for a close-up view, just as a filmmaker uses the camera. The absolute phrase is especially effective in writing description. Notice how the authors of the following passages use the main clause of the sentence as the wide lens and the absolute phrase as the close-up:

> There was no bus in sight and Julian, his hands still jammed in his pockets and his head thrust forward, scowled down the empty street.
> —FLANNERY O'CONNOR, *Everything That Rises Must Converge*

> The man stood laughing, his weapons at his hips.
> —STEPHEN CRANE, *The Bride Comes to Yellow Sky*

> To his right the valley continued in its sleepy beauty, mute and understated, its wildest autumn colors blunted by the distance, placid as a water color by an artist who mixed all his colors with brown.
> —JOYCE CAROL OATES, *The Secret Marriage*

> He smiled to himself as he ran, holding the ball lightly in front of him with his two hands, his knees pumping high, his hips twisting in the almost girlish run of a back in a broken field.
> —IRWIN SHAW, *The Eighty-Yard Run*

> Soon afterwards they retired, Mama in her big oak bed on one side of the room, Emilio and Rosy in their boxes full of straw and sheepskins on the other side of the room.

Soon the canyon sides became steep and the first giant sentinel red-woods guarded the trail, <u>great round red trunks bearing foliage as green and lacy as ferns.</u>

—JOHN STEINBECK, Flight

Silently they ambled down Tenth Street until they reached a stone bench that jutted from the sidewalk near the curb. They stopped there and sat down, <u>their backs to the eyes of the two men in white smocks who were watching them.</u>

—TONI MORRISON, Song of Solomon

APPOSITIVES

You'll recall that one of the nominals described in Chapter 4 is the appositive, a structure that in form is often a noun phrase:

> Our visitor, <u>a grey-haired lady of indeterminate age,</u> surprised us all when she joined in the volleyball game.

In this example, the appositive renames the subject of the sentence. But sometimes we use a noun phrase to rename, or, more accurately, to encapsulate the idea in the sentence as a whole. We call these structures sentence appositives; we often punctuate them with a dash:

> The musical opened to rave reviews and standing-room-only crowds—<u>a smashing success.</u>
>
> A pair of cardinals has set up housekeeping in our pine tree—<u>an unexpected but welcome event.</u>

Like the absolutes, which are also noun phrases in form, these sentence appositives are related to the sentence as a whole, but their purpose is quite different: They simply label, or restate, the idea of the main clause; they do not introduce a new, subordinate idea, as both kinds of absolute phrases do.

The rhetorical effects of sentence appositives are discussed further in Chapter 14.

===== *Exercise 33* =====

Underline any absolute phrases in the following sentences. Is the modifier of the headword an adjective, a prepositional phrase, a noun phrase, or a participle?

1. The cat lay by the fire, purring contentedly, her tail moving from side to side like a metronome.
2. Chuck and Margie kicked their way through the fallen leaves, their arms draped across each other's shoulders.
3. The rain having persisted for over an hour, the game was officially stopped in the sixth inning.
4. With the Grand Tetons looming majestically above, Jackson Hole, Wyoming, looks like a picture postcard.
5. Michelle lounged in front of the fire, her book open on the floor, her eyes intent on the flames.
6. He saw the city spread below like a glittering golden ocean, the streets tiny ribbons of light, the planet curving away at the edges, the sky a purple hollow extending into infinity. [Anne Tyler]
7. Having slipped on the ice three times already, I decided to wear sensible boots for a change.
8. Then the boy was moving, his bunched shirt and the hard, bony hand between his shoulder-blades, his toes just touching the floor, across the room and into the other one, past the sisters sitting with spread heavy thighs in the two chairs over the cold hearth, and to where his mother and aunt sat side by side on the bed, the aunt's arms about his mother's shoulders. [William Faulkner]

RELATIVE CLAUSES

Most relative clauses are modifiers of nouns, and most are introduced by a relative pronoun that refers to that noun:

> Joe's car, which he bought just last week, looks like a gas guzzler
> to me.

In this sentence the antecedent of *which* is the noun *car*; the noun is modified by the clause.

But in some sentences *which* refers not to a particular noun but to a whole idea; it has what we call *broad reference*. In the following sentence, the antecedent of *which* is the idea of the entire main clause:

Joe bought a gas guzzler, which surprised me.

All such broad-reference clauses are introduced by *which*, never by *who* or *that*, and all are nonrestrictive—that is, they are set off by commas:

Tom cleaned up the garage without being asked, which made me suspect that he wanted to borrow the car.

This summer's heat wave in the Midwest devastated the corn crop, which probably means higher meat prices for the next year.

Many writers try to avoid the broad-reference relative clause, instead using *which* only in the adjectival clause to refer to a specific noun. In inexperienced hands the broad-reference *which* clause often has the vagueness associated with dangling modifiers:

I broke out in a rash, which really bothered me.

In this sentence the referent of *which* is unclear; *which* could refer to either the *rash* or the *breaking out*. There are a number of alternatives in which the meaning is clear:

Breaking out in a rash really bothered me.
The rash I got last week really bothered me.

Even though they are not particularly vague, the earlier examples, too, can be paraphrased in ways that avoid the broad-reference *which*:

When Tom cleaned up the garage without being asked, I suspected that he wanted to borrow the car.
Tom's cleaning up the garage without being asked made me suspect that he wanted to borrow the car.
This summer's heat wave in the Midwest, which devastated the corn crop, probably means higher meat prices for next year.

═══ *Exercise 34* ═══════════

Rewrite the following sentences to eliminate the broad-reference *which*.

1. I had to clean the basement this morning, which wasn't very much fun.
2. Otis didn't want to stay for the second half of the game, which surprised me.
3. The president criticized the Congress rather severely in his press conference, which some observers considered quite inappropriate.
4. The first snowstorm of the season in Denver was both early and severe, which was not what the weather service had predicted.
5. We're having company for dinner three times this week, which probably means hot dogs for the rest of the month.

KEY TERMS IN CHAPTER 8

Absolute phrase	Interjection
Broad-reference clause	Relative clause
Direct address	Sentence appositive
Elliptical clause	Sentence modifier
Idiomatic expression	Subordinate clause
Independent modifier	Vocative

SENTENCES FOR PRACTICE

Draw vertical lines to set off sentence modifiers; identify them by form. If the sentence modifier is, or includes, a verb phrase or clause, identify its sentence pattern.

1. My brother will finish basic training next month if everything goes smoothly.
2. Last week stock prices scored surprisingly strong gains as Wall Street experienced one of the busiest periods in the market's history.
3. If you don't mind, I want to be alone.
4. Speaking of travel, would you like to go to Seattle next week to see the Seahawks play?

5. Incidentally, you forgot to pay me for your share of the expenses.

6. The weather being so beautiful last Sunday, we decided to go to Silver Creek Falls for a picnic.

7. The invitations having been sent, we started planning the menu for Maria's birthday party.

8. Jennifer stayed in bed all day, her fever getting worse instead of better.

9. If bread is kept too long in hot weather, mold will begin to grow on it.

10. The giant redwoods loomed majestically, their branches filling the sky above us.

11. It is impossible to enjoy idling thoroughly unless one has plenty of work to do. [Jerome K. Jerome]

12. Because the weather turned cold suddenly, we decided to postpone our Saturday morning walk.

13. Luckily, Sunday was a nice day, so we didn't miss our weekly hike.

14. Freddie suggested we take a taxi instead of the subway—a splendid idea.

15. Old Town was festive, indeed—the stores decorated with bright colored banners, the air alive with music, the streets crowded with people.

16. If I can stop one heart from breaking, I shall not live in vain. [Emily Dickinson]

QUESTIONS FOR DISCUSSION

1. Many of the simple and phrasal subordinators listed in Chapter 12 introduce clauses that could be interpreted as either sentence modifiers or verb modifiers. How would you classify the underlined clauses in the following sentences—as sentence modifiers or as verb modifiers? Why?

I'll return your book as soon as I finish it.

He'll lend me the money provided that I use it for tuition.

The dog looked at me as if he wanted to tell me something important.

Nero fiddled while Rome burned.

2. The following sentences are both illogical and ungrammatical. What is the source of the problem? Correct the sentences and diagram them, showing the complete structure of the elliptical clauses.

> The summer temperatures in the Santa Clara Valley are much higher than San Francisco.
> The Pirates' stolen-base record is better than the Cardinals.

3. The following sentence is less elliptical than those you just read, but it's equally fuzzy. What is the source of its problem?

> The people of Atlanta are much friendlier than they are in New York.

4. Consider the pronouns in these elliptical clauses. Are they the correct form? Is it possible that both sentences are correct?

> I think my little sister likes our cat better than me.
> I think my little sister likes our cat better than I.

5. A common subject for discussion among people who think about language and usage is the "problem" of *hopefully*. The following sentences are, in fact, avoided by many speakers and writers.

> Hopefully, we will get to the theater before the play starts.
> Hopefully, this play will be better than the last one we saw.

Is the adverb *hopefully* used incorrectly in these sentences? Should it be used only as a manner adverb? Or can it function as a sentence modifier? Make a case for both sides of the issue. (In considering *hopefully*, think also about other adverbs as sentence modifiers, such as *clearly*, *luckily*, and *admittedly*.

6. Rewrite the following sentences, turning the underlined absolute phrases into complete clauses. Note whether the clauses are main clauses or subordinate. Do any of the sentences offer a choice between the two?

> The fans surged onto the field, <u>their shouts of victory filling the stadium like the roar of an avalanche.</u>

The catamarans skimmed across the water, <u>their sails billowing like low-flying clouds</u>.

<u>The garage being full of outdoor furniture and garden equipment</u>, we had no room for the car.

7. We have seen several kinds of structures that can open the sentence:

<u>An ex-Marine who once played professional football</u>, the security guard in our building makes us feel secure, indeed.

<u>Having found the camp deserted</u>, we assumed that the hunters had returned to civilization.

<u>Quiet and peaceful</u>, the neighborhood slept while the cat burglars made their rounds.

Label the form and function of each; explain how these structures differ from the absolute phrases discussed in this chapter.

8. How do you explain the difference in meaning between the following sentences, which appear so similar on the surface? Discuss the effect of the understood elliptical clause in the second sentence. Are both sentences negative?

I have never been happy with our living arrangement.

I have never been happier with our living arrangement.

9

Coordination

In the three preceding chapters we have examined a variety of ways to expand sentences with modifiers. Another common technique for expanding sentences is **coordination:** joining two or more structures to form a pair or a series. All parts of the sentence can be coordinated— subjects, main verbs, auxiliaries, complements, modifiers, prepositions, objects of prepositions—as well as whole sentences.

COORDINATING PARTS OF THE SENTENCE

Within a sentence both **coordinating** and **correlative conjunctions** do the job of connecting parts. In the following sentence, for example, both the subject and the adverbial prepositional phrase are coordinate structures. The coordinating conjunction *and* connects the compound subject; the correlative conjunction *both–and* connects the two adverbial prepositional phrases of place.

John and Tim worked out on Saturday, both in the weight room and in the gym.

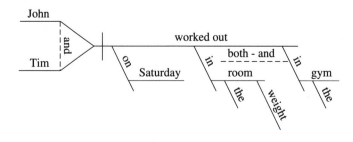

The diagram illustrates both the role of the coordinate structure and its form, with two or more lines in a particular slot instead of just one; a broken line for the conjunction connects them. The coordinating and correlative conjunctions are listed on pages 318 and 319.

The sentences that follow illustrate coordination in other sentence slots:

> **Compound Subjective Complement:** Molly's dessert was simple yet elegant.

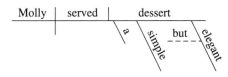

> **Compound Prenoun Adjective:** Molly served a simple but elegant dessert.

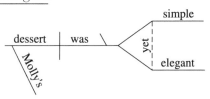

> **Compound Auxiliary:** He can and should finish the job before dark.

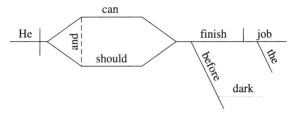

> **Compound Verb:** The whole gang laughed and sang and reminisced at the class reunion.

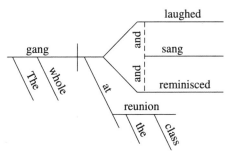

Note that in the last sentence the adverbial prepositional phrase modifies all three verbs, so in the diagram it is attached to a line that is common to all. In the following sentence each verb has a separate modifier; the conjunction connects complete verb phrases, not the verbs alone. The introductory prepositional phrase modifies both verb phrases, so it is shown on a line common to both.

> **Compound Verb Phrase:** On Homecoming weekend our frat party started at noon and lasted until dawn.

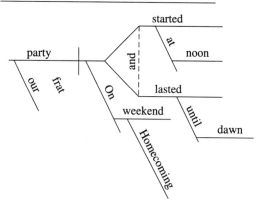

> **Compound Appositive:** I sometimes wonder if I could cook without my modern kitchen gadgets, the microwave and the food processor.

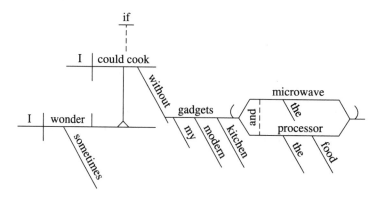

Punctuation of Coordinate Structures Within the Sentence.

As the preceding sentences illustrate, pairs of words, phrases, or clauses within the sentence need no commas with the conjunctions, nor does the series in which conjunctions join all of the coordinate elements. This rule applies even when the elements are long. For example, in the following sentence a pair of nominal clauses fills the direct object slot. Even though the clauses are long ones—and even though the reader might pause for a breath at the conjunction—the object is simply a compound structure within the sentence like those we have seen before; the sentence has no place for a comma:

He said that he would get here sooner or later and that I shouldn't start the rehearsal without him.

The diagram of this sentence with its compound nominal clause may look formidable—and take up a lot of space—but you can see that it simply has a branched slot for the direct object to accommodate the two nominal clauses.

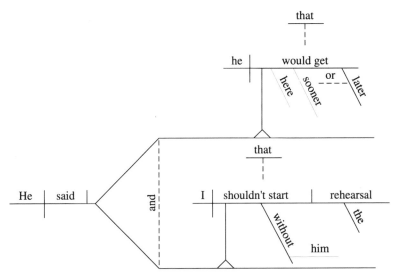

An exception to the rule against commas with compound elements occurs when the conjunction is *but*:

I have visited a lot of big cities, but never Los Angeles.

I worked hard all night, but just couldn't finish my project.

My new white dress is beautiful, but not very practical.

There's a clear disjunction with *but*, resulting, of course, from its meaning; it introduces a contrast. Furthermore, the phrase introduced by *but* could almost be thought of as an elliptical clause, another reason that the comma seems logical:

> I worked hard all night, but [I] just couldn't finish my project.
> My new white dress is beautiful, but [it is] not very practical.

Another exception to the comma restriction occurs when we want to give special emphasis to the second element in a coordinated pair:

> I didn't believe him, and said so.
> My new white dress is beautiful, and expensive.

This emphasis will be even stronger with a dash instead of a comma:

> I didn't believe him—and said so.
> My new white dress is beautiful—and expensive.

We also use commas with a series of three or more elements:

> We <u>gossiped, laughed, and sang</u> together at the class reunion, just like old times.

These commas represent the pauses and slight changes of pitch that occur in the production of the series. You can hear the commas in your voice when you compare the two—the series and the pair. Read them aloud:

> We gossiped, laughed, and sang....
> We laughed and sang....

You probably noticed a leveling of the pitch in reading the pair, a certain smoothness that the series did not have. In the series with conjunctions instead of commas, you'll notice that same leveling:

> We gossiped <u>and</u> laughed <u>and</u> sang together at the class reunion, just like old times.

When conjunctions connect all the elements, we use no commas.

In the series of three, some writers—and some publications as a matter of policy—use only one comma, leaving out the serial comma, the one immediately before *and:*

We gossiped, laughed <u>and</u> sang together at the class reunion, just like old times.

Perhaps they do so on the assumption that the conjunction substitutes for the comma. But it really does not. In fact, this punctuation misleads the reader in two ways: It implies a closer connection than actually exists between the last two elements of the series, and it ignores the pitch change, however slight, represented by the comma. The main purpose of punctuation, after all, is to represent graphically the meaningful speech signals—pitch, stress (loudness), and juncture (pauses)—that the written language otherwise lacks. That small pitch change represented by the comma can make a difference in emphasis and meaning.

===== *Exercise 35* =====

Punctuate the following sentences.

1. Pete sanded the car on Friday and painted it with undercoating on Saturday.
2. Even though the car's new paint job looks terrific now I suspect it will be covered with rust and scratches and dents before next winter.
3. I spent a fortune on new tires shock absorbers and brake linings for the car last week.
4. The car that my father had back in the 1960s and 1970s a 1959 Chevy required very little maintenance and no major repairs during the ten or more years he drove it.
5. I have decided to park my car until gas prices go down and to ride my bicycle instead.
6. I don't suppose I'll ever be able to afford either the down payment or the insurance on a new Corvette the car of my dreams.

Elliptical Coordinate Structures. Elliptical structures are those in which something has been left out. You'll recall from the discussion in the previous chapter that fuzziness or ambiguity sometimes results when the "understood" element is not, in fact, understood. The same kind of problem can occur with coordinate structures.

One common ellipsis is the elimination of the second determiner in a coordinate noun phrase:

> The cat and dog are sleeping on the porch.

A problem can arise when the noun phrase includes modifiers:

> Our new cat and dog are sleeping on the porch.

The clear implication of the noun phrase is that both the cat and the dog are new. If that's not the case, then *dog* needs its own determiner:

> Our new cat and our dog are sleeping on the porch.
> *or*
> Our dog and new cat are sleeping on the porch.

Postnoun modifiers can also be the source of ambiguity in coordinate structures:

> Visitors to this area always admire the flower gardens and stately elms on campus.

Without a determiner for *elms*, the reader is justified in inferring that both the flowers and trees are on the campus, although it's certainly possible that the writer had a different intention. The problem of ambiguity is much more blatant when both noun phrases have determiners:

> Visitors to this area always admire the flower gardens and the stately elms on campus.

Now the reader has no way to decide what *on campus* modifies. If only the elms are on campus, the writer can either reverse the two noun phrases or add another modifier so that both locations are clear:

> ...the stately elms on campus and the flower gardens.
> ...the flower gardens near City Hall and the stately elms on campus.

Here's a similar problem sentence, one with an ambiguous *by* phrase:

Penn State's administration building, Old Main, is best known for its presidential portraits and [its] murals by Henry Varnum Poor.

With or without the determiner for *murals*, this sentence is ambiguous. Another problem can occur with numbers as determiners:

There were six men and women waiting in line.
There were six dogs and cats on the porch.
There were six mothers and daughters at the mother–daughter reception.

We don't, of course, know whether the noun phrases include six or twelve people or animals. Compare these problem sentences with the following:

There were six husbands and wives waiting in line.
There were six knives and forks laid out on the table.

You'll recognize these two as unambiguous.

There are many possibilities for structural ambiguity, where the reader simply has no way of knowing the writer's intention. Coordinate structures are especially open to misinterpretation. It's the job of the writer to make sure that the meaning is clear.

Subject–Verb Agreement.   When nouns or noun phrases in the subject slot are joined by *and* or by the correlative *both–and*, the subject is plural:

My friends and relatives are coming to the wedding.

However, the coordinating conjunction *or* and the correlatives *either–or* and *neither–nor* do not have the additive meaning of *and;* with *or* and *nor* the relationship is called disjunctive. In compound subjects with these conjunctions, the verb will be determined by the closer member of the pair:

Neither the speaker nor the listeners were intimidated by the protestors.
Either the class officers or the faculty advisor makes the final decision.

Do the class officers or the faculty advisor make the final decision?

Does the faculty advisor or the class officers make the final decision?

If the correct sentence sounds incorrect or awkward because of the verb form, you can simply reverse the compound pair:

Either the faculty advisor or the class officers make the final decision.

When both members of the pair are alike, of course, there is no question:

Either the president or the vice-president is going to introduce the speaker.

Neither the union members nor the management representatives were willing to compromise.

For most verb forms, you'll recall, there is no decision to be made about subject–verb agreement; the issue arises only when the *-s* form of the verb or auxiliary is involved. In the following sentences, there is no *-s* form:

Either the class officers or the faculty advisor will make the final decision.

Either the faculty advisor or the class officers will make the final decision.

Another situation that sometimes causes confusion about number— that is, whether the subject is singular or plural—occurs with subjects that include a phrase introduced by *as well as* or *in addition to* or *along with*:

*The sidewalk, in addition to the driveway, need to be repaired.

*The piano player, as well as the rest of the group, usually join in the singing.

*Mike, along with his friend Emilio, often help out at the bakery on weekends.

These additions to the subject are parenthetical; they are not treated as part of the subject. To make the subject compound—to include them—the writer should use a coordinating conjunction, such as *and*:

> The sidewalk and the driveway need to be repaired.
>
> The piano player and the rest of the group usually join in the singing.
>
> Mike and his friend Emilio often help out at the bakery on weekends.

Parallel Structure.   An important requirement for coordinate structures is that they be **parallel**. A structure is parallel when all the coordinate parts are of the same grammatical form. The conjunctions must join comparable structures, such as pairs of noun phrases or verb phrases or adjectives:

> The little white-haired lady *and* her blonde poodle seemed to belong together.
>
> The stew smells delicious *and* tastes even better.
>
> The entire cast gave powerful *and* exciting performances.

Unparallel structures occur most commonly with the correlative conjunctions: *both–and, either–or, neither–nor,* and *not only–but also.* For example, in the following sentence, the two coordinators introduce structures of different forms:

> *Either* they will fly straight home *or* stop overnight in Dubuque.

Being able to picture the diagram can be helpful in preventing such unparallel structures. With the sentence above, you'll discover that the conjunction line would connect a complete sentence (*they will fly straight home*) and a verb phrase (*stop overnight in Dubuque*). Because the two structures are not parallel, the diagram simply won't work.

A diagram of the following sentence won't work either:

> *I'll *either* take a bus *or* a taxi.

The conjunction line would have to connect a verb phrase and a noun phrase; again the two structures are not parallel.

Such problems are easy to correct. It's just a matter of shifting one part of the correlative pair so that both introduce the same kind of construction:

> They will *either* fly straight home *or* stop overnight in Dubuque.
> I'll take *either* a bus *or* a taxi.

Further examples of the correlative conjunctions are given in Chapter 12. An exception to the rule of parallelism is explained on page 319 in connection with *either–or* and *neither–nor* as sentence connectors.

===== *Exercise 36* =====

Rewrite the following sentences, paying particular attention to correcting unparallel structures.

1. I can't decide which activity I prefer: to swim at the shore in July when the sand is warm or jogging along country roads in October when the autumn leaves are at their colorful best.
2. I almost never watch television. There is either nothing on that appeals to me or the picture disappears at a crucial moment.
3. I neither enjoy flying across the country nor particularly want to take the train.
4. The recipe was either printed wrong, or I misread it.
5. I was unhappy with what he said and the way he said it.
6. The coach announced an extra hour of drill on Saturday and that the practice on Sunday would be canceled.
7. Aunt Rosa has promised to fix her famous lasagna for my birthday dinner and will also bake my favorite cake.

COORDINATING COMPLETE SENTENCES

We have two principal methods of joining independent clauses to produce **compound sentences**: (1) using coordinating conjunctions and (2) using the semicolon, either with or without conjunctive adverbs.

Conjunctions. The compound sentence with a coordinating conjunction such as *and* shows up at an early stage of the writer's development:

> We went to the fair, and we had a good time.
> Robby is mean, and I don't like him.

Such sentences can, of course, be effective when they are used sparingly, but they will strike the reader as immature when overused. The compound sentence is most effective when the coordinate ideas have relatively equal importance—when the two ideas contribute equal weight:

> I disapprove of her spending money on lottery tickets, and I told her so.
> The curtain rose to reveal a perfectly bare stage, and a stillness settled over the audience.
> Pete filled the bags with hot roasted peanuts, and I stapled them shut.

Note that the punctuation rule that applies to the compound sentence differs from the rule regarding internal coordinate constructions. Between the sentences in a compound sentence we do use a comma with the conjunction; between the parts of a coordinate structure within the sentence we do not. When the clauses of a compound sentence are quite short and closely connected, however, we sometimes omit the comma. The following sentence, for example, would probably be spoken without the pitch change we associate with commas:

> October came and the tourists left.

The coordinators *and* and *or* can link a series of three or more sentences:

> Pete filled the bags, and I stapled them shut, and Marty packed them in the cartons.
> The kids can wait for me at the pool, or they can go over to the shopping center and catch the bus, or they can even walk home.

In these two sentences, the first conjunction can be replaced by a comma:

> Pete filled the bags, I stapled them shut, <u>and</u> Marty packed them in the cartons.

But usually joins only two clauses:

> Jill wanted me to wait for her, <u>but</u> I refused.

But can introduce the final clause when *and* or *or* joins the first two:

> Pete filled the bags, <u>and</u> I stapled them, <u>but</u> Marty refused to lift a finger.
>
> The kids can wait for me at the pool, <u>or</u> they can walk to the bus stop, <u>but</u> I really think they ought to walk home.

Semicolons.   When a semicolon connects two coordinate clauses, the conjunction can be omitted:

> Pete packed the hot roasted peanuts into bags; I stapled them shut.
> The curtain rose; a stillness settled over the audience.

The semicolon is also used when a **conjunctive adverb** introduces the second clause. Note, too, that the conjunctive adverb is set off by a comma:

> We worked hard for the Consumer Party candidates, ringing doorbells and stuffing envelopes; <u>however,</u> we knew they didn't stand a chance.
>
> We knew our candidates didn't have a hope of winning; <u>nevertheless,</u> for weeks on end we faithfully rang doorbells and stuffed envelopes.

Of all the adverbial conjunctions, only *yet* and *so* can be used with a comma instead of a semicolon between clauses:

> Several formations of birds were flying northward, <u>so</u> I knew spring was on the way.

Several formations of birds were flying northward, yet I suspected that winter was far from over.

In both of these sentences, a semicolon could replace the comma, depending on the writer's emphasis. The semicolon would put extra emphasis on the second clause. *So* and *yet* straddle the border between the coordinating conjunctions and the conjunctive adverbs; they are often listed as both. In meaning, *so* is similar to *therefore* and *yet* to *however;* but unlike these conjunctive adverbs, *so* and *yet* always introduce the clause, so in this respect they are perhaps closer to the coordinating conjunctions. Sometimes we use both the conjunction and the adverbial: *and so; but yet.*

Because they are also adverbials, most conjunctive adverbs are movable; they can appear in the middle of the clause or at the end, as well as at the beginning:

We worked hard for the Consumer Party candidates;

we knew, however, they didn't stand a chance.

or

we knew they didn't stand a chance, however.

These choices are examined further in Chapter 14. Other common conjunctive adverbs are listed on page 320.

═══ *Investigating Language 9.1* ═══

Combine the following groups of sentences into compound sentences, using conjunctions of your choice, including conjunctive adverbs. In each case there are a number of possible ways to combine them, depending on the emphasis.

1. The library closes at noon on Thursdays.
   It is open until 9:00 P.M. on Fridays.
2. The food at the new French restaurant is exceptionally good.
   The prices are exceptionally high.
3. I am going to take piano lessons this fall.
   I may take guitar lessons, too.

4. My first-period students are bright.
   They are wide awake at 8:00 A.M., too.
5. Our trip across Kansas was long and straight and uneventful.
   The trip across Kansas took an entire day.

Now turn your compound sentences into **compound–complex sentences** by adding a dependent clause to each one. The dependent clause can be nominal, adverbial, or adjectival. (You may have to make other changes to accommodate the dependent clauses.)

1. _____

_____

2. _____

_____

3. _____

_____

4. _____

_____

5. _____

_____

Elliptical Compound Sentences. We looked at elliptical coordinate structures earlier to recognize some of their potential problems. But certainly they are not always problems; they can, in fact, be very effective with their tight, controlled quality:

I haven't finished my project, but Amy has [finished her project].
I've finished my project, and so has Amy [finished her project].

In the next two examples, a comma (and, in speech, the pause that it represents) signals the omission:

> Jack roots for the Orioles, but Jane, the Oakland A's.
> Sue raises cocker spaniels, and Pam, whippets.

In the following quoted example, the author has omitted the conjunction; note too that he has not used a comma to signal the missing verb. If you read the sentence aloud, you may not hear as clear a pause as you do when reading the previous examples:

> The sea was a pearly turquoise, the far mountains ash-blue in the windless heat.
>
> —JOHN FOWLES, *The Magus*

You can compare the effect this tight structure has with a rewrite that includes the conjunction and the second linking *be*.

A similar method is used in these two passages describing Stonewall Jackson:

> His character was stern, his manner reserved and usually forbidding, his temper Calvinistic, his mode of life strict, frugal, austere. Black-bearded, pale-faced, with thin, compressed lips, aquiline nose, and dark, piercing eyes, he slouched in his weather-stained uniform a professor-warrior; yet greatly beloved by the few who knew him best, and gifted with that strange power of commanding measureless devotion from the thousands whom he ruled with an iron hand.
>
> —WINSTON CHURCHILL, *The Great Democracies*

In Chapter 14 we will examine further the rhetorical effects of such elliptical and coordinate elements.

Diagramming the Compound Sentence.   In the diagram a broken line connects the two verbs, with the connector on a solid line approximately halfway between the two clauses:

> Pete filled the bags, and I stapled them shut, but Marty refused to lift a finger.

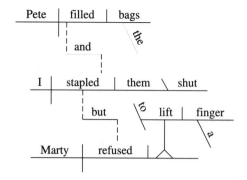

KEY TERMS IN CHAPTER 9

Compound sentence
Compound structure
Compound–complex sentence
Conjunction
Conjunctive adverb
Coordinating conjunction

Coordination
Correlative conjunction
Elliptical coordinate structure
Parallelism
Semicolon
Subject–verb agreement

SENTENCES FOR PRACTICE

Underline the sentence slots that have coordinate structures; circle the conjunctions. For further practice, identify the sentence patterns and diagram the sentences.

1. Despite the economic recovery, many auto workers in Detroit and many steelworkers in Pennsylvania are still unemployed.

2. I lent my son and daughter-in-law a sizable sum of money.

3. They have recently moved to Ohio and will soon be buying a new house.

4. To get your rebate, simply fill out the coupon and mail it to the company's headquarters in Michigan.

5. I have battled beetles and aphids and tent caterpillars for the entire summer.

6. Next month many students and tourists will be going to our nation's capital to visit the historical monuments or perhaps to stroll along the streets and simply enjoy that beautiful city.

7. My friends and I, finding the movie boring, left at intermission and adjourned to our favorite hangout.

8. Hope is the thing with feathers
That perches in the soul,
And sings the tune without the words,
And never stops at all.
—EMILY DICKINSON

9. Thousands of Americans, united by a deep and urgent concern about the quality of life for themselves and future generations, have given both their money and their time to the environmental movement.

10. The hundreds of separate groups that make up the environmental movement are demonstrating to get the support of their fellow citizens and their legislators.

11. Having found an apartment that was inexpensive, roomy, and close to the subway, we made a split-second decision and rented it on the spot.

12. The woods are lovely, dark, and deep,
But I have promises to keep,
And miles to go before I sleep.
—ROBERT FROST,
"Stopping by Woods on a Snowy Evening"

13. The boom in cosmetic surgery is apparently the result of new, more sophisticated procedures, safer anesthetics, and the desire for self-improvement.

14. Only two knots are required for most fly-fishing situations: a knot for tying on the fly and a knot for joining monofilament.

QUESTIONS FOR DISCUSSION

1. In the following sentences the coordinate ideas are unparallel in form. Do some seem more acceptable than others? Rank them in order of acceptability. Rewrite those that can be improved.

Almost every lineman on the squad was overweight and out of condition when the season started.

She volunteered her services at the Senior Citizens' Center frequently and with boundless enthusiasm.

The old man, broke and having no friends to turn to, simply disappeared from the neighborhood.

I have always loved sports of all kinds and jog regularly.

2. Consider the following compound sentences. Are they parallel? Can you find a way to improve them? What is their special problem?

I fixed three bowls of popcorn for the party, but it was eaten up before most of the guests even got there.

Burglars broke into the art museum last night, and three valuable paintings were stolen.

The television lost its sound last week, but luckily it got fixed before the World Series started.

3. Explain the ambiguity of the prenoun compound modifier in the following noun phrase:

six red and blue banners

4. Explain why the verbs or auxiliaries in the following sentences would not be the *-s* form even though the subject headwords *crime* and *stamina* are singular.

Blue collar and white collar crime are on the increase.

Both physical and mental stamina are required for long-distance running.

5. Officials of Lee County, Florida, adopted the following set-back ordinance, intending that it apply to all "buildings and structure":

All buildings and structure and all open areas used for any manufacturing process, for shipping and receiving, or for warehousing and storage shall be set back 100 feet from the boundary of any land zoned exclusively for residential land uses.

A property owner maintained that the ordinance did not apply to a retail establishment that he planned to build fifteen feet from the line. The county won the case by showing that the ordinance was poorly worded—that it was, in fact, ambiguous. The judge ruled that in the case of an ambiguous ordinance, the original intent would apply.

Explain the source of the ambiguity. Can you understand the property owner's point of view?

IV

WORDS
AND
WORD CLASSES

So far in this description of grammar we have been focusing on **syntax**—the structure of sentences—looking at the functions, or slots, that make up the sentence and at the variety of forms that fill those slots. Instead of starting with words, we have studied the way that words work together in phrases and in clauses. In this section, however, we will look at the words themselves.

In the next four chapters we will concentrate on differences in the forms of words and compare their functions in the sentence. These are the differences that determine the classification of words into categories known as the parts of speech.

The first division of words into groups is based on two different kinds of meaning. Suppose a stranger approached you and said, "Boy needs drink water." Your first response would probably be to recognize the person as a nonnative speaker of English. Your second would be to share your water supply, because in spite of the ungrammatical sentence you understood the message. Under the same circumstances, a native speaker would have said, "My boy needs a drink of water," or "This boy needs to drink that water," or "The boy needs a drink of your water." The message is more explicit, but the result would be the same: You'd share your water. The extra words wouldn't change the effect of the message, but they would provide a certain kind of meaning, a precision

261

that the nonnative speaker's sentence lacks. Clearly, then, different kinds of words function in different ways to contribute different kinds of meaning.

First consider the differences between the words the nonnative speaker used and those he left out. The ones he included are the content words, the words that give the sentence the lexical meaning necessary to get the message across: *Boy needs drink water*. What he omitted were certain grammatical signals. We don't know, for example, if *drink* is a noun or a verb; nor do we know the relationship of the speaker or the listener to the nouns *boy* and *water*. Nevertheless, the circumstances of the conversation, its setting or context, make the message clear.

This distinction between lexical and grammatical meaning determines the first division in our classification: form-class words and structure-class words. In general, the **form classes** provide the primary lexical content; the **structure classes** explain the grammatical or structural relationships. We can think of the form-class words as the bricks of the language and the structure words as the mortar that holds them together.

FORM CLASSES	STRUCTURE CLASSES	
Noun	Determiner	Pronoun
Verb	Auxiliary	Conjunction
Adjective	Qualifier	Interrogative
Adverb	Preposition	Expletive

Probably the most striking difference between the form classes and the structure classes is characterized by their numbers. Of the half million or more words in our language, the structure words—with some notable exceptions—can be counted in the hundreds. The form classes, however, are large, open classes; new nouns and verbs and adjectives and adverbs regularly enter the language as new technology and new ideas require them. They are sometimes abandoned, too, as the dictionary's "obsolete" and "archaic" labels testify. The structure classes, on the other hand, remain constant—and limited. We have managed with the very same small store of prepositions and conjunctions for generations, with few changes. It's true that we don't hear *whilst* and *betwixt* and *thy* anymore, nor do we see them in contemporary prose and poetry, but most of our structure words are identical to those that Shakespeare and his contemporaries used.

Another difference has to do with form. As their label suggests, the form classes are those that can undergo changes in form—that are, in fact, distinguishable by their form—whereas the structure classes are not. But, as with almost every "rule" of the language, we will encounter exceptions. For example, auxiliaries are among the structure classes, although some of them, because they are verbs, show form variations; *be*, *have*, and *do*, as you know, can be both auxiliaries and verbs. Some of the pronouns also have variations in form. On the other hand, there are many words in the form classes that have no distinctions in form and do not undergo change—nouns like *chaos*, adjectives like *main*, and adverbs like *there*.

Another complication in our two-part, form/structure division is the inclusion of the determiner and qualifier classes, both of which are more accurately described as *functions*, rather than word classes. The determiner class, as you will see in Chapter 12, includes words from other classes, such as pronouns; the fact that it also includes possessive nouns actually makes it an open class. The qualifier class, too, includes words from other classes, such as adverbs, so that class, also, is open to membership.

In spite of these problems of categories and labels, we are classifying our vocabulary into these two overall groups of form and structure words to help you distinguish the bricks and mortar, to help you classify those content words and grammatical signals that you have been studying in the context of sentences.

Before looking at the classes individually, we need to examine the basic unit of word formation, the morpheme; an understanding of the morpheme is central to the conscious understanding of words. Then we will take up the form classes, the structure classes, and, in a separate chapter, pronouns.

CHAPTER
10
Morphemes

Syntax refers to the arrangement of sentence elements into meaningful patterns. When we study sentence patterns and their transformations and expansions, we are studying syntax. But the structural linguist begins the study of grammar not with syntax but with **phonology,** the study of individual sounds. At the next level comes **morphology,** the study of **morphemes,** combinations of sounds with meaning. Then comes the study of **syntax,** the third level in the grammar hierarchy.

In this book we are concerned primarily with syntax, the systematic arrangement of words and phrases and clauses into sentences. But a thorough understanding of syntax depends on the understanding of the words that combine to form those larger units. So in this chapter, before taking up the word classes—known as the "parts of speech"—we will look briefly at morphemes, the units that make up words. (For an overview of phonemes, the individual sounds, see Appendix A.)

The definition of *morpheme,* a combination of sounds that has meaning, may sound to you like the definition of *word.* That's not surprising because many morphemes are, in fact, complete words; *head* and *act* and *kind* and *walk* (as well as *and*) are words consisting of a single morpheme, a single meaningful combination of sounds. But others, such as *heads* and *actively* and *unkindly* and *walking,* consist of two or more morphemes, each of which has meaning itself. The success you had years ago in learning to read and spell was in part dependent on your awareness of the parts of words. For instance, in spelling a word like *actively,* you probably break it into its three morphemes automatically:

Its stem, or **base,** is the verb *act;* the suffix *-ive* turns it into an adjective; and the suffix *-ly* turns the adjective into an adverb. Each of these three morphemes, the base and the two suffixes, has meaning itself; and each appears in other environments (other words) with the same meaning. These are the two primary criteria that we use to identify the morphemes in a word: They have meaning; they appear with the same meaning in other words.

We should also emphasize that *morpheme* and *syllable* are not synonymous—even though the morphemes discussed so far consist of a single syllable. There are, in fact, many two-syllable words in English that are single morphemes: *carrot, college, jolly, merit, over.* You can find them on every page of the dictionary. Furthermore, many two-morpheme words are single syllables: *acts, walked, dog's.* So even though it may be understandable to think of syllable boundaries as boundaries for morphemes, it is inaccurate to do so.

The individual morphemes in a word are not always quite as obvious as they are in words like *actively.* In the word *reflections,* for example, we can recognize the verb *reflect,* the *-ion* ending that turns it into a noun, and the *-s* that makes it plural: *reflect + ion + s.* But how about the word *reflect?* Is that a single morpheme, or is it two? Are *re* and *flect* separate morphemes? Do they both have meaning? Do they appear in other environments with the same meaning? Certainly there are many words that begin with the prefix *re-: reverse, rebound, refer.* In all these, *re-* means "back," so *re* passes the morpheme test. How about *flect?* We have *inflect* and *deflect.* The dictionary reveals that all three words with *flect* are based on the Latin verb *flectere,* meaning "to bend." So in the word *reflections* we can identify four morphemes: *re + flect + ion + s.*

Incidentally, it's not unusual to need the dictionary to understand the morpheme structure of a word. The meanings of words often change, and their origins become obscure. Take the word *obscure,* for example. How many morphemes does it have, one or two? What does *scure* mean? Does it appear in other words with the same meaning? And is *ob* the same morpheme we find in *observe?* What does it mean? And how about *observe?* Is that the verb *serve?* Such meanderings into the dictionary in search of clues about morphemes can heighten our awareness of words and appreciation of language. And certainly an awareness of morphemes can enhance the understanding of language essential to both reader and writer. When we study etymology or historical linguistics, we begin to understand the intricacies of morphemes, their changes, and their variations. But our interest in morphemes here is a limited one. We will look mainly at those that signal the form classes, that contribute to our understanding of the parts of speech.

BASES AND AFFIXES

All words, as we have seen, are combinations of morphemes, or, in the case of a word like *act* (as well as the eight words preceding it in this sentence), single morphemes. All morphemes are either **bases** (*act*), which we define as the morpheme that gives the word its primary lexical meaning, or **affixes** (*-ive, -ly*); and all affixes are either **prefixes,** those that precede the base (*re-*), or **suffixes,** those that follow it (*-ion*):

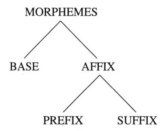

=== *Exercise 37* ===

The following four sets of words illustrate some of the relationships of morphemes. In each set find the common base. What does the base mean? Draw vertical lines in the words to show the separate morphemes.

nova	auditor	durable	conceive
renovation	audience	endure	capable
innovate	inaudible	duration	susceptible
novice	auditorium	during	capture
novelist	audio	endurance	intercept

BOUND AND FREE MORPHEMES

One other feature of morphemes concerns their ability to stand alone. Many cannot. For example, the affixes are **bound,** or attached, to another morpheme rather than **free** to stand alone; that's what *affix* means. In the word *actively,* only the first morpheme is free: *-ive* and *-ly* are bound. In *reflections,* even the base is bound; *flect* is not a word that can stand by itself. We call this a bound base. Other examples of words without free morphemes are *concur, conceive, depict, expel,* and many others with these common prefixes. There are also a few affixes that are free, such as *full* (spelled "ful" when used as an affix), *like,* and *less.* A free morpheme is a word; a bound morpheme is not. The solid arrows in the following diagram represent the most common circumstance, the broken ones the less common:

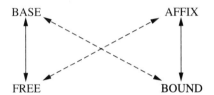

═══ *Exercise 38* ═══

Find a word to fit each of the following formulas. Include only the morphemes called for.

> **Examples:** free + bound = *birds*
> bound + free = *rerun*

1. free + bound
2. bound + free
3. free + bound + bound
4. bound + free + bound
5. free + free
6. bound + free + bound + bound
7. bound + bound
8. bound + bound + bound

DERIVATIONAL AND INFLECTIONAL MORPHEMES

Another feature of affixes we want to recognize is their classification as either derivational or inflectional:

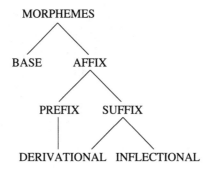

As the branching diagram shows, all prefixes are derivational, whereas suffixes are either derivational or inflectional. Although we have several hundred suffixes, distinguishing between the derivational and inflectional ones is easy to do. Only eight are **inflectional.** You'll recognize four of them from the discussion of verbs in Chapter 3.

-*s* (plural)
-*s* (possessive) } Noun inflections

-*s* (3rd-person singular)
-*ed* (past tense)
-*en* (past participle)
-*ing* (present participle) } Verb inflections

-*er* (comparative)
-*est* (superlative) } Adjective and adverb inflections

All the other suffixes, as well as all the prefixes, are **derivational.**

The term *derivational* refers to the change that a word undergoes when a derivational morpheme is added: Either the meaning of the word changes or the class, the part of speech, changes—or both. Take the word *inactivity*, for example. With the derivational morpheme -*ive*, the verb *act* becomes the adjective *active*—that is, we derive one class of word from another. When we add *in-*, the class remains the same—*active* and *inactive* are both adjectives—but the prefix does affect the meaning, as prefixes generally do; in other words, we derive a new meaning. Finally, with the addition of -*ity* the adjective becomes the noun *inactivity*.

The significance, then, of derivational morphemes is this ability they give us to derive new words: *Active* and *inactive* are two different words; so are *active* and *actively;* so are *act* and *action.*

The inflectional affixes also change words, of course, but the changes do not represent new words in the same sense that the changes with derivational morphemes do. It is probably accurate to consider the verb *acting* as simply a variation of *act;* likewise, the inflections we add to nouns—the plural and possessive—produce variations of the singular noun; we think of *dogs* and *dog's* simply as variations of *dog,* rather than as different words.

There are two other attributes of derivational morphemes that distinguish them from the inflectional morphemes:

1. Derivational morphemes are arbitrary. Unlike the inflectional morphemes, which apply in a systematic way to all, or at least to a significant number of, the words in a class, the derivational morphemes are quite unsystematic. For example, every verb—without exception—takes the inflectional *-s* and *-ing* endings (this may, in fact, be the only rule in our grammar without an exception); and almost all verbs have an *-ed* and *-en* inflection as well. However, there's nothing systematic about the derivational endings that we add to other word classes to form verbs: The adjective *able* becomes a verb with the addition of the prefix *en-* (*enable*); *sweet* takes the suffix *-en* (*sweeten*); *legal* takes *-ize* to become a verb (*legalize*); *active* takes *-ate* (*activate*). For many adjectives, however, we have no derivational morpheme at all for producing verbs; we have no way to turn such adjectives as *big, good, happy,* and *vicious* into verbs. On the other hand, we can derive nouns from these particular adjectives by adding *-ness*. As you might expect, however, *-ness* is not our only noun-forming suffix: Others include *-ity* (*generosity, activity, creativity*); *-acy* (*supremacy, literacy*); *-er* (*singer, helper*); or *-ion, -tion* (*action, preparation*); and *-ment* (*contentment, enlargement*). We have no rules to explain what goes with what, no system to account for these differences; that lack of system is what "arbitrary" means.

2. Derivational morphemes often change the class of the word. Most of the time, in fact, that change in class is their very purpose; they produce new words. Inflectional morphemes, on the other hand, never change the class. And, as mentioned earlier, we generally don't even consider the inflected form of a word as a different word.

If all these derivational and inflectional morphemes seem complicated to you, it's probably because you haven't thought about them before. If you're a native speaker, they're really not complicated at all; you use them without even thinking. In fact, there is probably no feature of English that illustrates more clearly the innate ability that native speakers have than this inventory of prefixes and suffixes that gives the language such versatility.

═══════ *Investigating Language 10.1* ═══════

Consider the following sets:

A. *X* can dorf; *X* dorfs; *X* is dorfing; *X* has dorfed already.
B. Give me that dorf. No, I mean those dorfs. Where's your dorf's snape?
C. You're pretty dorf, but *X* is dorfer, and *Y* is the dorfest of all.

1. In which set is *dorf* an adjective? What morphological—not syntactic—evidence tells you that?
2. In which set is *dorf* a verb? Again, what morphological evidence tells you that?
3. In which set is *dorf* a noun? Once more, what morphological evidence tells you that?
4. What type of morphemes have you been dealing with in these questions: inflectional or derivational?
5. The traditional definition of *noun* is "the name of a person, place, or thing" and that of *verb* is "a word that denotes action, being, or state of being." Instead of using those criteria of meaning, write your own definitions of *noun* and *verb* that are based on form.

ALLOMORPHS

In Exercise 37 the base morphemes *aud* and *dur* are pronounced and spelled the same in all five words in their lists. However, the morpheme *nov* in that same exercise has two pronunciations; in *nova* and *novelist* the vowels are different, comparable to the difference between *node* and *nod*. In the last group in the exercise, the difference from one word to the next is greater still, with variations in spelling as well as pronunciation. In fact, without the help of a dictionary we would be tempted to label *ceive* and *cap* and *cept* as different morphemes altogether, rather than variations of the same one. Such variations of morphemes, which are extremely common in English, are known as **allomorphs.**

Sometimes the base morphemes have allomorphic variations as the result of suffixes. For example, a word ending in *f* often takes a *v* in the plural:

leaf→ leaves   wife→ wives   elf→ elves

We would call *leav* and *wiv* and *elv* allomorphs of *leaf* and *wife* and *elf*. Here are some other examples in which the pronunciation of the base morpheme changes with the addition of a suffix: *type/typify*; *please/pleasant*; *press/pressure*; *able/ability*; *oblige/obligation*; *child/children*. And because these allomorphs of the base are not used without the suffix, we would include them in the category of bound bases.

Prefixes and suffixes, too, undergo such variation; that is, they also have allomorphs. For example, notice the negative prefix we add to these adjectives: *unkind, improper, illegal, irrelevant, ineligible*. All these prefixes mean *not*, so it is probably accurate to consider *im, il, ir*, and *in* as allomorphs of the prefix *un*, the most common among them. At any rate, their sounds are determined by their environment.

Suffixes also have allomorphic variation. Consider, for example, the sound you add to make nouns plural:

cat→ cats   dog→ dogs   kiss→ kisses

Even though the first two are spelled the same, the sounds are different: in *cats* the sound is an *s;* in *dogs*, it's a *z*. And in *kisses*, the *es* represents an unstressed vowel sound followed by *z*. These variations are discussed in further detail in Appendix A, "Phonology."

HOMOPHONES

You're probably familiar with the meaning of the word *homonyms:* words with different meanings that sound alike, such as *sail* and *sale, there* and *their*, or *to, two*, and *too*. These are also known as **homophones,** a label that refers not only to words but to morphemes as well—in some cases to parts of words that sound the same but have different meanings. Prefixes and suffixes, for example, can be homophones. The *ex* in *exchange* and the *ex* in *ex-wife* have two different meanings: "from" and "former." So do the *er* in *singer* and the *er* in *brighter:* "one who" and "more." In this case, one is derivational and one is inflectional. And the *s* endings we add to verbs and nouns also have different meanings. All of these are examples of homophones.

You might find it useful to think of homophones as simply an accident or a coincidence of language. It's accidental that *sale* and *sail* happen to sound alike when their meanings have no connection. It's coincidence that the word *bell* and the bound morpheme *bell* in *rebellion* sound alike. The dictionary will show that they have no connection: The free morpheme *bell* has its origin in the Old English word meaning roar; *rebellion* comes from the Latin word for war. And certainly it's coincidence that the name of the saw, a carpenter's tool, sounds the same and shares the same spelling as the past tense form of *see*.

Remember that morphemes are units of meaning—a single sound or a combination of sounds with meaning. Two morphemes that are unrelated in meaning are called homophones when their sounds happen to be the same.

═════════ *Exercise 39* ═════════

Draw vertical lines in the following words to indicate their morpheme boundaries. Identify each morpheme as follows: *bound* or *free; base* or *affix*. Identify each affix as *derivational* or *inflectional*. You will probably need to consult your dictionary.

precision	unaware	illegal
candidate	money	wealthy
detoured	sidewalks	television
excessively	promotion	revises

KEY TERMS

Affix	Homophones
Allomorph	Inflectional morpheme
Base morpheme	Morpheme
Bound morpheme	Morphology
Derivational morpheme	Prefix
Free morpheme	Suffix

QUESTIONS FOR DISCUSSION

1. Most morphemes are made up of combinations of sounds. Give some examples of morphemes that are single sounds.

2. Consider how the meaning of a word comes about. Explain the origin of the following words:

ambulance	cohort	fancy	mayhem
budget	daisy	hussy	meal
calculate	dial	infant	money
candidate	easel	lunatic	pilot
cigar	escape	magazine	vaccine

3. In Exercise 38 you came up with words containing various combinations of bound and free morphemes. Which of those sequences do you suppose is a compound word? Define *compound word* on the basis of its morpheme content.

4. Consider the difference between derivational and inflectional suffixes. What can you say about their positions when both appear on the same word? Is the rule fairly constant? Is it possible for more than one derivational and/or inflectional suffix to appear on a single word?

5. Which of the following words appear to violate the system that you described in Question 4?

inflectional   sportsmanship   microscopy   teaspoonsful

6. How can the awareness of morphemes be of help in spelling problem words, such as the following?

entirely	professor	inaudible	disappoint
safety	innovate	misspell	roommate

7. In his "On Language" column in the *New York Times Magazine* for October 14, 1984, William Safire cites four different meanings for the suffix *-ful*, as reported to him by the editorial director of Merriam-Webster, the dictionary publisher: (1) "full of;" (2) "characterized by;" (3) "resembling or having the qualities of;" and (4) "tending to or given to." Here are the four words he used as examples:

masterful   mournful
painful   eventful

Which word goes with which meaning?

8. Still on the subject of the suffix -*ful*, explain the difference between the words "painful" and "pained." Under what circumstances would the following sentences be accurate?

He had a pained expression on his face.
He had a painful expression on his face.

Now think about the difference between "healthy" and "healthful." Would you say that carrots are a healthy food to eat? And what's the difference between "masterly" and "masterful?"

9. Our vocabulary expands in many ways. Sometimes we give new meanings to old words or to their combinations, as in *waterbed, whistle-blower, gridlock,* and *moonshot.* And sometimes we combine the two into a completely new word: We made *brunch* from *breakfast* and *lunch.* What two words do you suppose were combined in the formation of these: *bash, clash, flare,* and *smash*?

11
The Form Classes

The contrast in the sentences of the native and nonnative speakers in the introduction to this section illustrates the difference in the kind of meaning that form-class words and structure-class words contribute to the sentence. The nonnative speaker communicated with nouns and verbs, the **form-class words** that provide the semantic content of the language: *Boy wants drink water*. The native speaker's version of that sentence includes such word classes as determiners and prepositions, the structure words that signal grammatical meaning: "*My* boy wants *a* drink *of your* water." One difference between the two kinds of words, then, is meaning.

The characteristic of form, introduced in the chapter on morphemes, is another difference between them. In general, the four form classes are distinguishable by their inflectional suffixes and by certain characteristic derivational suffixes and prefixes. In this chapter we will look at these features of nouns, verbs, adjectives, and adverbs.

NOUNS

We traditionally define *noun* on the basis of meaning, as the *name* of a person, place, thing, idea, event, or the like, and that definition works fairly well. After all, we've been learning names since we spoke our first words: *mama, daddy, cookie, baby*. The word *noun*, in fact, comes from *nomen*, the Latin word for "name."

But in distinguishing nouns from other parts of speech, meaning is only one clue. We also recognize nouns by the words that signal them. When we see a determiner—a word such as *the, my,* or *an*—we know what part of speech will follow, although not necessarily as the next word: *the* books, *my* sister, *an* honest opinion. Determiners are simply not used without nouns. Our third criterion for recognition of nouns, form, is somewhat more objective than the others; we can often differentiate the form classes from each other without reference to either meaning or context, simply on the basis of their derivational and inflectional suffixes.

Noun Derivational Suffixes.   Each of the four form classes has its own inventory of derivational suffixes. The *-ion,* for example, converts the verb *reflect* into a noun, so we call it—or its variations, *-tion, -sion, -cion,* and *-ation*—a noun-forming suffix. A quick check of the dictionary reveals that all the *-ion* words listed on the first few pages are also nouns formed from verbs:

abbreviation	abstraction	accusation
abolition	accommodation	acquisition
abortion	accumulation	action

Examples of *-ion* words that function as both nouns and verbs are *question, partition, mention,* and, yes, *function;* you may be able to think of others. But chances are you will find few, if any, *-ion* words that are not nouns; *-ion* is a reliable signal. Many other derivational suffixes do the same job, that of converting verbs into nouns:

accomplishment	breakage
acceptance	delivery
arrival	departure
assistant	teacher

This variety of noun-forming suffixes that we add to verbs—and, incidentally, there are many more than these—illustrates not only our versatility in changing one part of speech to another but also the sometimes arbitrary way in which we do so. Why, for example, do we say "delivery" and "deliverance" but not "deliverment"? Why "departure" rather than "departation"? Why "deportation" rather than "deporture"? There are no good answers to such questions.

The same arbitrariness runs through all the word classes. For example, many adjectives become nouns with the addition of -*ness:* pretti*ness*, lazi*ness*, strange*ness*, happi*ness*, helpless*ness*. But there is a long list of other suffixes that do the same job: tru*th*, wis*dom*, jus*tice*, partial*ity*. We also have a number of suffixes that simply alter the meaning of the word in one way or another without changing the class: boy*hood*, king*dom*, friend*ship*, Spani*ard*, garden*er*, terror*ism*.

Finally, the nouns *partiality* and *activation* illustrate another feature of derivational suffixes, where a noun-forming suffix is added to a word that already has one or more derivational suffixes:

part + -ial = partial +-ity = partiality
(noun)   *(adj.)*   *(noun)*

act + -ive = active + -ate = activate + -ion = activation
(verb)   *(adj.)*   *(verb)*   *(noun)*

The best-known example of this adding on is that legendary "longest word in English," *antidisestablishmentarianism*. This feature also illustrates another difference between derivational and inflectional suffixes. The inflectional suffixes do not add on in this way. With the exception of the plural and possessive morphemes of nouns, which may appear in combination, the form-class words will have only one inflectional suffix, and it will always come at the end of the word, after any derivational suffixes.

══════ *Exercise 40* ══════

Transform the following verbs into nouns by adding a derivational suffix. Are there any that have more than one noun form?

1. please   + _____ = _____

2. regulate   + _____ = _____

3. steal   + _____ = _____

4. heal   + _____ = _____

5. derive   + _____ = _____

6. inflect   + _____ = _____

7. form   + _____ = _____

8. revive   + _____ = _____

9. seize   + _____ = _____

10. retire   + _____ = _____

Noun Inflectional Suffixes.   The other aspect of form that differentiates the four form classes both from the structure classes and from each other is the set of inflectional morphemes that each form class has. In contrasting English and French verbs in Chapter 3, we saw how relatively free from inflections our verbs are; nouns, too, lack most of the case and gender inflections they once had, variations that make other languages seem so complicated when we study them. Our nouns have only two grammatical inflections, one indicating **number (plural)** and one indicating **case (possessive)**:

SINGULAR	PLURAL	SINGULAR POSSESSIVE	PLURAL POSSESSIVE
cat	cats	cat's	cats'
dog	dogs	dog's	dogs'
horse	horses	horse's	horses'
mouse	mice	mouse's	mice's

The nouns *cat* and *dog* and *horse* illustrate that in speech we can't always distinguish among inflected forms of nouns: *Cats, cat's,* and *cats'* are all pronounced exactly the same. Only in writing can we differentiate the plural from the possessive and from the plural possessive. In the case of *mouse*, with its irregular plural, we of course make the distinction in speech as well as in writing.

The preceding examples illustrate another point about noun inflections: Sometimes the plural inflection is not a single /s/ or /z/ sound, as in *cats* and *dogs*. It may be two sounds, an entire syllable, complete with vowel, as in *horses*. The sound we add is determined by the final sound of the noun. With words ending in what is called a sibilant sound—usually spelled with *s, z, sh, ch, dge*, or *ge*—we must add a syllable to pronounce the -*s* plural (as well as the possessive): kiss*es*, maz*es*, sash*es*, church*es*, judg*es*, pag*es*. (This system is discussed further in Appendix A.)

===== *Exercise 41* =====

The possessive marks are missing from the following noun phrases. Read each one aloud; then punctuate each phrase in two ways to show its two possible meanings.

all my teachers assignments	the horses sore legs
all my teachers assignments	the horses sore legs
my sisters husbands business	my sons problems
my sisters husbands business	my sons problems

Recognizing whether or not the added sound is a complete syllable can be a useful clue in spelling. Spelling the plural and possessive of words that end in an /s/ or /z/ sound is sometimes confusing; they not only sound strange, they tend to look strange when they're written:

Mr. and Mrs. Jones are the Joneses. (*Plural*)
Their cat is the Joneses' cat. (*Possessive*)

To turn *Joneses*, the plural of *Jones*, into the possessive case, we add only the apostrophe because we add no new sound, the usual procedure for possessive plurals: *cats', horses', leaders'*. The possessive of singular nouns ending in *s* can also look strange:

The cats of Ross and Kris are Ross's and Kris's cats.
The nephew of Sis is Sis's nephew.

Here we add the extra syllable when we pronounce the possessive of these words, so we add '*s* when we spell them, the usual procedure for the singular possessive. (We should note that some writers prefer to add only the possessive mark, the apostrophe, even though they add a syllable in speech—*Ross'* and *Kris'* and *Sis';* both spellings are acceptable.) But when the singular has more than one syllable and more than one /s/ or /z/ sound in the last syllable, we generally do not add a sound, so we do not add an *s* when we write the possessive:

> The followers of Jesus are Jesus' followers.
> The laws of Texas are Texas' laws.

A good rule of thumb is this: If the pronunciation does not change when you make a noun possessive, then do not add the *-s* inflection when you spell it; add only the apostrophe. If you're not sure how to pronounce the possessive—whether or not to add a syllable—listen to yourself say the word with that added *-s: the Williams's house* vs. *the Williams' house; Dukakis's running mate* vs. *Dukakis' running mate.* Then use your judgment. If it sounds awkward with the added syllable, then add only the apostrophe. Either choice you make will be "correct."

The plural and possessive inflections provide a test of sorts for "nounness." Can the word be made plural and/or possessive? If so, it's a noun. If not? Well, the possibility for nounness is still there. In applying the inflection test to the nouns in the preceding section, we find that all the words on the *-ion* list can take the plural inflection, but most of them will not take the possessive *-s.* With many nouns the *of* prepositional phrase is more common than the possessive *-s* inflection: In general, the more specific or concrete the sense of the noun, the more likely it is that the inflections will be acceptable.

═══ *Exercise 42* ═══

Transform the *of* possessive phrase into the inflected noun.

   1. The son of Mr. Price is Mr. ＿＿＿＿＿＿ son.

   2. The daughter of Ms. Hedges is Ms. ＿＿＿＿＿＿ daughter.

   3. The computer belonging to James is ＿＿＿＿＿＿ computer.

   4. The governor of Massachusetts is ＿＿＿＿＿＿ governor.

   5. The blanket belonging to Linus is ＿＿＿＿＿＿ blanket.

6. The garden of the neighbor is the _____ garden.

7. The garden of the neighbors is the _____ garden.

8. The curls on the head and tail of Miss Piggy are _____ curls.

9. The club the women belong to is the _____ club.

10. The wisdom of Confucius is _____ wisdom.

The Meaning of the Possessive Case. In the examples we have seen so far, the relationship between the possessive noun and the headword is actually one of possession, or ownership, but such a relationship is not always the case. As the following examples show, the possessive noun can be simply a description:

an evening's entertainment

a bachelor's degree

today's news

It can also be a measure of value or time:

a day's wages

a moment's notice

a dollar's worth

It can denote origin:

the teacher's suggestion

Lincoln's Gettysburg Address

And sometimes the actual relationship is unclear, even in context:

We admired Van Gogh's portrait.

This possessive could refer either to a portrait *of* the artist or to a portrait *by* the artist.

Irregular Plural Inflections.   Before leaving the noun inflections, we should note the many instances of irregular plurals, such as *mice*, in our lexicon. Some are old forms of English that have resisted becoming regularized: *foot–feet, tooth–teeth, man–men, child–children, ox–oxen*. A number of animal and fish names are irregular in that they have no inflection for the plural: *sheep, deer, bass, salmon, trout*. And a large number of borrowed words have retained their foreign plural inflections: *larva–larvae, criterion–criteria, alumnus–alumni, appendix–appendices*. Incidentally, some of these borrowings are now in the process of acquiring regular plurals. *Appendixes* appears along with *appendices; indexes* and *formulas* are even more common than *indices* and *formulae; stadiums* has all but replaced *stadia. Memorandum* is giving way to the shortened *memo*, along with its regular plural, *memos;* and the added complication of gender in *alumnus–alumni* (masculine) and *alumna–alumnae* (feminine) no doubt encourages the use of the simpler, gender-free—and informal—*alum* and *alums*. The borrowed words ending in *-s—analysis–analyses, nucleus–nuclei, hypothesis–hypotheses, stimulus–stimuli*—are less likely to lose their foreign inflections; the addition of *-es* to the singular would be cumbersome.

The irregularity of noun inflections, incidentally, applies only to the plural; the possessive follows the regular rule:

SINGULAR	SINGULAR POSSESSIVE	PLURAL	PLURAL POSSESSIVE
man	man's	men	men's
child	child's	children	children's
deer	deer's	deer	deer's
mouse	mouse's	mice	mice's
larva	larva's	larvae	larvae's

Note that these plural possessives look different from regular plural possessives (*dogs'*), only because for regular plural nouns we don't add an *-s* to make the word possessive; the regular plural already has one.

Plural-Only Forms.   Some nouns, even when singular in meaning, are plural in form. One such group refers to things that are in two parts—that are bifurcated, or branching: *scissors, shears, pliers, pants, trousers, slacks, shorts, glasses, spectacles*. As subjects of sentences, these nouns present no problems with subject–verb agreement: They take the same verb form as other plural subjects do. Interestingly, even though a pair of shorts is a single garment and a pair of pliers is a single tool, we use the plural pronoun in reference to them:

> I bought a new pair of shorts today; they're navy blue.
>
> I've lost my pliers; have you seen them?

A different situation arises with certain plural-in-form nouns that are sometimes singular in meaning. A noun such as *physics, mathematics,* and *linguistics,* when referring to an academic discipline or course, is treated as singular:

> Physics is my favorite subject.
>
> Linguistics is the scientific study of language.

But sometimes such nouns as *mathematics* and *statistics* are used with plural meanings:

> The mathematics involved in the experiment are very theoretical.
>
> The statistics on poverty levels are quite depressing.

These uses also call for plural pronouns.

Collective Nouns.   Nouns such as *family, choir, team, majority, minority*—any noun that names a group of individual members—can be treated as either singular or plural, depending on context and meaning:

> The family *have* all gone their separate ways.
>
> The whole family *is* celebrating the holidays at home this year.
>
> The majority of our city council members *are* Republicans.
>
> The majority always *rules*.

Other singular-in-form nouns, such as *remainder, rest,* and *number,* also have a plural meaning in certain contexts; their number depends on their modifiers:

> The remainder of the job applicants *are* waiting outside.
>
> The rest of the books *are* being donated to the library.
>
> A number of customers *have* come early.

This system also applies to certain indefinite pronouns, such as *some, all,* and *enough:*

> Some of the books *were* missing.
>
> All of the cookies *were* eaten.

Notice what happens to the verb in such sentences when the modifier of the subject headword is singular:

> The rest of the map *was* found.
>
> Some of the water *is* polluted.
>
> All of the cake *was* eaten.
>
> The remainder of this chapter *is* especially important.

The pronoun to use in reference to these noun phrases will depend on the meaning, and it will usually be obvious:

> They (some of the books) *were* missing.
>
> It (some of the water) *is* polluted.

One special problem occurs with the word *none,* which has its origin in the phrase *not one.* Because of that original meaning, many writers insist that *none* always be singular, as *not one* clearly is. However, a more accurate way to assess its meaning is to recognize *none* as the negative, or opposite, of *all* and to treat it in the same way, with its number (whether singular or plural) determined by the number of the modifier or of the referent:

> None of the guests *want* to leave.
>
> None of the cookies *were* left.
>
> None of the cake *was* eaten.
>
> All of the guests *are* staying; none of them *are* leaving.

Semantic Features of Nouns.   Nouns can be classified according to certain built-in semantic features that affect their distribution. At an early age children begin this process of classification, recognizing, for example, whether a noun can be counted. We can say "one cookie" or "two cookies"; but a noun like *milk* is not countable. This understanding is evident in the child's selection of determiners:

> I want milk.
>
> I want a cookie.
>
> I want some milk.

Within a few short years our linguistic computers have been programmed to make distinctions like this among noun classes that we are hardly aware of. The nonnative speaker, on the other hand, must work conscientiously to make such distinctions. The person who says "I need a new luggage" or "I have a lot of homeworks" or "I am looking forward to a peace and quiet this weekend" has not distinguished between **countable** and **noncountable** nouns. Linguists have described these features of our nouns in a hierarchy, each level of which has consequences for selecting determiners and other parts of the sentence:

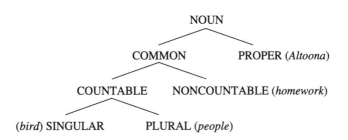

The restrictions built into the word determine its place in the hierarchy; each word carries with it only those features in the higher intersections (or *nodes*) that it is connected with: *Homework* is a noncountable, common noun; *bird* is a singular, countable, common noun. Determiners have related built-in features or restrictions; the determiner *a* (or *an*) includes the features "singular" and "countable," so we are restricted from using it with *homework*. It will signal only those nouns that fit in the lowest, left-hand branch, like *bird*. Some nouns appear in both branches of a node, depending on their meaning. For example, some nouns can be both countable and noncountable:

> I had a strange experience yesterday.
>
> I've had experience working with animals.

I baked a cake today.
I'll have some cake.

The term **proper noun** refers to a noun (or noun phrase) with a specific referent: Empire State Building, Grand Canyon, William Shakespeare, London, "The CBS Evening News," Aunt Mildred, November, Pearl Harbor Day, Thanksgiving. Proper nouns name people, geographic regions and locations, buildings, events, holidays, months, and days of the week; they are usually written with initial capital letters. Although most proper nouns are singular, exceptions occur in the case of mountain ranges and island groups—the Rockies, the Andes, the Falklands—which are plural.

Our store of words, or **lexicon**, is like a dictionary marked with restrictions and features that define each entry. The definitions not only carry information about the meaning of words, they carry information about the other parts of the sentence with which the word may be combined.

═══ Investigating Language 11.1 ═══

A careful writer would avoid writing sentences like these two:

*There have been less bicycle accidents in the county this year.
*I have also noticed an increase in the amount of bicycles on the roads.

But there's no problem with these:

There are fewer students enrolled in the advanced ceramics class this year.
There is an increase in the number of students enrolled in the beginning course.

Think about where in the noun hierarchy on page 285 you would find *accidents*, *bicycles*, *students*, and *attention*. How would a careful writer revise those first two sentences? If you were helping a nonnative speaker revise those sentences, how would you explain the changes?
Would that careful writer avoid any of these?

There were less than a dozen bicycle accidents in the county this year.
We had fewer accidents than last year.

We have less dollars than we need.
We have less money than we need.
We have less than ten dollars to last until payday.

You probably gave that nonnative speaker some advice about the use of *less/fewer* and *amount of/number of*. Should you revise your explanation? In what way?

<hr />

VERBS

The traditional definition of *verb*, like that of *noun*, is based on meaning: a word denoting action, being, or state of being. When we look for the verb in a sentence, we look for the word that tells *what is happening*, and most of the time this method works. But a much more reliable criterion for defining *verb* is that of form. Some verbs have derivational endings that signal that they are verbs; and all verbs, without exception, fit into the verb-expansion rule, the system of adding auxiliaries and inflections described in Chapter 3.

  Verb Derivational Affixes.   Many of the root words, or bases, that take noun-forming suffixes are verbs to begin with; for example, most of our nouns with *-ion* are formed from verbs. The opposite operation— deriving verbs from other form classes—is less common. We are more likely to turn a noun into a verb without changing its form at all, a process known as **functional shift**—in other words, shifting the function of the word. We *chair* meetings and *table* motions; the carpenter *roofs* the house; the cook *dishes* up the food; the painter *coats* the wall with paint; the gardener *seeds* the lawn and *weeds* the garden; we *butter* the *bread*, *bread* the *chicken*—and who among us hasn't *chickened out* at one time or another?

  But we also have a few verb-forming affixes that combine with certain nouns and adjectives:

  typi<u>fy</u>   dar<u>ken</u>   activ<u>ate</u>   legal<u>ize</u>

In addition to these suffixes, the prefixes *en-* and *be-* and *de-* and *dis-* can turn nouns and adjectives into verbs and can alter the meaning of other verbs: *enable, enact, enchant, encounter, encourage, encrust, endear, enforce, enlighten, enthrone, bedevil, bewitch, besmirch, dethrone, derail, disable.* But compared with the large number of derivational morphemes that signal nouns, the inventory of verb-forming affixes is fairly small.

Verb Inflectional Suffixes.   The verb-expansion rule describes the system of adding auxiliaries and inflectional suffixes to all verbs, without exception. So as a clue in identifying the part of speech we call *verb*, the inflectional system is completely reliable. All verbs, without exception—even those with irregular *-en* and *-ed* forms—have both *-s* and *-ing* forms. This is one of the few rules in English without an exception. This means we can identify a word as a verb simply by noting its *-s* and *-ing* forms. Every verb has the other three forms as well—the base, the *-ed* and the *-en*—but they may not be as recognizable: Verbs such as *hit* and *put*, for instance, show no changes in form from the base (*hit, put*) to the *-ed* form (*hit, put*) to the *-en* form (*hit, put*); others include *cast, hurt, shut, split,* and *spread.* Yet the *-s* and the *-ing* forms are exactly like those of every other verb: *hits, puts, hitting, putting.* The verb inflectional system is so regular, in fact, that we can define *verb* on that basis alone. A word that doesn't have an *-s* or an *-ing* form is simply not a verb.

===== *Exercise 43* =====

Add inflectional endings to demonstrate the "verb-ness" of the following words; then write a sentence using the form of the verb called for. Remember that the *-en* form will follow the auxiliary *have*. And if you begin your sentence with *yesterday*, you'll automatically use the *-ed* form.

BASE	-s FORM	-ed FORM	-ing FORM	-en FORM
1. GROUND	_____	_____	_____	_____
(-ed)				
2. WATER	_____	_____	_____	_____
(-s)				

3. AIR _____ _____ _____ _____

(-*ing*) _____

4. FIRE _____ _____ _____ _____

(-*en*) _____

ADJECTIVES

In terms of form, adjectives are not as easily identifiable in isolation as are nouns and verbs. Often we need either meaning or context for clues. In Chapter 2 we made use of a fairly reliable "adjective test" frame, a way to use the context of a sentence to discover if a word is an adjective:

The _____ NOUN is very _____.

Only an adjective will fit into both slots. But in some cases the form of the word also provides clues. A number of derivational suffixes signal adjectives.

Adjective Derivational Suffixes. The most reliable derivational suffix identifying a word as an adjective is -*ous*; we know that *gorgeous, famous, porous, courageous,* and *contagious* are adjectives simply on the basis of form. Here are some other adjective-forming suffixes:

merry, funny	childish, reddish
beautiful, wonderful	fragmentary, complimentary
terrific, ascetic	punitive, active
fortunate, temperate	variable, amenable

As clues to adjectives, these suffixes are not as reliable as -*ous* because they show up occasionally on other form classes too: hand*ful* (noun), pan*ic* (noun, verb), pun*ish* (verb). But it is safe to say that most words with these endings are adjectives.

Adjective Inflectional Suffixes. The inflectional suffixes that pattern with adjectives are -*er*, the sign of the comparative degree, and -*est*, the superlative:

Positive:	big	young	smart
Comparative:	bigger	younger	smarter
Superlative:	biggest	youngest	smartest

The *-er* form is used in the comparison of two nouns—that's why this form is called the **comparative** degree:

> Pat is <u>younger</u> than Phyllis.
> Phyllis is the <u>smarter</u> of the two.

The comparative degree with *than* can also be followed by a clause rather than a noun phrase:

> Pat is younger <u>than I suspected</u>.

The *-est* form, the **superlative** degree, is used when singling out one of more than two nouns:

> Tom was the <u>oldest</u> person in the room.
> Of the three candidates, Sarah is the <u>smartest</u>.

For many adjectives the comparative and superlative degrees are not formed with *-er* and *-est* but with *more* and *most*, which we can think of as alternative forms, or allomorphs, of the morphemes *-er* and *-est*. In fact, adjectives of more than one syllable generally pattern with *more* and *most*, with certain exceptions: two-syllable adjectives ending in *-y* or *-ly* (*prettiest, friendlier, lovelier*); some ending in *-le* (*nobler, noblest*), *-ow* (*narrower, narrowest*), and *-er* (*tenderest*).

But *more* and *most* are not exclusive to adjectives either. The *-ly* adverbs, those derived from adjectives, also have comparative and superlative versions: *more quickly, most frequently*. And there are some adjectives, such as *former, main,* and *principal*, that have no comparative and superlative forms.

A small group of words that have comparative and superlative forms can serve as either adjectives or adverbs, so the inflectional test is not completely reliable in identifying a word as an adjective:

early	fast	late	high
earlier	faster	later	higher
earliest	fastest	latest	highest

hard	long	low	deep
harder	longer	lower	deeper
hardest	longest	lowest	deepest

Another word we could add to this list is *near* (*nearer, nearest*), which can serve not only as an adjective and an adverb, but also as a preposition ("Our seats were *near* the fifty-yard line")—the only preposition that takes inflections. In short, the possibility of making a word comparative or superlative is not exclusive to adjectives.

In spite of all these limitations, we have no difficulty distinguishing adjectives in sentences. First, we know the positions they fill in the sentence patterns—as subjective and objective complements and in noun phrases as prenoun modifiers. And although nouns can also fill all these slots, the differences in the form of nouns and adjectives make it easy to distinguish between them.

On the subject of the comparative and superlative degrees, we should also note that adjectives can be compared in a negative sense with *as, less,* and *least:*

> This picnic is not <u>as exciting as</u> I thought it would be.
>
> This picnic is <u>less exciting than</u> I thought it would be.
>
> This is the <u>least exciting</u> picnic I've ever attended.

(A different version of the first sentence would be "The picnic is *about as exciting as* I expected" or, simply, "The picnic is *as exciting as* I expected," both of which may convey a somewhat negative meaning.)

We should also note some exceptions to the regular comparative and superlative forms:

good	bad	far	far
better	worse	farther	further
best	worst	farthest	furthest

===== *Exercise 44* =====

Fill in the blanks with the comparative and superlative degrees of the adjectives listed. Do any of them require *more* and *most*?

POSITIVE	COMPARATIVE	SUPERLATIVE
friendly	_____	_____
helpful	_____	_____
wise	_____	_____
awful	_____	_____
rich	_____	_____
mellow	_____	_____
expensive	_____	_____
valid	_____	_____
pure	_____	_____
able	_____	_____

Subclasses of Adjectives. The adjective test frame, which you saw in Chapter 2 (The _____ **NOUN** is very _____), is useful in identifying adjectives. It is also useful in helping distinguish subclasses of adjectives: those that are limited to the prenoun slot and those that are limited to the complement slots.

Adjectives actually fill three slots in the sentence patterns: as subjective and objective complements (where they are called **predicative** adjectives) and as modifiers in the noun phrase (where they are called **attributive** adjectives). Most adjectives can fill all three slots; the test frame uses two of them: attributive and subjective complements.

But a small number will not fill the complement slots. The following adjectives are attributive only: *main, principal, former, mere, potential, atomic, late* (meaning "dead"), and such technical adjectives as *sulfuric* and *hydrochloric.* These do not serve as either subjective or objective complements in the verb phrase, nor do they take qualifiers, such as *very:*

He is the former president.
*The president is former.

*My reason is main.

*My main reason is very main.

She is a mere child.

*The child is mere.

Many of the so-called A-adjectives—*ablaze, afraid, aghast, alone, awake*—are predicative only:

The house was ablaze.

*The ablaze house burned down in an hour.

The children were awake.

*The awake children were noisy.

There are a few others—*fond, ready, ill, well*—that rarely appear in attributive position in reference to animate nouns. We may refer to a "ready wit" but rarely to a "ready person." We may talk about an "ill omen" but rarely an "ill person"; we are more likely to say a "sick person."

Incidentally, not all predicative adjectives take *very*, the sample qualifier in the test frame. We probably wouldn't say "very afraid" or "very awake"; we would be more likely to say "very much afraid" or "very much awake." But these adjectives do combine with other qualifiers: *quite* afraid, *extremely* afraid, *completely* awake, *wide* awake.

A number of adjectives in predicative position appear frequently with complements in the form of phrases or clauses; some adjectives, such as *fond* and *aware*, are rarely used without them:

The children were afraid that the dog would bite.

The children were aware that the dog would bite.

The committee was certain that the rally would be a success.

The dog was fond of biting children.

We were conscious of the problem.

*The dog was fond.

He was crazy to jog on such a hot day.

Our team is certain to win.

We call these *complements* rather than, simply, modifiers or qualifiers because they complete the idea expressed by the adjective, in much the same way that direct objects are complements of verbs.

Another subclassification of adjectives relates to their ability to combine with qualifiers. Certain adjectives denote meanings that are **absolute** in nature: *unique, round, square, perfect, single, double.* These can fill both the attributive and predicate slots, but they generally cannot be qualified or compared. We can, of course, say "almost perfect" or "nearly square," but most writers avoid "more perfect" or "very perfect." In the case of *unique*, it has come to mean "rare" or "unusual," in which case "very unique" would be comparable to "very unusual." However, given the historical meaning "one of a kind," the qualified "very unique" makes no sense.

ADVERBS

Of all the form classes, adverbs are the hardest to pin down in terms of both form and position. Many of them have no distinguishing affixes, and except in Pattern I they fill no required slots in the sentence patterns. (Certain verbs in Patterns VI and VII, however—among them, *lay, put, place,* and *set*—often require adverbials.) The fact that adverbs are often movable is perhaps their most distinguishing characteristic.

Adverb Derivational Suffixes.   One common indicator of form we do have is the derivational suffix *-ly*, which we use to derive adverbs of manner from adjectives—adverbs that tell *how* or *in what way* about the verb:

> He walked <u>slowly</u>.
> She answered <u>correctly</u>.

But *-ly* is not completely reliable as a signaler of adverbs; it also occurs on nouns (*folly*) and on adjectives (*lovely, ugly*). But we are safe in saying that most *-ly* words are adverbs, simply because there are so many adjectives that we can turn into adverbs with this addition.

There are some restrictions on this derivational process, however: Not all adjectives can become manner adverbs. These restrictions are related to meaning. Some adjectives describe a state, such as *tall* and *old*, or a fixed or inherent characteristic, such as *Norwegian;* others describe characteristics that change, such as *weak, active,* and *industrious.* Another distinction can be drawn between objective characteristics, such as *tall* and *old,* and subjective ones, such as *nice* and *splendid.* The adjectives that refer to objective or stative or inherent qualities rarely become manner adverbs: *tall, old, fat, young, short, thick, large, flat, round, red.* When they do, they are likely to have a specialized, often metaphorical, meaning: *shortly, hardly, flatly, squarely, widely.*

Besides *-ly,* two other derivational suffixes produce adverbs: *-ward* and *-wise.* Words ending in *-ward* signal direction: *homeward, forward, backward, upward, downward.* Words ending in *-wise,* which indicate manner, include both old usages, such as *otherwise, lengthwise,* and *crosswise,* and new ones that are considered by some writers as unnecessary jargon, such as *budgetwise, weatherwise, moneywise,* and *profitwise.*

===== *Investigating Language 11.2* =======

One of our most reliable derivational suffixes is *-ly.* In most cases the message it sends is "adverb of manner": *Quickly* means "in a quick manner," and *slowly* means "in a slow manner." But, as with most rules in our language, there are exceptions to both parts of that message—both the "adverb" part and the "of manner" part.

Consider the *-ly* words in the following sentences. Are they adverbs? Are they adjectives? Could they be nouns or verbs?

1. We're leaving immediately and driving directly to Austin.
2. Bob will be leaving directly.
3. The natives around here are not always friendly.
4. One person I met tried to bully me.
5. He wasn't particularly neighborly.
6. My sister is uncommonly beautiful.
7. My brother, on the other hand, is rather homely.
8. Shedding tears is not considered manly.
9. That is hardly a universal belief, however.
10. My belly aches, but I flatly refuse to stay home.

Use your understanding of form to test these *-ly* words. Remember the inflectional paradigms for nouns and verbs; remember the "seems" test for adjectives. And is it possible that *-ly* adverbs have a meaning other than manner? Use your intuition, too!

Adverb Inflectional Suffixes. The comparative and superlative inflections, *-er* and *-est*, combine with adverbs as well as with adjectives, although in a much more limited way. The comparative form of *-ly* adverbs, usually formed by adding *more* rather than *-er*, is fairly common. The superlative degree—*most* suddenly, *most* favorably—is rare enough in both speech and writing to have impact when used; it invariably calls attention to itself, and in most cases will have the main focus and main stress of the sentence:

> The committee was most favorably impressed with the proposal.
> The crime was planned most ingeniously.

In the discussion of adjectives, we listed a few words that serve as both adjectives and adverbs: *early, late, hard, fast, long, high, low, deep,* and *near.* These are simply adverbs made from adjectives without the addition of *-ly;* they are referred to as **flat adverbs.** Except for a few others such as *soon* and *often,* they are the only adverbs that take *-er* and *-est;* most of the *-ly* adverbs take *more* and, occasionally, *most* in forming the comparative and superlative degrees.

A great many adverbs have neither derivational nor inflectional affixes that distinguish them as adverbs. Instead, we recognize them by the information they provide, by their position in the sentence, and often by their movability:

Time:	now, today, nowadays, yesterday
Duration:	already, always, still, yet
Frequency:	often, seldom, never, sometimes, always
Place:	there, here, everywhere, somewhere, elsewhere, upstairs
Direction:	away, thence

Concession: still, yet
Sequence: afterward, next, then

There are also a number of words without form distinctions that can serve as either prepositions or adverbs: *above, around, behind, below, down, in, inside, out, outside, up.*

===== *Investigating Language 11.3* =====

Here's a sentence with a message you may not understand:

The frabous gricks were brocking my miktations very botly.

As you see, it's filled with nonsense words. But even though the sentence has no semantic, or dictionary, meaning, it still sounds like English. It has structural meaning. In fact, you can probably figure out the classes of the separate words as well as the sentence pattern. Identify the derivational and inflectional clues that enable you to do so.

Noun(s):

Verb(s):

Adjective(s):

Adverbs(s):

The traditional definitions of *noun* (the name of a person, place, or thing) and *verb* (a word showing action) won't help you out here. Write new definitions based on those clues you identified.

Noun:_____

_____

Verb:_____

_____

===== *Exercise 45* =====

Fill in the blanks with variations of the words shown on the chart, changing or adding derivational morphemes to change the word class.

	NOUN	VERB	ADJECTIVE	ADVERB
1.	grief			
2.		vary		
3.				ably
4.		defend		
5.	economy			
6.			pleasant	
7.	type			
8.		prohibit		
9.				critically
10.			valid	
11.		appreciate		
12.	beauty			
13.		accept		
14.			pure	
15.		continue		

KEY TERMS IN CHAPTER 11

Absolute adjective
Adjective
Adjective complement
Adjective derivational suffix
Adjective inflectional suffix
Adverb
Adverb derivational suffix
Adverb inflectional suffix
Attributive adjective
Case

Collective noun
Common noun
Comparative degree
Countable noun
Flat adverb
Form classes
Functional shift
Indefinite pronoun
Noncountable noun
Noun

Noun derivational suffix	Predicative adjective
Noun inflectional suffix	Proper noun
Number	Superlative degree
Plural	Verb
Plural-only noun	Verb derivational suffix
Positive degree	Verb inflectional suffix
Possessive	

QUESTIONS FOR DISCUSSION

1. A government spokesperson recently used the following clauses in a discussion of the economy:

> When we were approaching crunch. . . .
> When push comes to shove. . . .

What part of speech are *crunch, push,* and *shove*?

2. In response to a question about Egypt's agreement with Israel, President Sadat made the following statement:

> Some parts we're not very glad with, and some we'd like to see with different languages.

What particular "rules" was he having trouble with? In what way do those problems illustrate the arbitrariness of English?

3. L. L. Bean's catalog offers "a fine wool pant" for sale. The dictionary lists *pant* only as an adjective, as in "pant leg." Do you think the noun *pant* will catch on? Why do you suppose the catalog writers changed the word's place in the hierarchy?

4. The traditional Latin term for possessive case is *genitive*. Consider the relationship between the possessive noun and its headword in the following noun phrases:

> the teacher's explanation
> the car's overhaul

Explain what is meant by *subjective genitive* and *objective genitive*.
   Now consider the following ambiguous sentence:

I was disturbed about Tom's punishment.

What is the source of the ambiguity?

5. We looked briefly at adjectives that pattern with complements:

We were <u>conscious</u> of the problem.

The kids were <u>afraid</u> that they would miss the party.

Joe is <u>determined</u> to win the race.

The dog was <u>fond</u> of biting children.

What do these adjectives have in common? Tell which of the following adjectives will pattern with complements: *young, big, pretty, green, slow, nice, splendid, British, disgusting, tired, cylindrical*. What generalization can you make about the system?

6. We often use verbs adjectivally, as noun modifiers, as you saw in Chapter 7. But many words that look like verbs—that were, in fact, originally verbs—now have the characteristics of adjectives. We have said that we can identify a word as an adjective if it can fit into the adjective test frame (The _____ NOUN is very _____). We also have an inflectional test for adjectives: Can the word be made comparative and superlative? Using these two tests, identify the underlined words in the following sentences: Are they adjectives or verbs?

Joe took the <u>broken</u> chair to the dump.

That <u>disgusting</u> movie wasn't worth five dollars.

The football rally was <u>exciting</u>.

I feel <u>tired</u>.

Joe was <u>drunk</u> last night.

Many <u>working</u> mothers have problems with day-care.

The <u>decorated</u> tree looks beautiful.

7. Sometimes verbs are used as nouns (gerunds), as you saw in Chapter 4. What test can you apply to the following words to test their part of speech? Are they verbs or nouns?

The <u>meeting</u> was boring.

Julie looked lovely at her <u>wedding</u>.

The committee's <u>finding</u> surprised everyone.

<u>Jogging</u> is good exercise.

8. Explain the ambiguity of the following sentences in terms of their possible sentence patterns and parts of speech:

My mother is always entertaining.
They are frightening people.

9. In the discussion questions following Chapter 3, we applied the terms *volition* and *nonvolition*—i.e., the power of choice—to adjectives. The adjective *careless* describes a condition under control of the will; such conditions as *short* and *tall*, on the other hand, cannot be willed. Can this distinction also be useful in describing the restrictions on deriving adverbs from adjectives? Which adjectives can or cannot take *-ly*?

10. Shakespeare, as you know, used language in all sorts of original ways. Here are two lines from *Romeo and Juliet*. What has he done with word classes?

Thank me no thankings nor proud me no prouds.
O flesh, flesh, how art thou fishified!

11. The dictionary labels *today* as both an adverb and a noun. Are those labels based on form or function? How should we define *yesterday* and *tomorrow*? Are they also members of both classes? Examine the following passage from *Macbeth* to see how Shakespeare used the words:

Tomorrow, and tomorrow, and tomorrow
Creeps in this petty pace from day to day
To the last syllable of recorded time,
And all our yesterdays have lighted fools
The way to dusty death.

12. And here are two lines from Groucho Marx, who also had a way with words:

Time flies like an arrow.
Fruit flies like a banana.

Use your understanding of both sentence patterns and word classes to explain the joke.

13. Nothing is more confusing to nonnative speakers just learning English than some of our idiomatic expressions. Explain why someone might have trouble understanding these expressions:

> I'll be right there.
> Never mind.
> You need self-confidence.
> Won't you please come.

14. In meeting a very tall person, you might ask the question, "How tall are you?" Strangely enough, we would ask the same question of a short person: We don't usually ask, "How short are you?" In this pair of adjectives, *tall* is called the unmarked version. Think of other adjectives we use for quantity or size or age or speed: *old/young, big/little, heavy/light, fast/slow*. Does our usage suggest a marked and unmarked version? Under what circumstances would we use the other?

CHAPTER
12
The Structure Classes

In contrast to the large, open form classes, the categories of words known as structure classes are small and, for the most part, closed. Although new words regularly enter the language as nouns and verbs as the need arises for new vocabulary, the structure classes—conjunctions, prepositions, auxiliaries, and the like—remain constant from one generation to the next. As native speakers, we pay little attention to the structure words, and until we hear a nonnative speaker struggling with them, we probably don't appreciate the importance of the grammatical sense that they contribute.

Part of that grammatical sense comes from the stress–unstress pattern of speech, the rhythm of the language. Most structure words are unstressed: They have the lowest volume, providing valleys between the peaks of loudness that fall on the stressed syllables of the form-class words. One reason we must listen so carefully in order to understand the inexperienced foreign speaker—and often the experienced one as well—is the breakdown of that signaling system. When structure words are given equal stress, their role as signaler tends to be lost.

The first three structure classes we will look at are those that signal specific form classes: determiners, the signalers of nouns; auxiliaries, the signalers of verbs; and qualifiers, the signalers of adjectives and adverbs. Then we will look at prepositions and conjunctions, both of which have connective roles; interrogatives, the signalers of questions; and expletives, which serve as structural operators of various kinds.

DETERMINERS

This section of the book, "Words and Word Classes," opened with a sentence lacking all of the structure words: *Boy needs drink water.* Most noticeably missing are the determiners, the signalers of nouns.

The **determiner** class is one of the structure classes that straddle the line between a word class and a function. On the one hand, our most common determiners, the articles, do indeed constitute a small, closed structure class. At the other end of the spectrum are the possessive nouns, which function as determiners while retaining their membership in the open class "noun." In between are the subclasses of determiners that belong to the closed pronoun class: Demonstrative, possessive, and indefinite pronouns all function as determiners; and, of course, as pronouns they also function as nominals (in fact, "pronominal" would be a more accurate label than "pronoun").

Determiners signal nouns in a variety of ways: They may define the *relationship* of the noun to the speaker or listener (or reader); they may identify the noun as *specific* or *general*; they may *quantify* it specifically or refer to quantity in general. Following are the most common classes of determiners, many of which have appeared in our sample sentences:

ARTICLES	POSSESSIVE NOUNS	DEMONSTRATIVE PRONOUNS	NUMBERS
the	John's	this/these	one
a(n)	my son's	that/those	two
	etc.		etc.

POSSESSIVE PRONOUNS			INDEFINITE PRONOUNS		
my	its	several	few	each	all
your	our	little	fewer	every	both
his	their	many	more	either	some
her	whose	much	most	neither	any
		enough	less	no	

We should note that possessive nouns as determiners retain their own determiners: *my daughter's* teacher; *the week's* groceries; *our cat's* fur.

Many of the features of nouns in the hierarchy shown on page 285 affect our selection of determiners. A noun appearing in the lowest, left-hand branch of the diagram, for example—a singular, countable noun—rarely appears without a determiner:

This cookie tastes good.

*Cookie tastes good.

John is my friend.

*John is friend.

There are certain exceptions to this rule. For example, the nouns *town*, *school*, and *car* are singular, countable nouns; nevertheless, in some prepositional phrases they appear without determiners:

the other side of town

going to school

the best kind of car

These exceptions present no problems for native speakers, of course. We're used to the sometimes arbitrary nature of the determiner:

We say, "I walked to town," but not "I walked to city."
We say, "I have a cold," but not "I have a flu."
We say, "I attend college," but not "I attend university."
We say, "I'm going into town," but not "I'm going into hospital."

(The British and Australians, incidentally, do "go into hospital," "attend university," and "look out of window.")

The difficulty for the nonnative speaker comes with learning which nouns are countable nouns and which are not. Other complications arise in selecting the determiners because, like all the words in our lexicon, determiners have built-in restrictions. Some will signal only plural nouns (*these, those, many, few, several*), some only singular nouns (*a, one, each, either, neither, every*), some only noncountables (*much, less*), and others only countables (*few, many, a, one*).

Another fairly regular rule concerns the limitation of determiners with certain noncountable nouns, sometimes called **mass nouns,** such as *luggage, furniture, beer, cake, sugar, rice, coal, steel, water*. When mass nouns are used as noncountable, they cannot be plural, so they do not combine with determiners that have either the "plural" or "countable" feature: *a, one, two, these, several, many.*

> *These furniture are sturdy.
>
> *Many furnitures are expensive.
>
> *Each furniture has its own charm.

Some determiners have both countable and noncountable features built into them (*this, some, most, all*), so they can combine with both kinds of nouns:

> This furniture is lovely.
>
> This chair is comfortable.
>
> Some furniture is expensive.
>
> Some chairs are expensive.
>
> Most chocolate cake is high in calories.
>
> Most coconut macaroons are delicious.
>
> All polluted water is undrinkable.
>
> Not all rules are necessarily good rules.

The nonnative speaker must consciously learn these features of both nouns and determiners. But a further complication arises when these mass nouns take on countable meanings:

> These whole-grain flours are popular now.
>
> The light beers are getting better all the time.

Abstract nouns also present problems for the nonnative speaker because they may appear either with or without determiners:

> I have finally regained peace of mind.
>
> I have finally regained my peace of mind.

In some cases the determiner is tied to the presence of a modifier, such as a *that* clause:

> *The peace of mind is hard to acquire in these insecure times.
>
> The peace of mind that comes with financial security is my goal.

Even a proper noun may require a determiner when it has certain kinds of modifiers:

The Altoona of my childhood was a railroad town.

And for some inexplicable reason, the article *a* changes the meaning in sentences with *few* and *little*:

I have few friends.	I've had little trouble with my car.
I have a few friends.	I've had a little trouble with my car.

Finally, some determiners are extremely versatile. The **definite article,** *the,* can signal all classes of nouns that can take determiners when the definite meaning is called for—unlike the **indefinite** *a,* which is restricted to countables. The possessives, too—both nouns and pronouns—are wide-ranging, without built-in distribution restrictions.

===== *Exercise 46* =====

Underline the determiners in the following sentences.

1. My sister doesn't have enough money for her ticket.
2. John's roommate went home for the weekend.
3. Every course I'm taking this term has a midterm exam.
4. Bill spent more money on the week's groceries than he expected to.
5. I spend less time studying now than I did last term.
6. I haven't seen either movie, so I have no preference.

The Expanded Determiner.   A determiner is not always a single word. In fact, we can think of the determiner slot itself as a series of slots with optional pre- and postdeterminers. The following formula will account for some fairly common **expanded determiners,** although a description that accounted for all the possibilities would be far more complex. This simplified scheme, however, should help you appreciate the intricacies of the grammar rules built into your linguistic computer.

(predeterminer) + DETERMINER + (postdeterminer)

		ORDINAL NUMBERS	CARDINAL NUMBERS
all (of)	the	first	one
both (of)	a	second	two
half (of)	my	etc.	etc.
only	these	next	
especially	etc.	last	
just			
double			

The pre- and postdeterminers are, of course, optional, so they are shown in parentheses in the formula.

In the following sentences, the pre- and postdeterminers are underlined; the determiner is written with capital letters:

All of THE cookies disappeared.

Only MY pretzels disappeared.

THE first ten students in line were chosen.

Only THE next two students complained.

Both (of) THESE students wrote A papers.

Half (of) THE class took part in the demonstration.

I have just ENOUGH gas for the trip.

Another type of expanded determiner is the phrasal quantifier; it can occur with either countable or noncountable nouns:

a lot of classes

a lot of homework

a great many friends

a large number of people

In terms of **subject–verb agreement,** it is the number of the noun—whether singular or plural—that determines the verb: homework *is;* classes (friends, people) *are.*

We also have a large open class of quantifying noun phrases that we use with noncountable nouns; they enable us to count those noncountables:

<u>a quart of</u> milk
<u>a pound of</u> butter
<u>a piece of</u> furniture
<u>a spoonful of</u> sugar

When these noun phrases are subjects, their number is determined by the number of the quantifier: *two quarts* of milk *are; a quart* of milk *is*. We might, in fact, be tempted to call the quantifiers the headwords of these noun phrases, just as we would call *end* and *back* the headwords in the following:

the end of the alley
the back of my hand

The traditional diagram would, in fact, treat these noun phrases and those with the quantifiers in the same way, with the *of* phrase as a modifier of the noun, even though the quantifiers are much more clearly functioning as determiners.

Despite such questions of analysis, however, native speakers know intuitively how to follow these determiner "rules," as complicated and arbitrary as they sometimes are.

AUXILIARIES

Like the determiners and the other structure classes, the **auxiliary** class is limited in membership and closed to new members. Counting the forms of *have* and *be*, the modals, and the forms of *do*, the list of regular auxiliaries numbers around two dozen:

have	be	can	do
has	is	could	does
had	are	will	did
having	am	would	
	was	shall	
	were	should	
	been	may	
	being	might	
		must	
		ought to	

The following modal-like verbs also function as auxiliaries; they are sometimes referred to as semi-auxiliaries.

have to	get	keep
has to	gets	keeps
had to	got	kept
be to	be going to	used to

He has to go.	I used to smoke.
She got started.	The bus is to leave at noon.
She got to go.	I'm going to take the bus.
They kept going.	

Two other modal-like verbs, *dare* and *need*, commonly appear in negative sentences and in questions:

She need not go.	Dare we go?
I don't dare go.	Need you go?

The auxiliaries differ somewhat from the other classes of structure words in both form and function. With only two exceptions, *must* and *ought to*, the auxiliaries have inflectional variations that signal changes in meaning. Because *have* and *be*, our most frequently used auxiliaries, can also fill the verb slot, they of course have all the usual verb inflections. *Be* has even more than usual, with its eight forms. Even the stand-in auxiliary *do* and the other marginal modals undergo inflectional variations in their auxiliary roles. So in terms of their form, auxiliaries are very much like the form-class words.

In function, the auxiliaries are perhaps more intimately connected to verbs than are determiners to nouns, because they alter the verb's meaning in important ways and often determine the form that it takes. Forms of *have* require the *-en* form of the main verb and forms of *be* the *-ing* form—or, in the case of the passive transformation, the *-en* form (see Chapter 3).

Another important difference between the auxiliaries and the other structure classes lies in their systematic distribution. Determiners and qualifiers are somewhat arbitrary in distribution; but with few exceptions every verb can be signaled (preceded) by every auxiliary. The modals *have* and *do* combine with every verb; only *be* is restricted in any way, as we saw in Chapter 3, where we noted a few verbs, such as *seem*, that rarely appear with *be* + *-ing*. This regularity accounts for the relative ease with which nonnative speakers are able to learn the compound verb forms of English.

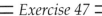

=== *Exercise 47* ===

Underline the auxiliaries in the following sentences. Circle the main verb.

1. I have been having problems with my car.
2. Many women don't dare walk alone in this neighborhood after dark.
3. I should not have eaten tomatoes.
4. Apparently some people can't even look at them.
5. Sally will be helping us with the party.
6. Margie has to leave early.
7. The kids are really frustrating me today.
8. The teens can be frustrating years for some adolescents.
9. The gymnasts should keep practicing their balance-beam routines.
10. I am keeping my opinions to myself.

QUALIFIERS

As the following lists demonstrate, many words can act as **qualifiers** or **intensifiers** to alter the meaning of adjectives and adverbs. (In the adjective test frame the word *very* is used to represent all the possible qualifiers.) On the diagram the qualifier is attached to the adjective or adverb:

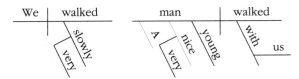

The following list of qualifers can be used with the positive form of most adjectives, such as *good* and *soft*, and with adverbs of manner, such as *rapidly*:

very	really	fairly
quite	pretty	mighty
rather	awfully	too

A second group of qualifiers can be used with the comparative degree of adjectives, such as *better* and *nicer*, and with comparative adverbs, such as *sooner, later, nearer,* and *farther*:

still	some	no
even	much	

And there are a number of others that have a limited distribution:

right now	just about there
wide awake	almost there
just so	

Many others are used in colloquial expressions:

right nice	darn right
damn sure	real pretty

Some of the adverbs of manner, the *-ly* adverbs, are themselves used as qualifiers with certain adjectives:

dangerously close	politically expedient
particularly harmful	technically possible
absolutely true	especially difficult

Because of the *-ly* adverbs in their ranks, the qualifier class, like that of the determiners, is not a closed class.

=== *Investigating Language 12.1* ===

You may recall that the title of Chapter 6 includes a definition of *adverbial*: "Modifiers of the Verb." And the discussion in that chapter takes you through the various forms that modify verbs—adverbs, prepositional phrases, noun phrases, verb phrases, and clauses. Note that the form-class "adverb" is one of five structures that function adverbially.

Now compare that definition with the traditional definition of *adverb*—one you may be familiar with: "a word that modifies a verb, an adjective, or another adverb." This definition clearly includes what we are calling qualifiers—that is, words that modify adjectives and adverbs.

Consider what you have learned about the form classes—nouns, verbs, adjectives, and adverbs; add to that what you know about structures that modify verbs—the adverbials. Then examine the following sentences, some of which are marked as ungrammatical:

> Quite slowly the old man climbed the stairs.
> *The old man quite climbed the stairs.
> *The old man slowly climbed the stairs quite.
> The girl is very young.
> That very young girl is coming over to babysit.
> That young girl is coming over soon.
> *That soon young girl is coming over very.

At this point you probably agree that these sentences suggest a difference between adverbs and qualifiers that justifies their membership in different classes. Three other words that are traditionally classified as adverbs are *quite*, *rather*, and *so*. Write several sentences to illustrate their use in sentences. Can you justify retaining them as members of the adverb class?

In their relationship to the form classes, the qualifiers are different from the determiners and auxiliaries in that they are optional; all the adjectives and adverbs they modify can appear without them. This is not true of the relationship of nouns and verbs to their signal words: Many nouns cannot appear without a determiner; and two of our verb forms—the *-en* and the *-ing* forms—require auxiliaries to function as the main verb. But like the other structure words, the qualifiers signal the form classes; they provide a useful test to differentiate adjectives and adverbs from other parts of speech.

PREPOSITIONS

The **preposition** (meaning "placed before") is a structure word found in pre-position to—preceding—a noun phrase or other nominal. Prepositions are among our most common words in English; in fact, of our twenty most frequently used words, eight are prepositions: *of, to, in, for, with, on, at,* and *by*.[1] Prepositions can be classified according to form as simple (one-word) or phrasal (multiple-word):

Simple Prepositions.   The following list includes the most common simple prepositions:

aboard	below	in	since
about	beneath	into	through
above	beside	like	throughout
across	between	near	till
after	beyond	of	to
against	but (except)	off	toward
along	by	on	under
amid	concerning	onto	underneath
among	despite	out	until
around	down	outside	up
as	during	over	upon
at	except	past	with
atop	for	per	within
before	from	regarding	without
behind			

Note that we label these words as prepositions only when they are followed by a nominal—that is, only when they are part of prepositional phrases. In the following sentence, for example, *up* functions as an adverb, not a preposition:

The price of sugar went <u>up</u> again.

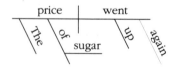

---

[1] This frequency count, based on a collection of 1,014,232 words, is published in Henry Kuçera and W. Nelson Francis, *Computational Analysis of Present-Day English* (Providence, RI: Brown University Press, 1967).

Words like *up* also function as particles in two-word, or phrasal, verbs, such as *hold up:*

A masked gunman held up the liquor store.

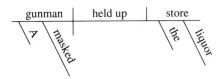

But in the following sentence, *up* is a preposition, part of a prepositional phrase:

We hiked up the steep trail.

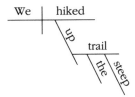

═══ *Investigating Language 12.2* ═══

Speaking of *up*, a "Dear Abby" correspondent sent in the following passage, which he had clipped from the *Reader's Digest* twenty-five years ago:

"It's easy to understand UP, meaning toward the sky or toward the top of a list. But when we waken, why do we wake UP? At a meeting, why does a topic come UP? And why are participants said to speak UP? Why are officers UP for election? And why is it UP to the secretary to write UP a report?

"The little word is really not needed, but we use it anyway. We brighten UP a room, light UP a cigar, polish UP the silver, lock UP the house and fix UP the old car.

"At other times, it has special meanings. People stir UP trouble, line UP for tickets, work UP an appetite, think UP excuses and get tied UP in traffic.

"To be dressed is one thing, but to be dressed UP is special. It may be confusing, but a drain must be opened UP because it is stopped UP.

"We open UP a store in the morning, and close it UP in the evening. We seem to be all mixed UP about UP.

"In order to be UP on the proper use of UP, look UP the word in the dictionary. In one desk dictionary, UP takes UP half a page; and the listed definitions add UP to about 40.

"If you are UP to it, you might try building UP a list of the many ways in which UP is used. It may take UP a lot of your time, but if you don't give UP, you may wind UP with a thousand."

Try your hand at writing a similar passage using DOWN or OUT or OFF.

Phrasal Prepositions.   Two-word, or **phrasal**, **prepositions** consist of a simple preposition preceded by a word from another category, such as an adverb, adjective, or conjunction:

according to	because of	next to
ahead of	but for	out of
along with	contrary to	prior to
as for	except for	thanks to
aside from	instead of	up to

Most three-word prepositions consist of preposition + noun + preposition:

by means of	in lieu of
in accordance with	in search of
in back of	in spite of
in case of	on account of
in charge of	on behalf of
in front of	

In a traditional diagram, we usually treat these phrases as we do the simple prepositions:

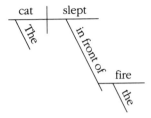

Because *in front of the fire* can also be analyzed as one prepositional phrase embedded in another, we can diagram it another way:

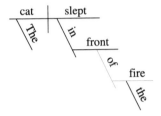

The foregoing lists include the most common, although certainly not all, of the prepositions. We use prepositions automatically, as we do the other structure words, in spite of the sometimes subtle differences in meaning they can express: *below* the stairs, *beneath* the stairs, *under* the stairs, *underneath* the stairs; *in* the room, *inside* the room, *within* the room. As native speakers we understand these distinctions, and, except for a few idioms that sometimes cause problems of usage, we rarely hesitate in selecting the right preposition for the occasion.

═══ *Exercise 48* ═══

Underline the prepositions in the following sentences.

1. The Renfords have lived in San Diego since 1985.
2. They like it there because of the climate.
3. I like Minnesota in spite of the cold winters.
4. Prior to 1985, the Renfords lived in Baltimore.
5. According to the latest government figures, the cost of rearing a child rose to $85,000 during the 1980s.
6. I look on such statistics with skepticism.
7. Except for eggs, which rarely go up in price, the cost of groceries is going out of sight.

8. Thanks to rice and beans, I manage to eat well without going broke.
9. Between you and me, my grocery money may not hold out until payday.
10. I am finding it hard to live within my budget.

CONJUNCTIONS

We use **conjunctions** to connect words and phrases and clauses within the sentence and to connect the sentences themselves. Within the sentence our most common connectors are the simple **coordinating** conjunctions and the **correlative** conjunctions. For joining sentences we use, in addition, the **subordinating** conjunctions, also called subordinators, and **conjunctive adverbs**. The relative pronouns and relative adverbs also function as connectors, joining relative, or adjectival, clauses to nouns.

Coordinating Conjunctions.   We can use a coordinate structure for any slot in the sentence by using a coordinating conjunction (*and, or, but, yet, nor, for*):

Riley and Tim worked out on Saturday.

I'll meet you at the ticket window or in the grandstand.

The dessert was simple yet elegant.

Eager to start her new job but sad at the thought of leaving home,
Kris packed the car and drove away from the familiar house on
Maxwell Avenue.

The coordinating conjunctions also join complete sentences:

I disapproved of his betting on the horses, and I told him so.
He claims to have won fifty dollars, but I suspect he's exaggerating.
She won't come to the party, nor will she explain why.

Notice that the clause introduced by *nor* requires a subject–auxiliary shift.

The coordinating conjunction *for* joins only complete sentences, not structures within the sentence. Even though it is close in meaning to *because*, it differs from the subordinating conjunctions: The *for* clause cannot open the sentence.

Correlative Conjunctions.   Like the coordinating conjunctions, the correlatives (*both–and, either–or, neither–nor, not only–but also*), connect both complete sentences and elements within the sentence. Within the sentence *either–or* and *neither–nor* are used alike:

$$\text{I will} \begin{Bmatrix} \text{either} \\ \text{neither} \end{Bmatrix} \text{meet you in the lobby} \begin{Bmatrix} \text{or} \\ \text{nor} \end{Bmatrix} \text{come to your room.}$$

As a connector of sentences, *neither–nor* requires the subject–auxiliary shift; *either–or* does not:

> Neither will I meet you in the lobby, nor will I come to your room.
>
> Either I will meet you in the lobby, or I will come to your room.

Structures connected by the correlatives should be parallel, with both members of the conjunction introducing structures of the same form, such as verb phrases or noun phrases:

> He both tried and succeeded.
>
> Either run slowly or walk fast.
>
> I want neither the pudding nor the shortcake.

But in the case of complete sentences, the following are also common, especially in speech, where the *either* and *neither* come after the subject in one clause, even though the *or* and *nor* come before it in the next:

> I will neither meet you in the lobby, nor will I come to your room.
>
> I will either meet you in the lobby, or I will come to your room.

Not only–but also can be used both within and between sentences.

> Not only the coaches and players but also the fans had high hopes of defeating the Crimson Tide.

Not only did the government's experts underestimate the economic downturn that the 1990s would bring, but they also delayed in taking action to change its course.

This sentence would be equally grammatical with either *but* or *also*, rather than both.

Both–and does not connect complete sentences; it connects elements within the sentence only:

Franco is a good sport, both on and off the playing field.

Both Jeanne and Marie worked hard to get their manuscript finished on schedule.

Conjunctive Adverbs (Adverbial Conjunctions). As their name suggests, the conjunctive adverbs join sentences to form coordinate structures as other conjunctions do, but they do so with an adverbial emphasis. The following list also includes some of the most common simple adverbs and adverbial prepositional phrases that function as sentence connectors:

Result:	*therefore, so, consequently, as a result, of course*
Concession:	*nevertheless, yet, at any rate, still, after all, of course*
Apposition:	*for example, for instance, that is, namely, in other words*
Addition:	*moreover, furthermore, also, in addition, likewise, further*
Time:	*meanwhile, in the meantime*
Contrast:	*however, instead, on the contrary, on the other hand, in contrast, rather*
Summary:	*thus, in conclusion, then*
Reinforcement:	*further, in particular, indeed, above all, in fact*

Conjunctive adverbs differ from other conjunctions in that, like many other adverbials, they tend to be movable within their clause; they need not introduce the clause:

My tax accountant is not cheap; however, the amount of tax she saves me is far greater than her fee.

My tax accountant is not cheap; the amount of tax she saves me, however, is far greater than her fee.

The punctuation of coordinate sentences with conjunctive adverbs is explained on pages 252–253. Their rhetorical effects are discussed in Chapter 14.

Subordinating Conjunctions.　The subordinators are con-junctions too, although their function is not to connect independent ideas as equals but rather to show a relationship between two ideas in which one of them is a **dependent** or **subordinate clause.** Like the conjunctive adverbs, the subordinators are both single words and phrases:

Time:	*when, whenever, after, as, before, once, since, till, until, now that, while, as long as, as soon as*
Concession:	*though, although, even though, if, while*
Contingency:	*if, once*
Condition:	*if, in case, as long as, unless, provided that*
Reason:	*because, since, as long as*
Result:	*so, so that*
Comparison:	*as, just as, as if*
Contrast:	*while, whereas*

Subordinate clauses come both before and after the main clause. This movability feature provides a test to differentiate between subordinators and coordinators. The coordinators—the conjunctive adverbs as well as the coordinating conjunctions—introduce only the second clause:

We decided to walk because we missed the last bus.
Because we had missed the last bus, we decided to walk.

We decided to walk, for we had missed the last bus.
*For we had missed the last bus, we decided to walk.

We missed the bus, so we decided to walk.
*So we decided to walk, we missed the bus.

When set off by commas, subordinate clauses can also come between the subject and the predicate, where they will get added emphasis:

The City Council members, <u>before they adjourned their meeting,</u>
voted to give a special award to the recycling center.

None of the players, <u>as they sat in the dugout,</u> heard the fans fighting in the stands just above them.

In addition to these simple and phrasal subordinators, we have a small
group of correlative subordinators—two-part structures, one of which is
part of the main clause: *as–so, the–the, no sooner–than.*

<u>As</u> General Motors goes, <u>so</u> goes the nation.

<u>The</u> more I go on fad diets, <u>the</u> more weight I seem to add.

He had <u>no sooner</u> arrived <u>than</u> he started to give orders.

Another two-part subordinator occurs in the clause of comparison:

There were <u>more</u> people at the political rally <u>than</u> we expected.

The governor gave a much long<u>er</u> speech <u>than</u> the program called
for.

Adverbial subordinate clauses are discussed in Chapter 6. Subordinate
clauses that are more clearly sentence modifiers and elliptical clauses
are discussed in Chapter 8.

Relatives.   **Relative pronouns**—*who* (*whose, whom*), *which,*
and *that*—and **relative adverbs**—*where, when, why*—perform a dual
function in the noun phrase: They introduce the relative, or adjectival,
clause, connecting the clause to the noun it modifies; and they play a part
in the clause, the pronouns as nominals and the adverbs as adverbials.

The price *that* <u>we pay for sneakers</u> keeps going up.

The man *who* <u>lives next door</u> rides a bicycle to work.

Nothing exciting ever happens in the small town *where* <u>I was born.</u>

Adjectival clauses are also introduced by the **indefinite relative pronouns,** such as *whoever* (*whomever, whosever*), *whichever, whatever,*
and *what* (meaning "that which"). These pronouns are called "indefinite" because they have no specific referent; instead, they have a general,
indefinite reference. See page 202.

All the adjectival clauses are discussed in detail in Chapter 7.

INTERROGATIVES

As their name implies, the **interrogatives**—*who, whose, whom, which, what, how, why, when, where*—introduce questions:

> <u>What</u> are you doing here?
>
> <u>How</u> did you get here?
>
> <u>When</u> are you leaving?

The function of such questions, of course, is to elicit particular information.

The interrogatives also introduce clauses that fill NP slots in the sentence patterns. Such clauses are sometimes referred to as *indirect questions:*

> Tell me <u>why he came</u>.
>
> I wonder <u>who came with him</u>.
>
> <u>Whose car he drove</u> is a mystery to me.

These clauses, which function as nominals, are discussed in Chapter 4. (We should note that the interrogatives are the same words that in other contexts are classified as relative pronouns or relative adverbs. For that reason the term *interrogative* more accurately labels a function than a word class.)

EXPLETIVES

Rather than providing a grammatical or structural meaning as the other structure-word classes do, the **expletives**—sometimes defined as "empty words"—generally act simply as operators that allow us to manipulate sentences in a variety of ways. In the diagrams of these sentences, the expletives are independent of the basic sentence.

There.   The *there* transformation, as we saw in Chapter 5, enables us to delay the subject in certain kinds of sentences, thus putting it in the position of main stress, which generally falls in the predicate half of the sentence:

> An airplane is landing   There's an áirplane landing
>   on the fréeway. $\longrightarrow$ on the freeway.

As the following diagram shows, the expletive *there* plays no grammatical role in the sentence. To analyze the sentence, you have to discover its underlying form by eliminating the expletive and shifting the subject in front of the *be:*

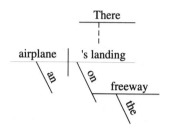

The *there* transformation as a rhetorical tool is discussed in Chapter 14.

That.   One of our most common expletives, *that*, introduces a nominal clause:

I hope that our exam is easy.

Unlike the relative pronoun *that*, which introduces adjectival clauses, the expletive *that* plays no part in the clause:

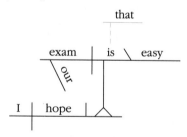

That can be left out when the clause is in object position:

I hope our exam is easy.

However, when the clause is in subject position, *that* cannot be omitted:

That we will have an exam is fairly certain.

We also use the expletive *that* to turn a direct quotation into indirect discourse:

He said, "I will come." ⟶ He said that he would come.

"Expletive" is not the only label given to this use of the word *that;* it is sometimes called a "nominalizer," because its function is to turn a clause into a nominal, that is, a noun phrase substitute. And sometimes it is called a "subordinator." The label "expletive" is used by traditional grammarians to emphasize the "empty word" quality of *that,* in that it serves strictly as an operator; it plays no role in the clause itself. The use of *that* in nominal clauses is taken up in detail in Chapter 4.

Or. The expletive *or* introduces an explanatory appositive:

> The study of sentences, or syntax, helps us appreciate how much we know when we know language.
>
> The African wildebeest, or gnu, resembles an ox.

This or should not be confused with the conjunction or, which indicates an alternative (as in coffee or tea). The expletive introduces an equivalent in an appositive role.

The diagram shows its expletive role:

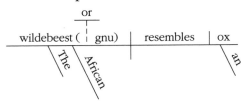

As. Another fairly common expletive introduces certain objective complements in Patterns IX and X:

> We elected him as president.

Again, the diagram shows the role of *as* outside of the grammatical structure of the sentence:[2]

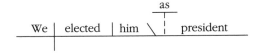

---

[2]An alternative analysis for these phrases with *as* is to consider them prepositional phrases:

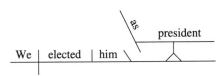

Leaving out the *as* does not change the meaning of this sentence; whether to choose it or not is usually a matter of emphasis or rhythm. With verbs like *refer to*, *think of*, and *know*, however, *as* is required with the objective complement:

> I refer to Professor Buck as a man of character.
>
> I think of him as a man of many talents.
>
> I think of him as exceptionally clever.
>
> I know him as a friend.

===== *Exercise 49* =====

Label the class of each underlined word.

1. I found some rare stamps and postmarks on an old envelope in the attic.

2. Four friends of mine from the dorm waited in line for sixteen hours, for they were determined to get tickets for the World Series.

3. As the experts predicted, the Republicans chose an ultraconservative as their party's candidate at the convention.

4. We should be arriving by six, but don't wait for us.

5. Our group of tourists will take off at dawn if the weather permits.

6. We are now studying the structure of sentences, or syntax, in our English class.

7. We will warm up with a game of one-on-one while we wait for the rest of the players.

8. We had too many problems with our two new puppies, so we gave them both to the neighbors.

---

n. 2 continued

Admittedly, the word *as* presents something of a problem; however, to call it an expletive, or operator, does help alleviate the problem somewhat. First, it makes clear the membership of these sentences in Patterns IX and X, pointing out the optional nature of *as* with some of the verbs. It also avoids the introduction of what would be a deviant prepositional phrase: a preposition followed by an adjective (I consider him *as exceptionally clever*). Other prepositions do not take adjectives as objects. Finally, it acknowledges the resemblance between the role of *as* in these sentences and the expletive role of *or* and *that* in the previous sections, where the *or* and *that* have no grammatical role in the sentence itself.

KEY TERMS IN CHAPTER 12

Adverbial conjunction	Indefinite pronoun
Article	Intensifier
Auxiliary	Interrogative
Conjunction	Modal-like verb
Conjunctive adverb	Number
Coordinating conjunction	Phrasal preposition
Correlative conjunction	Possessive noun
Definite article	Possessive pronoun
Demonstrative pronoun	Postdeterminer
Determiner	Predeterminer
Expanded determiner	Preposition
Explanatory appositive	Qualifier
Expletive	Relative
Expletive *as*	Semi-auxiliary
Expletive *or*	Simple preposition
Expletive *that*	Subject–verb agreement
Indefinite article	Subordinating conjunction

QUESTIONS FOR DISCUSSION

1. Prepositions and particles are among the most difficult words in the language for foreign speakers to master. Why do you suppose this is so? Look at the following sentences. How would you explain the selection of prepositions to a learner of English?

> Be sure to fill out the form carefully.
> Be sure to fill in the form carefully.
>
> I like to jog in the early morning.
> I like to jog on a sunny morning.
>
> Our house burned down last week.
> All of my books burned up.
>
> I'm working on my math.
> I'm really working at it.

2. Do the sentences in Question 1 say anything about the arbitrariness of English? Consider the following in light of the examples in Question 1.

We hope to reach the solution that we are dreaming for.
That is the solution we are hoping of.

Are these quotations from native speakers?

3. In what sense are *keep, dare, get,* and *have to* modal-like? How do they differ from modals? In thinking about this question, consider their place in the verb-expansion rule.

In what sense are these verbs *not* like the other modals? Consider the following examples:

He kept playing all afternoon.
Did he keep playing?

Do I dare walk alone?
You dare not walk alone around here at night.

He got fired.
He was fired.
He wasn't fired.
He didn't get fired.

4. In answering an interviewer's question, an economist recently said, "I do not foresee any improvement in the economy, absent any change in the elements that are driving it." What part of speech is *absent*?

5. In an article entitled "The Big Nine" (*Atlantic*, March 1988), Cullen Murphy reports on a 1923 study in which the lexicographer G. H. McKnight identified nine words in our language that comprise one-quarter of all spoken words. (A list of forty-three accounts for one-half.) Here are the nine: *and, be, have, it, of, the, to, will,* and *you*. Identify their word classes.

Murphy did his own research of written texts, ranging from an IRS document to the "Wizard of Id" comic strip and came up with similar results. You might find it interesting to evaluate your own writing. Then write a paragraph in which you use none of the nine—just to see if you can do it. Describe the difference—perhaps in tone or in rhythm—if any.

6. *The New Yorker* reported an apology printed by a Sydney, Australia, newspaper for inadvertently changing a word in a reader's letter to the editor. The correspondent had written, "The number of speakers became unmanageable." The paper changed *the* to *a*. How can one little structure word make such a difference?

7. One of the assessment tools commonly used in the field of English as a Second Language (ESL) is the "Cloze" test, which consists of a prose passage with deletions at regular intervals. Language proficiency is then judged on the student's ability to fill in the blanks correctly. Here are two Cloze passages with every fifth word deleted. The first is from the opening paragraph of Shelby Foote's first volume of *The Civil War: A Narrative.* The second is the last paragraph in a *Time* article about weather on the occasion of the 1993 Mississippi flood. Fill in the blanks with what you think has been deleted; then compare your answers with those of your classmates. Is there more agreement among you on the form class words or on the structure words? Which blanks do you think would be the most difficult for a nonnative speaker?

1. It was a Monday _____ Washington, January 21; Jefferson Davis _____ from his seat in _____ Senate. South Carolina had _____ the Union a month _____, followed by Mississippi, Florida, _____ Alabama, which seceded at _____ rate of one a _____ during the second week _____ the new year. Georgia _____ out eight days later; _____ and Texas were poised _____ go; few doubted that _____ would, along with others. _____ more than a decade _____ had been intensive discussion _____ to the legality of _____, but now the argument _____ no longer academic.

2. What is new about _____ weather is that, for _____ first time, some of _____ factors that help shape _____ may be man-made. Experts _____ it may be decades _____ we are certain what _____ the buildup of greenhouse _____ or the depletion of _____ ozone layer has had _____ the global climate. Last _____ flooding and heat wave _____ as a warning that _____ we wait for the _____ to tell us what's _____ with the weather, it _____ be too late to _____ anything about it.

CHAPTER
13
Pronouns

As their name suggests, pronouns are words that stand for nouns. Perhaps a more accurate label would be *pronominal,* because they actually stand for any construction that functions as a nominal in the sentence. We refer to the noun or nominal that the pronoun stands for as its **antecedent**.

Most pronouns replace an entire noun phrase:

The pistachio nut ice cream at Meyer's Dairy is delicious.
$\downarrow$
It   is delicious.

My friend Jan, who lives in Houston, is coming to visit.
$\downarrow$
She   is coming to visit.

Pronouns also substitute for other nominals, such as verb phrases and clauses:

The judge warned my brother to stay out of trouble.
$\downarrow$
He told me   that,   too.

330

Where you spend your time is none of my business.

$$\left\{\dfrac{\text{That}}{\underline{\text{It}}}\right\} \qquad \text{is none of my business.}$$

Not all pronouns are alike. The label **pronoun** actually covers a wide variety of words, many of which function in quite different ways. A brief description of the main classes of pronouns follows.

PERSONAL PRONOUNS

The **personal pronouns** are the ones we usually think of when the word *pronoun* comes to mind. We generally label them on the basis of person and number:

PERSON	NUMBER		
	Singular	*Plural*	
1st	I	we	[person(s) speaking]
2nd	you	you	[person(s) spoken to]
3rd	he she it	they	[person(s) spoken about]

For example, we refer to *I* as the "first-person singular" pronoun and *they* as the "third-person plural." In addition, the third-person singular pronouns include the feature of **gender**: masculine (*he*), feminine (*she*), and neuter (*it*).

The term **pronoun-antecedent agreement** describes our selection of the pronoun in reference to the noun or noun phrase (or nominal) it replaces: The personal pronoun "agrees with" its antecedent in both number and, for third-person singular, gender. Note that the second person (*you*) has neither gender nor number distinctions.

The forms given in the preceding set are in the **subjective** (traditionally called "nominative") case; this is the form used when the pronoun serves as the subject or subjective complement. The personal pronouns also inflect for the **possessive** ("genitive") case, as nouns do, and the **objective** ("accusative") case, an inflection that nouns do not have.

Subjective: I	we	you	he	she	it	they
Possessive: my	our	your	his	her	its	their
(mine)	(ours)	(yours)	(his)	(hers)		(theirs)
Objective: me	us	you	him	her	it	them

The possessive case forms of pronouns function as determiners. The objective case is used for pronouns in all the other NP slots: direct object, indirect object, objective complement, and object of the preposition.

Alternative forms of the possessive case, shown in parentheses, are used when the headword of the noun phrase is deleted:

> This is my book.   This is mine.
> This is her book.   This is hers.

Possessive nouns can also be used without headwords:

> This is John's book.   This is John's.
> Mary's book is missing.   Mary's is missing.

The third person singular *it*, the most neutral of the personal pronouns, is sometimes used as an "anticipatory" subject, as we saw in the discussion of cleft sentences and nominals. In some cases it has clear pronoun status:

> My little horse must think it queer
> To stop without a farmhouse near.

In this passage from Robert Frost's "Stopping by Woods on a Snowy Evening," the infinitive phrase is in apposition to the direct object *it*. In the following sentence, the infinitive is in apposition to the *it* subject:

> It is nice to be here with you.

And here the appositive is a nominal clause:

> It was unthinkable that the Nittany Lion defense couldn't stop the Wolverines.

In some cases the *it*, while acting as a grammatical subject, remains essentially an empty word:

> It is raining
> It's a nice day.

The plural pronoun *they* can also have neutral status:

> They say best men are moulded out of faults. [Shakespeare]

We should also note that our system of personal pronouns—or, to be more accurate, a gap in the system—is the source of a great deal of the sexism in our language. Missing from the system is a singular third-person pronoun that refers to either gender. Our plural pronoun (*they*) includes both male and female; but when we need a pronoun to refer to an unidentified person, such as "the writer" or "a student" or "the doctor," the long-standing tradition has been to use the masculine (*he/his/him*):

> The writer of this news story should have kept <u>his</u> personal opinions out of it.

Attempts to promote *s/he* in recent years have been unsuccessful. Perhaps someday the plural pronoun will be accepted for both singular and plural, a usage that has become quite common in speech:

> Someone broke into our car last night; <u>they</u> stole our tape deck and all our tapes.

(This issue is discussed further on pages 384–390.)

===== *Exercise 50* =====

Substitute personal pronouns for the underlined nouns and noun phrases in the following sentences.

1. <u>Luis and Maria</u> have bought a new house.
2. <u>Bev and I</u> will be going to the game with <u>Otis</u>.

3. Betsy bought that beautiful new car of hers in Charlotte.
4. Both of her cars are gas guzzlers.
5. There have always been uneasy feelings between the neighbors and my husband.
6. I want Tony to approve of the project.
7. The kids gave their father and me a bad time.
8. My brother, who works for the Navy in California, spends his weekends in Las Vegas.

═══ *Investigating Language 13.1* ═══

The difference between *who* and *whom* is identical to the difference between *I* and *me* or between *she* and *her* or between *he* and *him* or *they* and *them*. We say

I know him.	and	He knows me.
She helps them.	and	They help her.

And we also say

The man who loves me is coming to visit,

where *who* is the subject in its own clause, the subject of the verb *love*, and

The man whom I love is coming to visit,

where *whom* is the direct object of *love*.

The topic under discussion here, as you have probably guessed, is that of **case**. If you are a native speaker of English, nothing in the previous discussion comes as a surprise. Chances are you've never been tempted to say,

*Him knows I.   or   *Them helps she.

However, you may have been tempted to say—you may even have heard yourself say—

The stranger who I helped this morning was very grateful.

For some reason, that *who* doesn't sound as strange, or as ungrammatical, as

      *Amy knows I.   or   *They help she.

If you consider the position of *who* in its clause, you can probably figure out why that sentence about the stranger is so easy to say—and why it sounds o.k.

The point is that we do *say* it. The fact that we do is one of the differences between speech and writing. But in writing, you'll want to figure out the appropriate case for the object position:

      The stranger whom I helped this morning . . .

You can use your understanding of case to edit yourself.

Objects of prepositions. The direct object slot is, of course, not the only object slot in our sentences. The slot following prepositions—the object of the preposition—is probably even more common than the direct object. And it, too, requires the objective case when the object is a pronoun:

      I bought this for him.   Pam bought this for me.

      I gave it to them.   They came with her.

Again, you're probably not tempted to say "for he" or "to they" or "for I" or "with she." You automatically use the objective case of personal pronouns after prepositions. And native speakers are probably never tempted to say,

      *This secret is just between we.

So why do you suppose it's so common to hear,

      *This secret is just between Joe and I

           and

      *This secret is just between he and I?

It's a question worth considering.

REFLEXIVE PRONOUNS

Reflexive pronouns are those formed by adding *-self* or *-selves* to a form of the personal pronoun:

PERSON	SINGULAR	PLURAL
1st	myself	ourselves
2nd	yourself	yourselves
3rd	himself herself itself	themselves

The reflexive pronoun is used as the direct object, indirect object, and object of the preposition when its antecedent is the subject of the sentence:

John cut <u>himself.</u>

I glanced at <u>myself</u> in the mirror.

I cooked dinner for Shelley and <u>myself.</u>

Joe cooked dinner for Gary and <u>himself.</u>

The reflexive pronoun *myself* is also fairly common in certain spoken sentences where the standard written version would call for the objective case, *me:*

Joe cooked dinner for Gary and <u>myself.</u>

In Standard Written English the object of the preposition *for* would be *Gary and me* because the antecedent of *myself* does not appear in the sentence:

Joe cooked dinner for <u>Gary and me.</u>

Both versions are unambiguous; both forms of the first-person pronoun, *me* and *myself,* can refer only to the speaker. However, with third-person pronouns different forms produce different meanings:

Joe cooked dinner for Gary and <u>himself</u> (Joe).

Joe cooked dinner for Gary and <u>him</u> (someone else).

===== *Exercise 51* =====

Fill the blanks with the appropriate reflexive pronouns.

1. Gabrielle gave _____ a black eye when she fell.

2. Li and Mei-Ling cooked _____ salmon for dinner.

3. The ceramic figurine sat by _____ on the shelf.

4. We sat by _____ in the front row.

5. Paulo cooked a delicious Mexican feast for Rosa and _____.

6. Wearing our new designer jeans, Sheila and I admired _____ in the mirror.

INTENSIVE PRONOUNS

Also known as the *emphatic reflexive pronouns*, the **intensive pronouns** have the same form as the reflexives. The intensive pronoun serves as an appositive to emphasize a noun, but it need not directly follow the noun:

I <u>myself</u> prefer chocolate.

I prefer chocolate <u>myself</u>.

<u>Myself</u>, I prefer chocolate.

Because *myself* is in apposition to *I* in all three versions, the diagram will not distinguish among them:

I (myself)	prefer	chocolate

RECIPROCAL PRONOUNS

Each other and *one another* are known as the **reciprocal pronouns.** They serve either as determiners (in the possessive case) or as objects, referring to previously named nouns: *Each other* generally refers to two nouns; *one another* to three or more:

> Juan and Claudia help each other.
>
> They even do each other's chores.
>
> All the students in my study group help one another with their homework.

DEMONSTRATIVE PRONOUNS

In our discussion of determiners we noted that the selection of a determiner is based on certain inherent features, such as definite or indefinite, countable or noncountable. The **demonstrative pronouns**, one of the subclasses of determiners, include the features of "number" and "proximity":

PROXIMITY	NUMBER	
	Singular	*Plural*
Near	this	these
Distant	that	those

> That documentary we saw last night really made me think, but this one is simply stupid.
>
> Those trees on the ridge were almost destroyed by gypsy moths, but these seem perfectly healthy.

Like other determiner classes, the demonstrative pronoun can be a substitute for a nominal as well as a signal for one:

> These old shoes and hats   will be perfect for the costumes.
>
> These   will be perfect for the costumes.

To be effective as a nominal, the demonstrative pronoun must replace or stand for a clearly stated antecedent. In the following example, *that* does not refer to "solar energy"; it has no clear antecedent:

> Our contractor is obviously skeptical about solar energy. That doesn't surprise me.

Such sentences are not uncommon in speech, nor are they ungrammatical. But when a *this* or *that* has no specific antecedent, the writer can usually improve the sentence by providing a noun headword for the demonstrative pronoun—by turning the pronoun into a determiner:

> Our contractor is obviously skeptical about solar energy. <u>That attitude</u> (or <u>His attitude</u>) doesn't surprise me.

A combination of the two sentences would also be an improvement over the vague use of *that*:

> Our contractor's skepticism about solar energy doesn't surprise me.

The vague reference of *this* and *that* has the same fuzzy quality as the broad-reference relative clause, which you read about in Chapter 8:

> Our contractor is skeptical about solar energy, <u>which doesn't surprise me</u>.

A singular demonstrative pronoun can also function as a qualifier:

> I can't imagine being <u>that</u> rich.
> I can't believe I weigh <u>this</u> much.

RELATIVE PRONOUNS

The **relative pronouns** are *who*, *which*, and *that*; they introduce clauses that modify the nouns that are the antecedents of these pronouns. *Who* inflects for both possessive and objective cases: *whose* (possessive) and *whom* (objective). The case of *who* is determined by the part it plays (its function) in its own clause:

> The man <u>who lives across the street</u> sold me his car.

In this sentence *who* renames *man*, its antecedent, and plays the part of subject in the relative (adjectival) clause. In the next sentence the relative pronoun is in the possessive case form, *whose*:

The man whose car I bought was not very honest about the gas mileage.

Here *whose*, the possessive relative pronoun, again stands for *man*; in its own clause it acts as the determiner for *car*, the role that possessives normally play.

Whose also acts as the possessive form of *which:*

The wooded ridge across the valley, whose trees were infested by gypsy moths, turned brown in mid-June.

The relative pronoun *that* is generally subjective or objective, never possessive:

I lost the backpack that I bought yesterday.

That renames *backpack* and acts as the object within its own clause. In object position, *that* can be omitted:

I lost the backpack I bought yesterday.

When *that* is the subject of the clause, however, it cannot be omitted:

The route that will get us there fastest is straight across the mountain.

The *wh-* relative pronouns also have an expanded form with the addition of *-ever*, known as **indefinite relative pronouns:** *whoever, whosever, whomever,* and *whatever.* The expanded relatives have indefinite referents rather than specific ones as the simple relatives do:

I will give a bonus to whoever works the hardest.
I will pay you whatever you deserve.
I will call whomever the doctor recommends.

What is also considered an indefinite relative pronoun when it introduces adjectival clauses and means "that which."

I will pay you <u>what you deserve.</u>

The relative (adjectival) clauses are also discussed in Chapter 7.

INTERROGATIVE PRONOUNS

The list of **interrogative pronouns** is similar to that of the relatives: *who (whose, whom), which,* and *what*. The interrogatives, as their name suggests, are among the question words that produce information questions (in contrast to yes/no questions):

<u>What</u> do you want for lunch?

<u>Whose</u> car is that?

<u>Which</u> section of history did you get?

As we saw in Chapter 5, the interrogative word plays a part in the sentence. For example, in the first preceding sample sentence, *what* fills the direct object slot: "You do want *what* for lunch." In a sentence such as "What flavor do you prefer?" the interrogative *what* acts as a determiner for the noun *flavor*. In the other two examples listed, *whose* and *which* also act as determiners: *whose car, which section*. Because of this modifying function, *which, what,* and *whose* are sometimes classified as **interrogative adjectives**.

The interrogative pronouns also introduce nominal clauses and, like the relative pronouns, play a part in the clause. There is an indirect question involved in such clauses—either implied or stated, asked or answered:

Tell me <u>what you want for lunch.</u>

I know <u>who gave you that black eye.</u>

Nominal clauses are discussed in Chapter 4.

INDEFINITE PRONOUNS

The **indefinite pronouns** include a number of words listed earlier as determiners:

enough, few, fewer, less, little, many, much, several, more, most,
all, both, every, each, any, either, neither, none, some

One is also commonly used as a pronoun (as are the other cardinal numbers—*two, three,* etc.) along with its negative, *none.* As a pronoun, *one* often replaces only the headword, rather than the entire noun phrase:

> *The blue shoes that I bought yesterday* will be perfect for the trip.
>
> *The blue ones that I bought yesterday* will be perfect for the trip.

The personal pronoun, on the other hand, would replace the entire noun phrase:

> They will be perfect for the trip.

The pronouns *every, any, no,* and *some* can be expanded with *-body,* *-thing,* and *-one*:

some	body		every	body	
	thing			thing	
	one			one	
any	body		no	body	
	thing			thing	
	one			one (two words)	

These pronouns can take modifiers in the form of clauses:

> Anyone *who wants extra credit in psych class* can volunteer for tonight's experiment.

They can also be modified by verb phrases:

> Everyone *reporting late for practice* will take fifteen laps.

And by prepositional phrases:

> Nothing *on the front page* interests me anymore.

And, unlike most nouns, they can be modified by adjectives in posthead-word position:

I don't care for <u>anything</u> *sweet*.

I think that <u>something</u> *strange* is going on here.

=== *Exercise 52* ===

Underline the pronouns in the following sentences. Identify the subclass to which each pronoun belongs.

1. When Roberto ordered a pizza with everything, I ordered one too.
2. Millie and Bev shopped at almost every store in the mall but couldn't find any shoes they liked.
3. Someone was standing in the shadows, but we couldn't see who it was.
4. All that I had for lunch was that overripe banana.
5. Booker and Marcus didn't eat much either, but they both ate more than I did.
6. I myself will go along with whatever you decide.
7. One hour of studying was enough for me.
8. Quarreling among themselves, the committee members completely disregarded one another's suggestions.
9. Tell me what color I should paint your sign.
10. The employment office will find a job for whoever wants one.

KEY TERMS IN CHAPTER 13

Antecedent	Number
Case	Objective case
Demonstrative pronoun	Person
Emphatic reflexive pronoun	Personal pronoun
Gender	Plural
Indefinite pronoun	Possessive case
Indefinite relative pronoun	Pronoun
Intensive pronoun	Pronoun-antecedent
Interrogative adjective	agreement
Interrogative pronoun	Proximity

Reciprocal pronoun
Reflexive pronoun
Relative pronoun

Sexism
Singular
Subjective case

QUESTIONS FOR DISCUSSION

1. The relative pronoun agrees with its antecedent in person and number but not necessarily in case. How do the following sentences illustrate that statement?

I don't know the women who live next door.
It was I whom you spoke with on the phone.

2. Comment on the choice of pronouns in the following sentence. Are they correct?

I didn't know who felt worse: him or me.

3. In Chapter 2, Discussion Question 10, we looked at the following ambiguous sentence:

Rosa called her mother.

What is the source of the ambiguity? Would a sentence about Mario and father instead of Rosa and mother be equally ambiguous? What's the difference?

4. What is the difference in the meaning of *one* in the following sentences?

<u>One</u> farmer told me there hadn't been rain in eight weeks.
<u>One</u> can only hope that the weather changes soon.

5. The telephone rings and you answer it. When you hang up, your roommate asks, "What did they want?" Does your roommate really believe you were talking to more than one person? If not, what is there about our language that would produce such a strange question?

6. In the discussion of the expanded, or indefinite, relative pronouns, the following three sample sentences appear:

I will give a bonus to whoever works hardest.
I will pay you whatever you deserve.
I will call whomever the doctor recommends.

Explain why a traditional diagram of such sentences would look like this:

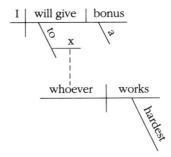

How should we diagram the sentences with *whatever* and *whomever*?

7. How do you explain the use of *we* and *us* in the following sentences?

We graduates lined up to go into the gym.
The speaker told us graduates that we were the hope of the future.

Is *we* used correctly in the following sentence?

It wasn't a good idea for we dishwashers to go on strike.

8. Explain the source of the ambiguity in the following sentence:

You know yourself better than anyone.

How would a spoken version clear up the ambiguity?

9. Here's a statement with a single, straightforward meaning:

I invited everyone in the class to my party.

The follow-up sentence is not quite as clear; in fact, it's ambiguous:

Everyone didn't come.

Here's another ambiguous sentence:

Everything doesn't cause cancer.

Paraphrase the two negative sentences in two ways to demonstrate their meanings. Then consider the meaning of *everyone* and *everything* and explain why their use with the negative should produce ambiguity.

10. Examine the following sentences; then explain the "rule" that a nonnative speaker learning English must understand in connection with *some* and *any.*

Mario wants some dessert. Rosa doesn't want any.
I lent someone my book. I didn't lend anyone my class notes.
Are you going somewhere special for lunch? I'm not going any-
    where.

Why would that student of English find the following sentences ungrammatical?

Anyone can have seconds on dessert.
I haven't given some of the volunteers their assignments yet.

What would happen to the meaning of those two sentences if that English student were to follow the "some/any rule"?

V

GRAMMAR FOR WRITERS

For some of you, this book has been your introduction to the study of grammar. Terms like *noun* and *adjective* and *predicate* and *participle* were completely new to you or, at best, distant echoes from a long-ago classroom. Others of you brought a fairly substantial understanding of parts of speech and sentences from grammar classes that may have begun in the fifth grade and continued through the twelfth, very likely starting every year with parts of speech and ending with complex sentences. The majority of you are probably somewhere in between, with memories of a grammar unit for a year or two, perhaps in the seventh and eighth grades. Those differing backgrounds reflect actual differences in the way in which grammar is taught throughout this country. Grammar is not a subject area that curriculum experts agree on; it is, in fact, an area fraught with controversy and misunderstanding.

Part of the misunderstanding is a problem of definition. What exactly do we mean by grammar? In this book we have defined grammar as that unconscious system of rules that enables a speaker of the language to produce grammatical sentences. We have emphasized the automatic and unconscious nature of those internalized rules, comparing the native speaker to a computer and the rules of grammar to a computer program that generates sentences. This definition was probably new to you.

For many people grammar is a set of do's and don't's, those traditional rules about correctness that they recall from their grammar classes. Unlike math or history or science, grammar is remembered in a negative way—as red marks on English papers, as comma splices and spelling

347

errors, and as prohibitions against ending sentences with prepositions and beginning them with conjunctions. It's understandable for people to assume that the purpose of studying grammar is to avoid error. That definition of grammar and that purpose—and the methods of teaching that reflect that definition and purpose—underlie the misunderstanding.

If the purpose of studying grammar is to avoid error, then it should follow that if you learn the rules of grammar you should be a better writer because you will avoid errors in your compositions. Research has shown, however, that there is little, if any, correlation between knowing the rules and writing well. There is no "transfer" from all those drills on the parts of speech to actual writing ability. If that's the case, then why teach grammar at all? For many years "why teach grammar?" is the question that curriculum planners have been asking. In many school districts, the response has been to downplay the teaching of grammar or eliminate it altogether.

The misunderstanding comes about because the goal of grammar study should not be simply to teach students to avoid error. (And surely we have moved beyond thinking that an error-free composition is by definition an effective one.) Rather, an understanding of grammar should enhance the students' confidence in their own writing ability; it should give them control over their writing by illuminating all the choices that are available to them. That control and those choices are the subject matter of Chapter 14, "Rhetorical Grammar." Understanding grammar from a rhetorical point of view means understanding the choices and recognizing the effects that those choices will have on the reader.

14

Rhetorical Grammar

A language has certain abilities or even inclinations which the wise user can draw into the service of his own rhetorical effort. Using a language may be compared to riding a horse: much of one's success depends upon an understanding of what it can and will do.

—RICHARD WEAVER, *The Ethics of Rhetoric*

Until now we have touched only briefly on the rhetorical aspects of grammar, including the placement of certain modifiers and a few punctuation rules that an understanding of grammar can illuminate. But the purpose of the first thirteen chapters has not been a rhetorical one; it has not focused on the choices that you as a writer may have in a given situation or the effects on a reader that a particular structure will have. Rather, the purpose has been to describe in an objective way the system of rules that underlies your language competence, to help you understand the structures of English in a conscious way. The purpose of this chapter, however, is to help you use that understanding of what language can and will do, to apply what you have learned.

COHESION: THE KNOWN–NEW CONTRACT

One of the first, and most important, concepts you studied in connection with the sentence patterns back in Chapter 2 was that of sentence slots—the recognition that sentences consist of required and optional slots, filled by various forms. Your undertanding of the slots can be especially helpful in thinking about sentence **cohesion**, the ties that connect each sentence to what has gone before—the glue that gives a paragraph unity.

Part of that glue is provided by information in the sentence that the reader already knows. This *known*, or given, information generally fills the subject slot; the *new* information—the real purpose of the sentence—generally comes in the predicate. For example, consider how often the subject slot of a sentence is filled by a pronoun; that pronoun, of course, stands for an antecedent that is known to the reader, a previously mentioned nominal.

The following paragraph, the opening of E. B. White's introduction to the second edition of Strunk and White's *The Elements of Style*, illustrates several principles of cohesion, including the use of the pronoun:

> At the close of the first World War, when I was a student at Cornell, I took a course called English 8. My professor was William Strunk, Jr. A textbook required for the course was a slim volume called *The Elements of Style*, whose author was the professor himself. The year was 1919. The book was known on the campus in those days as "the little book," with the stress on the word "little." It had been privately printed by the author.

The pronoun *it* serves as the subject of the last sentence, referring to the previously mentioned book. But there are other kinds of connections, too, that this paragraph exemplifies.

You can expect the first sentence of a paragraph to consist of new information; it will introduce the topic. But the second sentence will be connected to the first by means of known information—usually in the subject slot. Look at the information in the second and third sentences of the White paragraph. The subjects are "my professor" and "a textbook required for the course." Although neither has been mentioned before, both are in the area of what is "known" about college courses, the topic introduced in the first sentence. As a reader, you're not surprised to be reading about teachers and books; in fact, you expect to. In both cases the reason for the sentences is the information in the predicate—the new information: the professor's name and the book's title. The next sentence—*The year was 1919*—is all known information (the author assumes that the reader knows when World War I ended). Its purpose is to emphasize the timelessness of the book, its status as a classic in its field. The last two sentences begin with known information—*the book* and *it*; again the reason for the sentences is the new information in the predicate.

Linguists have found this known–new sequence to be so pervasive a feature of prose that it is sometimes referred to as the **known–new contract.** The writer has an obligation, a contract of sorts, to fulfill expectations in the reader—to keep the reader on familiar ground. The reader has every right to expect each sentence to be connected in some way to what has gone before, to include a known element.

How can the known–new principle of cohesion help you as a writer? Are you supposed to stop after every sentence and estimate the cohesive power of your next subject? No, of course not. That's not the way writers work. But when you are revising—and, by the way, revision goes on all the time, even during the first draft—the question of reader expectation is one you will want to keep in mind. You can learn to put yourself in your reader's shoes to see if you've kept your part of the bargain.

SENTENCE RHYTHM

One of the most distinctive features of any language—and one of the most automatic for the native speaker—is its sense of rhythm. Our language has a rhythm just as surely as music does—a regular beat. And that sense of rhythm is tied up with the grammar of sentences and with the known–new contract. If you read the opening sentence in this paragraph out loud, you'll hear yourself saying "one of the most" in almost a monotone; you probably don't hear a stressed syllable, a beat, until you get to *distinctive*:

one of the most disTINCtive

And you probably rush through those first four words so fast that you pronounce "of" without the *f,* making "one of" sound like the first two words in "won a prize."

The rhythm of sentences, what we call the **intonation pattern,** can be described as valleys and peaks, where the loudest syllables, those with stress, are represented by peaks:

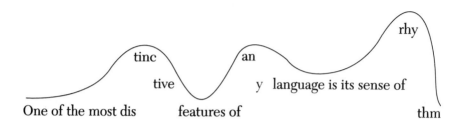

Not all the peaks are of the same height—we have different degrees of stress—but they do tend to come at fairly regular intervals. As listeners we pay attention to the peaks—that's where we'll hear the information that the speaker is focusing on. As speakers, we manipulate the peaks and valleys to coincide with our message, reserving the loudest stress, the highest peak, for the new information, which will be our main point of focus.

Such sentence manipulation is not something we ordinarily think about, nor is it a skill we were taught; it's automatic, part of our native language ability. In fact, one of the reasons that nonnative speakers are sometimes hard for us to understand—one feature of their "foreign accent"—is the absence of that rhythm. We often have to listen very carefully because their intonation clues are misleading, with peaks and valleys in unexpected places or missing altogether.

Sentence rhythm is a feature of all modes of language, not only speech. The peaks and valleys are there when we read silently, and they are there when we write, as we think of the words and phrases while moving our pen or punching the keyboard. Although philosophers may debate about whether it's possible to think in the absence of words, we're well aware that we do our conscious thinking with words. In fact, we hold silent conversations with ourselves; we rehearse what we plan to say to others; we remember what we should have said but didn't; we scold ourselves; we make mental lists. And that interior language of ours, the sentences and fragments of our inner voice, has all the peaks and valleys that our spoken language has.

Reading and writing, of course, are not intuitive behaviors like speaking and listening; they are learned. As with all learned behaviors, people vary widely in their ability to perform them. So when people read, there are undoubtedly differences in the intonation of their inner voices, variations in the degree to which their intonation interprets the writer's intention. We have no way of testing this assumption, of course; we can't record a reader's inner voice. But it seems safe to assume that an unskilled reader, one who struggles with the words, will surely miss a great deal of the meaning that sentence rhythm contributes. And the child who is just learning to read, who gives equal emphasis to nearly every syllable, is clearly not hearing the nuances of the writer's rhythm. It's obvious, too, that writers vary in the ability to use sentence rhythm to their best advantage—or, rather, to the reader's advantage. The writer who does not understand the rhythm, or who disregards it, who simply gives no thought to the peaks and valleys, will not be in complete control of the message the reader gets.

End Focus.   The rhythm of a sentence is closely tied both to its two-part subject–predicate structure and to the known–new contract. The topic, or theme, stated in the subject will usually be a valley or a low peak in the intonation contour; the prominent peak of stress, the focus on the new information, will come in the predicate; it will be close to the end of the sentence, often on the last or next-to-the-last slot. Linguists describe this common rhythm pattern as **end focus**. It is a rhythm that experienced writers are sensitive to. Good writers, you can be sure, are tuned into the rhythm of their own inner voice as they write; they understand how to manipulate sentences in order to control the way the reader reads them and to prevent misreading.

If you read the paragraph by E. B. White aloud, you will be able to hear that rhythm contour. Here are some of the sentences:

I took a course called English 8.

My professor was William Strunk, Jr.

The year was 1919.

It had been privately printed by the author.

In each case you probably put the main stress on the last word, the new information in the sentence.

Here's another example. Listen to the intonation pattern of the underlined sentence as you read the passage aloud:

> Did you hear what happened? <u>Barbara wrecked her motorcycle yesterday.</u> She was on her way to work when the car in front of her stopped suddenly—and she didn't.

You probably read that second sentence with the stress on *motor*. In a different context, however, the rhythm could change if the purpose of the sentence has changed. In the following passage, the known information has changed. Again, read it aloud and listen to the intonation:

> Sue told me that Barbara had an accident this morning on her way to work. But I think she got her facts wrong. <u>Barbara wrecked her motorcycle yesterday.</u>

This time you probably put the main stress on *yesterday*; in this context it would make no sense to stress *motorcycle*. Try reading the passage that way, and you'll easily recognize the problem: All the information in the last sentence up to the word *yesterday* is already known. In this context it is old information: "Barbara wrecked her motorcycle" is a repetition, albeit more specific, of "Barbara had an accident." As a reader, you know intuitively that it's not time to apply stress until you get beyond that old information, until you get to *yesterday*, the new focus.

You'll note, however, that the principle of end focus is still operating, with the main stress on the last sentence element. But imagine how awkward the sentence would be if the adverb *yesterday* were shifted to the beginning of the sentence. It would certainly be grammatical from a structural point of view; as you know, adverbials are movable, especially adverbials of time. Even in opening position the reader might recognize *yesterday* as the new information and give it main stress. But the sentence would certainly have lost its natural rhythm. Read the passage aloud, and you'll hear the problem:

> Sue told me that Barbara had an accident this morning on her way to work. But I think she got her facts wrong. Yesterday Barbara wrecked her motorcycle.

If you were an English teacher reading that sentence in a student's composition, you'd be tempted to write "awk" in the margin. What we call awkwardness is nearly always a case of something unexpected—in this case, an unexpected rhythm.

═══════ *Investigating Language 14.1* ═══════

Read the following passages, listening carefully to the intonation contour of each sentence. Indicate the words (or syllables) that get main stress. Compare your reading with that of your classmates. Identify the new information in each sentence. Does its position and emphasis fulfill the known–new contract?

1. "Never invest in something you don't understand or in the dream of an artful salesperson. Be a buyer, not a sellee. Figure out what you want (be it life insurance, mutual funds or a vacuum cleaner) and then shop for a good buy. Don't let someone else tell you what you need—at least not if he happens to be selling it." [Andrew Tobias, *Parade*]

2. "Plaque has almost become a household word. It is certainly a household problem. But even though everyone is affected by it, few people really understand the seriousness of plaque or the importance of controlling it. Plaque is an almost invisible sticky film of bacteria that continuously forms on the teeth. Plaque germs are constantly multiplying and building up. Any dentist will tell you that controlling plaque is the single most important step to better oral health." [Advertisement of the American Dental Association]

3. To simulate chance occurrences, a computer can't literally toss a coin or roll a die. Instead, it relies on special numerical recipes for generating strings for shuffled digits that pass for random numbers. Such sequences of pseudorandom numbers play crucial roles not only in computer games but also in simulations of physical processes. [I. Peterson, *Science News*]

4. In a report issued Nov. 30 [1992], a panel of scientists and public safety administrators tried to estimate the near-term chances of a large quake in southern California. They noted that the frequency of sizable quakes in this region has increased dramatically in the last six years. This trend, along with the boost in stress from the Landers quake, has raised concern about the next few years. Using several statistical analyses, the panel forecast an 18 to 47 percent chance that

a magnitude 7 earthquake will shake southern California in the next five years. [R. Monastersky, *Science News*]

5. Frank evaluation of its [caffeine's] hazards is not easy. There is a vast literature on the effects of caffeine on the body, and for every study reaching one conclusion, seemingly there is another that contradicts it. Although most major health risks have been ruled out, research continues at a steady clip. [Corby Kummer, *Atlantic Monthly*]

CONTROLLING RHYTHM

Because end focus is such a common rhythm pattern, we can think of it as a part of the contract between writer and reader. The reader expects the main sentence focus to be in the predicate unless given a signal to the contrary. And we do have several such signals at our disposal. You'll recall in Chapter 5 the discussion of transformations that allow the writer to shift the focus of the sentence, pointing the reader to a particular slot. The *it*-cleft transformation is one of the most versatile:

It was Barbara who wrecked her motorcycle yesterday.
It was her motorcycle that Barbara wrecked yesterday.
It was yesterday that Barbara wrecked her motorcycle.

If the last sentence in the preceding list had been included in that earlier passage about the accident, it would have been impossible for the reader to miss the new information; the emphasis is clearly on *yesterday*. And the sentence rhythm remains standard, with an opening valley. The *it*-cleft is not a structure you will want to overuse, but it certainly is useful—and almost foolproof—when it comes to controlling the rhythm of a sentence and directing the reader's focus.

Another cleft transformation, also described in Chapter 5, uses a *what* clause to direct the reader's attention:

Mike's cynical attitude toward the customers really bothers me.

Cleft: What bothers me is Mike's cynical attitude toward the customers.

Cleft: What bothers me about Mike is his cynical attitude toward the customers.

The purpose of these transformations is clearly to allow the subject to get the main focus by shifting it to the end of the sentence. Following is a context in which the transformed version is clearly needed:

> Apparently the shift supervisor has threatened to fire Mike because he hasn't been following procedures. But I don't see that as Mike's main problem. His cynical attitude toward the customers really bothers me.

The subject slot of the last sentence in the passage names the "main problem" referred to in the preceding sentence; it's the new information. But subject position is not where we normally expect the new information to be, so the sentence loses its natural rhythm. The *what*-cleft would shift the new information, giving it the end focus we expect:

> What bothers me is his cynical attitude toward the customers.

Another common sentence variation you saw in Chapter 5 is the *there* transformation, which allows the writer to focus on the subject by shifting it to the slot following *be*—either the predicating *be* or the auxiliary *be*:

> <u>Several hundred people</u> were crowding the courtroom.
> There were several hundred people crowding the courtroom.
>
> <u>Another big crowd</u> was in the hallway.
> There was another big crowd in the hallway.

The last paragraph in the previous Investigating Language exercise includes two *there*-transformations in the second sentence:

> There is a vast literature on the effects of caffeine on the body, and for every study reaching one conclusion, seemingly there is another that contradicts it.

Here the author undoubtedly wants the reader to put main stress on *vast literature* and on *another*.

Do writers consciously call up such rhythm-controlling devices from their grammar tool kits as they write? Do they deliberately say, "Time to use my trusty *it*-cleft, or should I delay this subject with the *there*-transformation?"

No, they probably don't. They may not even have labels like "transformation" and "cleft" to describe those structures. But as experienced writers and readers, they're tuned into sentence rhythm as they compose—especially as they revise. Published paragraphs such as those in the previous Investigating Language exercise did not spring fully developed from the heads of their authors. Those final drafts may have gone through many revisions. It's in the revision stage that writers experiment with such devices as the *it*- and *what*-clefts and the *there*-transformation and make decisions about their effectiveness. And you can be sure that in reading their own prose, whether silently or aloud, they are paying attention to sentence rhythm.

Unfortunately, the *there* and the cleft transformations are often misunderstood in handbooks and style manuals; they are seen as wordy, indirect ways of conveying ideas rather than as alternatives that give the writer a choice, that enable the writer to control the sentence focus. It's true, of course, that you won't want to overuse these transformations. You will want to consider the larger context, to pay attention to how many other *it* or *what* or *there* sentences occur in proximity. But certainly these kinds of sentence manipulations are valuable tools for the right occasion.

=== *Exercise 53* ===

Rewrite the following sentences, shifting the focus by using sentence transformations: the *it*-cleft, the *what*-cleft, and *there*. For example, you could use a cleft structure in the first sentence to focus either on Jody or on the flavor; in the second sentence, you could focus on the date or the place or the ship or the iceberg. Note that the various transformations will not work equally well with all the sentences.

1. Jody loves chocolate ice cream.
2. The *Titanic* hit an iceberg and sank in the North Atlantic in 1912.
3. Our defense won the Stanford game in the final three minutes with a crucial interception.
4. Florida's agriculture and tourism industries will feel the sting when the African "killer" bee arrives in the 1990s as scientists expect. [*Orlando Sentinel*]

5. Tuesday's earthquake started with a small slip of the earth eleven miles beneath the ground. [Glenda Chui, *San Jose Mercury News*]
6. Hundreds of angry women were protesting the senator's position on day care at yesterday's political rally in the student union.
7. A month of unseasonably warm weather almost ruined the ski season last winter.
8. In the last few months of 1989, a democratic revolution that swept Eastern Europe changed our foreign policy agenda.

THE PASSIVE VOICE

Another misunderstood structure is the passive sentence, which some English teachers simply declare out of bounds. Such edicts come about because students so often use passives when they shouldn't—and it's true that ineffective passives do stand out. But it is both simplistic and inaccurate to flatly rule out the passive voice; all good prose includes both active and passive.

As we have seen, all these transformations—the cleft sentences, the *there* transformation, and the passive voice—enable writers to shift the emphasis in the sentence, so that the reader will put the focus where it should be: on the new information. That shift, especially in the case of the passive voice, can also provide transition between sentences. You'll recall that in most sentences the new information, which is where the main focus will occur, is at or near the end, in object position, while the known information is in the subject slot. However, if the direct object is the known information, it can be shifted to the subject slot by means of the passive transformation. That opening information will provide transition from the previous sentence.

Here, for example, is a paragraph from *Time* about the destruction of the Brazilian rain forests. Note that in the second sentence, which is passive, the subject provides that transition:

If Americans are truly interested in saving the rain forests, they should move beyond rhetoric and suggest *policies* that are practical—and acceptable—to the understandably wary Brazilians. *Such policies* cannot be presented as take-them-or-leave-them propositions. If the U.S. expects better performance from Brazil, Brazil has a right to make demands in return. In fact, the U.S. and Brazil need to engage in face-to-face negotiations as part of a formal dialogue on the environment between the industrial nations and the developing countries. The two sides frequently negotiate on debt refinancing and other issues. Why not put the environment at the top of the agenda?

—MICHAEL D. LEMONICK

In the first sentence, *policies* is new information; in the second, it is known.

In many situations, of course, the purpose of the passive is simply to avoid mentioning the agent:

> It was reported today that the federal funds to be allocated for the power plant would not be forthcoming as early as had been anticipated. Some contracts on the preliminary work have been canceled and others renegotiated.

Such "officialese" or "bureaucratese" takes on a nonhuman quality because the agent role has completely disappeared from the sentences. In the foregoing example the reader does not know who is reporting, allocating, anticipating, canceling, or renegotiating.

This kind of agentless passive is especially common in official news conferences, where press secretaries and other government officials explain what is happening without revealing who is responsible for making it happen:

> Recommendations are being made to the Israeli government concerning the Middle East problem.
> A tax hike has been proposed, but several other solutions to the federal deficit are also being considered.
> The president has been advised that certain highly placed officials are being investigated.

The faceless passive does an efficient job of obscuring responsibility, but it is neither efficient nor graceful for the writing that most of us do in school and on the job.

Sometimes the inexperienced writer resorts to the passive voice simply to avoid using the first-person point of view. Here is a gardener's active account of spring planting written in the first person (*we*):

> In late April, when the ground dried out enough to be worked, we planted peas and onions and potatoes and prepared the soil for the rest of the vegetables. Then in mid-May we set out the tomato and pepper plants, hoping we had seen the last of frost.

Certainly the first person as used here would seem to be the logical choice for such a passage; nevertheless, some writers take great pains to avoid it (and, unfortunately, some writing texts, for no logical reason, warn against using the first person). The result is a gardener's passive account of spring planting—without the gardener:

> In late April, when the ground dried out enough to be worked, the peas and onions and potatoes were planted and the soil was prepared for the rest of the vegetables. Then in mid-May the tomato and pepper plants were set out in hopes that the frost was over.

This revision is certainly not as stilted as the earlier examples of agentless prose, but it does lack the live, human quality that the active version has.

Here's another example of the passive, typical of the student writer who has managed to avoid using *I*, perhaps because the paper has too many of them already or because the teacher has ruled out the first-person point of view:

> The incessant sound of foghorns could be heard along the water-
> front.

But English is a versatile language: First person is not the only alternative. Here's a version of the sentence using *sound* as the verb:

> The foghorn sounded along the waterfront.

And here's one that describes the movement of the sound:

> The incessant sound of foghorns floated across the water.

Many times, of course, the writer simply doesn't realize that the passive voice may be the culprit producing the vagueness or wordiness of that first draft. For example, the writer of the following sentence ended a family Christmas story with no awareness of voice at all:

> That visit from Santa was an occurrence that would never be forgotten by the family.

The active version produces a tight, straightforward sentence:

> The family would never forget that visit from Santa.

The writer could also have found an active sentence that retains *visit* as the subject:

> That visit from Santa became part of our family legend.

The passive voice certainly has a place in everyone's writing. It will be effective, however, only when the writer understands it and uses it in a conscious and controlled way.

THE ABSTRACT SUBJECT

As you know from your study of the passive voice, the agent—the perpetrator—is not always the subject of the sentence; in some passive sentences it doesn't appear at all. However, the more concrete and active the sentence, the more likely the agent will function as the subject—or at least make an appearance. The more abstract and passive the sentence, the more likely the agent will be missing.

One common cause of abstraction is **nominalization,** verbs that have been turned into nouns. The word *occurrence* in the previous discussion about Santa's visit is one such example; we saw other nominalizations in Chapters 10 and 11 in connection with derivational affixes, the word endings that change the class of the word. Remember that a verb is an action word. A verb *shows* the action; but a noun simply *names* the action:

> The governor's <u>opposition</u> to abortion has caused many pro-choice organizations to work against his reelection.

There is a growing <u>recognition</u> that forests are more valuable when
left standing.

Our language, of course, is filled with nominalized verbs—most of which
are useful, legitimate ways of expressing ideas. In the second sentence of
this paragraph, for example, you'll see *discussion* and *connection*, both of
which began as verbs (*discuss*, *connect*) and are now ordinary, everyday
nouns.

But because nominalized verbs are so common and so easy to produce,
they can become a trap for the unwary writer, introducing abstraction
where concrete ideas belong. It's during the revision stage of writing
that you'll want to be on the lookout. Ask yourself, is the agent there and,
if so, is it functioning as the subject? In other words, does the sentence
explain *who is doing what?* If the answer is no, your sentence may be a
prime candidate for revision.

Another source of abstraction and flabbiness is the sentence with a
verb phrase or a clause as subject, rather than the usual noun phrase.
You learned in Chapter 4 that these structures are grammatical, common
substitutes for noun phrases. But because they are abstractions, they too
may be pitfalls for the unwary writer. Again, the source of the problem
may be that of the missing or misplaced agent:

> The <u>buying</u> of so many American companies and so much real
> estate by the Japanese is causing concern on Wall Street.
> With the opening of the East Bloc nations to democracy and
> capitalism, <u>what is happening</u> is that American companies are
> looking for ways of expanding their markets and their product
> lines to take advantage of the situation.
> <u>Analyzing</u> the situation in Eastern Europe has shown that oppor-
> tunities for investment are growing.

Although we need context to tell us the best way to revise these
sentences, we can see and hear a problem. The sentences seem to be
about actions—but they can't show the action in a strong and concrete
way because the agents of those actions are not there in subject position.
This kind of agentless sentence should send up a red flag—a signal that
here's a possible candidate for revision.

===== *Exercise 54* =====

Here are some sentences that might sound familiar—that is, you may write like this yourself. Try to achieve a more direct style and tone as you revise the sentences. Be especially alert to unnecessary nominalizations and ineffective passives. The first three items are the examples from the preceding discussion. Remember to ask yourself, "Who is doing what?"

1. The buying of so many American companies and so much real estate by the Japanese is causing concern on Wall Street.
2. With the opening of the East Bloc nations to democracy and capitalism, what is happening is that American companies are looking for ways of expanding their markets and their product lines to take advantage of the situation.
3. Analyzing the situation in Eastern Europe has shown that opportunities for investment are growing.
4. In the biography of Lyndon Johnson by Robert Caro, an account of the Senate election of 1948 is described in great detail.
5. When Julie filled out an application for a work-study job, she was surprised to learn that a detailed financial statement would have to be submitted by her parents.
6. Getting his new pizza shop to finally turn a profit has meant a lot of hard work and long hours for Tim.
7. The broadening of one's view of life and the establishment of worthy goals are both important aims of education.
8. The encouragement of the thinking process is also an important educational aim. Strategies should be developed by students for the understanding of problems and for their solutions.

INTERRUPTING THE RHYTHM PATTERN

The sentence transformations with *it* and *what* and *there* and the passive voice are not the only ways we have to control the rhythm of sentences. Other ways, in fact, are much more common and, in most cases, more subtle. The phrase "in fact" in the preceding sentence illustrates one such method—a set phrase that interrupts the rhythm pattern. You'll recognize it from Chapter 8 as a sentence modifier. When it's inserted within the sentence, rather than at the opening, it adds a new intonation contour within the sentence while adding stress to the subject. We can illustrate the difference with a picture of the contours:

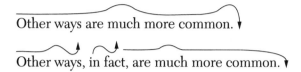

Other ways are much more common.

Other ways, in fact, are much more common.

The visual signal of the commas causes the reader to give added length and stress to the preceding word. And, as the contour lines illustrate, the sentence has gone from having one intonation contour to having three. The main focus is still on the new information at the end, but the sentence rhythm has changed, with part of the reader's attention shifted to the subject.

There are many such parenthetical elements that we add to sentences to control the reader's attention. Not all of them are set phrases, such as "in fact"; sometimes they are subordinate clauses or adverbials or other modifiers. For example, when you read the second sentence in the previous paragraph, with its inserted *as* clause, you lengthened the opening *and*. Because of the comma, you gave that one word its own contour:

And, as the contour lines illustrate, the sentence. . . .

Without the comma, the *and* would have been an unstressed valley.

The movability of conjunctive adverbs, which you saw in Chapter 9, also gives the writer a chance to change the way the reader will stress the sentence:

> Until recently Australia has seemed a strange and distant place to Americans, both geographically and mentally; however, an outpouring of books and television shows and movies has helped to close that distance.

> . . . ; an outpouring of books and television shows and movies, however, has helped to close that distance.

> . . . ; an outpouring of books and television shows and movies has helped to close that distance, however.

In the second version *movies* gets added stress and length, and in the third version *distance* does.

THE SHIFTING ADVERBIALS

One of the writer's most versatile sentence elements is the adverbial, in terms of both form and position. As you recall from Chapter 6, the adverbs and prepositional phrases and noun phrases and verb phrases and clauses that add adverbial information can open the sentence or close it, or they can interrupt it somewhere in the middle. Sentence variety by itself is, of course, not a reason for opening or closing a sentence with an adverbial structure. Rather, you should understand the effects on the reader that adverbials will have in different positions.

In Chapter 2 we labeled the adverbial function as "optional," but that label is somewhat misleading. Even though the adverbial information is rarely needed from a grammatical point of view, it is often the main idea—the new information of the sentence. For example, in the sentence,

> I got up <u>early</u> <u>to study for my Spanish test</u>,

the two adverbials are optional in terms of the sentence pattern: *I got up* is a grammatical Pattern VI sentence. But the person saying that sentence probably says it to convey time or purpose. It's the information in one or both adverbials that actually provides the main focus of the sentence.

The decision about placement of adverbials, then, is connected to sentence focus and to the concept of known and new information. If the adverbial is the main focus, it will probably be at or near the end of the sentence. We saw an example of this situation earlier in this chapter with the sentence "Barbara wrecked her motorcycle yesterday," where the adverb *yesterday* supplied the new information. In opening position, the adverbial will usually tie the sentence to what has gone before, either because it is the known information or because it is providing a cohesive element, such as time sequence, with an adverbial like *then* or *later that day* or *on the following afternoon*. The opening adverbial in the sentence you just read provides that cohesive tie: *In opening position* contrasts with the discussion in the previous sentence about closing position. In a sense it is known information, even though opening position had not been discussed in the paragraph up to that point: Common sense tells us that a sentence has an opening as well as a closing position.

The versatility of adverbials lies not only in the variety of positions they can occupy; it lies also in the variety of their forms. They can be short and brisk, or they can be long and relaxed, changing the tone and pace of the sentence.

> I haven't been feeling well <u>lately</u>.
>
> I haven't been feeling well <u>since September</u>.
>
> I haven't been feeling well <u>since the beginning of the semester</u>.
>
> I haven't been feeling well <u>since September, when the semester started</u>.

The Adverbial Clause.   In Chapters 6 and 8 we emphasized the movable nature of adverbial and subordinate clauses. They are both movable and versatile: Our long list of subordinators enables us to connect ideas for a wide variety of reasons. And certainly subordinate clauses are common structures in our language: In speech we use them often and automatically. In writing, of course, they are not automatic, nor are they always used as effectively as they could be. Two problems that show up fairly often are related to the meaning of the sentence: (1) The wrong idea gets subordinated; and (2) the meaning of the subordinator is imprecise.

Here, for example, are two related ideas that a writer might want to combine into a single sentence:

> We worked hard for the candidates.
> We suspected they didn't stand a chance.

Here are some possibilities for connecting them:

> <u>While</u> we worked hard for the candidates, we suspected they didn't stand a chance.
>
> <u>Although</u> we worked hard for the candidates, we suspected they didn't stand a chance.
>
> We worked hard for the candidates, <u>even though</u> we suspected they didn't stand a chance.

We need context, of course, to know precisely what the connection between the two ideas should be, but given no other information, the last version expresses what would appear to be the logical relationship.

Perhaps an even more common problem than the imprecise subordinator is the compound sentence with no subordination—the sentence with two independent clauses, two equal focuses, that would be more accurate and effective with a single focus. The most common culprit is the compound sentence connected by *but*:

> The prime rate went down two percentage points during the last quarter, but government economists are still worried about high inflation and low productivity.

Because *but* is a coordinating conjunction, just as *and* is, the sentence has two ideas that, by reason of the structure, can be considered only as equals. But are they? Probably not.

Here's another compound sentence with *but*, a paragraph opener in an article about sleep. The paragraph preceding this one gives examples of accidents on the job connected with work schedules:

> The biological clock is flexible enough to adjust to slight changes in a person's work schedule, *but* in many industries rotations in shift work are so drastic that they play havoc with body rhythms, leaving employees unable to sleep at home and impairing their productivity at work. (italics added)
>
> —ERIK ECKHOLM, *The New York Times Magazine*

Here the two clauses are clearly not equal: The main idea is the second clause. The idea in the first clause, although it has not previously appeared in the article, is presented as understood, as information the reader is assumed to know—the known information. The new information is in the second clause. Making the first clause subordinate will help the reader focus on the new idea:

> *Although* the biological clock is flexible enough to adjust to slight changes in a person's work schedule, in many industries rotations in shift work are so drastic that they play havoc with body rhythms, leaving employees unable to sleep at home and impairing their productivity at work.

Remember that a compound sentence has two points of focus that, in terms of structure, are equal. The compound sentence is effective only when that structure accurately reflects the relationship of the two ideas. If a single point of focus would be more accurate, then a subordinating conjunction should introduce one of the two ideas.

=== *Exercise 55* ==========================

Combine each of the following groups of sentences into a single sentence by using subordination. In some cases you will want to reword the sentence. Remember that the subordinator you select will signal the relationship between the two ideas. You can probably come up with more than one possibility for each.

1. The famous Gateway Arch is in St. Louis.
   Kansas City claims the title "Gateway to the West."
2. Our spring semester doesn't end until the second week of June.
   Many students have a hard time finding summer jobs.
3. Thomas Jefferson acquired the Ozark Mountains for the United States in 1803.
   That was the year of the Louisiana Purchase.
   We bought the Louisiana Territory from Napoleon.
4. Many attorneys are unacquainted with oil and gas laws.
   They are unable to offer advice concerning oil and gas leases to their clients.
5. The neighbors added a pit bull to their pet population, which now numbers three unfriendly four-legged creatures.
   We have decided to fence in our back yard.
6. The human circulatory system is a marvel of efficiency.
   It is still subject to a wide variety of degenerative diseases.
7. Carbohydrates—starches—are the body's prime source of energy.
   Fad diets that severely restrict the intake of starches are nearly always ineffective.
   Such diets can also be dangerous.
8. Our congressman knows that the majority of voters in this district are upset with their tax rates.
   They also don't like the way their tax dollars are being spent.
   He has made "No New Taxes" the main theme of his reelection campaign.

9. Auto companies offered enticing cash rebates to buyers of new cars last January.

Car sales increased dramatically.

10. By 1890 the buffalo population of the West had been nearly wiped out.

It now numbers about 60,000.

About 400 ranchers in Colorado are raising buffalo for meat.

The Adverbs of Emphasis.   As you know the adverbials are versatile structures. They provide their information of time, place, manner, and the like in a variety of shapes; and they give the writer special flexibility because they can fill so many different slots—at the beginning, the middle, and the end of sentences. But there's another group of adverbials, mainly single-word adverbs, whose purpose is to emphasize a particular structure and thus control the pace and rhythm of the sentence.

Read the following sentences and note where you apply the main stress:

I hardly slept last night.
I slept hardly at all last night.
My roommate also had trouble sleeping.
Some people are always looking for trouble.
Joe tells me that he rarely stays awake past midnight.
The country has never before faced the kind of crisis it faces with AIDS.
Scientists will surely find a cure for AIDS before long.
Many people assumed that by now the mystery of AIDS would have been solved.

You probably put the emphasis on *hardly, all, also, always, rarely, never, before, surely,* and *by now.*

Given these examples, you can think of other words that you use for emphasis: other negatives, such as *seldom, barely, scarcely;* other time and frequency words, such as *afterwards, finally, sometimes;* and others expressing duration, such as *already, no longer, still.*

It's possible, of course, to write sentences in which these words would not have main stress, where the principle of end focus, for example, would still be in effect. But certainly these are words that you, as a writer, need to recognize; they often wield the power in a sentence, controlling its intonation contour and making a difference in the message.

The Common Only.   One of our most versatile—but also most frequently misused—adverbials of emphasis is the common **only**. Like other emphasizers, *only* can change the focus of the sentence by directing the reader's attention to a particular word:

> I'm taking <u>only twelve</u> credits this semester.
> The car <u>only looks</u> old; it's really quite new.
> Joe isn't <u>only handsome</u>; he's rich too.
> Paul cleans house <u>only on Saturdays</u>.

When you read these sentences, you'll find yourself putting nearly equal emphasis on both *only* and the word that follows it.

But there's also a common problem with *only*: It's frequently misplaced—and most of the time we don't even notice!

> I'm only taking twelve credits this semester.
> Paul only cleans house on Saturdays.
> We're only going to be gone for two or three days.
> Jane refuses to watch the Super Bowl; she only likes baseball.

Even songwriters get it wrong:

> I only have eyes for you.

A well-placed *only* can strengthen the sentence focus. It sends a message to the reader that the writer has crafted the sentence carefully. The fuzzy *only*, even though it's a common mistake, is one you'll want to avoid.

APPOSITIVES

The Sentence Appositive.   The sentence appositive is a noun phrase that encapsulates the idea of the sentence in a tightly structured way. Here are two compound sentences, both of which are candidates for tightening:

> The musical opened to rave reviews and standing-room-only crowds; it was a smashing success.
> A pair of cardinals has set up housekeeping in our pine tree; we consider it a most welcome event, even though it was unexpected.

In these compound sentences, the second one can be turned into a noun phrase and added to the first as a sentence appositive:

> The musical opened to rave reviews and standing-room-only crowds—a smashing success.
> A pair of cardinals has set up housekeeping in our pine tree—an unexpected but welcome event.

Often the clue to that kind of revision is the sentence with a subjective complement—or, in the case of the second example, an objective complement. That complement can be turned into a summary statement that focuses the idea of the main clause; in other words, the original subjective or objective complement becomes a sentence appositive.

The Nominal Appositive.   The appositive that renames a nominal, which you studied in Chapter 4, provides the same kind of tightening effect that the sentence appositive does. It's an especially useful tool for helping novice writers avoid two common problems: short, choppy sentences and the overuse of *be* as a predicating verb.

> Alan B. Shepard *was* <u>the first American to fly in space</u>. He was launched on a 302-mile suborbital shot over the Atlantic in May, 1961.
> I'll never forget the birthday present my dad bought me when I was ten. It *was* <u>a new three-speed bike</u>.
> In August of 1992 Hurricane Andrew hit Florida and Louisiana with winds that clocked 175 mph; it *was* <u>the country's worst natural disaster in this century</u>.

In each of these examples, you'll notice that one of the two clauses has a form of *be* as its predicating verb followed by a noun phrase as subjective complement; the subject of the second clause in each case is *it*. This common situation is the ideal candidate for a combined sentence containing an appositive:

> Alan B. Shepard, <u>the first American to fly in space</u>, was launched on a 302-mile suborbital shot over the Atlantic in May, 1961.
>
> I'll never forget the birthday present my dad bought me when I was ten, <u>a new three-speed bike</u>.
>
> In August of 1992 Hurricane Andrew hit Florida and Louisiana with winds that clocked 175 mph, <u>the country's worst natural disaster in this century</u>.

It's possible that the context might call for a different emphasis:

> Alan B. Shepard, launched on a 302-mile suborbital shot over the Atlantic in May, 1961, was the first American to fly in space.
>
> I'll never forget my first three-speed bike, a birthday present from my dad when I was ten.

When the appositive renames the subject, it has another important feature. It is movable; it can open or close the sentence. At the end of the sentence, the appositive will be the point of focus. At the beginning, it will tend to put more stress on the subject, which will no longer be an opening valley in the intonation contour:

> The first American to fly in space, Alan B. Shepard was launched on a 302-mile suborbital shot over the Atlantic in May, 1961.
>
> Alan B. Shepard was launched on a 302-mile suborbital shot over the Atlantic in May, 1961, the first American to fly in space.

Of these three positions for the appositive, the "home base" position, the slot following the noun, gets the least emphasis. This is what is called the unmarked position; in other words, it is the expected one.

The Colon with Appositives.   To understand appositives is to understand that tricky mark of punctuation, the colon. The structure that follows the colon is, in fact, an appositive. The examples of closing appositives that we saw earlier could be signaled by the colon:

> In August of 1992 Hurricane Andrew hit Florida and Louisiana with winds that clocked 175 mph: the country's worst natural disaster in this century.
>
> I'll never forget the birthday present my dad bought me when I was ten: a new three-speed bike.

As we saw earlier, both of the foregoing sentences can also be written with a comma instead of a colon. With the comma, however, there is less anticipation; the appositive gets less emphasis.

One of the most common uses of the colon is to signal a list:

> Three committees were set up to plan the convention: <u>program, finance, and local arrangements.</u>

Here the list is actually a list of appositives renaming the noun *committees*. The colon is a way of saying, "Here it comes, the list I promised." Sometimes the list following the colon includes internal punctuation other than commas:

> The study of our grammar system includes three areas: phonology, the study of sounds; morphology, the study of meaningful combinations of sounds; and syntax, the study of sentences.

Here the list includes three nouns, each of which has a nonrestrictive postnoun modifier of its own. This is one of the two occasions in our writing system that call for the semicolon. (The other, the joining of clauses in compound sentences, is discussed on pages 252–53.)

When the appositive in its home base position is a list, we use a pair of dashes to set it off:

> Three committees—<u>program, finance, and local arrangements</u>— were set up to plan the convention.
>
> All three areas of our grammar system—<u>phonology, morphology, and syntax</u>—are covered in this book.

Dashes will add emphasis even when the appositive has no internal punctuation; the dashes announce the appositive with a kind of fanfare:

> Maria's latest purchase—<u>a new IBM computer</u>—has really pleased her.

The main stress of the sentence, however, remains on the predicate.

Notice that dashes within the sentence always come in pairs. At the end of the sentence we use a single dash:

> I ordered my favorite flavor—<u>pistachio nut</u>.
>
> Our visitor was a stranger with a long, jet-black beard—<u>a real mystery man</u>.

Avoiding Punctuation Errors. The use of the colon with appositives is the source of a common punctuation error, but one simple rule can resolve it:

A COMPLETE SENTENCE PRECEDES THE COLON.

Notice in the examples that the structure preceding the colon is a complete sentence pattern, with every slot filled:

> Three committees were set up to plan the convention.
> The study of our grammar system includes three areas.

Because the colon so often does precede a list, the writer may assume that every list should be preceded by one, but that is not the case. In the following sentences, the colons are misused:

> *The committees that were set up to plan the convention are: program, finance, and local arrangements.
> *The three areas of the grammar system are: phonology, morphology, and syntax.

Your understanding of the sentence patterns will tell you that a subjective complement is needed to complete these sentences in which a form of *be* is the predicating verb.

One common variation for the sentence with a list includes the phrase *the following*:

> The committees that were set up to plan the convention are the following: program, finance, and local arrangements.

That noun phrase, *the following*, fills the subjective complement slot, so the sentence is indeed grammatical. But it is not necessarily the most effective version of the sentence. If you want to use a colon in such a sentence for purposes of emphasis, the earlier version is smoother and more concise:

> Three committees were set up to plan the convention: program, finance, and local arrangements.

═══════ *Exercise 56* ═══════

Revise and/or combine the following sentences or groups by providing an appositive or by changing the focus. Experiment with commas, colons, and dashes.

1. The cost of repairs to the nation's public transportation facilities is an expenditure that cannot be delayed much longer if the system is to survive. Roads, bridges, and railroads are all in need of repair.
2. To many people, the mushroom is a lowly fungus. It has little food value. To other people, it is a gourmet's delight.
3. In the early 1980s the Chinese banned the import of certain American goods, such as cotton, synthetic fibers, and soybeans. The restriction had an adverse effect on the U.S. economy, especially on the farmers.
4. According to fashion experts, the crew cut will be back in style before long. That particular haircut was more or less the hallmark of the 1950s.
5. My favorite activities are skiing, playing golf, and bowling; unfortunately, they cost more than my budget can stand.
6. Alexander Graham Bell is remembered as the inventor of the telephone. Most people probably don't know that Bell succeeded his father-in-law as president of the National Geographic Society.
7. Cypress Gardens, Florida, comprises thirty acres of flowers, exotic plants, and wildlife. It is a year-round extravaganza of nature's bounty and beauty.

8. Many scientists believe that sightings of "cryptids" are mistakes. Cryptids include Big Foot, the Loch Ness monster, and Yeti, known as the Abominable Snowman. Mistaken sightings can be attributed to unfamiliarity with known animals, rather than to delusions.

STYLE

We all know the word *style* as it pertains to fashion and decor. When we say that a hat or a room "has style," we are judging it in a positive way, as appropriate and pleasing. We also use the word with modifiers: "1950s style" or "hippie style" or "L.L. Bean style" clothes; "Victorian style" or "early American style" or "late Salvation Army style" furniture. Such terms can be either positive or negative, depending on the writing or speaking situation.

What do we mean by style in writing? We don't say of a particular piece of writing that it "has style"; nevertheless, we do make judgments about the appropriateness of a certain style or about its clarity or its obliqueness. We also use the word *style* to characterize the writing of a particular author. The straightforward, seemingly simple prose of Ernest Hemingway, for instance—the "Hemingway style"—contrasts with complex embeddings of William Faulkner, as the following passage from Faulkner's "Barn Burning" illustrates:

> The boy, crouched on his nail keg at the back of the crowded room, knew he smelled cheese, and more: from where he sat he could see the ranked shelves close-packed with the solid, squat, dynamic shapes of tin cans whose labels his stomach read, not from the lettering which meant nothing to his mind but from the scarlet devils and the silver curve of fish—this, the cheese which he knew he smelled and the hermetic meat which his intestines believed he smelled coming in intermittent gusts momentary and brief between the other constant one, the smell and sense just a little of fear because mostly of despair and grief, the old fierce pull of blood.

Such publications as *Time*, *The New Yorker*, and *National Geographic* are also known for particular styles. And certain professions produce a characteristic style: *Official style* and *bureaucratese* and *educationese* are terms used to characterize the dehumanized communications that so often emanate from government officials, social scientists, and educators. The word *style,* then, refers to certain features of the writing of individuals and groups.

Learning to listen with your inner ear is one technique for becoming conscious of and improving your sentence style as you reread and revise your prose. Another is to apply what you know about sentence grammar. You have learned about a variety of ways to expand sentences using modification and coordination and subordination. In this section we will examine how deviations from the usual and expected sentence structure can affect a writer's style.

Word Order Variation.   Variation from the standard subject-verb-object word order is fairly common in poetry; it can be effective in prose as well, partly because it is uncommon. In the following sentence, Charles Dickens made sure that the reader would hear the contrast between *has* and *has not:*

Talent, Mr. Micawber has; money, Mr. Micawber has not.

Another fairly common rearrangement occurs when a clause as direct object opens the sentence:

Which of these calls seemed more mysterious, it is not possible to say.

—JAMES AGEE

Robert Frost used this variation, too, in the first line of his famous poem "Stopping by Woods on a Snowy Evening":

Whose woods these are, I think I know.

Notice that all these variations put special emphasis on the verb, the slot that would normally be in a valley when the sentence has a direct object.

With certain adverbs in opening position, a shift of subject and auxiliary is called for:

Never before had I seen such an eerie glow in the night sky.
Rarely do I hear such words of praise.

You'll notice that the opening adverbial is a peak of stress.

The following sentence, written by Winston Churchill, illustrates another kind of shift in word order. Here the very last noun phrase in the sentence is the grammatical subject:

Against Lee and his great Lieutenant [Stonewall Jackson], united for a year of intense action in a comradeship which recalls that of Marlborough and Eugene, were now to be marshaled *the overwhelming forces of the Union.* (italics added)

When you read this sentence aloud, you can hear your voice building to a peak of stress on *overwhelming forces,* just as Churchill planned. In fact, it's hard to read the sentence without sounding Churchillian.

Ellipsis. Another fairly common stylistic variation is the use of ellipsis, where part of the sentence is simply left out, or "understood," usually for the purpose of avoiding repetition. In the following description of Stonewall Jackson, which we saw in Chapter 9, Churchill used ellipses in both sentences. In the first, he left out the linking verb in all but the first clause. The tightness of the sentence actually reflects the description of Jackson's character:

His character was stern, his manner [was] reserved and usually forbidding, his temper [was] Calvinistic, his mode of life [was] strict, frugal, austere.

Black-bearded, pale-faced, with thin, compressed lips, aquiline nose, and dark, piercing eyes, he slouched in his weather-stained uniform a professor-warrior; yet [he was] greatly beloved by the few who knew him best, and [he was] gifted with that strange power of commanding measureless devotion from the thousands whom he ruled with an iron hand.

Notice also in the last sentence that in the clause after the semicolon both the subjects and the verbs are understood.

And here's a sentence that includes both ellipsis and a shift in word order:

Of time, I have plenty; of money, no need.

The Coordinate Series.   Many of the structural variations that writers use for special effects occur in connection with coordinate structures—pairs and series of sentences and sentence parts. One effective way of changing the emphasis in coordinate structures entails a small deviation from the usual way of using conjunctions. In a series of three or more structures, we generally use commas between the parts of the series, and we use a conjunction before the final member:

At the class reunion, we laughed, reminisced, and sang the old songs.

Here are two variations. Read them aloud and listen to the differences.

At the class reunion we laughed and reminisced and sang the old songs.
At the class reunion we laughed, reminisced, sang the old songs.

The differences are subtle, but meaningful. The first variation puts emphasis on each verb with a fairly equal beat: / and / and /. It also puts a lilt in your voice. The second variation, the one without conjunctions, has an open-ended quality, as though the list were incomplete. The writer seems to be saying, "I could go on and on; I could tell you much more."

The first sentence in Churchill's description of Jackson includes that second technique. The phrases themselves have no conjunctions, as a regular series would, nor does the final series of adjectives:

His character was stern, his manner reserved and usually forbidding, his temper Calvinistic, his mode of life strict, frugal, austere.

The omission of the conjunction contributes to the strictness and frugality of style that echo the words themselves. With conjunctions, the sentence would lose that echo:

His mode of life was strict and frugal and austere.

The Introductory Appositive Series. You'll recall from your study of nominals that the appositive is a noun phrase that renames another noun. In the following passages, the sentence opens with a series of noun phrases that act as appositives to the subject. In the first example, Churchill describes Queen Victoria:

> High devotion to her royal task, domestic virtues, evident sincerity of nature, a piercing and sometime disconcerting truthfulness— all these qualities of the Queen's had long impressed themselves upon the mind of her subjects.

Often the noun phrase series is in apposition to a pronoun as subject, as in this example from William Golding:

> Political and religious systems, social customs, loyalties and traditions, they all came tumbling down like so many rotten apples off a tree.

Notice, too, in these examples that the series does not include a conjunction before the last member.

The Deliberate Sentence Fragment. The sentence fragments that composition teachers flag with a marginal "frag" are the unintentional kind, usually the result of punctuation errors, the most common being the subordinate clause punctuated as a full sentence. But not all fragments are errors. Experienced writers know how to use them effectively—noun phrases or verb phrases that invariably call attention to themselves. The first two examples are from novels of John le Carré:

> They remembered the tinkling of falling glass all right, and the timid brushing noise of the young foliage hitting the road. And the mewing of people too frightened to scream.
>
> — *The Little Drummer Girl*

Our Candidate begins speaking. A deliberate, unimpressive opening.

— A Perfect Spy

In the following paragraph from *Love Medicine* by Louise Erdrich, we are hearing fragmented thoughts—ideal candidates for sentence fragments. You'll notice that some are simple noun phrases, some are absolutes—a noun with a modifier following—and some are subordinate clauses. But, obviously, all are deliberate:

Northern lights. Something in the cold, wet atmosphere brought them out. I grabbed Lipsha's arm. We floated into the field and sank down, crushing green wheat. We chewed the sweet kernels and stared up and were lost. Everything seemed to be one piece. The air, our faces, all cool, moist, and dark, and the ghostly sky. Pale green licks of light pulsed and faded across it. Living lights. Their fires lobbed over, higher, higher, then died out in blackness. At times the whole sky was ringed in shooting points and puckers of light gathering and falling, pulsing, fading, rhythmical as breathing. All of a piece. As if the sky were a pattern of nerves and our thought and memories traveled across it. As if the sky were one gigantic memory for us all. Or a dance hall. And all the world's wandering souls were dancing there. I thought of June. She would be dancing if there were a dance hall in space. She would be dancing a two-step for wandering souls. Her long legs lifting and falling. Her laugh an ace. Her sweet perfume the way all grown-up women were supposed to smell. Her amusement at both the bad and the good. Her defeat. Her reckless victory. Her sons.

Repetition.   Repetition has come up before in these pages—in both a positive and a negative sense. On the positive side, repetition gives our sentences cohesion: The known–new contract calls for the repetition, if not of words, then of ideas. It is part of the glue that holds sentences together. But we also have a negative label for repetition when it has no purpose, when it gets in the reader's way:

Then we call it redundancy. If you've heard warnings about redundancy, if you've seen "red" in the margins of your essays, you might hesitate to use repetition deliberately. But don't hesitate. It's easy to distinguish redundancy from good repetition, from repetition as a stylistic tool.

The Greek rhetoricians had labels for every conceivable kind of good repetition—from the repetition of sounds and syllables to that of words and phrases in various locations in the sentence. We'll confine our discussion to repetition in coordinate structures that will make the reader sit up and take notice.

Consider the Gettysburg Address. Which of Lincoln's words, other than "Fourscore and seven years ago," do you remember? Probably "government of the people, by the people, and for the people." It's hard to imagine those words without the repetition: "Of, by, and for the people" just wouldn't have the same effect. And think about President Kennedy's stirring words, with his repetition of *any:*

> [W]e shall pay any price, bear any burden, meet any hardship, support any friend, oppose any foe to assure the survival and the success of liberty.

(Notice, too, that the conjunction has been omitted before the last member of the series. He seems to be saying, "I could go on and on with my list.")

You don't have to be a president to use that kind of repetition, nor do you have to reserve it for formal occasions. Whenever you use a coordinate structure, there's an opportunity for you to add to its impact with repetition, simply by including words that wouldn't have to be included. The following sentence, from an essay in *Time* by Charles Krauthammer, could have been more concise, but it would have lost its drama:

> There is not a single Western standard, there are two: what we demand of Western countries at peace and what we demand of Western countries at war.

In the following sentence, from a *New Yorker* article on the Soviet Union by Jane Kramer, a great deal of the stylistic flair comes from repetition. Note the series of "for" phrases followed by a series of "no" phrases:

> The babel of languages has come to be a metaphor for the cultural confusion, for the lack of community, for the obvious, astonishing fact that five hundred years after the Moscow conquests began in earnest there is still no reason for the Soviet Union to call itself a country—no national dream, no shared "history," no identity that people can agree on to make them responsible to one another. [emphasis added]

A series of clauses, too, can be dramatized by repetition. The following sentence by Terrence Rafferty is from a review of the movie "Mountains of the Moon." It, too, appeared in *The New Yorker*:

> He [Sir Richard Burton] had travelled widely, in Europe, Asia, and Africa; he had mastered a couple of dozen languages; he had written seven books; and he had made a reputation as an intellectual adventurer, a man whose joy was to immerse himself in other cultures, to experience everything—even (or perhaps especially) things that his countrymen loathed and feared.

These uses of repetition, as well as the other stylistic devices we have taken up in this chapter, will invariably call attention to themselves. For that reason, you will reserve these structures for important ideas, for those times when you want your reader to sit up and take notice. But, like the gourmet cook who knows that too many spices can overwhelm a dish, you won't want to overwhelm your reader. But you will want to recognize that, like the spice that turns a bland sauce into fine cuisine, these stylistic tools can make the difference between ordinary and powerful prose.

AVOIDING SEXISM IN LANGUAGE

As you learned in Chapter 13, the system of personal pronouns has a gap. And it is that gap—the lack of a gender-neutral pronoun in the third-person singular slot—that is responsible for a great deal of the sexism in our language. You'd think that *he* and *she* and *it* would be up to the task of covering all the contingencies, but they're not. When we need a pronoun to refer to an unidentified person, such as "the writer" or "a student" or just "someone," our long-standing tradition has been to use the masculine:

The writer of this news story should have kept <u>his</u> personal opinion out of it.

Someone left <u>his</u> book on the table.

But that usage is no longer automatically accepted. Times and attitudes change, and we have come to recognize the power of language in shaping those attitudes. So an important step in reshaping society's view of women has been to eliminate the automatic use of *he* and *his* and *him* when the gender of someone referred to could just as easily be female.

In a paragraph we looked at earlier in this chapter in connection with sentence rhythm, the writer has made an effort to avoid sexism with the generic *salesperson,* a title that has all but replaced the masculine *salesman.* But notice the pronoun in the last sentence:

Never invest in something you don't understand or in the dream of an artful salesperson. Be a buyer, not a sellee. Figure out what you want (be it life insurance, mutual funds or a vacuum cleaner) and then shop for a good buy. Don't let someone else tell you what you need—at least not if <u>he</u> happens to be selling it.

—ANDREW TOBIAS

In speech we commonly use *they* for both singular and plural:

Don't let someone else tell you what you need—at least not if <u>they</u> happen to be selling it.

Eventually, perhaps, the plural pronoun will take over for the singular; in the second person (*you/your/you*), we make no distinction between singular and plural, so it's not unreasonable to do the same in the third person. But such changes come slowly. What should we do in the meanwhile?

One common, but not necessarily effective, way to solve the problem of the pronoun gap is with *he or she*:

. . . at least not if <u>he or she</u> happens to be selling it.

An occasional *he or she* will work in most situations like this one, but more than one in a paragraph will change the rhythm of the prose, slow the reader down, and call attention to itself when such attention is simply uncalled for.

The awkwardness of *he or she* in a passage becomes even more obvious when the possessive and objective case pronouns are also required. Avoiding sexist language by using *his or her* and *him or her* as well as *he or she* will quickly render the solution worse than the problem. Here, for example, is a passage from a 1981 issue of *Newsweek:*

> To the average American, the energy problem is mainly his monthly fuel bill and the cost of filling up his gas tank. He may also remember that in 1979, and way back in 1974, he had to wait in long lines at gasoline stations. For all of this, he blames the "Arabs" or the oil companies or the government, or perhaps all three. Much of the information that he gets from the media, as well as his own past experience, tells him that energy prices will continue to go up sharply and that gas lines are going to come back whenever a conflict flares up in the Middle East.
>
> —FRED SINGER, *"Hope for the Energy Shortage"*

Now imagine a version in which the problem of sexism has been solved with *he or she:*

> To the average American, the energy problem is mainly his or her monthly fuel bill and the cost of filling up his or her gas tank. He or she may also remember that in 1979, and way back in 1974, he or she had to wait in long lines at gasoline stations. For all of this, he or she blames the "Arabs" or the oil companies or the government, or perhaps all three. Much of the information that he or she gets from the media, as well as from his or her own past experience, tells him or her that energy prices will continue . . . *Enough!*

That's only one short paragraph. Imagine reading a whole essay! Clearly, there are better solutions to the problem.

Because we do have a gender-neutral pronoun in the plural, often that singular noun can be changed to plural. In the *Newsweek* article, for example, the writer could have started out by discussing "average Americans":

> To average Americans, the energy problem is mainly their monthly fuel bill and the cost of filling up their gas tank.

That revision, of course, has changed the relationship of the writer to the reader: The writer is no longer addressing the reader as an individual—a change the writer may not want. Often, however, the plural is an easy and obvious solution. For example, in the following passages from books about language, the change to plural does not affect the overall meaning or intent:

Of all the developments in the history of man [*the human race*], surely the most remarkable was language, for with it he was [*our ancestors were*] able to pass on his [*their*] cultural heritage to succeeding generations who then did not have to rediscover how to make a fire, where to hunt, or how to build another wheel.

–CHARLES B. MARTIN AND CURT M. RULON

It has been said that whenever a person [*people*] speaks, he is [*they are*] either mimicking or analogizing.

–CHARLES HOCKETT

We should emphasize that these three examples of sexist language were written at least a decade ago, when the masculine pronoun was the norm. Chances are, none of them would have been written in this way today. All of us who are involved with words, who are sensitive to the power of language, have gone through a consciousness raising in the matter of sexist language.

Let's assume that Fred Singer, the *Newsweek* writer, insists on maintaining the singular "average American." What other means would he have for eliminating the sexism for the masculine pronouns? In some cases, he could use different determiners. For example, he needn't write "*his* monthly fuel bill" and "*his* gas tank;" *the* will do the job. And in the last sentence, "his own past experience" could become "past experience" or, simply, "experience" without losing any information; "tells him" could become "says" or "suggests." He could probably get by with a single *he or she*, to replace the *he* of the second sentence; the other sentences with *he* can be revised with different subjects. Here's one possibility:

To the average American, the energy problem is mainly the monthly fuel bill and the cost of filling up the gas tank. He or she may also remember in 1979, and way back in 1974, waiting in long lines at the gasoline stations. Who gets the blame for all of this? The "Arabs" or the oil companies or the government, or perhaps all three. The media, as well as the consumer's past experience, suggest that energy prices will continue to go up sharply and that gas lines are going to come back whenever a conflict flares up in the Middle East.

In the last sentence we've substituted "the consumer" for "the average American."

Here, then, are some of the ways in which you can make up for the pronoun gap when you write and/or revise your own sentences:

1. USE THE PLURAL:
   Every writer should be aware of the power of language when he chooses his pronouns.
   Revision: Writers should be aware of the power of language when they choose their pronouns.
2. USE *HE OR SHE* **IF YOU CAN USE IT ONLY ONCE**.
   Revision: Every writer should be aware of the power of language when he or she chooses pronouns.
3. AVOID *HIS* AS A DETERMINER, EITHER BY SUBSTITUTING ANOTHER ONE OR, IN SOME CASES, DELETING THE DETERMINER:
   The writer of the news story should have kept his opinion out of it.
   Revision: The writer of the news story should have kept (all) opinion out of it.
4. TURN THE CLAUSE INTO A VERB PHRASE, THUS ELIMINATING THE PROBLEM SUBJECT:
   Every writer should be aware of the power of language when choosing pronouns.

This fourth method of revision is often a good possibility because the offending pronoun nearly always shows up in the second clause of a passage, often as part of the same sentence. In our example, we have turned the complete subordinate clause into an elliptical clause—that is, a clause with something missing. In this case what's missing is the subject. (The elliptical clause, which has some hidden pitfalls, is discussed in Chapter 8.)

5. REWRITE THE ADVERBIAL CLAUSE AS A RELATIVE (WHO) CLAUSE:
   When a person buys a house, he should shop carefully for the lowest interest rate.
   Revision: A person who buys a house should shop carefully for the lowest interest rate.

The relative clause with its neutral *who* eliminates the necessity of a personal pronoun to rename a *person*.

6. CHANGE THE POINT OF VIEW:
   2nd person: As a writer you should be aware of the power of language when you choose (your) pronouns.
   1st person: As writers, we should be aware of the power of language when we choose (our) pronouns.

===== *Exercise 57* =====

1. Rewrite the *Newsweek* passage using the second person. (*Note:* You might begin with "If you are an average American...")
2. The following passage was written at a time when the masculine pronoun was accepted as the generic singular. Revise it to reflect today's concerns about sexism in language.

   Of all born creatures, man is the only one that cannot live by bread alone. He lives as much by symbols as by sense report, in a realm compounded of tangible things and virtual images, of actual events and ominous portents, always between fact and fiction. For he sees not only actualities but meanings. He has, indeed, all the impulses and interests of animal nature; he eats, sleeps, mates, seeks comfort and safety, flees pain, falls sick and dies, just as cats and bears and fishes and butterflies do. But he has something more in his repertoire, too—he has laws and religions, theories and dogmas, because he lives not only through sense but through symbols. That is the special asset of his mind, which makes him the master of earth and all its progeny.
   —SUSANNE K. LANGER, "The Prince of Creation," *Fortune* (January 1944)

KEY TERMS IN CHAPTER 14

Absolute phrase
Abstract subject
Adverbial clause
Adverbial of emphasis
Appositive
Cohesion
Colon
Compound sentence
Coordinate series
Ellipsis
End focus
Intonation pattern

Introductory appositive series
Known–new contract
Nominalization
Passive voice
Repetition
Rhetorical grammar
Rhythm
Sentence rhythm
Sexist language
Shifting adverbial
Style
Word-order variation

PART

VI

GLOSSARY OF
GRAMMATICAL TERMS

(For further explanation of the terms listed here, check the index for page references.)

Absolute adjective. An adjective with a meaning that is generally not capable of being intensified or compared, such as *unique* or *perfect* or *square*. Careful writers avoid such usages as "very perfect" or "more unique."

Absolute phrase. A noun phrase related to the sentence as a whole that includes a postnoun modifier (often a participial phrase). One kind of absolute explains a cause or condition (*"The weather being warm,* we decided to have a picnic"); the other adds a detail or a point of focus to the idea in the main clause ("He spoke quietly to the class, *his voice trembling"*).

Accusative case. The Latin term denoting the case of nouns and pronouns functioning as direct objects and as objects of certain prepositions.

Active voice. A feature of transitive verb sentences in which the subject is generally the agent and the direct object is the goal or objective of the action. Voice refers to the relationship of the subject to the verb. See also *Passive voice.*

Adjectival. Any structure, no matter what its form, that functions as a modifier of a noun—that is, that functions as an adjective normally functions. See Chapter 7.

Adjectival clause. See *Relative clause.*

Adjective. One of the four form classes, whose members act as modifiers of nouns; most adjectives can be inflected for comparative and superlative degree (*big, bigger, biggest*); they can be qualified or intensified (*rather big,*

391

very big); they have characteristic derivational endings such as *-ous (famous)*, *-ish (childish)*, *-ful (graceful)*, and *-ary (complementary)*.

Adverb. One of the four form classes, whose members act as modifiers of verbs, contributing information of time, place, reason, manner, and the like. Like adjectives, certain adverbs can be qualified (*very quickly, rather fast*); some can be inflected for comparative and superlative degree (*more quickly, fastest*); they have characteristic derivational endings such as *-ly (quickly)*, *-wise (lengthwise)*, *-ward (backward)*, and *-like (snakelike)*.

Adverbial. Any structure, no matter what its form, that functions as a modifier of a verb—that is, that functions as an adverb normally functions. See Chapter 6.

Adverbial objective. The traditional label given to the noun phrase that functions adverbially: "Joe went *home*"; "It was cold *last night*."

Affix. A morpheme, or meaningful unit, that is added to the beginning (prefix) or end (suffix) of a word to change its meaning or its grammatical role or its form class: (prefix) *un*likely; (suffix) unlike*ly*.

Agent. The initiator of the action in the sentence, the "doer" of the action. Usually the agent is the subject in an active sentence: "*John* groomed the dog"; "*The committee* elected Pam."

Agreement. (1) Subject–verb. A third-person singular subject in the present tense takes the *-s* form of the verb: "*The dog barks* all night"; "*He bothers* the neighbors." A plural subject takes the base form: "*The dogs bark*"; "*They bother* the neighbors." (2) Pronoun–antecedent. The number of the pronoun (whether singular or plural) agrees with the number of its antecedent: "*The boys* did *their* chores"; "*Each girl* did *her* best."

Allomorph. A variation of a morpheme, usually determined by its environment. For example, the three allomorphs of the regular plural morpheme are determined by the final sound of the nouns to which they are added: /s/ *cats;* /z/ *dogs;* and /əz/ *churches.*

Ambiguity. The condition in which a structure has more than one possible meaning. The source may be lexical ("She is *blue*") or structural ("*Visiting relatives* can be boring") or both ("The detective looked *hard*").

Antecedent. The noun or nominal that a pronoun stands for.

Appositive. A structure, often a noun phrase, that renames another structure: "My neighbor, *a butcher at Weis Market,* recently lost his job." Clauses ("It is nice *that you could come*") and verb phrases ("My favorite hobby, *collecting stamps*, is getting expensive") can also function as appositives.

Article. One of the determiner classes, including the indefinite *a*, or *an*, which signals only countable nouns, and the definite *the*, which can signal all classes of nouns.

Aspect. A feature of the verb phrase in which auxiliaries designate whether the action of the verb is completed (*have* + *-en*) or in progress (*be* + *-ing*).

Attributive adjective. The adjective in prenoun position: "my *new* coat"; "the *big* attraction."

Auxiliary. One of the structure-class words, a marker of verbs. Auxiliaries include forms of *have* and *be*, as well as the modals, such as *will*, *shall*, and *must*.

Base form of the verb. The uninflected form of the verb. In all verbs except *be*, the base form is the present tense: *go*, *help*. The base form also serves as the infinitive, usually preceded by *to*.

Base morpheme. The morpheme that gives a word its primary lexical meaning: *help*ing, *reflect*.

be patterns. The sentence patterns in which a form of *be* is the main verb: Patterns I, II, and III.

Bound morpheme. A morpheme that cannot stand alone as a word. Most affixes are bound (help*ing*; *re*act); some base morphemes are also bound (con*cise*; *leg*al).

Case. A feature of nouns and certain pronouns that denotes their relationship to other words in a sentence. Pronouns have three case distinctions: subjective (e.g., *I*, *they*, *who*); possessive (e.g., *my*, *their*, *whose*); and objective (e.g., *me*, *them*, *whom*). Nouns have only one case inflection, the possessive (*John's*, the *cat's*). The case of nouns other than the possessive is sometimes referred to as common case.

Catenative verb. A transitive verb that can take another verb as its object: "I *like* to jog"; "We *enjoy* jogging."

Clause. A structure with a subject and a predicate. The sentence patterns are clause patterns. Clauses are either independent or dependent.

Cleft sentence. A sentence variation that provides a way of shifting the stress or focus of the sentence: "A careless bicyclist caused the accident" → "It was a careless bicyclist who caused the accident"; "What caused the accident was a careless bicyclist."

Cohesion. The grammatical, lexical, and semantic connections between sentences. Cohesive ties are furnished by pronouns that have antecedents in previous sentences, by adverbial connections, by known information, and by knowledge shared by the reader.

Collective noun. A noun that refers to a collection of individuals: *group, team, family.* Collective nouns can be replaced by both singular and plural pronouns, depending on the meaning.

Command. See *Imperative.*

Common case. See *Case.*

Common noun. A noun with general, rather than unique, reference (in contrast to proper nouns). Common nouns may be countable (*house, book*) or noncountable (*water, oil*); they may be concrete (*house, water*) or abstract (*justice, indifference*).

Comparative degree. See *Degree.*

Complement. A structure that "completes" the sentence. The term includes those slots in the predicate that complete the verb: direct object, indirect object, subjective complement, and objective complement. Certain adjectives also have complements—clauses and phrases that pattern with them: "I was *certain that he would come;* I was *afraid to go.*"

Complementary infinitive. An infinitive that functions as the main verb. "I'm going *to move* next week"; "I have *to find* a new apartment." There is a modal-like quality in "going to" and "have to."

Complex sentence. A sentence that includes at least one dependent clause.

Compound sentence. A sentence with two or more independent clauses.

Compound–complex sentence. A sentence that includes at least two independent clauses and one dependent clause.

Conditional mood. The attitude of probability designated by the modal auxiliaries *could, may, might, would,* and *should.*

Conjunction. One of the structure classes, which includes connectors that coordinate structures of many forms (e.g., *and, or*), subordinate sentences (e.g., *if, because, when*), and coordinate sentences with an adverbial emphasis (e.g., *however, therefore*).

Conjunctive adverb. A conjunction that connects two sentences with an adverbial emphasis, such as *however, therefore, moreover,* and *nevertheless.*

Coordinating conjunction. A conjunction that connects two or more sentences or structures within a sentence as equals: *and, but, or, nor, for,* and *yet.*

Coordination. A way of expanding sentences in which two or more structures of the same form function as a unit. All the sentence slots and modifiers in the slots, as well as the sentence itself, can be coordinated. See Chapter 9.

Correlative conjunction. A two-part conjunction that expresses a relationship between the coordinated structures: *either–or, neither–nor, both–and.*

Countable noun. A noun whose referent can be identified as a separate entity; the countable noun can be signaled by the indefinite article, *a,* and numbers: *a house; an experience; two eggs; three problems.*

Declarative sentence. A sentence in the form of a statement (in contrast to a command, a question, or an exclamation).

Deep structure. A term from transformational generative grammar that refers to the underlying semantic and syntactic relationships of the sentence, in contrast to surface structure, the sentence as it is actually written or spoken.

Definite article. The determiner *the,* which generally marks a specific or previously mentioned noun: "*the* man on the corner"; "*the* blue coat I want for Christmas."

Degree. The variations in adjectives that indicate the simple quality of a noun, or positive degree ("Bill is *a big* boy"); its comparison to another, the comparative degree ("Bill is *bigger* than Tim"); or to two or more, the superlative degree ("Bill is the *biggest* person in the whole class"). Certain adverbs also have degree variations, usually designated by *more* and *most.*

Demonstrative pronoun. The pronouns *this* (plural *these*) and *that* (plural *those*), which function as nominal substitutes and as determiners. They include the feature of proximity: near (*this, these*); distant (*that, those*).

Dependent clause. A clause that functions as an adverbial, adjectival, nominal, or sentence modifier (in contrast to an independent, or main, clause).

Derivational affix. A morpheme that is added to a form-class word, either to change its class (*friend → friendly; act → action*) or to change its meaning (*legal → illegal; boy → boyhood*).

Determiner. One of the structure-class words, a marker of nouns. Determiners include articles (*a, the*); possessive nouns and pronouns (e.g., *Chuck's,* *his, my*); demonstrative pronouns (*this, that*); quantifiers (e.g., *many, several*); indefinite pronouns (e.g., *each, every*); and numbers.

Direct object. A nominal slot in the predicate of the transitive sentence patterns. The direct object names the objective or goal or the receiver of the verb's action: "We ate *the peanuts*"; "The boy hit *the ball*"; "I enjoy *playing chess.*"

***Do* transformation.** The addition of the "stand-in auxiliary" *do* to a verb string that has no other auxiliary. The question, the negative, and the emphatic transformations all require an auxiliary. *Do* also substitutes for a repeated verb phrase in compound sentences: "Bryan liked the movie, and I *did* too."

Dynamic. Words that exhibit features related to qualities capable of change. Dynamic verbs can combine with the progressive aspect, *be* + *-ing*: "I *am leaving* now"; dynamic adjectives can follow the progressive form of *be*: "He is being *silly.*" See also *Stative.*

Elliptical clause. A clause in which a part has been left out but is "understood"; "Chester is older *than I (am old)*"; "Bev can jog farther *than Otis (can jog)*"; "When *(you are) planning your essay,* be sure to consider the audience."

Emphatic sentence. A statement in which the main stress has been shifted to the auxiliary: "I AM trying." When there is no auxiliary, the "stand-in auxiliary" *do* is added to carry the stress: "I DO want to go."

End focus. The common rhythm pattern in which the prominent peak of stress falls on or near the final sentence slot.

Exclamatory sentence. A sentence that expresses excitement or emotion. It may include a shift in the word order of a basic sentence that focuses on a complement: "What a beautiful day we're having!" It is characterized by heightened pitch and stress and is usually punctuated with an exclamation point.

Expanded determiner. The determiner, together with pre- and post-determiners that qualify and quantify and in other ways alter its meaning.

Expletive. A word that enables the writer or speaker to shift the stress in a sentence or to embed one sentence in another: "A fly is in my soup → *There is* a fly in my soup"; "I know *that* he loves me." The expletive is sometimes called an "empty word" because it plays a structural rather than a lexical role.

Finite verb. The main verb of the clause, one that fills the last slot in the verb-expansion formula. A finite verb can be marked for tense, mood, aspect, and voice (in contrast to gerunds, participles, and infinitives, which can be marked only for aspect and voice).

Flat adverb. A class of adverb that is the same in form as its corresponding adjective: *fast, high, early, late, hard, long,* etc.

Form classes. The large, open classes of words that provide the lexical content of the language: nouns, verbs, adjectives, and adverbs. Each has characteristic derivational and inflectional morphemes that distinguish its forms. See Chapter 11.

Free morpheme. A single morpheme that is also a complete word (in contrast to a bound morpheme, which is not).

Function. The role that a particular structure plays, or the slot that it fills, in a sentence (or in any larger structure). In "The book on the table is mine," "table" functions as the *object of a preposition* in the prepositional phrase "on the table"; the prepositional phrase functions as an *adjectival,* modifying book. The entire noun phrase "the book on the table" functions as the *subject* in its sentence.

Functional shift. The conversion of one word class to another, simply by changing its function. He *bottled* the wine (noun to verb); She *lowered* the curtain (adjective to verb); We took a *swim* (verb to noun).

Gender. A feature of personal pronouns and certain nouns that distinguishes masculine (*he*), feminine (*she*), and neuter (*it*). Nouns with gender distinctions include *waiter, waitress, actor, actress, girl, boy, man, woman, ewe, ram.*

Genitive case. The Latin term for possessive case.

Gerund. An *-ing* verb functioning as a nominal: "I enjoy *jogging*"; "*Running* is good exercise."

Gerund phrase. A gerund together with all of its complements and modifiers.

Grammatical. Usage that conforms to the rules that native speakers follow or that native speakers would find acceptable in a given situation. See also *Standard Written English.*

Headword. The word that fills the noun slot in the noun phrase: "the little *boy* across [the *street*]." The verb is the headword of the verb phrase; the preposition is the headword of the prepositional phrase.

Homophones. Morphemes, both bases and affixes, that sound alike but have different meanings: *sale/sail;* farm*er*/bright*er.*

Idiom. A combination of words, a set phrase, whose meaning cannot be predicted from the meaning of the individual words.

Imperative. The sentence—and also the verb—in the form of a command. The imperative sentence includes the base form of the verb and usually an understood subject (*you*): "*Eat* your spinach"; "*Finish* your report as soon as possible"; "You *go* on without me."

Indefinite article. The determiner *a*, or *an*, which marks an unspecified count noun. See also *Definite article.*

Indefinite pronoun. A large category that includes quantifiers (e.g., *enough, several, many, much*), universals (*all, both, every, each*), and partitives (*any, either, neither, no, some*). Many of the indefinite pronouns can function as determiners.

Indefinite relative pronoun. The relative pronouns with *-ever* added, which have indefinite referents; they introduce adjectival clauses: "I will give a bonus to *whoever* works the hardest" (i.e., to the person who works the hardest).

Independent clause. The main clause of the sentence; a compound sentence has more than one independent clause.

Indicative mood. The expression of an idea as fact (as opposed to probability). Verb phrases without modal auxiliaries and those with *will* and *shall* are considered the indicative mood: "We *will* go soon"; "We *are going* tomorrow." "When *are* you *going?*" See also *Subjunctive mood* and *Conditional mood.*

Indirect object. The nominal slot following the verb in a Pattern VIII sentence. In a sentence with a verb like *give*, the indirect object is the recipient; the direct object is the thing given: "We gave *our friends* a ride home." The indirect object can be shifted to the slot following the direct object with the preposition *to* or *for:* "Joe gave a message to Kim"; "Sam bought a ticket for his dad."

Infinitive. The base form of the verb (present tense), usually expressed with *to*, which is called the "sign of the infinitive." The infinitive can function adverbially ("I stayed up all night *to study* for the exam"); adjectivally ("That is no way *to study*"); or nominally ("*To stay up* all night is foolish"). The only verb with an infinitive form separate from the present tense is *be*.

Infinitive phrase. The infinitive together with all of its complements and modifiers.

Inflectional morpheme. Morphemes that are added to the form classes (nouns, verbs, adjectives, and adverbs) to change their grammatical role in some way. Nouns have two inflectional suffixes (*-s* plural and *-'s* possessive); verbs have four (*-s, -ing, -ed,* and *-en*); adjectives and some adverbs have two (*-er* and *-est*).

Intensifier. See *Qualifier.*

Intensive pronoun. A pronoun that serves as an appositive to emphasize a noun or pronoun. It is formed by adding *-self* or *-selves* to a personal pronoun: "I *myself* prefer chocolate."

Interjection. A word considered independent of the main sentence, often punctuated with an exclamation point: "*Ouch!* My shoe pinches"; "*Oh!* Is that what you meant?"

Interrogative. A sentence that is a question in form: "Are you leaving now?" "When are you leaving?" The term **interrogative** also refers to the "*wh*-words" in their roles as pronouns, adjectives, and adverbs, introducing questions and nominal clauses: "*Where* are you going?" "I wonder *where* he is going."

Intonation pattern. The rhythmic pattern of a spoken sentence, affected by its stress and pitch and pauses.

Intransitive verb. The verbs of Pattern VI sentences, most of which require no complement to be complete.

Irregular verb. Any verb in which the *-ed* and *-en* forms are not that of the regular verb; in other words, a verb in which the *-ed* and *-en* forms are not simply the addition of *-d, -ed,* or *-t* to the base form.

***It*-cleft.** See *Cleft sentence.*

Known-new contract. A common feature of prose in which the known information opens the sentence and the new information occupies the point of main focus at or near the end of the sentence.

Lexicon. The store of words—the internalized dictionary—that every speaker of the language has.

Linking verb. The verbs of Patterns IV and V, which require a subjective complement to be complete.

Main verb. The finite verb that fills the last slot in the verb-expansion formula.

Manner adverb. An adverb that answers the question of "how" or "in what manner" about the verb. Most manner adverbs are derived from adjectives with the addition of *-ly: quickly, merrily, candidly.*

Mass nouns. See *Noncountable nouns.*

Modal auxiliary. The auxiliary that occupies the opening slot in the verb-expansion rule and may affect what is known as the mood of the verb, conveying probability, possibility, obligation, and the like.

Mood. A quality of the verb denoting fact (indicative), a condition contrary to fact (subjunctive), and probability or possibility (conditional).

Morpheme. A sound or combination of sounds with meaning.

Morphology. The study of morphemes. See Chapter 10.

Nominal. Any structure that functions as a noun phrase normally functions. See Chapter 4.

Nominal clause. A clause that fills an NP slot.

Nominalization. The process of producing a noun by adding derivational affixes to another word class, commonly a verb: *legalize–legalization; regulate–regulation; friendly–friendliness.*

Nominative case. The Latin term for subjective case.

Noncountable noun. Nouns referring to what might be called an undifferentiated mass—such as *wood, water, sugar, glass*—or an abstraction—*justice, love, indifference.* Whether or not you can use the indefinite article, *a*, is probably the best test of countability: If you can, the noun is countable.

Nonfinite verb. A verb that functions other than as the main (finite) verb. Verbs and verb phrases acting as adjectivals, adverbials, and nominals within the sentence are called nonfinite verbs.

Nonrestrictive modifier. A modifier in the noun phrase that comments about the noun rather than defines it. Nonrestrictive modifiers following the noun are set off by commas.

Noun. One of the four form classes, whose members fill the headword slot in the noun phrase. Most nouns can be inflected for plural and possessive (*boy, boys, boy's, boys'*). Nouns have characteristic derivational endings, such as *-tion* (*action, compensation*), *-ment* (*contentment*), and *-ness* (*happiness*). Nouns can also function as adjectivals and adverbials (The *neighbor* children went home).

Noun clause. See *Nominal clause.*

Noun phrase (NP). The noun headword with all of its attendant pre- and postnoun modifiers.

Number. A feature of nouns and pronouns, referring to singular and plural.

Object of preposition. The nominal slot—usually filled by a noun phrase—that follows the preposition to form a prepositional phrase.

Objective case. The role in a sentence of a noun phrase or pronoun when it functions as an object—direct object, indirect object, objective complement, or object of the preposition. Although nouns do not have a special form for objective case, many of the pronouns do; personal pronouns and the relative pronoun *who* have separate forms when they function as objects. See Chapter 13.

Objective complement. The slot following the direct object, filled by an adjectival (Pattern IX) or a nominal (Pattern X). The objective complement has two functions: (1) It completes the idea of the verb; and (2) it modifies (if an adjective) or renames (if a nominal) the direct object: "I found the play *exciting*"; "We consider Pete *a good friend.*"

Optional slot. The adverbial information that can be added to all the sentence patterns; such information is not required for grammaticality.

Parallel structure. A coordinate structure in which all the coordinate parts are of the same grammatical form.

Participial phrase. A participle together with all of its complements and modifiers.

Participle. The *-ing* and *-en* verb (or verb phrase) functioning as an adjectival. See also *Present participle* and *Past participle.*

Particle. A word that combines with a verb to form a phrasal verb: look *up*; look *into*; put *up with.*

Passive voice. A feature of transitive sentences in which the direct object (the objective or goal) is shifted to the subject position and *be* + *-en* is added to the verb. The term *passive* refers to the relationship between the subject and verb: "Ed ate the pizza" → "The pizza *was eaten* by Ed." See Chapter 3.

Past participle. The *-en* form of the verb.

Past tense. The *-ed* form of the verb, usually denoting a specific past action.

Person. A feature of personal pronouns that distinguishes the speaker or writer (first person), the person or thing spoken to (second person), and the person or thing spoken of (third person).

Personal pronoun. The pronoun that refers to a specific person or thing: In the subjective case the personal pronouns are *I, you, he, she, we, you, they,* and *it*. The personal pronouns have variant forms for objective and possessive case.

Phoneme. The smallest unit of sound that makes a difference in meaning.

Phonology. The study of phonemes. See Appendix A.

Phrasal preposition. A preposition of two or more words that act as a unit: *according to, because of, out of.*

Phrasal subordinator. A subordinating conjunction of two or more words that act as a unit to subordinate one clause to another: *as if, even though, provided that.*

Phrasal verb. A verb-particle combination that produces a meaning that cannot be predicted from the meaning of the parts: *look up, put up with, make up.*

Phrase. A combination of words that constitutes a unit of the sentence.

Plural. A feature of nouns and pronouns denoting more than one, usually signaled in nouns by the inflectional ending *-s* (or *-es*).

Positive degree. See *Degree*.

Possessive case. The inflected form of nouns (*John's, the dog's*) and pronouns (*my, his, your, her, their,* etc.) usually indicating ownership.

Predicate. One of the two principal parts of the sentence, the comment made about the subject. The predicate includes the verb, together with its complements and modifiers.

Predicate adjective. The adjective that functions as a subjective complement.

Predicate nominative. The noun or nominal that functions as a subjective complement.

Predicating verb. The function of the verb slot in the sentence patterns, consisting of the main verb together with its auxiliaries. The verb-expansion rule in Chapter 3 accounts for all the possible auxiliary-verb combinations for the predicating verb.

Predicative adjective. The adjective that occupies a complement slot in the sentence as subjective or objective complement.

Prefix. An affix added to the beginning of the word to change its meaning (*un*likely, *il*legal, *pre*scribe, *re*new) or its class (*en*able, *be*little).

Preposition. A structure-class word found in pre-position to—that is, preceding—a nominal. Prepositions can be classed according to their form as simple (*above, at, in, of,* etc.) or phrasal (*according to, instead of,* etc.).

Prepositional phrase. The combination of a preposition and a nominal, which is known as the object of the preposition.

Present participle. The *-ing* form of the verb.

Present tense. The base form and the *-s* form of the verb: *help, helps.* The present tense denotes a present point in time ("I *understand* your position"), a habitual action ("I *jog* five miles a day"), or the "timeless" present ("Shakespeare *helps* us understand ourselves").

Pronoun. A word that substitutes for a noun—or, more accurately, for a nominal—in the sentence.

Pronoun–antecedent agreement. See *Agreement.*

Proper noun. A noun with individual reference to a person, a historical event, or other name. Proper nouns are capitalized.

Qualifier. A structure-class word that qualifies or intensifies an adjective or adverb: "We worked *rather* slowly"; "We worked *very* hard."

Reciprocal pronoun. The pronouns *each other* and *one another,* which refer to previously named nouns.

Referent. The thing (or person, event, concept, action, etc.)—in other words, the reality—that a word stands for.

Reflexive pronoun. A pronoun formed by adding *-self* or *-selves* to a form of the personal pronoun, used as an object in the sentence to refer to a previously named noun or pronoun: "I gave *myself* a haircut."

Regular verb. A verb in which the *-ed* form (the past tense) and the *-en* form (the past participle) are formed by adding *-ed* (or, in some cases, *-d* or *-t*) to the base. These two forms of a regular verb are always identical. "I *walked* home"; "I have *walked* home every day this week."

Relative adverb. The adverbs *where, when,* and *why,* which introduce adjectival clauses.

Relative clause. A clause introduced by a relative pronoun (*who, which, that*) or a relative adverb (*when, where, why*) that generally modifies a noun. The broad-reference *which* clause functions as a sentence modifier.

Relative pronoun. The pronouns *who* (*whom*, *whose*), *which*, and *that* in their role as introducers of a relative clause.

Restrictive modifier. A modifier in the noun phrase whose function is to restrict the meaning of the noun. A modifier is restrictive when it is needed to identify the referent of the headword. The restrictive modifier is not set off by commas.

Retained object. The direct object of a Pattern VIII sentence that is retained in its original position when the sentence is transformed into the passive voice: "The judges awarded Mary the prize" → "Mary was awarded *the prize.*"

Sentence. A word or group of words based on one or more subject–predicate, or clause, patterns. The written sentence begins with a capital letter and ends with terminal punctuation—a period, question mark, or an exclamation point.

Sentence modifier. A word or phrase or clause that modifies the sentence as a whole. See Chapter 8.

Sentence patterns. The simple skeletal sentences, made up of two or three or four required elements, that underlie our sentences, even the most complex among them. Ten such patterns will account for almost all the possible sentences of English. See Chapter 2.

Singular. A feature of nouns and pronouns denoting one referent.

Standard Written English. The level of English usage that is widely accepted as the norm for the edited public writing of newspapers, magazines, and books.

"Stand-in" auxiliary. The auxiliary *do* (*does*, *did*), which we add to sentences when we transform them into questions, negatives, and emphatic statements when there is no auxiliary in the original.

Stative. Words that exhibit features relating to an unchanging state, in contrast to those that change. Stative verbs do not pattern with the progressive aspect: *I am *resembling* my mother. Stative adjectives generally do not follow the progressive form of *be*: *He is *being tall.* See also *Dynamic.*

Structure classes. The small, closed classes of words that explain the grammatical or structural relationships of the form classes. See Chapter 12.

Subject. The opening slot in the sentence patterns, filled by a noun phrase or other nominal, that functions as the topic of the sentence.

Subjective case. The role in the sentence of a noun phrase or a pronoun when it functions as the subject of the sentence. Personal pronouns have distinctive forms for subjective case: *I, he, she, they,* etc.

Subjective complement. The nominal or adjectival in Pattern II, III, IV, and V sentences following the verb, which renames or modifies the subject. The passive version of a Pattern IX or X sentence will also have a subjective complement, the nominal or adjectival that in the active voice functions as the objective complement.

Subject–verb agreement. See *Agreement.*

Subjunctive mood. An expression of the verb in which the base form, rather than the inflected form, is used (1) in certain *that* clauses conveying strong suggestions or resolutions or commands ("We suggest that Mary *go* with us"; "I move that the meeting *be* adjourned"; "I demand that you *let* us in"), and (2) in the expression of wishes or conditions contrary to fact ("If I *were* you, I'd be careful"; "I wish it *were* summer"). The subjunctive of the verb *be* is expressed by *were,* or *be,* even for subjects that normally take *is* or *was.*

Subordinate clause. A dependent clause introduced by a subordinating conjunction, such as *if, since, because,* and *although.*

Subordinator. A subordinating conjunction that turns a complete sentence into a subordinate clause and expresses the connection between the subordinate clause and the main clause.

Substantive. A structure that functions as a noun; a nominal.

Suffix. An affix added to the end of a form-class word to change its class (act → action; laugh → laugh*able*) with derivational suffixes or to change its grammatical function (boy → boys; walk → walk*ing*) with inflectional suffixes. See also *Derivational affix* and *Inflectional morpheme.*

Superlative degree. See *Degree.*

Surface structure. A term used by transformational grammarians to designate the sentences of the language as they are spoken and written. See also *Deep structure.*

Syntax. The structure of sentences; the relationship of the parts of the sentence.

Tense. A grammatical feature of verbs and auxiliaries relating to time. Tense is designated either by an inflectional change (*walked*), by an auxiliary (*will walk*), or both (*am walking, have walked*). Note that "tense" in relation to the modal auxiliaries refers to form, not to time.

***There* transformation.** A variation of a basic sentence in which the expletive *there* is added at the beginning and the subject is shifted to a position following *be:* "A fly is in my soup" → *"There is a fly in my soup."*

Third-person singular. The personal pronouns *he, she,* and *it.* The term is also used in reference to the *-s* form of the verb.

Transformational grammar (also called Transformational Generative, or T-G). A theory of grammar that attempts to account for the ability of native speakers to generate and process the sentences of their language. See Appendix B.

Transitive verb. The verbs of Patterns VII through X, which require at least one complement, the direct object, to be complete. With only a few exceptions, transitive verbs are those that can be transformed into the passive voice.

Ungrammatical. Usage that does not conform to the rules that native speakers follow. Usage that varies from one dialect or speech community to another is not necessarily ungrammatical. "I ain't coming" is an unacceptable usage to many, although it follows the "rules." However, it is not part of the prestige, or standard, dialect and would be inappropriate in most formal and business situations. See also *Grammatical* and *Standard Written English.*

Verb. One of the four form classes, traditionally thought of as the action word in the sentence. A better way to recognize the verb, however, is by its form. Every verb, without exception, has an *-s* and an *-ing* form; every verb also has an *-ed* and an *-en* form, although in the case of some irregular verbs these forms are not readily apparent. And every verb, without exception, can be marked by auxiliaries. Many verbs also have characteristic derivational forms, such as *-ify (typify), -ize (criticize),* and *-ate (activate).*

Verb phrase (VP). A verb together with its complements and modifiers; the predicate of the sentence is a verb phrase. See also *Gerund phrase, Infinitive phrase,* and *Participial phrase.*

Verb-expansion rule. The formula that describes our system for expanding the verb with auxiliaries to express variations in meaning: T + (M) + (have + -en) + (be + -ing) + V. See Chapter 3.

Vocative. The noun or noun phrase of direct address, considered a sentence modifier: *"Mike,* is that you?"

***What*-cleft.** See *Cleft sentence.*

***Wh*-question.** A question that is introduced by an interrogative, such as *who, which, when, where, why,* or *how,* that asks for information of content, in contrast to a *yes/no* question.

***Yes/no* interrogative.** The words *if* and *whether* (*or not*) that introduce nominal clauses that ask or suggest a *yes/no* question: "I wonder *if Kim is coming*"; "I wonder *whether or not she's coming.*"

***Yes/no* question.** A question that calls for a *yes* or *no* response. It is characterized by the opening auxiliary, in contrast to the interrogative that opens the *wh*-question: "*Are* you being served?" "*Did* the Orioles win?"

APPENDIX

A

Phonology

For the structural linguist, the study of language begins not with the grammar of sentences nor even with the parts of speech. It begins with the study of sounds, the smallest units of language. We call these **phonemes** and the study of them **phonology**.

PHONEMES

An important first step in the study of phonology is to recognize the parts of words and syllables as sounds rather than as letters of the alphabet and to hear these sounds separately. If you can isolate the sounds, you should have no trouble in learning the system of phonemes that make up the morphemes and words and sentences of English.

First, let's define *phoneme*. A phoneme is not just any sound: It is a sound that can make a difference in meaning. In English the inventory of distinctive sounds numbers around three dozen. Our vocal apparatus is capable of making many more sounds than this, of course; we make many more than this every day. We whistle and hum and groan and hiss and click our tongues and giggle and howl with laughter. All such sounds, of course, convey messages, so in that sense they are meaningful. However, when we say that sounds are distinctive, or that they distinguish meaning, we are referring to their role in the production of words.

Every language has its own inventory of distinctive sounds, or phonemes. Many of our three dozen phonemes are the same as those of other languages, but the sets for even closely related languages are not identical. For example, imagine the following conversation with a student from Venezuela:

> *Joe:* How was your trip, José? Did you fly?
> *José:* No, I came by sheep.
> *Joe:* You mean "ship."
> *José:* That's what I said—"sheep."

In pronouncing *ship* exactly like *sheep*, José is imposing the phonemes of Spanish on his pronunciation of English. In English the vowel sound in *ship*, /ɪ/, is different from the vowel in *sheep*, /i/. But Spanish does not have both of these vowels, so the difference between them makes no difference in meaning. In English the difference between /ɪ/ and /i/ is what is known as a *phonemic difference*; that is, it makes a difference in meaning because *ship* and *sheep* are different words. In Spanish the difference is not phonemic because /ɪ/ and /i/ are not separate phonemes. In fact, Spanish speakers may not even hear the two sounds as different, as the conversation with José demonstrates.

(Note: Because we have to deal with sounds in the written language, we use the convention of slashes to represent phonemes. /ɪ/ represents the vowel sound in *ship*. When you see a symbol written between slashes, remember that it represents a sound, not a letter of the alphabet.)

Another example illustrates a difference between Norwegian and English. The Norwegian speaker may have a hard time distinguishing between *yam* and *jam*; to the Norwegian they may sound alike. In English, of course, /ǰ/ and /y/ are separate phonemes, but Norwegian has no /ǰ/, only a /y/; consequently, Jack's Norwegian friend calls him "Yak" most of the time.

THE PRODUCTION OF SOUNDS

Speech sounds are actually disturbances of the air as it travels from the lungs through the larynx and out of either the mouth or the nose. Differences in these disturbances—along with variations in the size and shape of the mouth, the resonating chamber—create the differences in the sounds. The illustration on the next page shows the various parts of the speech apparatus.

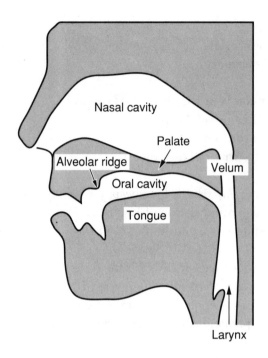

THE INVENTORY OF PHONEMES

It is not possible to pin down our inventory of phonemes with absolute precision; certainly, the description we are using here is not the only way of categorizing the sounds of English. The vowels are especially elusive, as you will discover in trying to distinguish between *ham* and *hem* or *fear* and *fair* and *fire*. It is important to recognize that each of the phonemes represents a range of sound. For example, the positions of the vowels on the vowel chart (page 418) represent the actual physical feature of tongue and lip placement, so there are bound to be differences among speakers. Especially obvious are the differences that we hear in different parts of the country.

This inventory of thirty-five phonemes includes eleven vowels and twenty-four consonants, including two glides; the three diphthongs are combinations of a vowel and a glide. We will begin our description with the consonants, which are categorized on the basis of three physical features: the manner of articulation, the place of articulation, and voicing. These are the features you will be able to recognize—to hear and to feel—as you pronounce the consonants.

CONSONANTS

We will first classify the consonant phonemes on the basis of their manner of articulation—that is, the way in which the air is disturbed. The two main classes are *stops*, where the air is completely stopped in its passage, and *fricatives*, where the air is only partially obstructed. We can further subdivide the consonants by noting if they are *voiced* or *voiceless*—that is, whether or not the vocal cords vibrate as the air passes through the larynx, or voice box.

Stops.* /p/ *and* /b/—*The Bilabial Stops.   In the production of these two sounds, the air is stopped at the lips. The only difference between them is voicing: /p/ is voiceless; /b/ is voiced. When you say the following pairs of words aloud, you can probably feel the vibration in those with /b/:

tap	tab
pit	bit
pup	bub
cup	cub

You will detect the difference between /p/ and /b/ even more clearly if you put your fingers over your ears when you say the words.

You'll probably notice another difference besides voicing as you listen to these two sounds. The pitch of your voice drops as you go from /p/ to /b/. For example, say the word *pub*. You'll notice that your voice ends up lower than it began; compare the pitch pattern of *pub* with that of *pup*, in which your voice stays at one level.

/t/ *and* /d/—*The Alveolar Stops.   In the production of this pair of stop consonants, the tip of the tongue stops the air at the alveolar ridge, the ridge you can feel just behind your upper teeth. Again the difference between the two sounds is voicing—with its attendant pitch change. Say the following pairs aloud:

pat	pad
trip	drip
tat	dad

/k/ *and* /g/—*The Velar Stops.   In the production of these two sounds, the back of the tongue stops the air at the velum, or soft palate.

When you say the following words, you can feel the closure in the back of your throat as the air is being stopped. You can also feel the difference between the voiceless /k/ and the voiced /g/:

tack	tag
core	gore
pick	pig

These three pairs comprise the stop consonants. They are easy to differentiate and, except for /k/, which is not always spelled with the letter *k*, the stops also correspond to the written alphabet. (Notice that in the word *core* the /k/ sound is represented by the letter *c* and in *tack* by *ck*.)

Fricatives.   In the production of fricative consonants, the air is not completely stopped, but it is obstructed in some way on its passage through the oral cavity, the mouth. One obvious difference between this class and the stops is that the sound of a fricative can be sustained, whereas a stop cannot. Because fricatives, like the stops, are either voiced or voiceless, we will look at them in pairs.

/f/ and /v/—The Labio-Dental Fricatives.   In the production of these two sounds, the air passes freely until it reaches the front of the mouth, where it is obstructed by the lower lip and upper teeth. Say the following pair of words, sustaining the last sound:

leaf	leave

You should be able to hear the difference between the voiceless /f/ and the voiced /v/. Here are some other pairs that show the contrast between these two sounds:

fat	vat
feel	veal
fife	five

/θ/ (theta) and /ð/ (eth)—The Interdental Fricatives.   You can think of these two fricatives, in which the air is obstructed with the tongue between the teeth, as the "th" sounds. In studying the consonant sounds, you may find these two the most difficult to differentiate since you are used to seeing them written exactly alike. Consider the following pair:

thigh   thy

The difference you hear in their opening sound is a difference in voicing: *thigh* begins with the voiceless /θ/; *thy* begins with the voiced /ð/. The physical difference in their production is identical to the physical difference between /t/ and /d/ or between /p/ and /b/.

Say the following words aloud; then identify the "th" sound in each as either voiced or voiceless:

1. myth	_____	5. both	_____	9. path	_____
2. mother	_____	6. bother	_____	10. thick	_____
3. bathe	_____	7. ether	_____	11. stealth	_____
4. thirsty	_____	8. either	_____	12. rather	_____

In the list you should have identified 2, 3, 6, 8, and 12 as voiced, the others as voiceless. If you had a problem making the distinction, sustain the "th" in a pair such as *bath* and *bathe* and listen for the difference. You should feel the voicing as a kind of buzzing in your head.

/s/ and /z/—The Alveolar Fricatives. In the production of this pair, the air is obstructed at the alveolar ridge. In fact, the placement of the tongue for these sounds is almost identical to the placement for /t/ and /d/, with the tongue tip on the alveolar ridge. The air passes along the sides of the tongue as either a buzz, with the voiced /z/, or a hiss, with the voiceless /s/:

sip   zip
bus   buzz
sap   zap

/š/ and /ž/—The Alveopalatal Fricatives. The voiceless /š/ can be thought of as the "sh" sound, as in words like *ship* and *sheep*, although it is not always spelled with the letters sh: It appears also in *Chicago*, *ocean*, and *sugar*, as well as in the "shun" words: *action*, *mansion, mention*. The voiced counterpart of /š/ is one of two consonants that does not appear in initial position in English words—that is, at the opening of a syllable. However, we do hear /ž/ at the opening of certain words recently borrowed from French, such as *genre* and *gendarme*. It is the second consonant sound in *measure* and *seizure*; for some people it is the final sound in *garage*. You can hear the contrast between /š/ and /ž/ in the following pairs:

š	ž
Aleutian	allusion
pressure	pleasure

/h/—The Voiceless Glottal Fricative.

This fricative, the sound at the beginning of *hot, hear,* and *ham,* is caused by the air rushing through the glottis, the space between the vocal cords. It alone of the fricatives has no voiced counterpart in English.

Affricates.   A third group of consonant phonemes is that of the affricates, a combination of a stop and a fricative:

/č/, *the voiceless alveopalatal affricate*, represents the "ch" sound. It combines the voiceless alveolar stop /t/ and the voiceless alveopalatal fricative /š/.

/ǰ/, *the voiced alveopalatal affricate*, combines the voiced counterparts of those two phonemes, /d/ and /ž/.

č	ǰ
batch	badge
rich	ridge
chug	jug

===== *Exercise 1: Consonants* =====

Identify the opening and closing consonant sound in each of the following words:

1. shrug	5. cards	9. dropped
2. circus	6. thatch	10. that
3. Thomas	7. pledge	11. judge
4. tax	8. huff	12. chord

13. crash	15. click	17. thrice
14. blush	16. chance	18. cage

(You can check your answers on page 423.)

Nasals. The consonants described so far are all oral sounds; that is, the air passes through the oral cavity. But we articulate three consonants by allowing the air to pass through the nasal cavity. (The diagram on page 410 shows a clear passage behind the velum; this passage is closed for the production of the oral consonants you have just been studying.)

/m/, /n/, and /ŋ/—The Nasal Consonants. You can easily demonstrate the physical difference between oral and nasal sounds: First say the word *ham*, sustaining the /m/; then pinch your nose, cutting off the air. You have also cut off the sound.

The three nasals, all of which are voiced, are articulated exactly as the three pairs of stops are: /m/ is bilabial, corresponding to /b/; /n/ is alveolar, corresponding to /d/; and /ŋ/ is velar, corresponding to /g/:

tam   tan   tang

The letters *m* and *n*, of course, represent the sounds /m/ and /n/. The combined letters *ng*, in such words as *tang* and *sing*, stand for the velar nasal sound, /ŋ/, even though it is a single sound; in words like *finger*, *linger*, and *wink*, however, /ŋ/ is spelled with *n*. Incidentally, /ŋ/ is the other phoneme (along with /ž/) that does not appear in initial position. Other words with /ŋ/ are *think*, *ink*, and *mingle*.

Liquids. The two liquids are /l/, the lateral consonant, so called because the air escapes at the sides of the tongue, and /r/, called the retroflex, because of the backward, or bending, movement of the tongue tip:

late   rate
leer   reel

Glides. The glides, /w/ and /y/, are characterized by lip and tongue movement:

> wet   yet

The difference between the following pair is the presence of the /y/ glide in *cue*:

> coo /ku/   cue /kyu/

Glides also combine with vowels in the formation of diphthongs; we will take these up after the discussion of vowels.

The following chart shows the consonants according to their place and manner of articulation.

	BILABIAL	LABIO-DENTAL	INTER-DENTAL	ALVEOLAR	ALVEO-PALATAL	VELAR	GLOTTAL
Stops							
voiceless	p			t		k	
voiced	b			d		g	
Fricatives							
voiceless		f	θ	s	š		h
voiced		v	ð	z	ž		
Affricates							
voiceless					č		
voiced					ǰ		
Nasals	m			n		ŋ	
Liquids							
lateral				l			
retroflex				r			
Glides					y	w	

(The broken line encloses those consonants known as sibilants.)

SIBILANTS

The consonants identified on the chart as *sibilants*, you'll notice, are *s*-like or *z*-like sounds. This feature makes a difference when the sibilant comes at the end of a noun or verb; the sibilant determines both pronunciation and spelling of the plural and possessive morphemes for nouns and the *s*-form of the verbs. When a word ends in a sibilant, we add a complete syllable for the "*s*" endings:

church → churches	judge → judges
kiss → kisses	buzz → buzzes
splash → splashes	page → pages
garage → garages	

Notice also that when these "*s*" morphemes are added to other nouns and verbs (run → runs; dog → dogs; cat → cats; hit → hits; walk → walks; head → heads; sofa → sofas) they are not always pronounced /s/, no matter how they are written. Following vowels (which are always voiced) and following voiced consonants, the letter *s* is pronounced /z/; it is only after voiceless consonants that the *s* is actually pronounced /s/. However, when the ending is added to sibilants, as described in the preceding paragraph, the sound is never /s/, because we add a complete syllable, including the voiced vowel; the voicing of the vowel carries over to the *s*, producing a /z/ sound.

VOWELS

With few exceptions, every syllable has a vowel; to count the syllables in a word, you can count the vowel sounds, which form the peaks of loudness in the syllable. The vocal cords vibrate in the production of all English vowels, so they are all voiced phonemes.

The differences in the vowel sounds are caused by the differences in the size and shape of the mouth, which acts as a resonance chamber for the sound. These differences are caused by changes in the placement of the tongue, in the action of the lips, and in the opening and closing of the mouth.

The easiest way to differentiate and to remember the vowels is to learn a sample word for each:

	FRONT	CENTRAL	BACK
HIGH	/i/ (beat)		/u/ (boot)
	/ɪ/ (bit)		/ʊ/ (put)
MID	/e/ (bait)	/ə/ (but)	/o/ (boat)
	/ɛ/ (bet)		/ɔ/ (bought, caught)
LOW	/æ/ (bat)		/a/ (father, cot)

The vowels are classified as to position—from front to central to back and from high to mid to low. The position labels refer to tongue placement. For example, a designation such as "high front vowel" or "low back vowel" refers to the sound produced when the highest part of the tongue is in that position.

As you say the front vowels, from high to low—from *beat* to *bat*—you can feel your mouth opening wider and your tongue lowering. As you say the vowels from front to back—from *bait* to *but* to *boot*—you can feel your lips rounding.

Before going on, we should note some common variations in the pronunciation of vowels among people from different parts of the country. One difference occurs in the following pairs:

cot	collar	don	hock
caught	caller	dawn	hawk

For many speakers the vowel sounds in these pairs represent the contrast between /a/ (the first member of each pair listed) and /ɔ/, sometimes called the "open o"; but for other speakers these pairs of words are homophones, words that sound identical. For this latter group, in fact, the open o is not a phoneme (except for its occurrence in the diphthong /ɔy/, described in the next section); in other words, it is not a sound that makes a difference in meaning. People who live in Washington, Oregon, and parts of northern California, for example, do not make the distinction between /a/ and /ɔ/; this is also true of an area extending several hundred miles with Pittsburgh at its center. For these speakers the vowels in the words *cot*, *caught*, *don*, *dawn*, *law*, and the first syllable of *father* are all pronounced the same. There are a great many other regional differences in the production of vowel sounds. New Englanders and Southerners, for example, have very distinct accents to people outside of their regions, caused mainly by differences in vowels.

DIPHTHONGS

In addition to the simple vowel sounds, we produce diphthongs by combining a vowel and a glide:

/ay/ (bite)   /aw/ (bout)   /ɔy/ (boy)

The diphthong is a vowel sound combined with lip and tongue movement to produce a new sound. In the production of /ay/, for example, we begin with the low back vowel, /a/, and move the position of the tongue and lips toward the position for the high front vowel, /i/, which is the region of the /y/ glide. Likewise, in producing /aw/, we begin with the same sound, /a/, and move to the position for the high back sound, the region of /w/. The diphthongs are characterized by this movement toward closure from the open position of the vowel.

The following exercises will give you practice with vowels and diphthongs. To transcribe the sounds in the word, say the word aloud and listen for the sound of the vowel—and try to disregard spelling. If you have trouble identifying a vowel, isolate it by dropping the sounds before and after it, one at a time. For example, to identify the vowel sound in *mad*, pronounce the word; then say it without the /d/, sustaining the vowel; then drop the /m/. You're left with the vowel. Now match it with the chart on page 418; you'll probably decide that the vowel in *mad* is most like the vowel in *hat*.

===== *Exercise 2: Vowels and Diphthongs* =====

Transcribe the following words as you pronounce them.

1. deep _____	6. pest _____	11. laid _____
2. drop _____	7. food _____	12. lad _____
3. chug _____	8. feud _____	13. ice _____
4. good _____	9. gripe _____	14. breeze _____
5. pout _____	10. grip _____	15. crouch _____

16. seize _____   18. chance _____   20. push _____

17. shrug _____   19. peace _____

(You can check your answers on page 423.)

==

Exercise 3 will give you practice with longer words. Each of the words listed has two or more vowel sounds, one for each syllable. You'll find that the loudest syllable, the one that gets the main stress, will be the easiest to identify. You'll also discover that the mid central vowel on the vowel chart, /ə/, the sound in *but* (called the schwa), turns up frequently in syllables without main stress. This "uh" sound is our most common vowel.

===== Exercise 3: Vowels and Diphthongs =====

Transcribe the following words as you pronounce them. (Note: The "er" sound in such words as *consider*, *mother*, and *bird* is conventionally transcribed /ər/.)

1. meadow _____   11. teacup _____

2. consider _____   12. flowers _____

3. female _____   13. brightly _____

4. common _____   14. January _____

5. persecute _____   15. parasite _____

6. paranoid _____   16. pressurize _____

7. easy _____   17. embroider _____

8. consent _____   18. rebounding _____

9. Idaho _____   19. humorous _____

10. loudest _____   20. sixty _____

21. frequent _____	24. creatures _____
22. skewer _____	25. machine _____
23. beautiful _____	26. chaperone _____

As you have probably discovered, the vowel sounds are harder to pin down than the consonants. And some of your answers were probably different from those given on page 423. That's understandable. Each of the phonemes actually represents a range of sounds, with variations depending on the environment—on the sounds that surround another particular sound—and on the individual speaker.[1] Certain consonants, especially /r/ and /l/, often make the vowel sounds hard to identify. For example, pronounce the following words; then identify the vowel in each:

fit _____	pet _____
fear _____	pair _____

The /r/ has the effect of a glide, causing movement during the production of the vowel, thus making the sound difficult to identify precisely. (In fact, in some descriptions of phonology the /r/ is included with the glides.) You probably had no problem with the vowels in *fit* /fɪt/ and *pet* /pɛt/, but for *fear* and *pair* the /ɪ/ and /ɛ/ are not as clear. In fact, you may have made a different decision—perhaps /fir/ and /per/.

ASSIMILATION

The pronunciation of words in isolation is often quite different from the pronunciation in connected speech. Say the following sentences aloud:

I have to leave now.
I have two dollars.

---

[1] These variations in phonemes—differences that make no difference in meaning—are called **allophones**. The distinction between phonemes and allophones is comparable to the distinction between morphemes and allomorphs.

You'll notice that *have to* /hæftə/ in the first sentence is quite different from *have two* /hævtu/ in the second. Now say the following:

I must tell Lucy about Tom.

You probably said something like this:

/ay məstɛlusi əbawtam/

Notice how the *t*'s and *l*'s run together. These changes in the pronunciation of connected speech are called *assimilation*. Here are some further examples:

He bought it for me.
Bill and Pam left town.
Did you make it yourself?
Would you give me a cup of coffee?

If you first pronounce the words in the sentences separately, as though they were in a list, and then say the sentences as you would in conversation, you'll notice the difference that assimilation produces. Here's how your conversational sentences might be transcribed:

/hi bat ɪt fər mi/
/bɪl ən pæm lɛftawn/
/dɪju mek ɪt yərsɛlf/ or /ǰumekɪčərsɛlf/
/wʊǰu gɪmi ə kəp əv kafi/ or /ǰu gɪmi ə kəp əv kɔfi/

ANSWERS TO EXERCISES

EXERCISE 1

1. /š/ /g/
2. /s/ /s/
3. /t/ /s/
4. /t/ /s/
5. /k/ /z/
6. /θ/ /č/
7. /p/ /ǰ/
8. /h/ /f/
9. /d/ /t/
10. /ð/ /t/
11. /ǰ/ /ǰ/
12. /k/ /d/
13. /k/ /š/
14. /b/ /š/
15. /k/ /k/
16. /č/ /s/
17. /θ/ /s/
18. /k/ /ǰ/

EXERCISE 2

1. /dip/
2. /drap/
3. /čəg/
4. /gʊd/
5. /pawt/
6. /pɛst/
7. /fud/
8. /fyud/
9. /grayp/
10. /grɪp/
11. /led/
12. /læd/
13. /ays/
14. /briz/
15. /krawč/
16. /siz/
17. /šrəg/
18. /čæns/
19. /pis/
20. /pʊš/

EXERCISE 3

1. /mɛdo/
2. /kənsɪdər/
3. /fimel/
4. /kamən/
5. /pərsəkyut/
6. /pɛrənɔyd/ or /pærənɔyd/
7. /izi/
8. /kənsɛnt/
9. /aydəho/
10. /lawdəst/
11. /tikəp/
12. /flawərz/
13. /braytli/
14. /ǰænyuɛri/
15. /pærəsayt/ or /pɛrəsayt/
16. /prɛšərayz/
17. /ɛmbrɔydər/
18. /ribawndɪŋ/
19. /hyumərəs/
20. /sɪksti/
21. /frikwənt/
22. /skyuwər/
23. /byudəfʊl/
24. /kričərz/
25. /məšin/
26. /šæpəron/

APPENDIX

B

An Introduction to Transformational Grammar

The theory of **transformational generative grammar** (often abbreviated T-G or called simply transformational grammar) has itself gone through several stages of transformation since 1957, when it was first presented by Noam Chomsky in his book *Syntactic Structures* (The Hague: Mouton). But despite the changes, its goal remains the same: to account for the ability that native speakers of a language share in generating and processing sentences, to account for our knowledge of language.

Although its origin is not pedagogical or practical like that of traditional and structural theory, transformational theory has practical value for the student of grammar. Many of the ideas in this book are taken directly from transformational grammar: the verb-expansion rule in Chapter 3, for example, and the idea of sentence transformations discussed in Chapter 5 and elsewhere.

One of the most useful concepts from transformational theory is the idea that a sentence has both a "deep structure" and a "surface structure." The **deep structure** consists of the semantic and grammatical relationships that underlie the surface structure; the **surface structure** is the form the sentence takes when we speak it. This concept of a deep structure underlying all our sentences accounts for our ability to perceive more than one meaning when a sentence is ambiguous. Consider the following sentence:

Visiting relatives can be boring.

Who is doing the visiting, you or your relatives? The sentence is structurally ambiguous because there is more than one possible deep structure underlying the opening noun phrase, *visiting relatives*. In one, *relatives* is the subject of *visiting;* in the other, it is the object. The transformations that the two different deep structures go through result in the same surface structure:

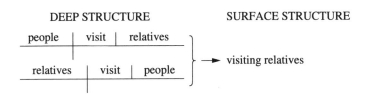

DEEP STRUCTURE   SURFACE STRUCTURE

people | visit | relatives

relatives | visit | people   → visiting relatives

===== *Investigating Language B.1* =====

If you have studied the nominals in Chapter 4 and the adjectivals in Chapter 7, you understand the difference between gerunds and participles. One way to illustrate the two possible deep structures underlying these sentences is to diagram each of them in two ways.

1. Flying planes can be dangerous.
2. I don't like burping babies.

However, the traditional diagram will not illustrate the ambiguity of this third sentence. What is different about it?

3. The shooting of the hunters was astonishing.

The passive transformation illustrates the opposite situation—two different surface structures that mean the same thing:

Howard Hughes built *The Spruce Goose.*
The Spruce Goose was built by Howard Hughes.

We are able to recognize these two sentences, these two different surface structures, as synonymous because they share the same deep structure. The relationship between Howard Hughes and *The Spruce*

Goose remains the same no matter what the surface structure: Howard Hughes is the agent or actor (in this case, the builder); *The Spruce Goose* is the object of the action.

DEEP STRUCTURE   SURFACE STRUCTURE

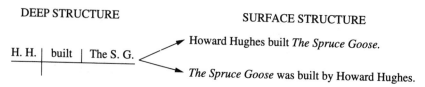

It was Chomsky's belief that the descriptive methods of the traditional and structural grammarians were simply inadequate to account for or explain this important aspect of language: this intuitive recognition of ambiguity and synonymy in sentences. One of his classic examples illustrates still another aspect of this inadequacy. The following sentences, neither ambiguous nor synonymous, are outwardly identical in structure:

John is easy to please.
John is eager to please.

A traditional analysis confirms their similarity:

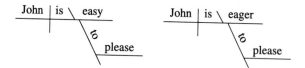

But think about the underlying meaning. Think about the relationship of *John* and *please* in the two sentences. They are not the same. In one sentence John is doing the pleasing; in the other, someone is pleasing him. The first sentence can be paraphrased:

It is easy to please John.

The second cannot:

*It is eager to please John.

The theory attempts to describe how it is that a native speaker knows that those two sentences have different meanings. It is concerned with the underlying logical relations and the way in which the deep structure, the meaning, gets transformed into the outward surface structure.

The sentences about John are similar to the ambiguous sentence about the shooting that you considered in the Investigating Language exercise:

> The shooting of the hunters was astonishing.

Both interpretations of this sentence—whether the hunters did the shooting or were themselves shot—will produce the same traditional diagram: In both, shooting is a gerund. Transformational grammar, however, will account for the ambiguity by generating two different deep structures underlying this one surface structure.

Deep structure is described in terms of *phrase-structure rules* such as the following:

RULE 1:   S → NP + VP

This rule says that a sentence can be rewritten as, or consists of, a noun phrase and a verb phrase. We used the branching diagram of this rule in Chapter 2 to describe the sentence patterns:

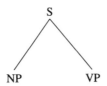

Our second rewrite rule describes the noun phrase, which begins with the determiner. We know that not every noun takes a determiner: Proper nouns do not, nor do all plural nouns. So we'll show the determiner as optional. And of course many of our noun phrases include modifiers; we commonly add adjectives and prepositional phrases. All of the following formulas represent possible noun phrases:

1. N (students)
2. Det + N (the students)
3. Det + Adj + N (the weary students)
4. Adj + N (weary students)
5. Det + N + Prep Phr (the students in the dorm)
6. Det + Adj + N + Prep Phr (the weary students in the dorm)

The one thing that all of these noun phrase variations have in common is, obviously, the noun. So taking advantage of parentheses, which mean "optional," we can come up with a rule that will account for all possibilities:

RULE 2:   NP → (Det) + (Adj) + N + (Prep Phr)

You'll recall that we used this same technique in the verb-expansion rule in Chapter 3. Now the NP rule says that the one requirement is the noun, the headword—the only element without parentheses; we can add a determiner and/or an adjective in prenoun position and a prepositional phrase in postnoun position if we wish.

We haven't quite finished the rewrite rule for NPs. We'll come back to it after we examine the expanded VP.

The VP rule describes how to generate a grammatical verb phrase.

RULE 3:   VP → AUX + V + (COMP) + (ADV)

The required components are the auxiliary and the verb; the complement and the adverbial are optional, as indicated by the parentheses. The rule simply states in terms of a single formula what you have learned in your study of the sentence patterns: Some sentence patterns have a complement (a noun phrase or an adjective), and some don't, depending on the class of the verb.

You will understand why the AUX is shown as required instead of optional when you consider the next phrase-structure rule:

RULE 4:   AUX → T + (M) + (*have* + *-en*) + (*be* + *-ing*)

This rule should look familiar. It is, of course, the verb-expansion rule without the main-verb slot at the end. In other words, it is the rule that describes how the auxiliary is generated. AUX is shown in the VP rule as required because, as you will recall from Chapter 3, every verb phrase includes tense, T. And in this rule, T is a component of the auxiliary.

Two more rules, which rewrite the complement and the adverbial, will enable us to generate skeletal versions of most of our sentence patterns:

RULE 5:   COMP → $\begin{Bmatrix} NP \\ Adj \end{Bmatrix}$

RULE 6:   ADV → $\left\{ \begin{array}{l} \textbf{Adv} \\ \textbf{Prep Phr} \end{array} \right\}$

The complement will be either an adjective or a noun phrase; the adverbial will be either an adverb or a prepositional phrase. Our final two rules describe the form of the prepositional phrase and the choice of tense:

RULE 7:   Prep Phr → Prep + NP

RULE 8:   T → $\left\{ \begin{array}{l} \textbf{Pres} \\ \textbf{Past} \end{array} \right\}$

The clearest way to picture how the phrase-structure rules work is to draw a branching tree. Here, for example, is a tree that represents the deep structure of our sample Pattern VII sentence from Chapter 2: *The students studied their assignment.*

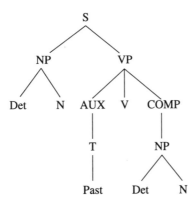

None of the symbols now at the bottom of the tree can be rewritten; that is, none of them appear on the left side of the arrows in the phrase-structure rules. We have thus generated what is known as a *terminal string*:

Det + N + Past + V + Det + N

We now insert words from our lexicon—the inventory, or dictionary, we have in our heads—and produce "The students studied their assignment." If we had wanted to generate the deep structure of "The students studied their assignment in the library," we would have selected ADV as well as COMP in rewriting the VP, then Prep Phrase in rewriting the ADV:

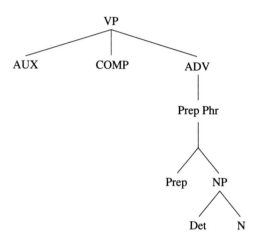

───── *Exercise B.1* ═════════════════════════════

Follow the phrase-structure rules to generate terminal strings that represent the deep structures of the following sentences. You will find it helpful to identify the sentence pattern and the forms of the structures that fill each slot. Do a branching tree. (Answers to the odd-numbered items are on pages 437–438.)

1. The soup tastes salty.
2. My new car should be in the shop.
3. The car has developed a strange noise in the engine.
4. My roommate became a good friend immediately.
5. My sister is coming for a short visit.
6. The weary students in the library finally finished their homework.

These eight rules enable us to generate most of our sentence patterns—certainly the first seven. When we select *be* as the predicating verb, we can generate I, II, and III by selecting the ADV for I, an adjective as COMP for II, and an NP as COMP for III. To generate Patterns IV and V, again we choose an adjective or an NP as the complement. And for VI we can choose an adverbial if we wish. But a bare Pattern VI such as "The children giggled" would require only the following:

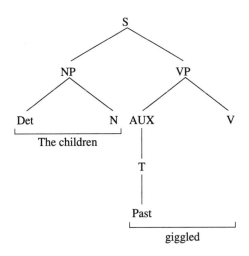

And to generate Pattern VII, we can simply select COMP in the VP and rewrite the complement as a noun phrase.

Pattern VIII is a little trickier. You'll recall that it has two NPs in the predicate—an indirect object, followed by a direct object. You'll recall, too, that the indirect object sometimes appears as the object of a preposition:

Pam gave *Joe* a present → Pam gave a present *to Joe*.

We could make the case that the version with *to* is the deep structure and that the one with the indirect object is the transformation. Clearly, the two sentences mean the same thing; they have the same deep structure. So to generate Pattern VIII, we will select both the COMP and the ADV:

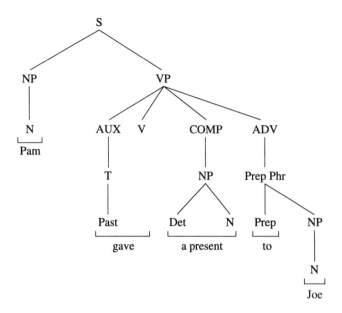

We would have to go beyond this limited introduction to transformational theory to include the rules that generate Patterns IX and X and to generate such structures as gerunds, nominal clauses, appositives, coordinate structures, and sentence modifiers. However, we will add one more detail to the phrase-structure rules to illustrate the embedding feature that underlies a great many of our sentence expansions.

Consider the postnoun modifier in the subject noun phrase of the following sentence:

The people <u>who live across the street</u> are noisy.

Who live across the street is clearly a sentence in form; we can pick out its subject and predicate; we can identify its sentence pattern; and in the traditional diagram we analyze it as a sentence:

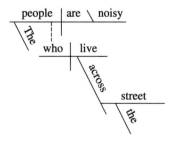

The simple addition of an optional S to our NP rewrite rule will produce the modifying clause. So here is the final form for Rule 2:

RULE 2:   NP → (Det) + (Adj) + N + (Prep Phr) + (S)

We can now recognize the noun phrase with the *who* clause in the previous example as Det + N + S:

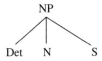

the people [the people live across the street]

The relative pronoun *who* is a feature of the surface structure only; its antecedent, *the people*, is what underlies it in the deep structure of the clause. The embedded **S**, the modifier, will always include an occurrence of the **N** headword, the noun being modified, although not necessarily as the subject. In the following sentence the **N** appears as the direct object in the embedded **S**:

The neighbors whom we met yesterday are nice.

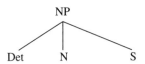

the neighbors [we met the neighbors yesterday]

Even when we leave out *whom* from the surface structure, as we probably would in this sentence, we recognize it as a part of the deep structure. The traditional diagram, too, you will recall, includes a slot for the relative pronoun even though it does not appear in the surface structure:

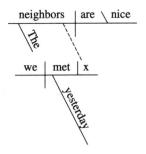

Not all modifiers in the noun phrase, of course, are clauses. The same information, or nearly so, can be conveyed if we reduce the clause to a participial phrase:

The people living across the street are noisy.

We can still identify the sentence pattern of the modifier, however, because sentence patterns are, in effect, verb phrase patterns; this one is Pattern VI, the intransitive verb pattern. Its subject is the noun being modified, *the people*. These two forms of modifiers, the clause and the participial phrase, have the same deep structure; only their surface structures are different. The participial phrase has undergone a transformational operation that deletes the subject.

The notion of the participle or participial phrase as a sentence should be obvious; in Chapter 7 we identified the sentence patterns underlying both pre- and postnoun participles. And we saw that the diagram of the participial phrase looks just like the verb half of a sentence:

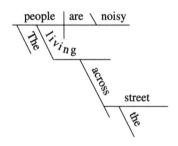

═══════ *Exercise B.2* ═══════

Draw a tree to illustrate the deep structure of the following sentences. Make sure that you have reached a terminal string—i.e., that none of the elements at the bottom of the tree can be rewritten. (Answers to the odd-numbered items are on pages 438–440.)

1. The car that my sister bought in June needs four new tires already.
2. Peter recognized that man standing at the edge of the crowd.
3. Our house was designed by my father.
4. My father has been an architect for forty years.
5. The neighbors are building their new puppy an elegant doghouse.

6. On Saturday our furniture will be delivered.
7. That young woman rowing the boat toward the pier is holding a rabbit on her lap.
8. The woman with the rabbit looks familiar.

===== *Exercise B.3* =====

The following sentences are ambiguous. Illustrate their two possible deep structures by doing a phrase-structure tree to illustrate one meaning and a traditional diagram to illustrate the other:

1. Mary washed the stones she found in the river.
2. We discussed our problem with the teacher.
3. My roommate is always entertaining.
4. My parents live near the school on Main Street.

Recognizing the relationship between deep and surface structure can help us understand the effect that misplaced and dangling modifiers can have. In Chapter 7 we saw dangling modifiers in opening position, participial phrases without subjects:

*Having swung his five iron too far to the left, Joe's ball landed precisely in the middle of a sand trap.

Linguists don't, in fact, make any claims that transformational grammar actually describes what goes on in the mind of a speaker or listener. Nevertheless, the recognition of the difference between deep and surface structure could account for reader expectation; it could account for the source of interference that misplaced and dangling modifiers introduce into the communication process. In the previous example with the dangling participle, for example, the reader expects to find a subject for the verb *having swung;* "the golfer," perhaps, or "Joe."

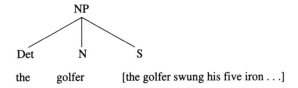

So the reader does a double-take when *Joe's ball* shows up as the subject. The reader may understand the sentence with no problem, but such double-takes are bound to interfere with readability.

Sometimes the reader is led astray because the path from surface to deep structure could go in either of two directions—an ambiguous sentence:

I know the driver of the bus standing on the corner.

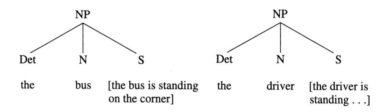

And sometimes the modifier is merely misplaced—a temporary detour:

The doctor examined the patient lying in bed with a stethoscope.

Writers who are the clearest are the most effective. They will keep their readers moving smoothly along the path, and they will make the trip as fresh and interesting as possible with precise language, with sentence variety, with modifiers that add detail clearly and vividly. They will not hinder readers with unnecessary sidesteps nor misdirect them into paths that should be marked "wrong way" and "no exit."

Appendix B: Answers to the Exercises

Exercise 1

1.

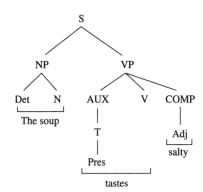

3.

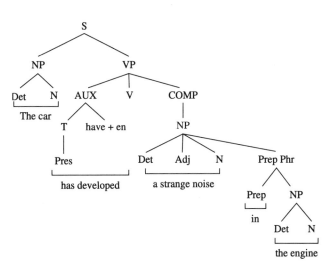

5.

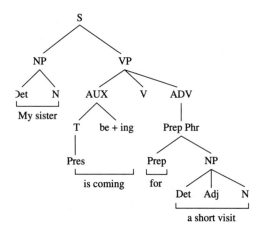

Exercise 2

1.

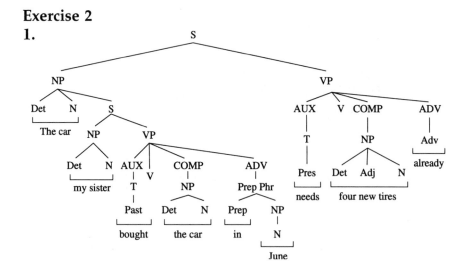

3.

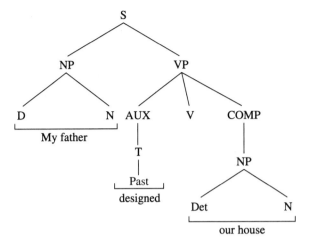

5.

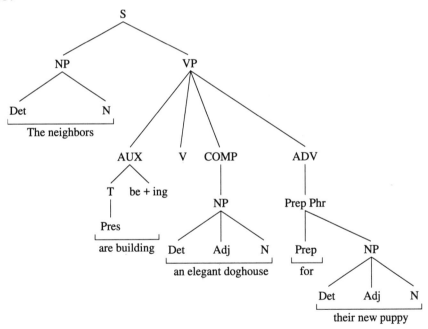

7.

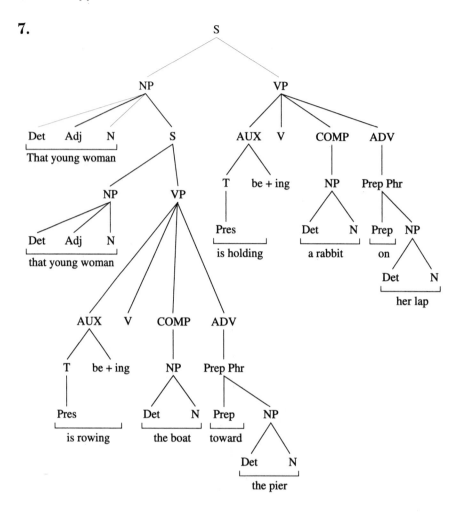

ANSWERS
TO THE EXERCISES

CHAPTER 2

Exercise 1, page 32

1. Brian's problem | is | serious. (Pattern II)
     NP₁   be   adj
     subj   pred subj comp
              vb

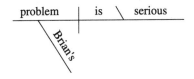

2. The horses | are | at the gate. (Pattern I)
     NP   be   prep phr
    subj   pred   ADV/TP
           vb

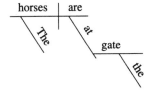

3. The excitement of the fans | is | really contagious. (Pattern II)
           NP   be   adj
           subj   pred   subj comp
                    vb

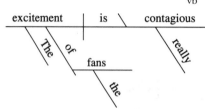

4. Brevity | is | the soul of wit. (Pattern III)
   NP₁   be   NP₁
   subj   pred   subj comp
          vb

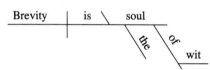

5. The final exam | will be | at four o'clock. (Pattern I)
      NP   be   prep phr
     subj   pred vb   ADV/TP

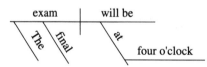

6. The kids | are being | unusually silly. (Pattern II)
    NP   be   adj
    subj   pred vb   subj comp

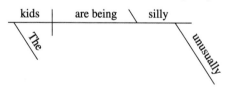

7. The Wongs | have been | terrific neighbors. (Pattern III)
    NP₁   be   NP₁
    subj   pred vb   subj comp

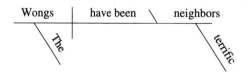

8. Those joggers | are | out of shape. (Pattern II)
    NP   be   prep phr
    subj   pred   subj comp
              vb

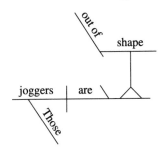

9. The basketball team | is | on a roll. (Pattern II)
    NP   be   prep phr
    subj   pred subj comp
             vb

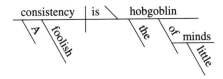

10. A foolish consistency | is | the hobgoblin of little minds. (Pattern III)
    NP₁   be   NP₁
    subj   pred   subj comp
            vb

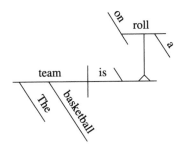

Exercise 2, page 34

1. The baby | looks | healthy. (Pattern IV)
    NP   lnk vb   adj
    subj pred vb subj comp

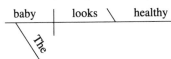

2. The old neighborhood gang | has remained | good friends. (Pattern V)

NP₁ .... lnk vb .... NP₁
subj .... pred vb .... subj comp

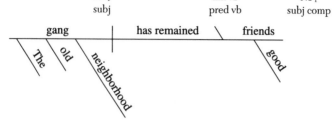

3. Exotic birds | are becoming | popular family pets. (Pattern V)

NP₁ .... lnk vb .... NP₁
subj .... pred vb .... subj comp

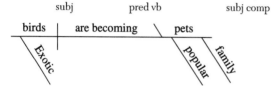

4. The piano | sounds | out of tune. (Pattern IV)

NP .... lnk vb .... prep phr
subj .... pred vb .... subj comp

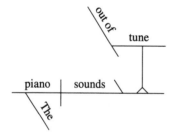

5. Ryan | looks | like his older brother. (Pattern IV)

NP .... lnk vb .... prep phr
subj .... pred vb .... subj comp

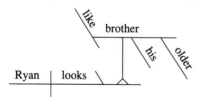

6. You | look | a mess! (Pattern V)

pro .... lnk vb .... NP₁
subj .... pred vb .... subj comp
(NP₁)

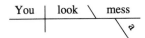

7. That spaghetti | smells | wonderful. (Pattern IV)
      NP   lnk vb   adj
      subj   pred vb   subj comp

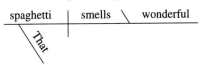

8. Your idea | seems | very sensible. (Pattern IV)
     NP   lnk   adj
     subj   pred vb   subj comp

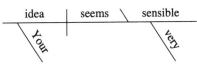

Exercise 3, page 39

1.

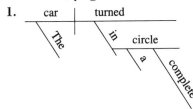

2.

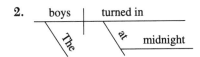

3.

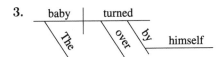

4.

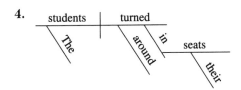

5.

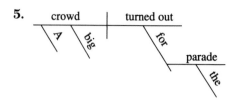

6.

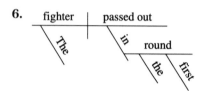

7.

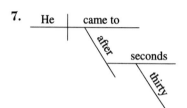

8.

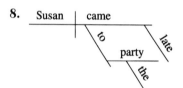

9.

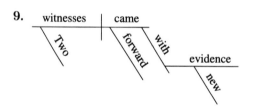

10.

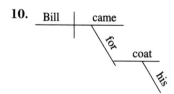

Exercise 4, page 42

1. The boys │ prepared │ a terrific spaghetti dinner. (Pattern VII)
  NP₁   tr vb   NP₂
  subj   pred vb   dir obj

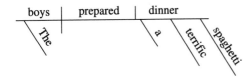

2. An old jalopy | turned | into our driveway. (Pattern VI)
       NP   int vb   prep phr
       subj   pred vb   opt ADV

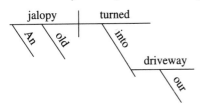

3. The ugly duckling | turned into | a beautiful swan. (Pattern V)
        NP$_1$ lnk vb   NP$_1$
        subj   pred vb   subj comp

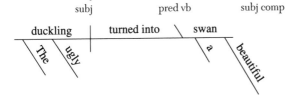

4. The fog | comes | on little cat feet. (Pattern VI)
      NP   int vb   prep phr
      subj   pred vb   opt ADV

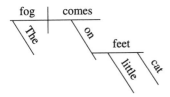

5. On Sundays | the neighbor | walks | his dog | at 6:00 A.M.
    prep phr   NP$_1$ tr vb   NP$_2$ prep phr
    opt ADV   subj   pred vb dir obj   opt ADV

    (Pattern VII)

6.   I | can't make out | the address on this envelope. (Pattern VII)
    pro   tr vb   NP₂
    subj   pred vb   dir obj
    (NP₁)

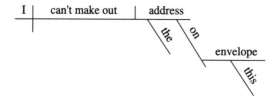

7. After two months | the teachers | called off | their strike. (Pattern VII)
    prep phr   NP₁   tr vb   NP₂
    opt ADV   subj   pred vb   dir obj

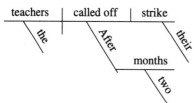

8. Everyone | was recalling | the good old days | at our class reunion.
    pro   tr vb   NP₂   prep phr
    subj   pred vb   dir obj   opt ADV
    (NP₁)

(Pattern VII)

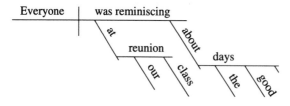

9. My best friend from high school | plays | in the band | at Portland State.
               NP   int vb   prep phr   prep phr
               subj   pred vb   opt ADV   opt ADV

(Pattern VI)

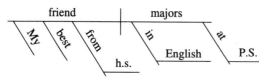

10. The mass of men | lead | lives of quiet desperation. (Pattern VII)
$\qquad$ NP₁ $\qquad\quad$ tr vb $\qquad$ NP₂
$\qquad$ subj $\qquad\quad$ pred vb $\qquad$ dir obj

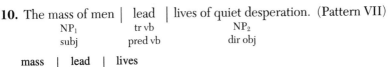

Exercise 5, page 47

1. The neighborhood kids | drive | my mother | crazy. (Pattern IX)
$\qquad$ NP₁ $\qquad\qquad$ tr vb $\quad$ NP₂ $\qquad$ adj
$\qquad$ subj $\qquad\qquad$ pred vb $\;$ dir obj $\;$ obj comp

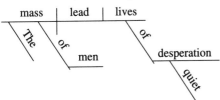

2. She | describes | them | as a menace to the neighborhood.
$\;$ pro $\qquad$ tr vb $\qquad$ pro $\qquad\qquad\qquad$ NP₂
$\;$ subj $\qquad$ pred vb $\quad$ dir obj $\qquad\qquad$ obj comp
(NP₁) $\qquad\qquad\qquad$ (NP₂)

(Pattern X)

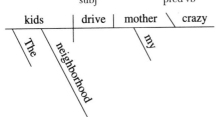

3. On Friday | the weather | suddenly | turned | colder. (Pattern IV)
$\;$ prep phr $\qquad$ NP $\qquad\quad$ adv $\qquad$ lnk vb $\quad$ adj
$\;$ opt ADV $\qquad$ subj $\qquad$ opt ADV $\;$ pred vb $\;$ subj comp

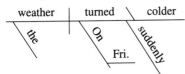

4. Yesterday | Luis | bought | himself | an expensive leather coat |
     adv   NP₁   tr vb   pro   NP₃
    opt ADV   subj   pred vb   ind obj   dir obj
                                  (NP₂)

    at Nordstrom's. (Pattern VIII)
     prep phr
     opt ADV

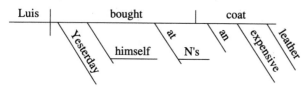

5. England's soccer fans | have | a reputation for wild behavior.
        NP₁   tr vb   NP₂
        subj   pred vb   dir obj

   (Pattern VII)

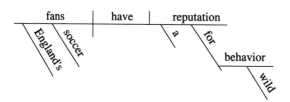

6. My boss at the pizza parlor | promised | me | a raise. (Pattern VIII)
        NP₁   tr vb   pro   NP₃
        subj   pred vb   ind obj   dir obj
                                (NP₂)

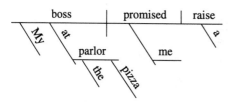

7. Hector's party | broke up | at midnight. (Pattern VI)
       NP   int vb   prep phr
      subj   pred vb   opt ADV

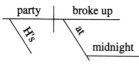

8. The voters | elected | Bill Clinton | president | in 1992. (Pattern X)
    NP₁   tr vb   NP₂   NP₂   prep phr
    subj   pred vb   dir obj   obj comp   opt ADV

9. Joe | cut | himself | a huge piece of cake. (Pattern VIII)
  NP₁   tr vb   pro   NP₃
  subj   pred vb   ind obj   dir obj
               (NP₂)

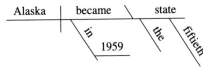

10. Alaska | became | the fiftieth state | in 1959. (Pattern V)
    NP₁   lnk vb   NP₁   prep phr
    subj   pred vb   subj comp   opt ADV

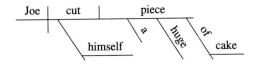

11. Acc. to the 1980 census, | Wyoming | is | our least populous state.
         prep phr   NP₁   be   NP₁
         opt ADV   subj   pred vb   subj comp

(Pattern III)

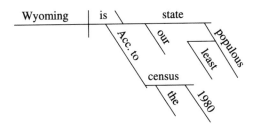

12. Some people | consider | Minnesota winters | excessively long.
    NP₁   tr vb   NP₂   adj phr
    subj   pred vb   dir obj   obj comp

(Pattern IX)

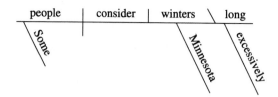

13. Our team | plays | Indiana | in the HIT | on Saturday night.
      NP₁   tr vb   NP₂   prep phr   prep phr
      subj   pred vb   dir obj   opt ADV   opt ADV

(Pattern VII)

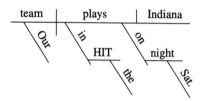

14.   I | ordered | you | a cheeseburger with onions. (Pattern VIII)
      pro   tr vb   pro   NP₃
      subj   pred vb ind obj   dir obj
    (NP₁)   (NP₂)

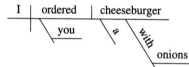

15. Professor Moore | assigned | the class | six chapters | for Monday.
       NP₁   tr vb   NP₂   NP₃   prep phr
       subj   pred vb   ind obj   dir obj   opt ADV

(Pattern VIII)

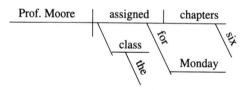

CHAPTER 3
Exercise 6, page 62

1. go	goes	went	going	gone
2. break	breaks	broke	breaking	broken
3. come	comes	came	coming	come

4. move	moves	moved	moving	moved
5. expect	expects	expected	expecting	expected
6. put	puts	put	putting	put
7. drink	drinks	drank	drinking	drunk
8. think	thinks	thought	thinking	thought
9. like	likes	liked	liking	liked
10. feel	feels	felt	feeling	felt
11. lose	loses	lost	losing	lost
12. pass	passes	passed	passing	passed
13. meet	meets	met	meeting	met
14. beat	beats	beat	beating	beat (en)
15. lead	leads	led	leading	led
16. read	reads	read	reading	read
17. say	says	said	saying	said
18. drive	drives	drove	driving	driven

Exercise 7, page 69

1. has worked
2. was working
3. has been playing
4. was being
5. is having
6. has had
7. had had
8. had been being

Exercise 8, page 71

1. shall be going
2. should have gone
3. would come
4. may have been playing
5. might play
6. could have drunk

Exercise 9, page 80

1. The lead article in today's *Collegian* was written by my roommate.
2. Some of our most intricate fugues were composed by Bach.
3. The most expensive houses in town are built by my brother-in-law.
4. That expensive apartment complex on Allen Street is being built by him.
5. A new tax collection system will be discussed by the county commissioners at their next meeting.

1. The cheerleading squad led the football team onto the field.
2. A committee chooses the cheerleaders in the spring.
3. Someone has burglarized several apartments in our building recently.
4. Someone should deliver a shipment of fresh lobsters soon.
5. We held a special election on Tuesday.

Exercise 10, page 84

1. A Republican will probably be elected as mayor next year.
2. Prospectors had found gold in Alaska long before the Gold Rush in California.

3. The school is giving some older students academic credit for "life experience."
4. The potholes in our street were finally repaired.
5. The subway fare is being raised to sixty cents next week.
6. People sometimes refer to remedial math courses in a pejorative way as "bonehead math."
7. People have sighted dozens of UFOs in our area during the past few years.
8. You should study six chapters before the next exam.
9. People sometimes call Lake Michigan America's inland ocean.
10. In the 1970s casino gambling was legalized by New Jersey.
11. Maria has finally been given the recognition she deserves.
12. In 1993 the Senate confirmed Janet Reno as our first female attorney general.

Exercise 11, page 102

1. I wonder <u>where I put my math book</u>. (dir obj)
2. <u>Why you stayed out so late</u> is no business of mine. (subj)
3. The counselor couldn't remember <u>who had volunteered for cleanup duty</u>. (dir obj)
4. Percy wondered <u>if we could come for the weekend</u>. (dir obj)
5. My problem in English class is <u>that I don't really understand poetry</u>. (subj comp)
6. I can't decide <u>which gym class I should take</u>. (dir obj)
7. It doesn't seem fair <u>that an exam is scheduled on the day before Thanksgiving break</u>. (appositive to *it*)
8. I wish <u>he would explain his explanation</u>. (dir obj)
9. <u>How the Panama Canal was built</u> is a story of high drama. (subj)
10. Our basketball fans think <u>it's great ²that we're getting a new athletic center</u>.¹

(1. dir obj) (2. appositive to *it*)

1.

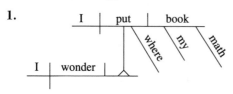

2.

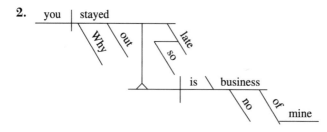

3.

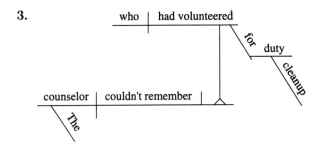

4.

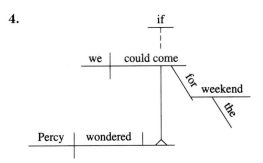

5.

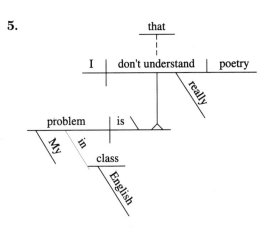

6.

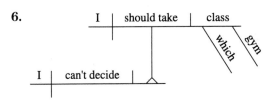

7.

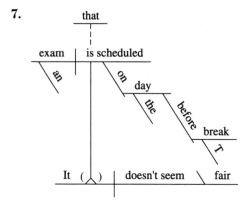

8.

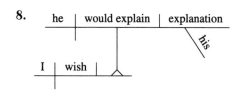

9.

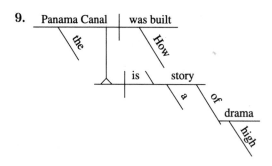

10.

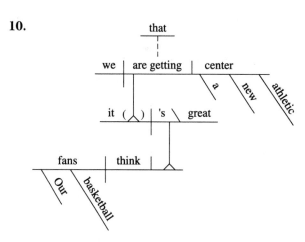

Exercise 12, page 107

1. your complaining to the boss—Pattern VI; subject
2. going . . . light—Pattern VI; object of preposition
3. weeding the garden—Pattern VII; direct object
4. growing roses—Pattern VII; subjective complement
5. Finding . . . roses—Pattern VII; subject
6. giving . . . time—Pattern VIII; direct object
7. being here with you—Pattern I; appositive to *it*
8. swimming there—Pattern VI; direct object
9. feeling angry with me—Pattern IV; object of preposition
   being so honest—Pattern II; object of preposition
10. painting the house green—Pattern IX; appositive to *project*

1.

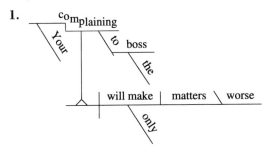

2.

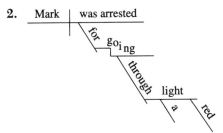

3.

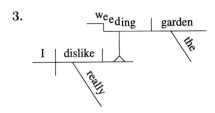

4.

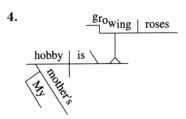

5.

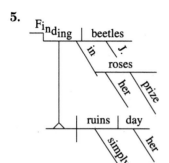

6.

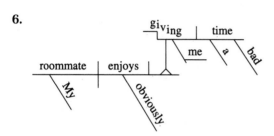

7.

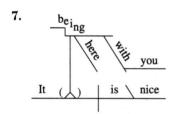

8.

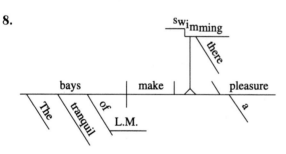

9.

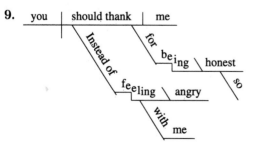

10.

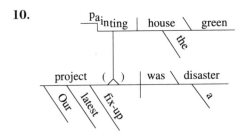

Exercise 13, page 110

Here are some possibilities; you may find others.

1. Before starting to bake a cake, first assemble the ingredients.
2. You should avoid heavy meals before swimming.
3. When I was making a career decision, my counselor was a big help.
4. After we stored the outdoor furniture in the garage, there was no room left for the car.
5. Our backpacks got really heavy after we hiked up that steep mountain trail.

Exercise 14, page 112

1. To put off ... tasks—Pattern VII, subject; main clause—Pattern VII
2. to see myself ... today—Pattern VII, appositive to *it*; main clause—Pattern II
3. to fight—Pattern VI, direct object; main clause—Pattern VII
4. To survive midterms—Pattern VII, subject; main clause—Pattern III
5. to tie—Pattern VI, subjective complement; main clause—Pattern III
6. to show up another team—Pattern VII; main clause—Pattern VII
7. To tie—Pattern VI, subject; to save face—Pattern VII, subjective complement; main clause—Pattern III
8. to be ... friendship—Pattern II, subjective complement; main clause—Pattern III
9. to become a vegetarian—Pattern V, subjective complement; main clause—Pattern VII
10. to paint ... purple—Pattern IX, appositive to *it*; main clause—Pattern III

1.

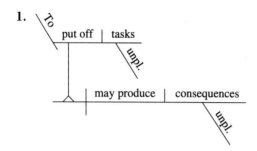

2.

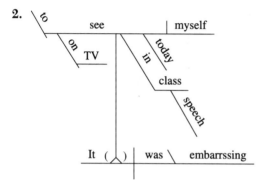

3.

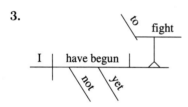

4.

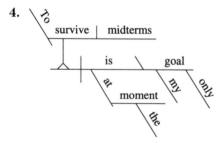

5.

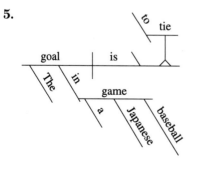

6.

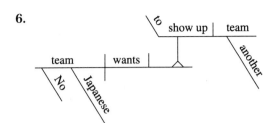

7.

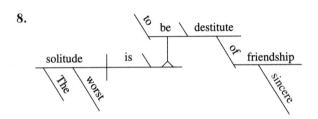

8.

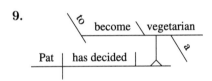

9.

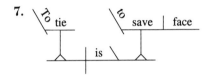

10.

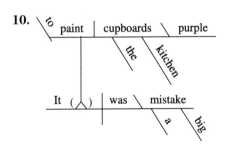

Exercise 15, page 132

1.

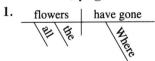

2.

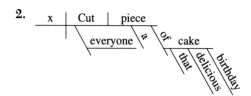

3.

4.

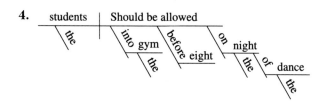

5.

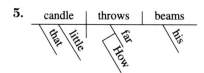

6.

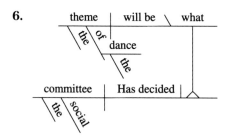

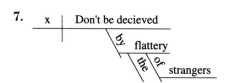

7.

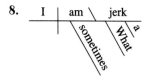

8.

9.

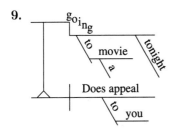

10.

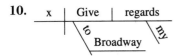

Exercise 16, page 136

1. expletive (Pattern I)
2. adverb (Pattern I)
3. expletive (Pattern I)
4. expletive (Pattern I)
5. adverb (Pattern I)
6. adverb (Pattern VI)
7. expletive (Pattern I)
8. adverb (Pattern VI)

CHAPTER 6
Exercise 17, page 154

1.

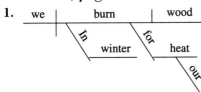

2.

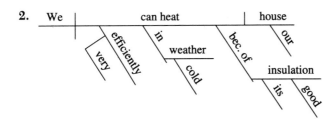

3.

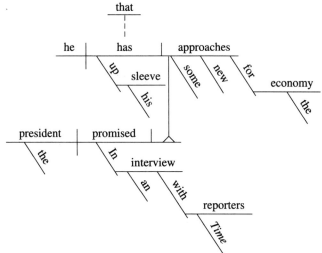

4.

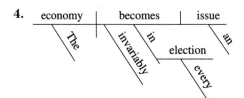

5.

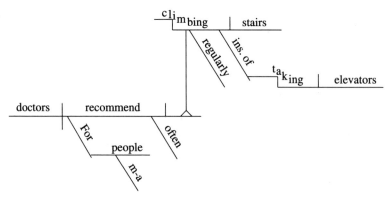

6.

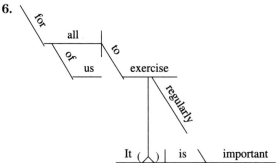

7.

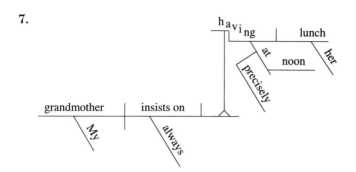

8.

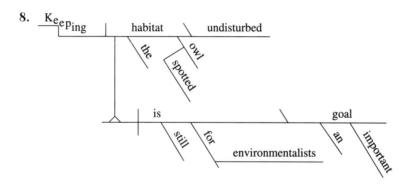

9.

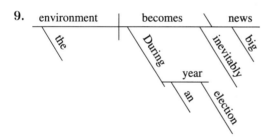

10.

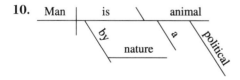

Exercise 18, page 156

1. I'm going to wax the car parked in the garage.
   I'm going into the garage to wax the car.
2. We watched the game from the porch.
   We watched the game being played on the porch.

3. I hid from the neighbors who live upstairs.
   I went upstairs to hide from the neighbors.
4. Fred tripped his teammate who was holding the bat.
   Fred stuck the bat out and tripped his teammate.
5. Susan washed the stones she found in the riverbed.
   Susan went to the river to wash the stones she found.

Exercise 19, page 159

1. Pete is working nights this week. (Pattern VI)
   <u>N</u>   <u>NP</u>

2. I was awake the whole night. (Pattern II)
   <u>NP</u>

3. I'll see you soon. (Pattern VII)
   <u>adv</u>

4. This morning Pam threw away the leftover spaghetti. (Pattern VII)
   <u>NP</u>

5. George will do dishes next time. (Pattern VII)
   <u>NP</u>

6. I love weekends. (Pattern VII)

7. Bill works weekends. (Pattern VI)
   <u>N</u>

8. At the first sign of winter the birds flew south. (Pattern VI)
   <u>prep phr</u>   <u>adv</u>

Exercise 20, page 163

1. Our cat often jumps up on the roof to reach the attic window. (main clause:
   Pattern VI; infinitive: Pattern VII)

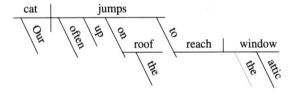

2. Sometimes she even climbs the ladder to get there. (main clause: Pattern
   VII; infinitive: Pattern VI)

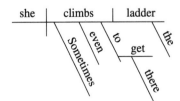

3. Last night the television set buzzed strangely during an electrical storm. (Pattern VI)

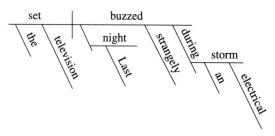

4. I had just gone into the kitchen to fix some popcorn. (main clause: Pattern VI; infinitive: Pattern VII)

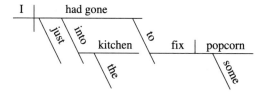

5. We went downtown last Saturday to check out the sidewalk sales. (main clause: Pattern VI; infinitive: Pattern VII)

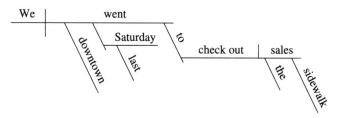

6. First I bought the children winter boots at the new shoe store. (Pattern VIII)

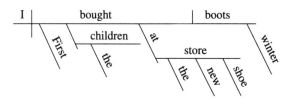

7. Afterward we stayed home to watch the playoff game with Uncle Dick. (main clause: Pattern VI; infinitive: Pattern VII)

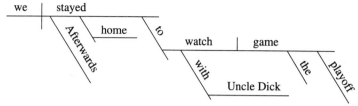

8. To keep my weight under control this winter, I have decided to give up popcorn. (main clause: Pattern VII; nominal infinitive: Pattern VII; adverbial infinitive: Pattern IX)

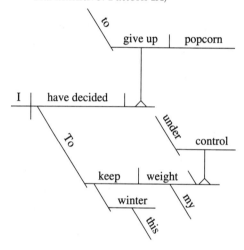

Exercise 21, page 166

1. Main clause: Pattern VII; nominal *where* clause (direct object): Pattern VII
2. Main clause: Pattern VII; adverbial *when* clause: Pattern VII
3. Main clause: Pattern IV; adverbial *when* clause: Pattern VI
4. Main clause: Pattern VII; nominal *when* clause (subject): Pattern VI; nominal *that* clause (direct object): Pattern III
5. Main clause: Pattern VI; adverbial *where* clause: Pattern VI
6. Main clause: Pattern VIII; adverbial *when* clause: Pattern VII; nominal *where* clause (direct object): Pattern VII
7. Main clause: Pattern VI; adverbial *where* clause: Pattern VI
8. Main clause: Pattern VII; nominal *where* clause (subject): Pattern VII

CHAPTER 7
Exercise 22, page 180

1. The department's personnel committee
   (determiner)   (noun)   (headword)
   the main office   Monday night
   (d)   (adj)   (H)   (n)   (H)

2. the new Sunday brunch menu   the cafeteria
   (d) (adj) (n) (n) (H)   (d) (H)

3. an expensive-looking copper-colored bracelet
   (d) (adj) (part) (n) (part) (H)
the subway station
(d) (n) (H)

4. The committee   this year's homecoming celebration
   (d) (H)   (d) (n) (H)
  a really festive occasion
(d) (qualified adj) (H)

5. The bicycle safety commission   the new regulations
   (d) (n) (n) (H)   (d) (adj) (H)
their regular meeting   this noon
   (d) (adj) (H)   (d) (H)

6. Her lovely, gracious manner   the start
   (d) (adj) (adj) (H)   (d) (H)

7. My poor old cat   another extreme winter
   (d) (adj) (adj) (H)   (d) (adj) (H)

8. a splendid old table   the auction
   (d) (adj) (adj) (H)   (d) (H)

9. dessert   Connie   a creamy, delicious chocolate mousse
   (H)   (H)   (det) (adj) (adj) (n) (H)

10. A commonly held notion   my cynical friends
   (d) (adv) (part) (H)   (d) (adj) (H)
big-business lobbyists   this country
(adj) (n) (H)   (d) (H)

Exercise 23, page 184

1. with a cast on his left foot

2. of the museum (*Near the visitors' information booth* could modify either *museum* or *meet.*)

3. after the game (*At Bob's* could modify either *party* or *game.*)

4. of computer viruses

5. from within

6. for my science course, from Stanford

Exercise 24, page 186

1. Bill owns that expensive sports car standing in the driveway. (Note that the indefinite *an* becomes definite with *that.*)

2. There will be no sleep tonight for the students cramming for their history test.

3. I am babysitting for <u>the baby sleeping upstairs in the crib</u>.

4. Some of the fans <u>lining up at the ticket office</u> will probably be disappointed.

5. A hush settled over <u>the huge crowd watching the parade</u> when the magnificent Percherons pranced by.

6. The students, <u>feeling upset about their tuition increase</u>, decided to organize a protest.

Exercise 25, page 191

1. The award <u>given every year to the outstanding volunteer</u> has been
VIII (passive)
announced.

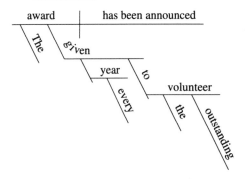

2. <u>Carrying their supplies on their backs</u>, the Boy Scout troop trudged up the
VII
mountain to find a campsite.

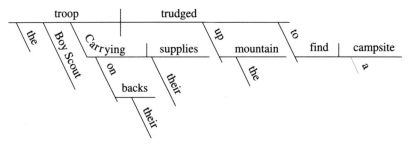

3. We gave the <u>singing</u> waiters at Ziggy's an extra big tip.
VI

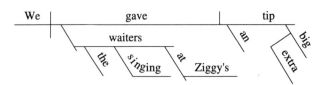

4. A noisy crowd of students gathered yesterday to demonstrate against the
tuition hike recently approved by the college trustees.

VII (passive)

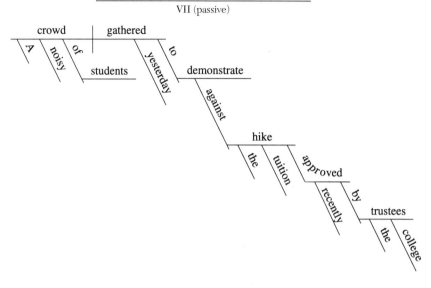

5. Finding the price reasonable, we rented the apartment on the spot.

IX

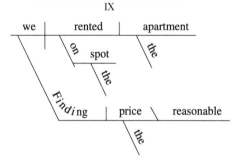

6. We planned our class picnic for Saturday, hoping that the good weather
would hold.

VII

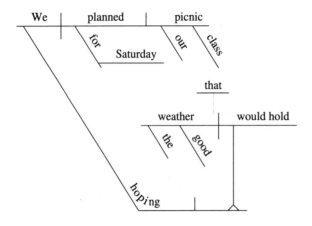

7. Having felt sick all night, I decided to skip my morning classes.
<u>IV</u>

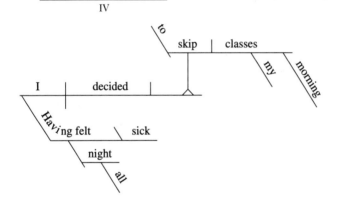

8. The teachers' union has finally approved the last two <u>disputed</u> sections of
VII (passive)

the contract <u>offered by the school district.</u>
VII (passive)

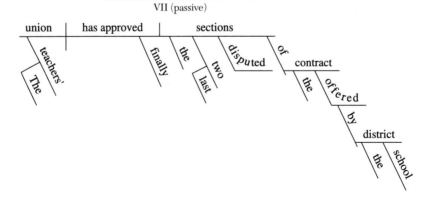

Exercise 26, page 194

Here are some possibilities; you will probably think of others.

1. Having endured rain all week, we weren't surprised at the miserable weather on Saturday.
2. Having hiked five miles uphill, I was sure my backpack weighed a ton.
3. Hoping for the sixth win in a row, the fans in the grandstand could not contain their excitement as the band played "The Star Spangled Banner."
4. The dog's reaction to strangers was fascinating to watch; he guarded his bone as if it were his very last meal.
5. Working ten hours a day six days a week, Jan completely finished her first novel in six months.
6. Exhausted by the hot weather, we could do nothing but lie in the shade.
7. Wearing their new uniforms proudly, the band marched across the field and formed a huge "O."
8. Having spent nearly all day in the kitchen, I nevertheless decided that my superb gourmet dinner was worth the effort.

or

Even though I spent nearly all day in the kitchen, that superb gourmet dinner was worth the effort.

Exercise 27, page 201

1. that we bought (that = direct object; Pattern VII)
2. (whom) I love (whom = direct object; Pattern VII)
3. that she had borrowed last month (that = direct object; Pattern VII)
4. which . . . cold (which = direct object; Pattern X)
5. (whom) he loved (whom = direct object; Pattern VII)
6. that make fine birds (that = subject; Pattern VII)
7. who . . . University (who = subject; Pattern VII)
8. that . . . lawn (that = direct object; Pattern VII)
9. whose . . . discovered (whose = determiner; Pattern VII)
10. which . . . north (which = subject; Pattern VI)

Exercise 28, page 202

1. whom
2. whoever
3. whom
4. whomever
5. Whoever
6. whom

Exercise 29, page 209

1. My parents, who retired to Arizona in 1992, love . . .
2. (no commas)
3. My favorite television show, which I watch every chance I get, is "Cheers."

4. (no commas)
5. Neither the senator nor his wife, sitting next to him on the speakers' platform, looked...
6. Westerners...the Middle East, where much...
7. ...my oldest sister, who runs a day-care center.
8. (no commas)
9. The I.D. Line, which is an imaginary line at 180° longitude, was fixed...
10. (no commas)

CHAPTER 8
Exercise 30, page 223

1. Amazingly
2. (none)
3. Well
4. (none)
5. Strangely

6. (none)
7. Without a doubt
8. no doubt
9. (none)
10. my friend

Exercise 31, page 226

1. (no commas)
2. us, although
3. over, we
4. coffee, since (optional)

5. rent, even
6. (no commas)
7. apartment, even (optional)
8. heat, get

Exercise 32, page 229

A. When you are late for work, the subway is better than the bus.
B. If bread is kept too long in hot weather, mold will grow on it.
C. While we were driving to the game on Saturday, an accident tied up traffic for over an hour.
1. I picked up a Midwestern accent while *I was* living in Omaha.
2. My accent is not as noticeable as Carlo's *accent is* [noticeable].
3. Holmes hit Ali harder than Norton (*hit Ali* or *Holmes hit Norton*).
4. If *it is* necessary, strain the juice before adding the sugar.
5. While *I was* waiting...
6. If *your paper is* handed in late...
7. Love goes toward love, as schoolboys *go* from their books. But love *goes* from love, *as schoolboys go* toward school with heavy looks.
8. The weather in Little Rock is not as humid as *it is in* New Orleans.

Exercise 33, page 234

1. her tail...metronome (participle)
2. their arms...shoulders (participle)

3. The rain having...hour (participle)
4. (no absolute phrase)
5. her book...floor (adjective phrase); her eyes...flames (adjective phrase)
6. the streets...light (noun phrase); the planet...edges (participle); the sky...infinity (noun phrase)
7. (no absolute phrase)
8. bunched shirt...blades (prepositional phrase); his toes...floor (participle); the aunt's arms...shoulders (prepositional phrase)

Exercise 34, page 236

1. Cleaning the basement this morning wasn't very much fun.
2. It surprised me that Otis didn't want to stay for the second half of the game.
3. The president criticized the Congress rather severely in his press conference; some observers considered his criticism quite inappropriate.
4. Contrary to the prediction of the weather service, the first snowstorm of the season in Denver was both early and severe.
5. Our having company for dinner three times this week probably means hot dogs for the rest of the month.

CHAPTER 9
Exercise 35, page 245

1. (no commas)
2. now, I
3. tires, shock absorbers, and brake linings
4. 1970s, a 1959 Chevy, required
5. (no commas)
6. Corvette, the car

Exercise 36, page 250

There's more than one possibility in each case.
1. I can't decide which activity I prefer: swimming...or jogging....
2. I almost never watch television. Either there is nothing on that appeals to me or the picture....
3. I don't enjoy flying, and I don't feel like taking the train.
4. Either the recipe was printed wrong, or I misread it.
5. I was unhappy with what he said and how he said it.
6. The coach announced an extra hour of drill on Saturday and no practice on Sunday.
7. For my birthday dinner, Aunt Rosa has promised to fix her famous lasagna and to bake my favorite cake.

CHAPTER 10
Exercise 37, page 266

n o v|a
re|n o v|a t|i o n
i n|n o v|a t e
n o v|i c e
n o v|e l|i s t
  nov = new

a u d|i t|o r
a u d|i e n c e
i n|a u d|i b l e
a u d|i t|o r|i u m
a u d|i o
  aud = hear

d u r|a b l e
e n|d u r e
d u r|a t i o n
d u r|i n g
e n|d u r|a n c e
  dur = hard

c o n|c e i v e
c a p|a b l e
s u s|c e p t|i b l e
c a p|t u r e
i n t e r|c e p t
  cap (cept) = take

Exercise 38, page 267
Check your answers with the dictionary and/or your instructor.

Exercise 39, page 272

1. pre cis ion (bound + bound + bound; affix, base, affix)
   d   d
  (**Note:** d = derivational; i = inflectional)

2. candid ate (free + bound; base, affix)
        d

3. de tour ed (bound + free + bound; affix, base, affix)
   d   i

4. ex cess ive ly (bound + bound + bound + bound; affix, base
   d   d d   affix, affix)

5. un a ware (bound + bound + free; affix, affix, base)
   d d

6. money (free; base)

7. side walk s (free + free + bound; base, base, affix)
        i

8. pro mot ion (bound + bound + bound; affix, base, affix)
   d   d

9. il leg al (bound + bound + bound; affix, base, affix)
   d   d

10. weal th y (free + bound + bound; base, affix, affix)
      d d

11. tele vis ion (bound + bound + bound; affix, base, affix)
    d   d

12. re vis es (bound + bound + bound; affix, base, affix)
    d   i

CHAPTER 11

Exercise 40, page 277

1. pleasure
2. regulation, regulator
3. stealth
4. health, healer
5. derivation
6. inflection
7. formula, formation
8. revival
9. seizure
10. retirement, retiree

Exercise 41, page 279

1. teacher's, teachers'
2. horse's, horses'
3. sister's husband's, sisters' husbands'
4. son's, sons'

Exercise 42, page 280

1. Price's
2. Hedges'
3. James's (or James')
4. Massachusetts'
5. Linus's
6. neighbor's
7. neighbors'
8. Miss Piggy's
9. women's
10. Confucius'

Exercise 43, page 288

ground, grounds, grounded, grounding, (My parents grounded me for a week.)
water, waters, watered, watering, watered (Joe waters the plants every day.)
air, airs, aired, airing, aired (They are airing their grievances in public again.)
fire, fires, fired, firing, fired (The overseer has fired the entire crew.)

Exercise 44, page 291

friendly	friendlier	friendliest
helpful	more helpful	most helpful
wise	wiser	wisest
awful	more awful	most awful
rich	richer	richest
mellow	mellower	mellowest
expensive	more expensive	most expensive
valid	more valid	most valid
pure	purer	purest
able	abler (more able)	ablest (most able)

Exercise 45, page 297

grief	grieve	grievous	grievously

variation	vary	variable	variably
variance		various	variously
variety			

ability	enable	able	ably
defense	defend	defensive	defensively
economy	economize	economical	economically
		economic	

pleasure	please	pleasant	pleasantly
type	typify	typical	typically
prohibition	prohibit	prohibitive	prohibitively
critic	criticize	critical	critically
criticism			

| validation | validate | valid | validly |
| validity | | | |

appreciation	appreciate	appreciative	appreciatively
beauty	beautify	beautiful	beautifully
acceptance	accept	acceptable	acceptably
purity	purify	pure	purely

| continuation | continue | continuous | continuously |
| continuity | | continual | continually |

(**Note:** You may think of other possibilities.)

CHAPTER 12
Exercise 46, page 307

1. my, enough, her
2. John's, the
3. Every, this, a
4. more, the week's
5. less, last
6. either, no

Exercise 47, page 311

1. have been (having)
2. don't dare (walk)
3. should have (eaten)
4. can't (look)
5. will be (helping)
6. has to (leave)
7. are (frustrating)
8. can (be)
9. should keep (practicing)
10. am (keeping)

Exercise 48, page 317

1. in, since
2. because of
3. in spite of
4. Prior to, in
5. According to, of, to, during
6. with (on = particle)
7. Except for, in, of, out of
8. Thanks to, without
9. Between, until
10. Within

Exercise 49, page 326

1. and—coordinating conjunction; on—preposition; an—determiner; in—preposition
2. Four—determiner; from—preposition; for—preposition; for—coordinating conjunction; for—preposition
3. As—subordinating conjunction; an—determiner; as—expletive; at—preposition
4. be—auxiliary; by—preposition; but—coordinating conjunction
5. of—preposition; off—particle (part of verb); if—subordinating conjunction
6. are—auxiliary; of—preposition; or—expletive; our—determiner
7. will—auxiliary; with—preposition; while—subordinating conjunction
8. too—qualifier; two—determiner; to—preposition

CHAPTER 13
Exercise 50, page 333

1. They
2. We, him
3. it
4. them
5. them
6. him, it
7. us
8. He, them

Exercise 51, page 337

1. herself
2. themselves
3. itself
4. ourselves
5. himself
6. ourselves

Exercise 52, page 343

1. everything—indefinite; I—personal; one—indefinite
2. every—indefinite; any—indefinite; they—personal
3. Someone—indefinite; we—personal; who—interrogative; it—personal
4. All—indefinite; that—relative; I—personal; that—demonstrative
5. much—indefinite; they—personal; both—indefinite; more—indefinite; I—personal

6. I—personal; myself—intensive; whatever—relative; you—personal
7. enough—indefinite; me—personal
8. themselves—reflexive; one another's—reciprocal
9. me—personal; what—interrogative; I—personal; your—personal
10. whoever—relative; one—indefinite

INDEX